Consumption and the Making of Respectability,

1600–1800

by

Woodruff D. Smith

routledge
new york   london

Published in 2002 by
Routledge
29 West 35th Street
New York, NY 10001

Published in Great Britain by
Routledge
11 New Fetter Lane
London EC4P 4EE

Routledge is an imprint of the Taylor & Francis Group.
Copyright © 2002 by Routledge

Printed in the United States of America on acid-free-paper.

Library of Congress Cataloging-in-Publication Data
Smith, Woodruff D.
Consumption and the making of respectability, 1600–1800 / Woodruff D. Smith.
p. cm.
Includes bibliographical references and index.
ISBN 0-415-93328-5 — ISBN 0-415-93329-3 (pbk.)
1. Consumption (Economics)—Europe—History. 2. Culture—Economic aspects—
Europe—History. 3. Europe—Social life and customs. I. Title.
HC240.9.C6 S65 2002
339.4'7—dc21
2001058877

For Janie

CONTENTS

ACKNOWLEDGMENTS

A great many people have assisted me with this book, in many different ways. I thank them all. I would like to give particular thanks to those who have read and commented on parts of the text: Ralph A. Austen, Jane H. Smith, Anthony W. Smith, and two anonymous reviewers; to individuals with whom I have had extensive conversations or exchanges about aspects of the topic: K. N. Chaudhuri, Pieter Emmer, Jordan Goodman, Paul Lovejoy, Dierdre McCloskey, and Janna M. Smith; to audiences and commentators at many scholarly conferences; and to students and colleagues at the University of Massachusetts Boston and the University of Texas at San Antonio, who have contributed suggestions and challenged my thinking—especially Victoria Hadfield, David Johnson, Peter Noble, David M. Schneider, and Malcolm Smuts. Research for this book was supported by Fulbright and National Endowment for the Humanities fellowships and by grants from the University of Texas at San Antonio. I must also thank the following for providing facilities for research: the Center for the History of European Expansion at the University of Leiden; the Davis Center at Princeton University; the library of the University of Massachusetts Boston and its director, Sharon Bostick; the libraries of the University of Texas at San Antonio, the University of Texas at Austin, Harvard University, Princeton University, the University of London, Frankfurt University, and the University of Leiden; the Royal Library in The Hague; Houghton Library at Harvard University; the Goldsmiths' Library at the University of London; Boston Public Library; the British Library; the Library of Congress; the Amsterdam Municipal Archives; the Netherlands National Archives in The

Hague; the Guildhall Library and the India Office Library and Records (now the Oriental and India Office Collections of the British Library) in London; and the British Public Record Office.

ABBREVIATIONS

The following abbreviations are used in the text, notes, and bibliography:

ARA   *Algemeen Rijksarchief* (Netherlands National Archives)

CCM   *A Calendar of the Court Minutes Etc. of the East India Company*, 11 vols., ed. E. B. Sainsbury (Oxford: 1907–38).

GAA   *Gemeente Archief Amsterdam* (Amsterdam Municipal Archives)

GL   Goldsmiths' Library, University of London

GLBC   Goldsmiths' Library Broadsides Collection

IOLR   India Office Library and Records, London (now the Oriental and India Office Collections, British Library)

Kn.   W. P. C. Knuttel, *Catalogus van de Pamfletten-Versameling berustende in de Koninklijke Bibliotheek*, 9 vols. (Utrecht: HES Publishers, 1978).

VOC   *Verenigde Oostindische Compagnie* (Netherlands East India Company)

ABBREVIATIONS

The following abbreviations are used in the text, notes, and bibliography:

ARA   *Algemeen Rijksarchief* (Netherlands National Archives)

CCM   *A Calendar of the Court Minutes Etc. of the East India Company*, 11 vols., ed. E. B. Sainsbury (Oxford: 1907–38).

GAA   *Gemeente Archief Amsterdam* (Amsterdam Municipal Archives)

GL   Goldsmiths' Library, University of London

GLBC   Goldsmiths' Library Broadsides Collection

IOLR   India Office Library and Records, London (now the Oriental and India Office Collections, British Library)

Kn.   W. P. C. Knuttel, *Catalogus van de Pamfletten-Versameling berustende in de Koninklijke Bibliotheek*, 9 vols. (Utrecht: HES Publishers, 1978).

VOC   *Verenigde Oostindische Compagnie* (Netherlands East India Company)

INTRODUCTION

The publication in 1993 of a major collection of essays edited by John Brewer and Roy Porter marked a turning point in the historiography of consumption, a new field that had hardly existed before 1980. In his contribution to the volume (actually an article written some years previously), Jean-Christophe Agnew set a task for the other authors. "The last decade of research has boldly challenged and immeasurably enriched our picture of consumer culture, but the very richness of that work—the thickness of its description and the detail of its maps—has at times submerged important questions of periodization, of power and, if you will, of principle—questions that historians can ill afford to ignore."[1] Agnew wondered whether "consumerism" and the "consumer society" could be accurately treated as autonomous historical phenomena, as much of the pioneering work had done.[2] He suggested that historians should try to investigate the connections between alterations in consumption patterns and other sociocultural changes—especially ones that may have given ethical and political meaning to consumer actions. He saw little moral content in such actions themselves: "there is nothing in the literature I have reviewed here that would support the view that commodity consumption has enhanced our appreciation of the remote consequences of our acts or has clarified our responsibilities for them."[3]

Whether or not they agreed with Agnew's last point, most of the other contributors to the volume did precisely what he called for: they paid close attention in their chapters to matters of moral, intellectual, and political embeddedness. Colin Campbell, for instance, analyzed the importance of models of "character" contained in early modern English culture as bases for consumer actions.[4] T. H. Breen continued his ongoing investigation of relationships between consumption and political ideology in the eighteenth century.[5] Lorna Weatherill, implicitly taking issue with a number of Agnew's statements, moved from examining the employment of specific goods to deriving inferences about their meanings.[6] Since 1993, most of the best new research on consumption in history has similarly concerned itself with contextualizing the subject, following a wide variety of interpretive models. Maxine Berg and her colleagues have developed a new understanding of relationships between luxury and consumption. John Brewer has published a major work on the consumption of art in eighteenth-century Britain. Amanda Vickery and others have placed consumption in the framework of women's history.[7] What is still lacking is a way of investigating the history of consumption *comprehensively*, of identifying the range of contexts of consumer behavior and their changes since the prototype of the modern global economy was constructed in the sixteenth and seventeenth centuries. We also need models for exploring the implications of alterations in consumption patterns across a broad spectrum of human thought, discourse, and action.

The present book is in part a contribution to filling these needs. I began working on the subject slightly more than two decades ago—at the dawn of consumption history—as a sideline to my primary research in an entirely different field. I did so because of an experience I had in a course I was teaching on imperialism. At the end of a lecture on the slave and sugar trades of the eighteenth century, a student asked, "But why did people in Europe *want* all that sugar?" I responded with a reference to "Europe's sweet tooth" and then talked about a natural human propensity to enjoy sugar and about Say's Law—the assertion that supply creates its own demand. It was not a very good answer. In reality, I had no idea what the answer was, and after consulting the literature, I discovered that no one else did, either. The question was seldom even asked. Apparently, a number of other scholars uncovered similar gaps at about the same time, which resulted in the new historiography of consumption.[8] In my case, I started by focusing on the manipulation of desires and behavior by business organizations (especially the East Indies companies in the seventeenth century) to create demand in Europe for goods produced overseas. But as my research deepened and as a barrage of excellent studies of early modern European and American consumption appeared, it became clear that market manipulation was only part of the story, that the strategies of marketers and the behavior of consumers were both embedded in very broad and very complex cultural patterns. Gradually, my interest shifted from the consumption of overseas commodities to early modern consumption in general, and then

from consumption to the cultural and social frameworks that shaped it and were in turn shaped by it.

This book is a result of a realization that struck me as soon as my focus had changed: that a very large portion of the demand in Europe and the Americas for consumer goods in the nineteenth century arose from people's use of those goods to signal and maintain their respectability. It is not uncommon to connect Victorian behavior of all sorts, from sex to purchasing, with respectability, but few systematic attempts have been made either to analyze precisely what "respectability" is or to trace its history.[9] It is normally linked discursively to the "middle class" or to "bourgeois society," but the history of the linkage is seldom pursued. I decided to focus my attention on respectability. I discovered that the set of sociocultural phenomena to which the word *respectability* (and its cognates in other languages) came to be applied in the late eighteenth century constituted a distinct and enormously significant cultural pattern that was central to the "modernity" of the Western and imperial worlds. Respectability gave meaning—moral and political as well as social and economic—to consumption, thereby permitting the construction of a host of connections between purchasing commodities and thinking and acting appropriately. In other words, by looking at the relationships between respectability and consumption, it is possible to place the latter in many of its historical contexts.

In addition, it became clear that respectability itself had a history. In fact, it was an aggregation of several sets of cultural traits, each of which had its own history and which only became connected firmly together in the eighteenth century. In early modern western Europe, each of these components acted in its own right as a context for the consumption of commodities—especially, as we shall see, goods produced overseas, which played a crucial role in the construction both of respectability and of modern consumption patterns. As the individual contexts changed between 1600 and 1800, the meanings and uses of certain key commodities altered, and so, accordingly, did demand for them. As certain commodities became available to fill new, vaguely defined cultural roles, their nature and availability helped to clarify, in a sense to reify, those roles. Tea, for example, entered European usage in the seventeenth century as an exotic elite fashion and a support for health—that is, as a commodity that possessed meaning in two quite distinct contexts. In the late seventeenth and eighteenth centuries, however, tea (with sugar) came to be a bridge between rapidly changing contexts of gentility and morality. Its use in the ritual of tea-taking gave practical, observable meaning to its altered contexts and also played a significant part in attaching those contexts to the larger composite pattern of respectability. What could be a more meaningful exercise in respectability than an English tea?

This book traces part of the process by which Europeans (primarily in northwestern European countries and their colonies) constructed a culture of respectability in the seventeenth and eighteenth centuries—first by creating or redefining a number of individual cultural contexts, and then by linking them together into a single framework. The book uses evidence about the consumption of products originally imported from overseas in order to explore the contexts of which respectability was composed and the process of their amalgamation. In so doing, it presents explanations for some of the massive changes in demand for such products that occurred in Europe between 1600 and 1800. This not only places the history of consumption in a larger context, but also has implications for understanding other phenomena fundamental to the construction of the modern world: industrialization, the global economy, the bourgeoisie, capitalism, imperialism—even political developments such as democracy. We can, unfortunately, pursue these implications only to a limited extent in the present book.

The next chapter begins with the questions about the consumption of overseas goods in seventeenth- and eighteenth-century Europe that originally interested me. We will see how quickly these questions reveal a need to understand the cultural contexts of consumption.

1

CONSUMPTION AND CULTURE

What was the nature of the extensive changes in European patterns of consumption that took place in the seventeenth and eighteenth centuries? How and why did these changes come about? Why did commodities imported from outside Europe play a central role in the reshaping and expansion of consumption, and what was the nature of that role? What were the effects, economic and otherwise, in Europe and elsewhere, of alterations in European consumption patterns?

Even a superficial consideration of these questions reveals that they cannot be answered without following trails of evidence that lead in multiple directions, into many, perhaps most, of the corners of early modern European life, crossing and crisscrossing each other in the process. Trying to understand changes in consumption requires that they be examined in connection with a host of other major phenomena with which they were interwoven, such as European overseas expansion and the elaboration of a global economy, the development of public opinion, changes in social organization and in definitions of gender, the processes of commercialization and industrialization, and so forth. This would be an impossible undertaking without an appropriate conceptual approach and analytical structure, which the present chapter is intended to provide.

CHANGES IN CONSUMPTION PATTERNS IN EARLY MODERN EUROPE

Some historians have written of a "consumer revolution" in the eighteenth century, with its origins in the seventeenth. Although others have questioned whether the term can be applied accurately to the period (not enough consumption, not rapid enough change for a revolution), there can be no doubt that major alterations occurred in the quantity and types of consumer goods demanded in western Europe, and that some of these alterations helped to lay the foundations for European industrialization, the consumer society, and much more.[1] What happened, and why?

Between the beginning of the seventeenth century and the conventional onset of British industrialization in the late eighteenth century, a period of rising consumption in general in western Europe, an increasingly large proportion of the commodities that satisfied European consumer demand were produced overseas. Although many consumer goods of entirely European origin also experienced growth in demand, many of the most important changes that occurred in consumption centered on the use of non-European products. Several of the staple commodities of the Industrial Revolution, most notably cottons, were imported massively from abroad before they were produced in quantity in Europe.[2] Hence the importance of paying close attention to the roles of overseas imports and, by implication, of European expansion and the construction of global economies in any attempt to understand European consumption patterns.

The significance of non-European consumer goods did not, as might be supposed, arise immediately from the European discovery of America. For a century after Columbus, the main object of European attention in America was precious metals. When silver was found in the 1540s in territories claimed by Spain, the whole enterprise of America (Spanish and non-Spanish alike) oriented itself around its extraction and transportation. A transatlantic consumer-oriented trade did develop in the fifteenth century, but it was small potatoes compared to the silver business, and of course the potatoes themselves, once brought across the ocean, required little further importation. Most of the consumer trade moved from Europe to America, to supply settlers in New Spain and Peru.[3]

Before 1600, it was the commerce between Europe and Asia, not America, that revolved around consumer goods—at least from the European perspective. That commerce, although modified by the entry of the Portuguese into maritime trade and extortion in the Indian Ocean around 1500, retained most of its centuries-old characteristics. It was precarious, inelastic, and opaque, featuring goods of low volume and high price. And although commodities brought to Europe from Asia spread fairly widely in Europe in the fifteenth and sixteenth centuries, few were in any way central to the daily lives of Europeans, even at the highest social levels.[4]

This situation changed dramatically in the period between 1600 and 1800. In the seventeenth century, America became a major supplier of consumer goods (mainly sugar and tobacco) to Europe and much of the rest of the world. The American trade affected almost every element of European commercial life. The Asian trade, too, was transformed with the entry of the Dutch and English East India companies and the construction of direct links between Asian commerce and the major centers of developing capitalism in the West. Asian commodities—again, mostly consumer goods—became available in Europe, America, and Africa in large quantities and (for the most part) at falling prices, while the transparency and elasticity of the trade increased markedly. By the middle of the eighteenth century, tea, coffee, sugar, tobacco, and cotton had all become staples of daily life for Europeans of great and middling means and were not uncommon among the poorer classes. There existed by that time a worldwide commercial network centered in northwestern Europe and built on the exchange of consumer goods—a network that differed structurally from the intercontinental linkages of the immediate post-Columbian period and dwarfed them in volume and impact.[5]

Not only did the size and centrality of the overseas commodity trade increase between about 1600 and the late eighteenth century, but the composition of the trade—the relative proportions and amounts of goods imported into Europe—changed substantially as well. Textiles had replaced pepper and spices as the mainstay of the Asian trade by the late seventeenth century, only to be in turn shouldered aside by tea and coffee.

What caused these changes in consumer demand? Economists have generally looked across the relatively short spectrum of explanatory factors that their discipline provides and fixed on one or another of two sets. There are those who emphasize supply factors: improvements in maritime technology and commercial organization, the establishment of efficient plantation agriculture in the West Indies using slave labor, the growing availability of investment capital, and so forth.[6] And there are those who focus on demand factors: changes in the amount and distribution of disposable income in western Europe, changes in levels of taxation on goods (and in the effectiveness of means of circumventing import duties through smuggling), and the growth of demand for imported goods to be reexported as a way to balance commercial payments.[7] What these explanations do not explain is what the student mentioned in the introduction wanted to know: Why did people in Europe *want* all that sugar, tea, and coffee, those imported fabrics and porcelain? Such questions lie outside the normal purview of economic theory, which deliberately avoids analyzing consumer motives except in terms that are quantifiable and commensurable. (Economics can explain reasonably well why English people in the eighteenth century would, all else being equal, buy smuggled tea rather than tea on which duty had been paid—it was considerably cheaper—but not why they wanted tea in the first place or why they wanted it so vehemently that they would risk legal penalties to obtain more of it at a lower price.) Economists build explanations around the concept of demand, which is an abstract, aggregate, and (theoretically) quantifiable market force, rather than around the much more complex concept of consumption, which is the set of behaviors that constitute the using of a commodity.[8] This is fine, as long as one does not assume that factors that fall within the economists' usual range of study must, simply because they are so situated, take explanatory priority over others.

Unfortunately, economic historians have often made precisely that assumption. It is not uncommon among them to argue, for example, that if changes in the factors that determine aggregate demand (personal income, income distribution, and so on) can be shown not to account for a phenomenon, then by elimination the cause must be found among the factors that conventionally define supply and production (investment rates, introduction of new technology, and so forth).[9] This makes sense only if one either ignores all the other factors that might be involved or claims that the other factors are of little significance—a claim typically justified by stating that the other factors cannot be subjected to economic analysis, not by demonstrating that they have no effect.

Most of our attention here will be focused on the other factors. The conventional economic factors are obviously of great significance and cannot be ignored, but we are interested in why people decided to consume the things they did, and such decisions are vastly more complicated and involve far more motives than are effectively recognized in economic theory.

Having said that, it is now necessary to admit that no other body of theory touching on consumer behavior is alone adequate to the task, despite the recent flurry of interest in consumption among scholars in a wide variety of fields. There is a well-pedigreed literature supplied by sociologists, historians, and some economists that emphasizes the importance of class and status distinctions, of desire to emulate social superiors or compete with peers, as generators of motives for consumption. This category includes, for example, Thorstein Veblen's theory of conspicuous consumption by the "leisure class," Georg Simmel's classic account of fashion as a recurring cycle of innovation by hegemonic classes and imitation by others, and Harold Perkin's explanation of British economic expansion as the result of consumption by social strata emulating the people just above them in a society with a peculiar multiplicity of class levels.[10] (The last provides much of the conceptual basis for McKendrick's "consumer revolution.") As we shall see in chapter 2, these class-based approaches can help to account for many consumption patterns in the seventeenth and eighteenth centuries, but far from all of them. It is difficult to apply Veblen, for example, to a society in which capitalism was not fully formed, and even then the range of motives he and Perkin examine is clearly too narrow. Simmel cannot explain why some fashions become permanent customs. Furthermore, all these approaches are so dependent on the concept of "class" and the assumption that classes exist more or less unambiguously that the recent critique of class as a unit of social analysis has compromised their viability as the primary bases for interpretation, at least with respect to early modern Europe.[11]

Another set of approaches concentrates on the inherent qualities of consumer goods themselves. Until recently, much of the writing on particular products imported into Europe from overseas during the era of European expansion, however analytical it might have been on the supply and transportation sides of the story, tended to revert to narrative when it came to the reception of the item in Europe—apparently on the assumption that there is nothing much to explain except perhaps the marketing of the product, that simple exposure was sufficient to make people want to buy it in ever increasing quantities.[12] This obviously begs the question of why they wanted to buy it. A further refinement in the case of sugar has been to argue that the human body has a "natural" desire for sweetness, perhaps associated with infantile experiences with mother's milk. But why cane sugar as opposed to other sweet substances, such as honey?[13] Recently, excellent research has been done on stimulants and addictive substances imported into early modern Europe, but the conclusion to which many of these studies have come is that such substances replaced or supplemented domestic European equivalents and that the reasons for their adoption have to be sought apart from their intrinsic qualities (or their prices, because they were almost always more expensive than their European equivalents when they were first introduced and for a good while afterward).[14] These studies, like other recent work, point toward a need to explain the meanings of consumption in order to understand changes in consumer choices. To explain meaning in human affairs, nowadays it is customary to look to the study of culture.

CULTURE AND THE CONTEXTS OF CONSUMPTION

Using "culture" as a framing concept for the kind of project envisioned here might seem to be attractive not only because it brings the vital factor of meaning to center stage, but also because there is less consensus among scholars about what culture actually is than with regard to almost any other important term in human studies. One might therefore hope to avoid conceptual imprisonment by the better-defined disciplinary paradigms. Unfortunately, at the present moment the academic study of culture is in such dynamic disarray that it presents rather too much of a good thing.[15] Within anthropology, the discipline that traditionally takes culture as its primary object of study, there are several bodies of theory and research that deal with consumption as an aspect of material or economic culture. Some of them, including the work of Mary Douglas and the structuralist anthropology of Claude Lévi-Strauss, are formulated ahistorically, although they can be adapted for historical use.[16] Other anthropologists, such as Marshall Sahlins, look overtly at historical change in economic patterns, including consumption.[17] In recent years, however, the whole concept of culture has been called into question by many anthropologists. To the lack of consensus that has always existed in anthropology as to what "culture" is has been added uncertainty about whether it exists at all, except as a theoretical concept developed in the nineteenth and twentieth centuries to justify Western hegemony over the rest of the world.

In what might seem an ironic twist of intellectual fashion, as anthropology has been experiencing its crisis of culture, practitioners of many other disciplines, including history, have been turning enthusiastically to culture as a framework for understanding. In part, this has been a reaction to a perceived failure of social science to deliver the kind of knowledge it once seemed to promise. In part, it has been a response to radical criticism of academic modes of inquiry in general, especially by deconstructionists. Many historians have also been attracted by the possibilities presented by the explosive growth of new fields such as culture and gender studies and by the "New Historicism" and postcolonialism in literary studies, all of which heavily feature cultural analysis in historical context.[18] In history and related fields, an emphasis in the 1980s on treating culture as language (either directly or by analogy) has expanded to include an interest in material culture, to some extent as a way of getting beyond limitations of the "linguistic turn." All this has been very exciting and extraordinarily productive of new approaches to consumption. What it has not done has been to create consensus about the meaning of culture or about the best ways to understand it. The richness of contemporary cultural studies makes it more attractive than ever before to confront the questions with which this book is concerned by focusing on culture, and at the same time more difficult. It appears that a new approach must be created specifically to address those questions.[19]

There are certain stipulations that must be laid down for such a vehicle. It must avoid prescribing the outcome of the inquiry through its own structure and forcing an inappropriately narrow hierarchy of explanatory priorities onto the data. It should, as much as possible, avoid tautology. Many of the more global approaches to creating context for historical events tend to be tautologous, typically tying the events together into a single developmental pattern. The pattern is then named, given the status of a self-generative historical force or process, and ascribed as the cause, or at least the explanation, of the events of which the pattern was originally composed. A notable example of this is modernization, which is an extraordinarily useful concept for identifying similarities among sequences of social and economic changes but which was unfortunately turned into a metahistorical explanation for those changes and became largely tautological. The vehicle should afford a sufficiently comprehensive view of the landscape that we can examine in detail similarities and connections among a host of very different features without presupposing an overarching explanation that links everything to everything else. It should allow the employment of models and theories from different disciplines without giving a priori explanatory precedence to any of them, and it should permit the use of such models and theories in cases in which they are valuable without creating an obligation to adopt them in cases in which they are not.

Above all, the approach should provide some reasonable way of dealing with the problems of causality. The way in which the questions at the beginning of this chapter were framed implies (indeed, requires) an attempt to identify causes. This is the traditional task of "scientific" history—which is precisely the kind of history most subject to the danger of theory dictating outcome. Scientific history has come under attack from proponents of "postmodern" approaches to cultural study, in part because of its emphasis on locating the causes of historical events. The postmodernist assault has certainly rendered most traditional assumptions about historical causation problematical. Some critics have gone so far as to deny the possibility of establishing chains of cause and effect as explanations of historical change. In their view, what passes for causal explanation in history is usually a myth, often derived from the system of power relations that obtains in the society of the interpreter. Such myths can never be objectively accurate, if for no other reason than that they are subverted by the very nature of the language in which they must be framed. Perhaps all that can be done is to try to comprehend the circumstances that led to the myth-building.[20]

The postmodern critique has cast doubt on the validity of historical explanation, but it has at the same time opened vast new avenues for exploring culture as something that is continually constructed rather than simply given. Is it necessary to abandon the attempt to put together a causal explanation for the kinds of change with which the present book is concerned, and instead to focus on exposing the ambiguities and contradictions of the linguistic fabric into which historical patterns of consumption are embroidered? Or is it possible to find a way of incorporating such analysis into an effort to find causes and explain change—if necessary, by treating causality as a much more uncertain category than historians have been accustomed to doing, but not eliminating it altogether? Can social theory and the constructions of social science be employed in full consciousness of their limitations, without dismissing them completely as delusional products of, say, the Enlightenment mania for science? I think it is possible to do all of these things. Comprehensive, objective, "scientific" understanding of historical causation and change may be impossible, but there is no reason that we should not try to understand in part, to make tentative approximations. That, after all, is what science actually does, and at least historians are not required to frame their (approximate) results in the rather awkward form of general laws. As long as we understand the problematical character of what we are doing, the effort to extract understanding of causation in history is not completely different from our efforts to understand anything else.

So what should be done? We should adopt a way of looking for causes and defining effects that does not assume that only one cause, or even a small number of causes, predominates in any process of change. We should not presume that something that seems important as a cause when we look back from the present must originally have been important in the dynamics of an earlier period. (Great oaks may grow from little acorns, but little acorns are still little acorns.) We should accept the fact that causal relationships may not always be confined within conventional interpretive categories. (One should not, for example, necessarily assume that economic effects always derive from economic causes.) We should also recognize the multiplicity of subject positions in any cultural construction, the ways in which linguistic and ideological incoherence often subvert meaning and belief, the likelihood of ambiguity in any significant statement—without, because of such recognition, giving up altogether on the search for causes in history.

These are commonsense guidelines for constructing a vehicle for investigation and a framework of interpretation. But there is also the problem of the vehicle itself: an apparatus that conforms to the guidelines, that permits discussion of cause and change without subjecting the discussion to a single, hegemonic body of theory, and that takes into account the discursively constructed subject positions of the people who are being studied as well as the people who are doing the studying (that is, us). Obviously, no analytical framework can provide everything required. The approach taken in this book is similar to one suggested by Marshall Sahlins.[21] It is built around categories that, for want of a better name, will be called *cultural contexts*.

CULTURAL CONTEXTS

A cultural context can be defined as an assembly of factors or traits that make "sense" as an ensemble to people living in a particular time and area, as elements of their world *meaningfully* linked to one another. Elements of a single cultural context might include items as diverse as an institution, a set of customary practices or behaviors, particular modes of cognition and discourse, and material objects. People in modern societies conduct their lives in the midst of a large number of cultural contexts, which they share with most of the people around them and which help to define their relationships with those people. People who live in American suburbs, for example, share a context of commuter transportation that has a distinctive set of institutions, a recognized range of practices and behavioral rules (many of them informal), an established discourse, conventional attitudes, and an array of material objects that are central to the context (automobiles, commuter trains, or, occasionally, commuter boats). Most people could describe several contexts that they negotiate on a regular basis that have clearly different cultures. The ones that would probably come to mind first would be those with strong institutional identities, such as family life, employment, and religion, but others would appear on further reflection (for instance, the commuter example).

For the most part, we are aware of cultural contexts even if we do not always have names for them—or at least we are conscious of what appear to be meaningful relationships among elements of a context and of the exclusion from particular contexts of items that do not appear to "belong." In day-to-day life, cultural contexts are not normally treated as objects for critical examination or regarded as problematical. We simply accept their existence unless we are forced to examine them more closely, typically by events that threaten to expose their incoherent aspects. Because much of what makes up a cultural context is consciously perceived, contexts are usually matters of record. This means that a scholar should be able to recover some of the "sense" of past contexts and thereby connect his or her own consciousness with records of the consciousness of participants in a historical culture no longer extant. A modern consciousness cannot, of course, apprehend all aspects of a past context and all the ways in which it might once have been meaningful. On the other hand, it is not clear that even an observant contemporary can understand every aspect of a context within which he or she lives, either. A person looking back in time may be able to perceive some aspects of it more clearly.

Like most other objects of historical study, cultural contexts possess a dual reality. On the one hand, historians may postulate that they existed in the minds and manifested themselves in the behavior of the people they study. On the other hand, past contexts must also have a reality in the contemporary minds of historians—a reality that, for the most part, must be constructed. The precise degree of correspondence between these realities can probably never be determined. This is, of course, merely a restatement of a difficulty that confronts all historians one way or another, as it does anyone trying to understand how other people think and why they act as they do. An obvious danger that arises for historians of cultural contexts is that they may impose on the past a sense of meaning that they themselves possess and then claim to have "found" it there—to which the remedy (at best a partial one) is to insist on good evidence that the people being studied possessed a similar sense.

Given the explosion of cultural studies across the academic disciplines in recent years, it goes without saying that we will not be giving automatic priority to anthropological theory in the chapters that follow. Anthropologists do not have a monopoly on the study of culture. Nevertheless, some of the clearest analyses of cultural contexts have come from anthropologists such as Sahlins. Moreover, cultural contexts resemble in some ways the concept of the "cultural complex" in the anthropological tradition of Franz Boas and his followers.[22] Cultural contexts (as they are described here) and Boasian complexes both contain a wide variety of elements, material and nonmaterial; both depend on interpreting the meanings of connections among elements; and neither confers interpretive privilege on any particular range of elements. But there are major differences as well.

Boasian cultural complexes are identified as the *dominant* patterns of culture in particular geographical areas or among particular ethnic groups. They may not include all cultural elements (there may be subcultures or random elements), but they contain a large proportion of them within a single, more or less coherent structure of meaning, so that a cultural complex designates the culture as a whole and permeates the social order with which it is identified. A cultural complex thus claims to be a single unifying framework for analysis of a particular people. Cultural contexts are much narrower in scope and more modest in their claims. Contexts vary greatly in the number of elements they contain and in their geographical or temporal coverage. None can be held, by itself, to define the culture of an area—or even the culture of its ruling elite. Rather, a number of cultural contexts (probably a large number) exist *simultaneously* within a particular area at a particular time. In the following chapters, we will see in early modern Europe a great many autonomous but overlapping contexts, some more or less static and some changing, some covering the whole continent and some quite local. The focus will be on a few changing contexts that crossed the boundaries of many countries but were particularly concentrated in the core areas of northwestern Europe, especially France, the Netherlands, and Britain. We will follow the process by which these contexts were reformulated as parts of a single, new context—respectability—that in the nineteenth century became essentially global in scope.

COMPONENTS OF CULTURAL CONTEXTS

What sort of item might belong in a cultural context? Almost anything, as long as it was seen to possess a set of meaningful connections to other elements of the context. These connections need not be thoroughly articulated. It may suffice that two things "go together" (tea and sugar, for example) as part of a larger set. Evidence that the people we are studying are conscious of coherence and connectedness among certain things is our primary clue to the existence, as well as the nature, of a specific cultural context. As we shall see, contexts are so varied and their boundaries and internal maps are so loosely drawn that we could fit practically any object, behavior pattern, or concept into one, and we could describe any set of cultural traits as a cultural context. That we could do so, however, does not mean that we should. We could, for instance, treat "liberalism" in the eighteenth century (before its ideology was formalized and named) as a cultural context. It possessed a wide variety of components, the connections among which were not always certain. But in fact, we possess plenty of methods for analyzing ideologies, even in their early forms. All we would be likely to gain would be a realization that there was more to liberalism than its cognitive structure, which would not be precisely a revelation, although it is often forgotten. What *would* be useful would be to look at early liberalism as an ideology against a background of cultural contexts. No ideology can function unless it is able to draw from the store of meanings arrayed in cultural contexts and available to the audiences—if one likes, the consumers—of ideology. One could argue that part of the phenomenal success of liberalism as an ideology was due to its relationships to many of the contexts that comprised respectability, something that would not be easily recognized if we made too extensive a claim for cultural contexts and tried to encompass everything of interest into them.

On the other hand, we should not try too eagerly to portray every ensemble of ideas and behaviors as an ideology or articulated body of theory unless there is good evidence that those models fit. For example, we shall see that it is misleading to speak of "consumerism" before the middle of the nineteenth century. Even to consider "consumption" as an autonomous, meaningful set of acts with its own coherence is probably incorrect anywhere in the world before the nineteenth century. Except in the writings of a few economic theorists, there is little evidence from the eighteenth century of that kind of consciousness of consumption. In the chapters that follow, consumption will be treated as a range of meaningful behaviors that, in early modern Europe, derived most of their meaning from their places in certain cultural contexts. Not all types of consumption were meaningful in all of the contexts that are discussed, and the consumption of a single item might be a part of several different contexts (although not always with the same meaning). Identifying contexts and their relationships to consumption allows us to construct a basis for explaining consumption history without recourse to inappropriate models, and yet without having to give up models altogether.

It may be useful to categorize the types of elements that might belong to a cultural context, as long as we do not take the categories too seriously. Their boundaries are porous, and the relationships that usually matter are those between specific elements, not between their types. Let us say that in a cultural context, one might expect to find cognitive, discursive (or perhaps linguistic), behavioral, structural, and material elements. In general, we can identify the components of each of the categories as follows:

Cognitive

These are the mental frameworks, typically manifested in words or images, within which people attempt to order data about, and thus to understand, themselves and the world around them. The category might include pictures, ideas, paradigms, and similar phenomena. Ideas can take many forms, although most commonly the term refers to propositional statements that purport to explain some aspect of reality. We could also include the more ____ ns that make up much of the consciousness of commu- ____, collective narratives and ideologies—although as we ha__ ____ usually better treated as separate entities. Together with discursive elements, cognitive frameworks traditionally occupy most of the attention of cultural historians. They are the prime foci of theoretical attempts to model the factors that "underlie" consciousness: *mentalités*, the *épistèmes* of Michel Foucault, the paradigms of Thomas Kuhn, and the like.[23]

Discursive

These are modes of verbal communication, spoken or written, together with words that are characteristic of particular contexts or that bear peculiar conventional meanings in those contexts. Modes of discourse convey meaning, but they may also conceal it. Words can deceive as well as inform the hearer, and they can certainly betray the user. Language frequently (some say inevitably) involves ambiguity. The meanings of words constantly change, more by a process of barely perceptible "slippage" than by conscious redefinition. Discursive elements are vital to a cultural context, but they are not the sole conveyors of meaning. Elements of *all* the categories we are discussing, when connected with each other, are meaningful. Close attention must be paid to language, but it must not be emphasized to the exclusion of everything else.

Behavioral

This category contains somatic factors, physical acts in a literal sense, actions of human bodies. It might appear that the difference between behaviors and items in the cognitive and discursive categories resembles the distinction between the "semiotic" and the "symbolic" in the early work of Julia Kristeva, but this is not the case. Kristeva's "symbols" would include *all* our categories; the "semiotic" is excluded because it cannot be regarded as being meaningful in the way that elements of cultural contexts are meaningful.[24] Not all physical actions are behaviors in our sense—only ones that are characteristic of a great many people, that are repeated on a regular basis, and that are recognized as being meaningful (although not necessarily legitimate) by the people who perform or observe them. The kinds of behavioral elements with which we are concerned include habits, fashions, and, above all, practices: customs, rituals, the accepted ways of using a material object, and so forth. Because this study focuses on the consumption of certain types of goods, the behaviors that are particularly featured are mainly consumption practices, but these are usually embedded in some larger behavior pattern, which is in turn part of a cultural context.

Structural

In a sense, a social structure is nothing more than a pattern of behaviors, a set of practices, repeated by many people at high levels of frequency and similarity, made meaningful by being attached to a particular cognitive framework that explains and legitimates the behavior (and sometimes by more or less conscious analogies to constructed edifices).[25] The category includes organized institutions—government, church, business firm, army—as well as less formal collective entities such as social classes, status groups, professions, and families. Under most circumstances, if one wants to understand how an institution or other collectivity works, it is not particularly helpful to analyze it as an element of a cultural context. If, however, one wants to analyze a cultural context, it is often vital to treat certain structures as functioning members. As we shall see, the context that will be called "domestic femininity" in chapter 6 would be unintelligible if families (not just the idea of "the family") were excluded from the context.

Material

Material objects require treatment as elements of cultural contexts on much the same footing as the factors that belong in the other categories. Material objects have meanings. The meanings of objects (even the same objects) are often different in different cultural contexts. This is not news. A whole anthropology of material objects exists that analyzes objects as economic goods and as bearers of meaning that parallel spoken and written language.[26] Historians of everyday life have long recognized the varying significance of material objects under different, but simultaneous, circumstances. John Demos, in his study of family life in the Plymouth Colony, writes that household objects "must be considered in a variety of different ways. . . . How did people *feel* about this or that object? What kind of value did they place upon it? What associations, voluntary or involuntary, did it call up in them? How might it influence, or reflect, the pattern of relationships that obtained between different members of the household? These are matters that we take for granted with respect to the familiar 'objects' of our own lives; they belong to an area of unspoken, and sometimes unconscious, assumptions, habits, and beliefs. They represent a kind of underlying *context*, from which each particular object derives much of its true meaning."[27] Demos goes on to describe how a common household item—a sieve—had a very different meaning in the context of seventeenth-century cooking from the one it held in contemporaneous occult practices (in which it was used for divination and related magical purposes).

Among the kinds of material objects with which we shall be concerned are foods and drinks. These, of course, can be subdivided into types based on physical composition, but it is sometimes more useful for analytical purposes to consider the functions a food may perform. In discussing the history of sugar, for example, Sidney Mintz distinguishes among the following functions, all of which have been performed by sugar: medicine, spice-condiment, decorative material, sweetener, and preservative.[28] The important point (well known to anthropologists) is that the acts of eating and drinking can be meaningful in many different ways besides the simple biological function of keeping the body alive. (Even that function is not so simple, because there are many different things one can eat to stay alive. People have starved to death because they have refused, on grounds of culturally derived distaste or prohibition, to eat things that are technically edible—for instance, each other.) And of course a single act of eating or drinking can, and usually does, have meaning in a variety of contexts simultaneously.

Obviously, this book cannot deal with the whole range of consumable objects available in Europe in the seventeenth and eighteenth centuries. It will focus on *commodities*—material objects produced for sale in markets, which can be exchanged for money or for other commodities. Although practically any physical object can play a role in a cultural context, the most significant material items in modern and early modern Western cultural life have been commodities, which display the same variability of meaning that other objects do.[29] For reasons that have been discussed, the commodities to which we will pay particular attention are items that were imported into Europe from the outside: sugar, pepper, other spices, tea, coffee, cotton, silk, porcelain, and tobacco. These cover several conventional classifications of consumer goods: foods and drinks, clothing, consumer durables, and drugs. European products will be discussed mainly in cases in which their use paralleled or derived from the consumption of imported goods.

MEANING IN CULTURAL CONTEXTS

The whole point of identifying cultural contexts is to lay out a perceptible area within which items that vary greatly in type have meaning in relation to one another. What, then, is "meaning"?

It is not possible to consider this question in any depth here or to address adequately the issue of whether or not there exists such a thing as noncontingent meaning. For present purposes, it is sufficient to consider meaning to be a phenomenon observable in human thought and behavior. It is apparently essential to (and perhaps arises from) the interaction of humans with each other and the negotiation of their physical environments. Meaning appears to be closely related to the ways human societies adapt to the circumstances they confront, and the kinds of meanings their members perceive may be a significant factor in determining whether or not their adaptations are effective.[30] Seen in this way, the kinds of meaning with which we deal here are always relational and contingent. In order to have meaning, one thing must be understood to bear some sort of relationship to another thing or things. This holds true for actions, objects, ideas, and most especially words, which can only mean something in terms of something else. Some meaningful relations among things can be quite simple, while others are immensely complex, involving layers and intersections of connections within which a single action, object, idea, or word can have multiple significations that are not always completely distinct from one another.

What kinds of relationships produce or contain meaning? This is an immense question, but for present purposes it will suffice to say that the essence of a meaningful cultural relationship is that it is constantly replicated and is perceived in similar ways by large numbers of people. A cultural context is characterized by high frequencies of repetition of connections between certain sets of items. The most common forms of connection within contexts appear to be symbolism (one item suggests another, usually by convention or analogy), association (which includes the classical relations of cause and effect, comparison, extension, and sympathy), utility (several things are used together or in sequence to perform a task), and inclusion/exclusion. It is rare for the hodgepodge of relations within a single cultural context to be free of contradictions, inconsistencies, or ambiguities. Indeed, we can identify many cultural contexts through the presence of characteristic inconsistencies. These may be recognized as contradictions, usually in the form of "problems" to be solved (as in Kuhn's "paradigms"). More frequently, however, there is a tacit agreement to ignore contradictions and to employ certain discursive techniques to get around them (for example, by understanding a single word in more than one way, while treating the word in logical construction as though it had but one meaning).

It would be possible, I suppose, to develop an abstract "theory" of cultural contexts by continuing in this vein, but their heterogeneity is such that I doubt that doing so would be very productive. Instead, let us consider a modern example. Most people today recognize the existence of a context we call "sports" or "sport." "Sport" denotes a particular range of behaviors, practices, types of dress, modes of discourse, words, ideas, values, goals, institutions, and material objects. It also refers to a specific set of meaningful connections that are assumed to exist between these elements. The "world of sports," although wide, is quite distinct as an ensemble from, say, the context bounded by the work environment of managers, professionals, and office employees in a bureaucratically organized corporation. The latter context has no conventional name, but it is also easily recognized. Most of the elements of the two contexts are entirely separate. An American football helmet is not normally found in a corporate office. In terms of its main use, it does not belong. As a cue to imagining a context, it suggests sport, not corporate business—even though professional football is a substantial business in its own right. A football helmet therefore has its primary meaning in the context of sport; it is connected, mainly by links of utility and symbolism, to other elements of the context. This is not, however, quite the same as saying that the helmet would be wholly meaningless in a corporate office. If the office were the headquarters of a professional football team, a helmet with the logo of the team might serve as a corporate symbol. Even in another office, a suitably mounted football helmet might be found on the desk of an executive who was once a football player. If its only function was to stimulate private, nostalgic reflections (or possibly fantasies) on the part of the executive, its meaning would still be exogenous to the context of the office. However, it might also represent a claim by its owner to a generalized high status on the basis of having proven his manhood on the playing field. Building on a set of conventional analogies among business competition, team sports, and war, it might suggest that the owner of the helmet is particularly valuable in his organization because he has demonstrated his competitiveness and ability to be a team player in the context of sport. (Analogy is one of the main modes of relationship between items in different contexts.) It might also be a crude attempt to intimidate rival executives. This example shows, in a small way, how material objects, social structures, and cognitive patterns can be connected within a cultural context, and also how different contexts can share elements while giving them separate (although not necessarily completely different) meanings.

Cultural contexts create both limits and opportunities for human thought and action. Because of the multiplicity of contexts, because a thing can have different meanings in different contexts, people can exercise choice among contexts within which to think and act. They cannot exercise unlimited choice, because meaning is effectively restricted to contexts that are available at any particular place and time. But a crucial point about cultural contexts is that they *change*, mainly through human exercise of choice with regard to small matters.

CHANGES IN CULTURAL CONTEXTS

One of the reasons that, until fairly recently, most historians were reluctant to make the concept of culture (in its various "anthropological" uses) a central feature of their research was the problem of change. Historians took the explanation of change as their major task, whereas students of culture tended to construct a timeless "anthropological present" for the people they studied. In the latter case, the traditional way of dealing with the huge amount of evidence that practically all peoples have experienced substantial cultural change has been to portray change in terms of "stages" of development, typically marked off from each other by some critical transformative experience. Here, at least, there could be interaction between historians and cultural scientists, for many historians thought in terms of stages as well. But most peoples and societies (with the significant exception of western Europe) were seen as changing as a result of factors largely exogenous to their own cultures—most recently, through conquest and colonial rule by Western societies, which destroyed the traditional bases of the anthropological present and ushered in the era of "history" (that is, change). In the case of the West, movement between stages was usually held to be generated within Western society, but by factors that lay outside culture (typically economic or political changes) or by changes in a narrow range of elite thinking. The notion of culture as a source of fundamental change in itself was alien to all parties.

In recent years, this situation has altered. Among many historians, the question of whether or not change should in fact be the center of their enterprise has become legitimate, while the idea of analyzing change in terms of stages or even eras has become questionable. Anthropologists have become more conscious of the variability of culture and the ubiquity (as well as the complexity) of cultural change. These developments, although disquieting to some, have made it possible to discuss a multiplicity of simultaneous changes in history. Explanations can be proposed for these changes without having to identify transcendental or underlying causes that tie them all together. We can focus instead on how connections between ongoing changes are constructed—not just by historians, but by contemporaries of the changes themselves. The present book explores some of the possibilities inherent in this readjustment of perspectives by making use of cultural contexts as frameworks for change.

It would be difficult and probably unnecessary to give a comprehensive, abstract account of change in cultural contexts. Just as each context contains a unique set of components, so each displays a unique pattern of change. It is useful, however, to think in general about some of the ways in which contexts might change. We can envision two patterns (although in most actual cases they appear to intersect): change within a context and change in the relationships between contexts.

Changes within a context may occur because one or more of its elements alter, either (1) as a result of some dynamic inherent in the context (such as the recognition of incompatibility between certain constituent elements) or because of willful acts of creation or destruction by individuals, or (2) because an exogenous element intrudes itself. In the first case, since elements are already connected in a meaningful pattern, change in some elements can have a substantial effect on others, ultimately altering the pattern and even the definition of the whole context. In the second case, new relations of meaning have to be created to incorporate the new element. Because most of the existing bodies of theory that deal with social and cultural change focus (in the terminology used here) on changes within contexts, finding an appropriate framework for interpreting a particular case is usually not difficult.

Unfortunately, analysis within a single context often has distinct limitations. As was pointed out previously, it is possible to explain why tea became fashionable in seventeenth-century Europe within a fairly clear context of status-seeking and fashion, but without reference to other contexts one cannot explain why it was imported in the first place or why its consumption was transformed from a fashion into a permanent, defining constituent of respectability.

It is therefore necessary to take into account changes that occur because of the intersection of contexts. Cultural contexts are seldom completely separate from each other; many intersect because they share some of the same elements. Changes within one context that affect a shared element may thereby create an intrusion into the other context. In the case of tea, at least two distinct contexts (one defined by status, the other by popular ideas and behavior concerning health and virtue) intersected in the late seventeenth and eighteenth centuries to produce both a huge growth in tea consumption and fundamental changes in the context of status. (This is, of course, a shorthand way of describing what happened; it may be excessively abstract and mechanical but it gets the job done. What actually happened was that a great many people consciously made a connection between the meanings that tea-taking possessed in two more or less separate sets of practices and ideas with which they were familiar.) Very few theories have much to say about these transfer processes, and those that do usually impose, a priori, a causal hierarchy among contexts—something that we are trying to avoid. In these cases it is necessary to go beyond conventional theory and improvise explanations.

The next five chapters describe particular cultural contexts that existed or formed in western Europe in the seventeenth and early eighteenth centuries and that continued to exist (although with substantial changes) into the nineteenth. The contexts are identified and explored primarily through the ways in which they constructed the consumption of non-European commodities, so that we obtain both an idea of each context and a grasp of its role (often through interaction with another context) in stimulating changes in demand. The contexts to be examined are:

• the context of *gentility* through which the complex status hierarchy of Europe manifested itself in, among other things, fashionable consumption behavior (chapter 2)

• a context of *luxury* in which sensuality (defined very broadly) was accommodated to morality through an aesthetic of consumption and the development of the concepts of comfort and convenience (chapter 3)

• a context of *virtue* in which ideas about health, cleanliness, and morality were attached to each other, helping, among other things, to define what it meant to be bourgeois (chapter 4)

- a context in which *masculinity* was connected to notions of rationality, public life, and voluntary association (chapter 5)

- a context in which *femininity* was constructed around a culture of domesticity, producing an ideology that emphasized the maintenance of civilization (chapter 6)

Chapter 7 will examine the process in the eighteenth century whereby all these contexts intersected or were more or less deliberately attached to each other to form a new, very broad, and well-defined cultural context to which the name *respectability* is most commonly given. Respectability became, by the nineteenth century, probably the primary factor defining consumption in Western economies. It also constituted a substantial part of the general phenomenon of modernity.

2

GENTILITY

STATUS AND CONSUMPTION

According to one of the most familiar myths of American culture, consumption occurs primarily in a context defined by the Joneses: the people down the street with whom all middle-class families supposedly attempt to keep up. This is one version of status consumption, a cultural pattern that overtly connects the possession of material goods with prescribed modes of behavior held to be appropriate for particular levels of social standing. Practically all modern societies practice status consumption. Its significance as one of the bases for the "consumer economy" and "consumer society" is generally accepted.[1] However, it is also now accepted that the notion of competitive consumption for purposes of signifying individual status—the idea promulgated by Thorstein Veblen at the turn of this century and explicit in the practice of "keeping up with the Joneses"—accounts for only a part of the modern phenomenon of status consumption. Pierre Bourdieu, for example, suggests that people seek to construct or reproduce "distinction" in what they buy and use, an intention that centers less around individual competition than on self-identification, class definition, and solidarity within classes.[2] Whatever its general nature, status consumption is not a simple phenomenon.

It is also not a universal aspect of human social life. Status differences have existed in most societies of which there are historical records, but they have been constituted in many different ways and not all of them have involved the kind of consumption as a sign of status that developed in the modern West. The Western pattern of status consumption is supposed to have emerged sometime between the sixteenth and the nineteenth centuries, depending on the interpretation one follows and the criteria one accepts for identifying the presence of the pattern.[3] Among its most-cited identifying features are the following.

The importance of rapidly changing fashions in designating products that confer status. Fashionability is not unique to modern status consumption, but the extent to which it has taken the place of the distinctive class uniforms and lifestyles found in earlier societies—both Western and non-Western—is quite remarkable. Except in unusual, transitory circumstances, being up with fashion (although not necessarily at the cutting edge) is an important part of claiming status at most levels and in most areas of social life.

The generality and relative homogeneity of status consumption patterns. Modern status consumption is not (as its predecessor in Europe before the sixteenth century was) an activity limited to certain prestigious social classes. It is a cultural practice in which people at practically all social levels engage, to the extent that their incomes allow. Moreover, although there are qualitative and cost differences between the status commodities consumed by the wealthy and those purchased by the less wealthy, the general types of the goods and the ways in which they are used are remarkably similar. This could be described as a "democratization" of taste and consumption in modern times. Whatever one calls it, the phenomenon illustrates the problematical nature of some of the ways in which status consumption is analyzed—whether in the style of Veblen or in that of Bourdieu. How does "distinction" arise from consuming in essentially the same ways as people of other (especially lower) income levels? This should serve as a warning that differences in consumption are often quite subtle, a matter of nuances, and are evidence of complex cultural codes at work that extend well beyond class structure (or, indeed, any other kind of social structure).

The high level of commercialization of status consumption and its close relationship to distinctively modern economic phenomena such as industrial production, technology, and mass advertising.[4] This aspect is often connected to an assertion that status consumption is essentially a behavioral characteristic of the "bourgeoisie" or "middle class" and that its generality is due to the economic and cultural hegemony of the bourgeoisie in the modern world.[5] As we shall see, identifying modern status consumption with the bourgeoisie is not historically incorrect, but it raises more questions than it answers. For example, the basic patterns of status consumption in the Western world clearly predate the existence of the bourgeoisie as a self-conscious social class. Most of the behavioral traits usually associated with "bourgeois" status consumption—especially with regard to dress—derive from a cultural pattern characteristic, until the late seventeenth century at the earliest, of the hereditary aristocracy of Europe, not the professional and commercial classes. What, then, makes them distinctively "bourgeois"?[6] In other words, how did they come to be part of a cultural context of status ordered in terms of bourgeois concerns and values—without, for some time, losing their relevance to the hereditary aristocracy?

These and related questions will be confronted throughout this book, but a brief preview of some of the answers can be given now. What will appear is that an aristocratic cultural context that revolved around a view of status defined by *gentility* was made to intersect with other contexts, so that elements of the original context that framed the pattern of status consumption for aristocrats became, by the late eighteenth century, part of a broader context in which the link between status and consumption was defined by *respectability*. Members of European elites who wanted to adhere to patterns based on something like the old gentility could do so until well into the nineteenth century, while quite a lot of people (theoretically, without regard to ascribed social level) who wanted and could afford to live, think, speak, and consume according to patterns based on respectability had the option of doing so from sometime in the eighteenth century—and could on that account be described accurately as "bourgeois."[7] In a sense, then, it was not so much that the European bourgeoisie adopted the cultural patterns of the traditional hereditary elite as it was that the bourgeoisie formed itself as a self-conscious class around a culture of respectability constructed from, among other sources, the older aristocratic context of gentility.

Let us look more closely at that earlier context in the third quarter of the seventeenth century—a time when, in the Netherlands and England at least, substantial tensions within gentility and influences from other contexts were producing observable changes. The principal instrument for this investigation will be one of the most observant and self-revealing people of the period.

SAMUEL PEPYS, GENTLEMAN

On December 3, 1661, Samuel Pepys, over a year into his appointment as secretary to the English Navy Board, visited Lady Sandwich, the wife of his patron, at the Earl of Sandwich's London house. Lady Wright, another guest, held forth with vigor on a subject of great interest to her. "And all our talk," Pepys wrote in his diary afterward, "about the great happiness that my

Lady Wright says there is in being in the fashion and in variety of fashions, in scorn of others that are not so, as citizens wifes and country-gentle-women—which though it did displease me enough, yet I said nothing."[8] On December 9, Lady Wright visited Pepys's office at the Wardrobe. (Pepys held two state jobs simultaneously.) While there, she "did talk much upon the worth and the desert of gallantry; and that there was none fit to be Courtiers but such as have been abroad and know fashions; which I endeavored to oppose and was troubled to hear her talk so, though she be a very wise and discreet lady in other things."[9]

Fashion was obviously very important in the social world in which Pepys found himself, and also an object of some ambiguity. The Pepys of the *Diary* was a classic social climber. A young university graduate from a "middling" family background, he had used a distant kinship with Sandwich to obtain government jobs. Pepys's social position was very uncertain. The early part of the *Diary* is full of references to slights he experienced, balanced by occasions on which he was treated with "respect" by distinguished people.[10] It also records Pepys's adoption of fashionable dress and a genteel public lifestyle as a conscious strategy for securing his social standing. Yet when Lady Wright praises fashionable behavior, Pepys disagrees.[11] The situation is complicated by the fact that, whatever Lady Wright's status may have been, Lady Sandwich had only been a countess for a few months herself. (Her husband was a country gentleman and Cromwellian officer rewarded by Charles II with a peerage for helping arrange the Restoration.)[12] Pepys was not the only one engaged in social self-promotion. Compared to his patron, he was a rank amateur.

Just how was Pepys affected by the relationship between status and fashion, especially fashionable consumption as manifested in dress? An answer to this question can be attempted by looking through Pepys's eyes at the context of gentility, near the edge of which he stood in 1660 and 1661 and within which he had to function in order to pursue the kind of career he desired.

The most obvious feature of any cultural context featuring status is "social structure" in its generic sense: a set of perceived group relationships that inform the ordering of people and the distribution of prestige among them. Pepys knew about social structure. He understood that high status, political power, and wealth were linked, and he wanted all three. Pepys accepted the notion of a fixed, natural social hierarchy with grades established by birth, but at the same time he planned a career of social climbing and believed he should be promoted on the basis of his merits. This suggests that Pepys's conception of social structure was neither uniform nor particularly consistent—not an unusual circumstance in his day or in ours. There is evidence in the *Diary* that Pepys's simultaneous adoption of different views of social structure and his use of the language of social stratification in contradictory ways sometimes led to a kind of cognitive dissonance. Dissonance between social conceptions was not uncommon in an England that had, in less than a generation, undergone the Civil War, the Puritan Commonwealth, the suggestion (not implemented) of radical social reform, and the Restoration.[13] Pepys, like many of his contemporaries, had observed the mutability of the social order and concluded that it was desirable to assert its permanence. Pepys appears to have reconciled his personal pursuit of social promotion with his support for a fixed social order by seeing his behavior not as an attempt to jump, say, from the "bourgeoisie" to the aristocracy, but rather as a means of confirming the status he believed he already possessed: that of "gentleman."

Pepys and his contemporaries perceived several kinds of distinction among status groups: between the noble and the non-noble landed aristocracies, between the urban professional and commercial elites and the landed aristocracy, and between all of the above and the various classes of nonelite persons. Such distinctions were significant in politics and sometimes in law. But people also thought in terms of status categories defined more broadly and fuzzily. In England, this was particularly true of the term *gentleman* and its correlatives *gentry* and *gentility*. Observers in the seventeenth century (like historians today) sometimes tried to fit the gentry snugly into a single hierarchy, somewhere between the nobility and the citizenry of towns. This was one perfectly acceptable use of the terminology.[14] More often, however, social discourse treated them as a class that transcended many of the internal boundaries of the formal social hierarchy to include in one large category all the adult males who had a claim to prestige, elite status, and a share of political power—together with their female and minor dependents.[15] In England, the status of gentleman had formal implications for public service liabilities and informal implications in terms of social and political opportunities. In essence, gentlemen were the people who ran politics and whose opinions about issues mattered. They were the natural leaders of society, at whatever level (local, regional, national) was appropriate to their birth, income, titles, and perhaps talents. Pepys would have liked eventually, through successful government service, to have been awarded a knighthood—an overt, legal badge of gentle status. (He never was.) In the 1660s, however, he was concerned with being accepted informally as a gentleman.

But who were gentlemen? In England, baronets, knights, male members of families with extensive landholdings, and sons of noblemen were all certainly gentlemen, as were, in a general sense, noblemen and the king himself (the "first gentleman" of the realm). With others it was less clear, but there were accepted criteria that could be applied. Conventionally, the broad status of gentleman was ascribed according to the status of one's family, not earned. So to someone like Pepys, one prerequisite for acceptance as a gentleman was the ability to claim a familial connection to people with the appropriate standing. This Pepys could do, although only distantly.[16] He had more difficulty with two other vital, connected prerequisites: income and independence. Pepys had little private income, and his prospects for inheritance were meager. Because of his lack of income and standing, he had begun his career as an obvious dependent of Sandwich and was treated as such by other members of the Navy Board.[17] Pepys was caught in a vicious circle. Secure possession of genteel status required a degree of independence, independence required income, income (in Pepys's case) could only be derived from public office, and full exploitation of office required that Pepys be accepted as a gentleman. Following the advice of his aristocratic patrons, Pepys decided (not without misgivings) to break out of his bind by being fashionable, by participating in a highly complex cultural pattern in which he could, with effort and luck, present himself as he wanted to be and thereby achieve his goals. Among other things, this decision required that Pepys and his household shape their behavior as consumers to certain norms.

Even before the previously noted conversations about fashion that Pepys recorded in his diary, he had been subjected to pressure from Lady Sandwich and others to spend more money on clothing for his wife, "Which I think it best to do, for her honour and my owne."[18] Mrs. Pepys may have had a hand in stimulating the delivery of such advice, but Pepys's acquiescence was consistent with his outlook on his career in the early 1660s. In October 1661, Pepys dined with other members of the Navy Board and felt uncomfortable. "I not being neat in clothes, which I find a great fault in me, could not be so merry as otherwise and at all times I am and can be, when I am in good habitt; which makes me remember my father Osborne's rule for a gentleman, to spare in all things rather then [sic] in that."[19] To fit in as a gentleman, you had to dress like one. A few days later, before going to the lord mayor's feast, Pepys wrote: "This day I put on my half-Cloth black stockings and my new Coate of the fashion, which pleases me well."[20] Pepys's concern with fashion for his wife, presumably pursuant to the aristocratic advice he had received, continued into the next year. In April 1662, they both visited the New Exchange to look at petticoats, and in May, after buying a new livery for his servant, Pepys and his wife walked to Gray's Inn "to observe fashions of the ladies, because of my wife's making some new clothes."[21]

Pepys had deliberately thrust himself and his wife into a social world that involved adopting, in public at least, a peculiar and complex pattern of behavior. As can be seen from the citations from the *Diary*, the pattern had at least three aspects: consuming manifestly expensive commodities (connected by Pepys to "honour"); conforming to the rules of dress that governed the personal deportment of a gentleman (which elicited internal anxieties and satisfactions); and following fashion. There were, of course, other modes of gentility that Pepys was expected to adhere to if he could, but these three appear to be the ones most directly connected to consumption practices.

MODES OF GENTILITY

Conspicuousness and Honor

The conspicuous consumption of expensive goods as a sign of status is classically explained in Veblen's *Theory of the Leisure Class*, which argues that such consumption arises from the stratified and competitive nature of society.[22] Social standing depends on the class in which a person is categorized by other people. In a capitalist society, class membership is essentially a function of wealth rather than, for example, individual accomplishments or birth. However, it is insufficient simply to have money; you must let other people know you have it. For this reason, people at all levels try, through ostentatious purchasing and display, to indicate that they have a great deal of money relative to the wealth of their immediate competitors. The wealthiest people of all, those who wish to be accounted members of the highest classes, not only spend the most on display but frame their display within a lifestyle that emphasizes expenditure on leisure—indicating both that they possess money and that they do not need to work for it. This last phenomenon is an obvious link to a precapitalist, aristocratic past.

How much of Veblen's "conspicuous consumption" model explains Pepys's behavior? Some elements certainly apply. Pepys's strategy required public, hence conspicuous, display. "Private life" in the modern sense may or may not have been invented by the 1660s, but in order to succeed at being fashionable, Pepys had to disinguish consciously between his public and private worlds, economizing on expenses for the latter in order to be able to cut the appropriate figure in the former.[23] Pepys's interest in his wife's clothing is limited to what she wears for appearances in public, as at church on Sunday or when she is entertaining wives of aristocratic colleagues. Pepys himself carefully avoids wearing his lace sleeve-bands except on important public occasions.[24]

Pepys often represents his fashion behavior as keeping up with the Joneses (or in his case, with the Penns and the other members of the Navy Board). Pepys does not seem to be as interested in claiming individual superiority to his aspirational peers as he is in being accepted by them as a member of their "club"—the gentry.[25] He wants to share the symbols of the gentry's "distinction," as Bourdieu explains. And the issue of leisure, of not having to work? Pepys is (and was) famous for his industry. Could such a person belong to a "leisure class"? In a sense, yes. Work, to Pepys as to any other gentleman of his time, was a matter of individual choice. One could spend one's days hunting or in affairs of the heart. Or one could do the work of one's state offices (if one couldn't afford a deputy), pursue appropriately genteel profitable enterprises, and spend time at a coffeehouse exchanging news and discussing matters of interest.[26] The point was that Pepys could *choose* how to spend his time, even in the relatively straitened circumstances under which he began his career. Like many of the American millionaires of the Gilded Age on whom Veblen focused, the practitioners of gentility in early modern Europe demonstrated their status not by ostentatiously refusing to work, but by actively showing that they could decide what they wanted to do or not do, unlike other people (regardless of income level) who were supposed to spend their working lives performing prescribed tasks. (In anticipation of a later chapter, it should be noted that "other people" here refers also to many, probably most, of the female members of the gentry in the seventeenth century, who did not share the options or the leisure of their menfolk.)

So Veblen's concept works to a degree for Pepys and probably for many of Pepys's contemporaries. Where Veblen fails is in explaining the *reasons* for early modern conspicuous consumer behavior. In Pepys's case, we are not observing the intensely and unabashedly individualistic competition to display wealth Veblen ascribes to capitalist society, perhaps because there is not yet any such thing as capitalist society. Although wealth was displayed (often garishly) by those who had it, the display was explained and justified in terms incompatible with Veblen's theory. Conspicuous display advertised and promoted the *honor* of the family that did the displaying, rather than the simple fact of individuals' wealth.

Honor—or familial repute, in which individuals participated—was one of the connections that bound members of an elite family together, linking contemporaries, framing their behavior, and (notionally, at least) placing them in a coherent relationship with their ancestors and descendants.[27] It was something that a gentleman or lady was obliged to defend. Males defended the full range of items that constituted honor by force and law. Females defended a narrower range by protecting their chastity and their marriage commitments (or at least by protecting themselves from the public imputation that they acted unchastely), ostensibly because only through the maintenance of a gentle or noble bloodline could the essence of the family be preserved.

Much of early modern public life, including politics, revolved around the idea of honor. Honor derived not just from one's personal standing, but even more from the standing of one's family and lineage, from the official positions one's ancestors had held and for which one therefore felt eligible, from one's titles, and from the place one occupied as a result of these things somewhere near the upper end of an assumed hierarchy of esteem that incorporated everyone. In this sense, honor defined the pool of people who should exercise authority. In the eighteenth century, Montesquieu identified the pursuit and defense of honor as the fundamental principle that motivated the nobility in a monarchy.[28]

Thus, part of Pepys's context of genteel status consumption consists of public display of wealth as a means (notionally) of supporting (or in Pepys's case, announcing) the honor of one's family—Veblen's conspicuous consumption, but in a cognitive world quite different from the one Veblen describes. The extent of conspicuous elite consumption in seventeenth-century Europe is very well known: the building of elaborate country houses, which bankrupted noble families all over the continent; extremely large expenditures on fashionable clothing, on unneeded retainers, on wasteful feasting; investments in honorific but not necessarily well-conceived business enterprises; and so forth.[29] It is not difficult to place Pepys at the edge of this behavior pattern. Nor is it difficult to see in his adoption of a limited version of it the efforts of a "new man" to find status, legitimacy, and success, in such a way that the elements of the pattern tended to be redefined. (In theory, a person behaved as a gentleman because he *was* one, not because he wanted to *become* one.)

And yet, on this subject (as opposed to the issue of income) Pepys gives no hint of conscious hypocrisy. He really believes he is a gentleman, playing a game that gentlemen play and seeking to do it successfully. He is not conscious of belonging in any other pool than the one in which he is attempting to swim. He is conscious of being connected by kinship, acquaintance, and business to the commercial and professional elite of the city of London, but he sees no apparent derogation of his assumed genteel status in that. He obviously considers many of his City associates to be gentlemen as well.[30] Members of older, better-established country families probably would not have agreed with Pepys's assessment of himself and his acquaintances, even though at one time—probably not far in the past—their own ancestors might have been in much the same situation.[31] There was, in other words, space within the context of gentility for cognitive flexibility and structural mobility, if not unlimited space. That this space existed was due both to the complexity of the actual histories of gentry families and to the fuzziness, ambiguity, and multiplicity of articulated social boundaries. What appears to be ambiguity from one person's perspective may be opportunity from another's.

We should be particularly careful not to assume that conspicuous consumption in Pepys's time was characteristic of a "new" as opposed to an "old" elite (or vice versa). Many well-established aristocrats engaged in astonishingly expensive forms of consumption in the seventeenth century, as did many people whose elite status was not so well established. Alternative patterns of moderation and parsimony were adopted by families of quite varied antiquity.[32] As we shall see, religious outlook and personal career strategy (and, to some extent, income) seem to have had more to do with encouraging the alternative patterns than did the standing of a person or family within the aristocracy relative to others. In the 1660s, Nicolas Fouquet and Jean-Baptiste Colbert were both upstarts, as far as the old French nobility (the *noblesse d'épée*) were concerned. But Fouquet emphasized conspicuous consumption and fashionability in his strategy for rising to power, while his rival sought a reputation for moderation in personal expense, regarding conspicuous consumption as something appropriate for his royal master and something that, in other people and countries, created opportunities for exploitation.[33] The difference was not one of pedigree, but of conscious choice among alternatives.

Conformity to Genteel Convention

People of status in the seventeenth and eighteenth centuries spent a great deal of time and effort attempting to conform to the standards of behavior expected of the genteel by the genteel. This can be readily understood in the case of someone like Pepys. Convinced of his own gentility but uncertain about how others rated him, Pepys felt constrained to behave properly and to avoid gaffes. *Constrained* is perhaps too mild a term for the force that lay behind the extreme discomfort Pepys felt and confided in his diary when he was caught, as it were, out of uniform. On one occasion in 1662, excited by a rather bizarre project on which he had become engaged, Pepys rushed from his house to the Tower of London without his cloak. At the Tower, he was required to leave his sword at the gate. Because a swordless gentleman out of doors was supposed to wear a cloak (presumably to disguise the fact that he was unarmed), Pepys hid in a corner, ap-parently for some time, until his servant returned with the missing item.[34]

There were many people in Pepys's situation in early modern Europe (and in the colonies; the young George Washington is an obvious American example). These were probably the most avid readers of the many guidebooks that are our best sources for the theory of genteel behavior in the seventeenth and eighteenth centuries.[35] But even people who were quite secure in their gentility went to considerable lengths to conform fully to its conventions. As social and cultural historians have emphasized in recent years, this was no easy task, because the conventions of European gentility changed substantially and frequently between 1600 and 1800.[36] The adoption of practices emphasizing "politeness" and "civility" (the changes that have attracted the greatest amount of historical attention) was not a matter simply of fashion, although, as we shall see later in the present chapter, fashion was certainly involved in the process. Nor can genteel conventions be understood wholly within the framework of "honor" that we have just discussed, although the notion of honor was one of several that were employed to construct them. Rather, they were an immensely complex, sometimes inconsistent set of practices, all of them with implications for social structures and for the consumption of material objects, and all of them with a variety of cognitive and discursive representations. They were adopted for many reasons, not least of which was that they were central to the self-image, and thus the self-esteem, of people who thought themselves to be gentlemen or gentlewomen. Historians have not yet fully explored the range of phenomena and the dynamics of change within this set. What can be done here is to focus on certain tensions, certain cognitive dissonances within the context of gentility that can be seen as motives for change, and on three very significant patterns of conformity that can be analyzed as partial responses to these tensions. These three patterns, which we will call "maintaining order," "magistracy," and "courtesy, politeness, and civility," strongly influenced (and in the third case was strongly influenced by) changes in genteel consumption. They also greatly affected the process through which much of the context of gentility was incorporated into the culture of respectability in the eighteenth century.

Maintaining order. Much of the historical literature on the cultural aspects of elite social behavior—especially consumption—treats them as means of reproducing or reinforcing the existing social order. Let us consider the sword about which Pepys was so worried. In sixteenth- and seventeenth-century England, only gentlemen were legally entitled to wear swords, to bear arms in the traditional sense. A whole industry had grown up around the mysteries of genealogy by which the College of Heralds "discovered" the ancestry of newly risen gentry families and provided them with coats of arms, which were in theory the licenses for males in those families to carry swords. The symbolism of the sword was obvious: it displayed the power of the ruling classes and the violence they could readily employ, just as the laws that regulated the bearing of arms displayed the authority of the state to limit violence and the diffusion of power. But it was not all symbolism. A gentleman was expected to use his sword when necessary, to maintain discipline among the lower classes, to protect himself and his property, to defend his honor and, in war, that of his sovereign. It is somewhat difficult to imagine Samuel Pepys actually brandishing an unsheathed blade, but plenty of his contemporaries did so on the slightest provocation.[37]

Not only weapons, but other items of status consumption, such as dress, food, and housing, symbolized the power that supported the social order. Louis XIV and other seventeenth-century monarchs consciously tried to create a hierarchy of fashionable behavior topped by themselves as a way of bolstering their political authority.[38] The thinking that lay behind sumptuary laws clearly saw a correspondence between the legitimate distribution of power in society and the wearing of appropriate class uniforms—a correspondence that seems to have been recognized by people at all social levels.

But in reality, the relationship between hegemony and genteel convention was very complicated, especially with regard to the role of fashion in status consumption. In May 1662, Pepys saw the king at Whitehall "in a suit laced with gold and silver, which it was said was out of fashion."[39] Charles II was apparently no more above fashion than he was (according to the soon to be Whigs) above the law. There were many models for fashion and many different ways in which consensus was established among the fashionable. The fact that fashion involved change—often quite rapid change—meant that anyone could be out of fashion, even the king. Conversely, people of uncertain standing within the structures of power could be in fashion. The key to being accounted fashionable lay in dressing, eating, and otherwise acting in accordance with the present mode and in being able to perceive which way the fashion was going. The latter task was one for which Pepys was quite well suited, as he was intelligent and observant. But Pepys was not, certainly in the 1660s, a powerful person or one far up the social ladder. He was clearly using fashion as a way of advancing, or at least defining, himself.

The widespread adoption of certain conventions of genteel behavior, often involving very particular forms of consumption and the following of fashions, was therefore connected to the process of replicating the social order in early modern Europe, but in a complicated way. Individuals adhered to the conventions not just because they wanted to maintain the existing status hierarchy and the hegemony of the ruling classes, and not just because they wanted to distinguish themselves as members of the

power elite, but also so that they could pursue their own life strategies—which might include achieving office for themselves and their relatives or even advancing the aims of political factions to which they adhered. From this multiplicity of purposes arose part of a dynamic of change both in the context of gentility and in early modern status consumption. We will see the dynamic in operation when the consumption of imported textiles is discussed in the second part of this chapter, and we will also look more closely at the related role of fashion. Before that, however, it is necessary to consider another set of genteel conventions that also concerned governance and order but operated in a different way from symbolic displays of power.

Magistracy. The term *magistracy* is used here to denote the conventions that framed the role of the gentleman as leader, community arbiter, and participant in the exercise of state authority. Much of the early modern literature on authority takes as its subject the ideal "magistrate," who is invariably assumed to be a gentleman.[40] The conventions of magistracy were linked to the body of "republican" political theory discussed by John Pocock and Quentin Skinner, but for the moment we will avoid the latter terminology because the connection was far from complete.[41] A gentleman did not have to accept republican political ideology as a consequence of conforming to the behavioral and cognitive pattern of magistracy, and discussion of the ideal magistrate ranged beyond the boundaries of the republican theoretical framework.

Magistracy differed significantly from the maintenance of hegemonic order and from elite behavior framed in terms of the conspicuous display of honor. Its central features were practices, concepts, and forms of discourse that emphasized the specific responsibilities of members of the upper classes to the people beneath them in society, as opposed to the assertion of other people's subordination and one's own membership in the superordinate class. As usual, the precise margin between magistracy and other elements of gentility was fuzzy, but the core differences were sufficiently clear as to create significant dissonance in the minds of gentlefolk.[42] Some standard aspects of honorific and hegemonic behavior could easily be seen as incompatible with the model of the ideal magistrate. The perceived need to resolve this dissonance was a considerable force for change in the culture of gentility and in the consumption patterns associated with it.

The cognitive aspects of magistracy developed between the fifteenth and the seventeenth centuries from a number of sources. One of the most important was the ancient notion of mutual obligation, part of the cultural foundation of feudal society. Within this framework, the deference that the nongentle owed to the gentle was supposed to be repaid by the gentle in various ways, such as generosity, forgiveness of dues on occasions of hardship, public entertainment and feasting, patronage, and so forth, as well as political benefits such as the local maintenance of justice and public order. Both in theory and in the hundreds of ways in which they were embodied in practice, the conventions of feudal reciprocity were vital to the stability of European society in the late Middle Ages. They continued to be vital (in modified form) throughout the early modern era. Among other things, they created a substantial amount of consumption and thus of economic demand because of the food, drink, and other commodities provided by the gentry to their subordinate neighbors on feast days and because of the informal obligation to patronize the skilled.[43]

Although magistracy developed in part from the practices of reciprocity and existed alongside them throughout the early modern era, it was different in ways that reflected a number of broader changes in society. Protestantism brought with it a close examination of the role of the bearers of civil authority, resulting in the Calvinists' emphasis on the duties of the magistrate and his relationship to divine election.[44] The magistrate was "called" to authority by God; his actions toward his inferiors were to be guided not by mutual obligations, but by his responsibilities toward God embodied in magisterial duties. Equally important were the structural changes in politics that we now describe as the emergence of the state. In the fifteenth and sixteenth centuries, there was a need to redefine the governmental and juridical roles of local elites in nonfeudal terms, placing them in an appropriate relationship to the state. In England, the structural locus of authority shifted from the manorial court to the magistrate's court, while the primary holder of local authority became the justice of the peace instead of the lord of the manor (even though they were generally people of the same status and families).[45] In France, an analogous shift occurred from manorial courts to the array of royal judicial institutions dominated by the *noblesse de la robe*.[46] Under such circumstances, the discourse of authority also shifted, from an emphasis on family honor and noblesse oblige, on conspicuous living, symbolic hegemony, and aristocratic largesse, to actual performance of a magistrate's duties to the state and to those he governed on behalf of the state. At the same time, it has been argued, there was a notable shift in genteel attitudes away from the traditional cultural ties that connected specific aristocratic families to specific inferior families and toward a view of inferiors as "others" to be governed (justly) by gentlemen as a class.[47]

These shifts brought with them a change in emphasis in ideals of behavior and in the image of the gentleman as magistrate. The virtues that counted were honesty (not just keeping one's word—the traditional *honnêteté* of the gentleman—but judging impartially and without reference to self-interest), sobriety, and moderation. Through his behavior more than through fostering fear, the magistrate was expected to maintain respect for the law and for the state. He was expected to set an example for everybody else. This was at least potentially inconsistent with conspicuous honorific behavior. The latter aimed at distinction, at setting the gentleman apart from others, whereas the magistrate could serve as an exemplar only if there were at least a categorical resemblance between his way of life and those of the people subject to his authority. It was not so much that the elements of the magistrate's character were alien to the honorific aspects of gentility. Few nobles or gentlemen would have argued that a person exercising authority should behave other than honestly, soberly, and so forth. The difference was one of emphasis. Nevertheless, even this created a problem. By the seventeenth century, the status of "magistrate" had become a significant part of the status of "gentleman," and the notion of "honor" was beginning to be redefined to include the traits of character of the ideal magistrate.[48] This exposed the apparent incompatibility between some of the honorific aspects of gentility (conspicuous consumption, liberality, willingness to defend honor whatever the law might say) and the ideal behaviors of magistracy.

Parallel changes in urban society and government also created tensions around the role of magistracy as an element of gentility. As urban elites became more closely connected to national politics and to the state in France, the Netherlands, and England in the sixteenth and seventeenth centuries, they, too, tended to adopt cultural frameworks that corresponded to their new roles and self-images. Taking on the pattern of magistracy was easy. It was already part of the culture of status in most self-governing cities.[49] (Indeed, much of the content of magistracy may have been suggested by the conventions of urban-dwelling elites in the first place.) The problem was that in order to validate their status and create an appropriate image on a national stage, urban elites moved strongly in the seventeenth and early eighteenth centuries to adopt as much as possible of the culture of gentility—especially its honorific aspects—and thereby experienced the same sort of cultural dissonance as the nonurban gentry.

The problems that arose from the coexistence of honorific behavior and magistracy as equally valid aspects of the context of gentility were not merely implicit in the elite culture of early modern Europe. They were the subject of a substantial public discussion in most countries of western Europe between the sixteenth and eighteenth centuries. Shakespeare focused on them in several plays (for example, in *Measure for Measure* and both parts of *Henry IV*).[50] One of the differences between "Puritan" or "Calvinist" notions of upper-class behavior and those of their "Cavalier" opponents was that the former tended to emphasize magistracy while the latter often projected honorific excess. And of course these differences were manifested in consumer behavior. The representation of magistracy required dressing soberly (although not cheaply) and following fashion only at a decorous distance. A magistrate charged with enforcing sumptuary laws would hardly set a good example if he violated them either in letter or in spirit, whereas in frameworks of honor and hegemony the whole point of sumptuary laws was that they were for other people, not the elite. Magistracy demanded a lifestyle that remained within a gentleman's means, whereas the more traditional notion of honor meant spending with a very free hand, under circumstances in which excessive attention to solvency was considered bad form.

Courtesy, civility, and politeness. One of the most interesting recent developments in the historiography of early modern Europe has been the appearance of studies of a cluster of aristocratic practices known as courtesy, civility, and politeness. The initial impetus to this development came primarily from the work of sociologist Norbert Elias. Elias and others influenced by him described the emergence of a behavioral pattern called "courtesy" in the courts of late medieval and Renaissance Italy, its spread to Burgundy and then to other courts in the fifteenth and sixteenth centuries, and its articulation in more refined forms (sometimes called "civility" and "politeness") as it was adopted by the European upper classes in general in the seventeenth and eighteenth centuries.[51] Courtesy's ideal practices and its principles were embodied in a large literature of which Castiglione's *The Courtier* was the classic. The earliest versions of courtesy presented it as a code of behavior for courtiers, which emphasized deference rather than self-assertion, acting agreeably and with restraint rather than in the boisterous fashion long associated with aristocratic males in Europe, and skill in conversation. It expanded in the sixteenth century to include a host of behaviors that featured refinement as the badge of gentility, including the ancestors of modern table manners. The last affected consumption by specifying the use of an increasingly large array of equipment for genteel dining: utensils, ceramic or metal plates, tablecloths, and (eventually) napkins. New items of genteel dress appropriate for the rituals of courtesy appeared, outfits designed to assist in maintaining proper posture while performing bow or curtsy. The possession and display of exotic items—spices, fine silks, objects of aesthetic, scientific, or magical interest—were means of establishing distinction among courtiers. In this respect, the advent of courtesy was closely linked to the development of early modern conceptions of luxury and a precursor to the construction of taste—subjects that will be considered in the next chapter.[52]

Elias and his followers interpret the rise of courtesy as a process by which "civilization" advanced itself. The central dynamic of the process was a conscious attempt to promote self-restraint and social control among a male aristocracy that was traditionally violent, selfish, petulant, gross, and, by modern standards, extraordinarily juvenile.[53] Courtesy produced the kinds of tension within gentility that were discussed above under the heading of "magistracy," but Elias says it went beyond that. By "civilization," he means the internalized cultural processes through which individuals (primarily elite males) increased their control over their own behavior and their own bodies in a general way, in accordance with an ideal that saw such self-control as desirable in itself, not just as instrumentally useful for gentlemen in the role of magistrate.[54]

Other research, some of it consciously breaking away from Elias's model, has shown that the development of courtesy was closely allied to the emergence by the early seventeenth century of a coherent view of the gentry as a class incorporating the whole of the early modern elite (titled, landed, bureaucratic, and urban). Although the term *civility* came to be more widely used than *courtesy* in England and bore the broader connotation of applying to genteel society overall rather than focusing on courts, Anna Bryson has shown that the overlap between the meanings of the words was and remained substantial through the end of the eighteenth century (as it does to this day).[55] A terminology centered around *politeness* developed in France in the eighteenth century. Initially, it suggested that polite or "polished" people were those conversant with a detailed set of fashionable manners that differentiated the gentle from everyone else (the kind of knowledge M. Jourdain seeks in Molière's *Bourgeois Gentilhomme*). By the eighteenth century, however, the terminology of politeness, the practices associated with all three terms (*courtesy*, *civility*, and *politeness*), and published guides had begun to emphasize ease and naturalness in behavior aimed at displaying gentility and showing concern for the sensibilities of others.[56] In England in the early eighteenth century, Joseph Addison took as one of his goals the spread of politeness and civility. Lawrence Klein has shown that the third Earl of Shaftesbury tried to create a political and social theory in which politeness was simultaneously the principal distinguishing attribute of the gentlemen who governed, the justification for their governance, and the mode in which governance was to be conducted.[57]

There are several important points to be made about the courtesy-civility-politeness cluster. By the beginning of the seventeenth century, the cluster had become a significant element of gentility and a major part of the set of practices to which the gentle were expected to conform. It had a substantial effect on consumption. In the eighteenth century, the culture of politeness, together with its close ally, the practice of good taste, shaped demand for a wide variety of items, including manufactured goods from China and

India.[58] It was yet another dynamic aspect of gentility, altering between the sixteenth and eighteenth centuries in connection with changes in aristocratic life (the diffusion of notions of good manners from court to country, the changing relationship of the upper classes to the state, an increase in the variety of goods able to convey status, and so forth) and innovations in ideas of what refinement meant. Most significant, although it obviously intersected in many ways with the other behavioral norms of gentility, it was seriously incompatible with some of the them.

This was particularly true of the relationship between the courtesy-civility-politeness cluster and the modes of gentility that emphasized the maintenance of honor through conspicuous consumption and violence.[59] Part of the rationale of the former was to counter the latter. In essence, courtesy attempted to redefine honor in terms of practices that emphasized deference to others as individuals within the large category of gentry. In this respect, there was a close connection between the courtesy cluster and magistracy. Early modern guidebooks to polite behavior often featured magisterial moderation and sobriety as aspects of their subject.[60] The link was even more apparent in overtly political formulations such as Lord Shaftesbury's. However, courtesy and its cognates existed in a certain amount of tension with magistracy as well. The magisterial mode focused on practices that manifested the judicial and political obligations of a class of people—gentlemen as magistrates—to the state and to the subjects whom they governed on the state's behalf. As a set of behavioral norms, it could readily be associated with "republican" notions of society and polity, which tended to disparage excessive individualism. Courtesy, civility, and politeness, on the other hand, although clearly aristocratic in concept and practice, focused much more on the individual and his or her relationships to other individuals.[61] A polite gentleman was as he was because of his training and personal application. His politeness, and thus by implication his gentility, was evidenced in the way he exercised self-control not for the good of the community, but in order to avoid offending the sensibilities of others.

It was perhaps this last feature of the courtesy cluster more than any other that promoted instability in the context of gentility. The fact that gentlemen and ladies were expected to act in a certain way did not automatically mean that anyone who acted that way was a gentleman or lady. Nevertheless, courteous practices, precisely because they were presented and understood in individual terms, were clearly attractive to people whose status with respect to gentility was uncertain, as well as to people who may not have thought of themselves as aristocratic at all but who sympathized with the principles that underlay those practices and saw no reason that they should not, as individuals, obtain some kind of distinction and self-esteem from adopting them. Just as clearly, adopting the conventions of polite behavior was absolutely necessary for people of nonaristocratic origins who wanted to pass for gentry. Even more important in this regard was fashion.

Fashion

Running throughout the preceding discussion of honor and conformity to convention as aspects of gentility has been fashion, which remains a major constituent of status-oriented consumption today. Fashion was obviously not the only impetus to change in consumption in early modern Europe, but its operation followed a dynamic of its own that cannot be fully understood if it is subsumed wholly within other patterns such as honor, convention, courtesy, or even taste.

Students of fashion as a social process have focused primarily on the rapid succession in styles of dress, food, housing, and other material objects that we associate with fashionable behavior. The classic explanation of the successional nature of fashion is that of Georg Simmel.[62] According to Simmel, fashions derive from the selection by an elite of certain material objects as public symbols of status. Fashions must change constantly because other groups, those excluded from the elite but desiring a share of status, are forever imitating elite fashions as soon as they become known. When a fashion generalizes to groups lower in the social hierarchy, the elite must look for a replacement. Then the whole process starts all over again.

Simmel's theory accounts for part, at least, of the phenomena of early modern fashion. The imitative and iterative aspects of fashion, depending on the upper classes as trendsetters, are clearly described by Pepys, as they are by other writers of the seventeenth and eighteenth centuries. But the theory is much too limited. If what Simmel discusses were all there were to it, the king and senior aristocrats could not be accounted out of fashion; the fashion hierarchy would closely replicate the social and political hierarchy. In fact, however, this was not the case, as we saw in Pepys's reference to Charles II. Power and inherited standing do not guarantee fashionability. Monarchs such as Louis XIV became centers of fashion not just by being monarchs, but by deliberately working hard to stay up with fashion trends and by consciously (and expensively) intervening in a fashion process they could never fully control.[63] In our own time, and at least as early as the late eighteenth century, a fashion establishment seen as being excessively dominated by the power elite has often been confronted with counterfashions that appeal even to the elite itself.

The process by which fashions are established is complex and partly consensual.[64] Starting in the seventeenth century, it became a subject of attempted manipulation by large-scale commercial organizations—manipulation that sometimes succeeded and sometimes failed. Even today, when anticipating and creating fashions is a major part of business enterprise, the fashion process is still not fully understood, probably because it alters when other aspects of culture change. Simmel's description of fashion change is much more effective at explaining short-run alterations within the same general fashion framework than it is at accounting for long-term, noncyclical changes that break out of the behavioral frameworks of earlier fashions or that introduce radically new material objects. In order to understand the latter, we have to consider the roles of fashion in specific cultural contexts prevailing at the time and place we are studying, as well as interactions between contexts. In the case of early modern Europe, one of the relevant contexts was gentility. The other was luxury, which will be the subject of chapter 3.

In the seventeenth century, fashions in dressing, in building and furnishing houses, in food and manner of dining, and in hundreds of other aspects of daily and occasional behavior heavily influenced the extent to which any particular purchase or any ensemble of purchases succeeded in conveying honor and supporting gentility. Fashion was a game primarily for the established elites—not only because it was expensive but also because the kind of information necessary to play it successfully was difficult to obtain outside very narrowly defined social boundaries. But fashion offered a playing field that was open, to a certain extent, to contestants of a variety of backgrounds. It allowed some people of both sexes who had taste, physical attractiveness, good manners, and a sharp eye for opportunities for self-advertisement to become trendsetters and in some cases to create an appearance of gentility that they might not otherwise have been able to bring off. Fashion could be manipulated not only by monarchs like Louis XIV, but also by persons like Pepys and the minor noblewomen and wives of officials in early-seventeenth-century Paris who laid the foundations of French salon culture.[65] Fashion was neither democratic nor intentionally subversive, but it did insert a conscious element of flexibility and change into a cultural context whose basic assumptions were permanence and stability. Perhaps most important, it created a space for *individual* activity, for people of both sexes to advance careers—a pattern of behavior that the standard conventions about status and display did not encompass.[66] At the same time, fashion provided a means by which the established order could absorb and disarm potentially hostile elements—a fact Louis XIV understood well. All these aspects of fashion will be seen at work when we explore changes in genteel consumption of overseas products in seventeenth- and eighteenth-century Europe.

Some of the salient characteristics of the context of gentility have now been laid out, at least as these can be reproduced from the observations of one person in one part of Europe in the third quarter of the seventeenth century. As references to other examples have shown, there is reason to think that the main features of the context were fairly general. Pepys's perceptions are useful for several reasons, not the least of which is that we have them. It is difficult to obtain such a firsthand account of attitudes and the motives for behavior in any period, especially from a person who appears simultaneously to be so intelligent and so ordinary. Apart from that, Pepys gives us a slant on the world of status that comes not from a self-conscious apologist, analyst, or critic, but from someone trying to negotiate that world in order to advance himself. In a sense, Pepys is an outsider trying to be an insider, but the boundary between "outside" and "inside" is very difficult to draw. Pepys thought himself to be, in a fundamental sense, a member of the establishment. Even people born into more illustrious families had to work the system to get ahead in the era of Louis XIV and Charles II. Pepys should probably not be seen as a member of a "new class" challenging the older elite or worming his way into it, but rather as a person attempting to understand the complexities of a game he has decided to play.

To summarize, the main characteristics of the context of gentility—the game and the playing field that confronted Pepys and thousands of his contemporaries—were:

- a social structure involving many distinctions and (often inconsistent) notions of rank, but within which the ascribed status of being gentle by birth was the main criterion for membership in the elite;

- a conceptual framework, with corresponding language and discourse, that emphasized honor, magistracy, courtesy, civility, and their cognates as elements of gentility;

- a behavioral pattern, featuring at least three major, overlapping sets of practices with implications for consumer behavior: conspicuous consumption, adherence to genteel norms, and observance of fashions.

The context was neither static nor unambiguous. The very fact that it permitted (indeed, required) manipulation by those who participated in it is testimony to its ambiguities. It contained, as all cultural contexts do, inconsistencies and contradictions, such as the dissonance between the behaviors associated with conspicuous consumption and violent defense of honor on the one hand and the notion of moderation subsumed within magistracy on the other. Some of these inconsistencies are probably inherent in any cultural construction of status based on birth. Others arose because of factors that impinged from outside the boundaries of gentility: the formation of the modern state, for instance, and the effects of changes in the global commercial economy. Such inconsistencies helped to change the nature of genteel ideas and practices more or less continuously in the seventeenth and eighteenth centuries. In the eighteenth century, the desire to resolve inconsistencies helped lead to an amalgamation of gentility with other contexts, especially with what will be called in chapter 4 the context of virtue. One result of these changes was the partial replacement of standard notions of gentility with status markers associated with respectability. To obtain an idea of how this happened, and also to observe the dynamic relationship between cultural change and consumption, let us turn to another category of elements of a cultural context: material objects. The focus will be on commodities imported from outside Europe—especially Asian textiles. It will be seen how demand for these commodities was shaped by their changing roles within the early modern context of gentility and by the intersections be-tween gentility and other contexts.

SILKS AND CALICOES

Europe has been importing textiles from the Far East for more than two thousand years. During the time of the Roman Empire, the export of precious metals in order to pay for silk from China was so extensive as to impinge upon the consciousness of the Roman imperial authorities, who occasionally tried (without success) to reduce the consumption of silk.[67] Throughout the Middle Ages, up to the end of the fifteenth century, Asian textiles followed essentially the same routes to Europe as pepper and spices and employed essentially the same marketing structures in Europe. The most important continued to be silk, mainly from China but also from Bengal and Persia. By the sixteenth century, raw silk was produced in substantial quantities on Genoese and Venetian plantations in the eastern Mediterranean, which permitted an increase in European production of silk cloth and of fabrics in which silk thread was interwoven with threads of other materials. In the seventeenth century, silk weaving became a major industry in Italy, France, and England. All this had a considerable effect on Europe's Asian trade. Whether they came to Europe by the old routes or by the new ones around Africa, Asian silks had (at least theoretically) to confront European competition in European markets. European silk weavers and entrepreneurs became a significant interest group in the politics of several countries. However, Chinese silks still had enormous appeal as imported status items, and for much of the seventeenth century they could genuinely be touted as incorporating a higher quality of workmanship than their European counterparts.[68]

Cotton cloth, both white and colored (dyed, printed, or painted), had been imported into Europe from India and the Near East since the twelfth century. It constituted a minor element of the direct seaborne intercontinental trade of the Portuguese during the sixteenth century.[69] Europeans also brought cotton plants to the West Indies and the American tropical mainland during the first decades of conquest and occupation. By the end of the sixteenth century, small-scale cotton weaving industries, fed by supplies of cotton fiber from Asia and America, existed at various European centers (including the town of Manchester in England).[70] The growth of the slave trade in the seventeenth century, which produced a demand for cotton cloth as a trade item in West Africa and as clothing for slaves in the Americas, stimulated some commerce in cotton, but much of the demand was filled by cloth produced in India. All things considered, cotton was a very small part of European consumption and of global trade until the middle of the seventeenth century.

Why the emphasis on silk rather than cotton? The main reason was that silk was an archetypal status commodity, and the traditional trade from Asia to Europe focused on status commodities and luxuries. Silk combined qualities of a luxury good (sensual appeal and exotic origin, which we will discuss at length in chapter 3) with scarcity, high cost, difficulty of maintenance, and impressive public display, which made it ideal as an item of conspicuous consumption. Silk was an obvious marker of distinction for the highest classes because it could be made part of the garments for practically any ritual, public or domestic. And it was, up to a point, suitable for a dynamic fashion situation. Not only could silk, as a soft, flexible material, be tailored into a vast array of garment styles for both sexes, but it was produced in many different weaves and could be altered, both in the weaving and by painting, so as to produce or follow fashions. When the Portuguese opened their direct trade to India and the Far East, they responded to existing patterns of European demand rather than promoting new ones, so it is not surprising that they focused their textile-buying endeavors on Chinese silk. Besides, two-thirds of Asian imports continued to flow into Europe as before through traditional (that is, non-Portuguese) channels and in traditional forms.[71]

This situation altered substantially in the seventeenth and early eighteenth centuries. A great deal of the change had to do with a revolution in the supply mechanism—in particular, the founding and development of the Netherlands and English East India companies. The two companies, especially the larger and initially more successful Netherlands East India Company (VOC, for *Verenigde Oostindische Compagnie*), dislodged the Portuguese from their monopoly of direct trade with the East Indies and established extensive "country trades" (carrying trades from point to point in Asia) as supports for their intercontinental business. They expanded the amount and range of goods transported to Europe and permanently disrupted the traditional commerce between Europe and the East Indies.[72] One of the main reasons that the companies were able to do this was that they were both (again, especially the VOC) closely connected to the primary business structures that supplied all of Europe with commercial capital and to the central nodes of the networks that distributed overseas imports in Europe. The Portuguese overseas enterprise had always been peripheral to these entities, whereas the East India companies were directed by the same people who oversaw the other major commercial operations. These circumstances had significant, largely unforeseen consequences, most of which were evident by the middle of the seventeenth century.

For one thing, contrary to their founders' intentions, the companies developed as permanent, extensive organizational structures, in part because business leaders in the Netherlands and England became aware of the potential inherent in permanent institutions for manipulating sources of supply in Asia and responding flexibly to demand changes in Europe. The VOC was the largest international business operation in the world under at least nominal central direction in the seventeenth century, and it was, within limits, able to formulate policies in Europe that would be carried out in Asia. We should not exaggerate the effectiveness of the companies' executive mechanisms. The first move by the VOC to push the sale of tea in Europe in the last third of the seventeenth century was probably the result of independent decisions by officials in India to buy large quantities of tea contrary to orders from home—perhaps so as to get the company to expand the market for a product that its agents in Asia already sent back on their private accounts.[73] In most cases in the first two-thirds of the century, it was not the companies acting as such which introduced new or modified consumer products into Europe, but rather company employees moonlighting as private traders and using space on the companies' ships to transport their goods. Nevertheless, once a product was introduced into Europe and once company directors—mostly merchants themselves—had determined that there was a market for it, the companies could order appropriate changes in the allocation of purchases in Asia with at least some degree of assurance that their orders would be carried out. In other words, the companies made the Asian goods market much more transparent and flexible on both continents, which meant that demand and supply could more quickly and accurately respond to each other than ever before.

Also, because the companies were closely connected to the largest wholesale markets in Europe (in the case of the VOC, to Amsterdam, the largest single point of product distribution on the continent), they could systematically acquire information about international marketing conditions and attempt to affect demand by active marketing.[74] English and Dutch overseas trading companies of the seventeenth century were probably the first commercial enterprises to organize marketing on an international basis and to recognize it as a corporate activity distinct from regulation. One of the reasons that both East India companies turned quite early to regular public auctions as their primary means of selling their products was that the auctions provided a great deal of current information about the state of demand, information that was more likely to be untainted by special private deals and collusion than if the goods had been sold by contract. The companies often tried to keep their information secret, but they usually failed. The companies could also, to a limited extent, operate as organizations to affect consumption patterns, and more than that, they and other new institutions (exchanges, newspapers, *prix courants*, and so on) provided media for rapid passage of information about fashions, consumption trends, and the like.[75]

Like their Portuguese predecessors, the VOC and the English East India Company both concentrated primarily on spices and pepper for many decades after their establishment at the beginning of the seventeenth century. The VOC, in fact, retained much of its focus on spices into the eighteenth century, mainly because it had acquired, at enormous expense in military overhead, a substantial degree of hegemony over their procurement in Southeast Asia.[76] The English company had not been so successful. Pushed out of the most profitable areas of the spice trade by the Dutch, it had been forced to concentrate its efforts along the coasts of India, the traditional center of Eurasian seaborne commerce. Contrary to its directors' original desires, it had to pay more attention than the VOC did to the secondary elements of the trade, especially textiles. And thus it happened, through a combination of ill success in competition with the Dutch, good luck in the timing of its ill success, and excellent marketing judgment, that the English East India Company found itself the main beneficiary of the most profitable consumer fad of the second half of the seventeenth century: the calico craze.[77]

Calico eventually came to mean any of a wide range of cotton textiles, but before the eighteenth century the term usually referred to a particular kind of heavy cotton fabric, usually printed or painted with distinctive designs. Calicoes had been among the first commodities brought by the Portuguese to Europe from Calicut, on the Malabar coast of India, hence the name they gave the textile.[78] Calicoes were used primarily for tablecloths, wall hangings, and window treatments throughout Europe until about the middle of the seventeenth century. Then something happened. As Daniel Defoe wrote disapprovingly in 1708, chints and painted calicoes, which before were only made use of for carpets, quilts, etc., and to clothe children and ordinary people, [became] now the dress of our ladies; and such is the power of a mode, as we saw some of our persons of quality dressed in Indian carpets, which a few years before their chambermaids would have thought too ordinary for them, the chints were advanced from lying upon their floors to their backs; from the footcloth to the petticoat; and even the queen herself from this time was pleased to appear in China and Japan, I mean China silks and Calico. Nor was this all, but it crept into our houses, our closets, and bedchambers: curtains, cushions, chairs, and at last beds themselves, were nothing but calicoes and Indian stuffs.[79]

As the passage indicates, although strictly speaking calicoes were cottons, the calico craze in fact extended to printed and painted silks. The wearing of printed Asian silks appears to have been the initial focus of an elite fashion that spread from Paris to much of the rest of western Europe around the middle of the seventeenth century. The idea of actually wearing printed cottons may have been a side effect of the silk fashion, or it may have been an adaptation of a fashion for cotton dressing gowns developed in southern Europe. In either case, the key factors involved in giving shape to the vastly expanded wearing of calicoes from the late 1660s onward were two: the increased availability of calicoes due to the imports of the English East India Company, and the dynamics of fashion in the French capital, which was just in the process of assuming its role as the source of fashions in dress for the rest of Europe.

One reason that Paris was becoming Europe's fashion center was that a set of institutions had developed there, outside and parallel to the royal court, that created venues for individual competition in display of talent, taste, and gentility. These were the famous Parisian salons, a product of the reign of Louis XIII (1610–43).[80] The pioneering salons were located in the town houses not of the great nobility, but of officials and members of the *noblesse de la robe*. Typically, the ladies of the houses organized and presided over the salons, thereby assuming leadership over the establishment of standards of taste, not only for dress but for other forms of conspicuous behavior as well. The salons created opportunities for genteel persons of a wide variety of backgrounds to mix with current and potential celebrities in the arts (thereby establishing a broader brokerage system for patronage than had previously existed) and to practice in appropriate surroundings the rituals of gentility. Guests could display expensive garments, and their hostesses could show off costly table settings, furniture, tapestries—under circumstances in which consensus could quickly be formed as to whether or not such displays were in good taste. Indeed, the Parisian salon was one of the prime contexts within which the concept of "taste" was defined in the seventeenth and eighteenth centuries. Habitués of the salon were expected to identify and conform to the latest fashions and contribute to the establishment of even newer ones. In a sense, a salon was like one of the commercial exchanges that appeared in many early modern European cities. Each made transactions in a particular context easier and more efficient for a larger number of people than previously, and each facilitated arrival at consensus about the things that mattered within the context: prices of commodities in an exchange, fashions in a salon. There were salons in cities other than Paris in the late seventeenth century and eighteenth centuries (London, for instance), but they tended to look to the French capital for intelligence about fashions.[81]

This was the setting within which printed silk and calico garments first became objects of fashion in the mid-seventeenth century, going through cycles of being in and out of favor. But the dynamics of the salon did not by themselves convert the wearing of calicoes into a craze in the latter part of the seventeenth century and into a long-term habit of consumption that was still going strong in Britain in the middle of the eighteenth century, despite legal prohibition.[82] Rather, it was the connection between the networks of fashion centering around the salons and the commercial capabilities of the East Indies companies (especially the English one) that made the craze and its extension possible. Equally important, it was the *meaning* of printed cottons in a changing context of gentility that made them an element of eighteenth-century culture strong enough to defend itself against the full brunt of mercantilism, and to emerge as a vital stimulant to the Industrial Revolution.

The innovative engagement of the English East India Company in the calico craze was shaped by its management's recognition of the essential feature of the fashion: that it focused primarily on unusual and changing print designs, and only secondarily on the fabric itself. The exotic nature of Asian silk and cotton was important, but their ability to carry and hold designs was paramount. What fashion-conscious people emulated was fashionable designs, and the way fashion leaders competed with each other was by sporting ever more unusual patterns. This led the English East India Company actually to try to anticipate and to influence the direction that fashions in calicoes would take.[83] In the late 1660s and 1670s, the company attempted to keep up with fashions emanating from Paris by sending samples of patterns in silk and cotton that had found acceptance in France to English factors in India and by encouraging a reorganization of the system of production in India.[84] The company enjoyed some success in this, but its management, led by its most active figure and eventual governor (chairman), Sir Josiah Child, thought it could do better. In the early 1680s, the company directors began annually ordering the factors to procure an array of full-sized silk and cotton cloths (not the usual small samples) with particularly striking and novel designs, radically different from each other. In a much-quoted instruction, they explained the theory thus:

> Note this for a constant and General Rule That in all flowered Silks you change the fashion and flower every yeare, as much as you can—for English ladies, and they say the french, and other Europeans—will give twice as much for a new thing not seen in Europe before the worse, than they will give for a better Silke of the same fashion worne the former yeare.[85]

The sample materials were sent from India to England with the regular load of textiles. Merchants in London and especially Paris received the material. Drapers in Paris made the new designs available to ladies figuring prominently in the leading salons. The mechanism of the salon went to work, acting as a test to see which designs would set the fashion and which would not. As soon as the result was clear, the company sent orders by the quickest means possible (often by dispatch through Italy to Aleppo, and thence overland by post riders to India) for large amounts of cloth printed with the Paris-approved designs. The factors in India gave the orders to their Indian wholesaler-suppliers, who circulated the desired patterns to weavers and dyers in the hundreds of villages where silk and cotton fabric was produced. Ideally, the required amount of fabric in the required patterns would be ready for the company's ships soon after their arrival from Europe.[86] This system increased silk sales, but when applied to calicoes the results were phenomenal. Colored and figured cottons quickly became the mainstay of the company's business.

The story of the English company's successful attempt to reap huge profits from the fashion game is interesting because it shows in detail the close relationship between supply and demand factors in a real commercial situation. Clearly, the scheme would have failed had the company not possessed the structure and the global reach that it did, and it would not have been remotely possible without the elaborate indigenous commercial system of India and the enormous skill and productivity of Indian spinners, weavers, and dyers. But it would also not have existed without a structure of fashion and conspicuous consumption that covered a large part of the European continent, and without the cultural context to which that structure belonged. The whole of the company's marketing scheme rested on the assumption that what was fashionable one year in Paris would be fashionable in other nearby major centers (London and Amsterdam) the next, in more distant centers (Hamburg, Copenhagen, Dublin) the year after, and so forth. So the real key was to use Paris as a guide to what would be bought on a much larger scale in the years to come, in other places where the real profits would be made. Like the modern fashion industry, its seventeenth-century ancestor could attempt to predict and influence the direction of consumption in the present and future, but it could by no means control it.

The English East India Company's scheme did not, in its classic form, at least, survive the decade of the 1680s (see table 1, page 299). In 1686, the French government banned the import of calicoes and even the printing of cotton cloth in France itself.[87] It did so primarily at the behest of domestic manufacturers of textiles to which the calicoes offered competition. The ban was not easily or well enforced with respect to imports because of the relative ease of smuggling, but it did upset the coherence of the East India Company's tightly organized scheme.[88] Nevertheless, the elements of the scheme remained in place well into the eighteenth century. Fashions in textile patterns tended to start in Paris, were imitated, reinforced, and often revised in other cities (especially London), and the main beneficiary was the English East India Company, which decided to base its business primarily on Asian textiles and which was able, because of the profits it made during the calico craze, to allocate a substantial amount of capital to that end. The mechanisms for assembling and transmitting fashion information also became more efficient.

The English company's huge success in calicoes and its heavy importation of cottons evoked violent opposition, not just in France but also in England, where the "calico question" was one of the major issues of national politics between the 1690s and the 1720s.[89] In 1700, Parliament responded to the issue by banning the importation of printed textiles into England. In 1721 (1720 Old Style, which is the year often cited), it passed a much more sweeping measure, prohibiting the sale and use of most cottons, whether imported or not. (White cotton and fabrics made of mixtures of cotton and linen were exempted, as was cloth for reexport.) The importance of the calico debate is well known in the history of economic theory. Its relevance to the Industrial Revolution and the formulation of liberalism is often cited.[90] For our immediate purposes, it provides a way to obtain perspectives on the meaning of calico in Europe at the start of the eighteenth century—on the significance calico had for its opponents, on the ways in which its role in the context of gentility made it important in politics and in the economy as a whole.

Until very recently, most approaches to explaining the genesis of the Calico Acts in Britain emphasized the rivalry of producers' interest groups and the technology of textile production.[91] Both these "supply-side" factors were vitally important. The constant complaints of the silk-weavers of London's Spitalfields about competition from Asian textiles, and their willingness to manifest their complaints in rioting, provided the immediate impetus to legislative action. By themselves, the silkweavers would have accomplished little, but they had allies: wool-weavers, merchants who dealt in wool and woolens, and a wide range of people with commercial and political interests who were jealous of the profits of the East India Company or who feared the power of chartered monopoly companies in general. The 1700 Calico Act must be understood to a considerable extent in a political context of interest group and party rivalries at the end of William III's reign, while its 1721 successor was influenced by the furor over the South Sea Bubble and the subsequent reaction against joint-stock companies.[92]

Political economy intersected with technology. Underlying the positions of many of the interest groups was the inability of British spinners, weavers, and textile printers to produce reasonable equivalents to Asian printed fabrics. Like their French counterparts, English silk-weavers could create materials of relatively high quality with a variety of patterns in the cloth itself. They could not, however, produce a fabric that could take prints very well, and the printing technology itself was clearly inferior in terms of clarity and colorfastness to those of China and India. Cotton was even more of a problem. India, with thousands of skilled cotton spinners, could by extremely labor-intensive methods produce thread strong enough to be used as warp in all-cotton textiles that could be made into fine outer garments, carpets, hangings, and so forth. European cotton spinners could not. They possessed neither the skill nor the traditions that underlay the skill, and there were not enough potential spinners willing to work for sufficiently low wages that direct competition with Indian calicoes was even remotely conceivable without a major technological breakthrough. In 1700, the breakthrough was more than half a century in the future. English cotton cloth could be used for sacking, wrapping, bandages, and cheap clothing for slaves, but not for garments of any quality. English-spun cotton thread could be woven together with warps made of stouter material, such as silk, wool, or linen, but the problem of printing remained. Technological limitations also affected other purely European-produced textiles. English woolen manufacturers could produce a very wide variety of qualities and weights of cloth, but there was still the printing problem. In any event, woolens were not easily suited to many of the uses to which calicoes and silks were put, whether printed or not. The linen industry had similar limitations.[93]

So technology and politics played a major part in the calico controversies. But there are other aspects that have to be considered in order to understand why the calico issue was so important to so many people and why, even in the face of legal prohibition, the fashion for calicoes maintained itself in Britain and France to the end of the eighteenth century and helped to inspire some of the central technical innovations of the Industrial Revolution. These other aspects have to do with the connection of calicoes to the cultural context of gentility.

Let us consider the situation of the English silk-weavers, who could produce high-quality silk fabric that could not, however, be effectively printed and therefore could not compete against Asian prints. They obviously had immediate reason to want to ban the importation and use of printed silks in England. Because they had only a small export trade (except to the colonies—see table 2, page 300), they had no reason to oppose importation of printed silks for reexport—which was politically useful, because they could argue that they were not damaging any national interest in the East India Company's business outside of England.[94] But two questions arise: Why were they, as silk-weavers, so concerned about *cottons*—more so, apparently, than about imported silks? And why did the silk-weavers and their allies not focus more of their attention on improving English methods of printing or on marketing positively the silk fabrics already produced in England? This was, after all, the era of "projects," of the enthusiastic exploration of technology as a means of getting out of just such a bind as the one the English silk interest thought it was in.

The answers to these questions depend on the silk-weavers' (and others') perceptions of the nature of the demand for English silks and Asian textiles. To the extent that English silks were intended for the upscale status market (that is, were expected to be used for conspicuous display of gentility, for keeping up with fashions, for polite presentations of good taste, and for the reproduction of the social order), they suffered under obvious disabilities in competition with Asian silk.[95] For purposes of conspicuous consumption, they could not match the exotic appeal of real Chinese silks (or the quality of lighter Chinese fabrics). Because the fashion environment was dominated by rapidly changing print patterns, English silks came up short once again. What was left to them was a share of the market for hegemonic signs (such as silks for judges' robes) and for tasteful upholstery. Until the printing problem was dealt with, fashions changed, or Asian competition was eliminated by law, English silks were not fully viable as status commodities.

Why not do something to improve production or to market English silks more effectively instead of resorting to protection? The comparative lack of interest in a technological solution may have been due partly to a distrust of innovation among skilled workers, and partly to a suspicion that, even with the ability to do high-quality printing, English silks could not match the appeal of exotic textiles from the mysterious East at the top end of the market. As for creating a fashion, opponents of calicoes did cite patriotic and moral reasons for buying English silks and woolens, but the argument seemed to make little difference except in the context of legal proscription.[96] It appears that not many people switched to nonprinted garments on nationalist grounds. The fact was that English silk was not very suitable to a regime of rapid fashion changes.

This brings us to calicoes. Why did even the Spitalfields weavers direct their attacks mainly against printed cottons rather than against the silks with which one would think they were directly competitive? The answer is that, as we have just seen, English silks were *not* competitive with Asian silks. Their primary competition was *calicoes*, because English silks and printed cottons had similar consumption uses within the context of status and bore similar relationships to Asian silks: both were *substitute status commodities*.

Substitute status commodities are goods that, for one reason or another, are adopted by people who want to demonstrate their claims to relatively high status but who cannot or will not allocate a sufficient amount of their disposable income to employ the commodities that the wealthiest people use—or at least, not as many of them.[97] Clearly, calico was a substitute for Asian silk in this sense because it could be used in essentially the same kinds of garment and the same fashion processes, but was cheaper and easier to care for. Domestic silk had a parallel, although not identical, role. It was a product the use of which conveyed status—not as clearly as Asian silk, and not in the same variety of ways, but as it was generally cheaper, it could be combined with Asian silk in the same suits and used in a wardrobe to supplement a limited array of more fashionable garments.

Substitute status commodities were far from unusual in the early modern period. Much of the North American fur trade depended on fashionable demand for fur for clothing and hats in place of European furs that had become prohibitively expensive for all but the wealthiest to buy in large quantities.[98] Such commodities acquire their places in this category by a wide variety of means, often including active marketing by vendors. In general, substitute status goods require the prior acceptance of a similar (but more expensive) set of physical objects by fashion-setters before vendors can successfully create demand for them. A substitute status commodity will normally not be as scarce or expensive as the commodity for which it is a substitute, but it will still be dear enough to have meaning for conspicuous consumption. Typically, the purchaser of a substitute good will also make some purchases of the original status commodity, thereby trying to show that he or she belongs to a social group whose members can choose what their symbols will be. A substitute commodity will be capable of being tailored to whatever practices are meaningful within the status context, and it will be suitable for use and exploitation within the structure of fashion. A substitute status commodity will generally *not* dislodge the commodity for which it is a substitute from its role as a high-level status good—unless there is a radical change in the behavior patterns and the cognitive structures that give the goods meaning. Such a change occurred in European dress styles on the occasion of the French Revolution, but not at the time of the fashion for calicoes. To state the same point somewhat differently: substitute status goods do not normally compete with the commodities for which they are substitutes; they compete with each other. Asian silk was safe from calico competition; English silk was not. Hence the particular vigor of the silk-weavers' attack on calicoes between the 1690s and 1721, and hence the fact that the woolen interest also lined up against calicoes. Fine English and Netherlands woolens (embellished with fur, lace, and so forth) had been, up to the mid-seventeenth century, the staple material for status garments. They had not, of course, been completely displaced, but a large proportion of woolen fabrics had by the early eighteenth century acquired some of the properties of substitute status goods.[99]

The furor that led to the Calico Acts therefore provides clues about relationships between fabric consumption and gentility. Clearly, the role of calicoes as a substitute status commodity was not to allow certain classes (for example, the "bourgeoisie") to mark out a difference between themselves and the recognized elite; nor did calicoes, in and of themselves, have that effect. At the same time, they cannot be explained as mere imitations of elite fashions. The initial fashion of wearing calicoes in the seventeenth century does seem to have started among certain segments of the social elite in England and France, but calicoes remained fashionable for generations throughout society—including among the highest strata. If we envision calicoes as substitute status goods, as material objects that possessed meaning in conjunction with other fabrics within the cultural context of gentility, what was happening becomes a little more intelligible. People at all social levels who had sufficient discretionary income wore both calicoes and Asian silks; the proportion of one to the other (or to European silk) in a person's wardrobe depended in part on how much money he or she had to spend, but the cultural framework was essentially the same for everyone.[100] The point of wearing calicoes was the same as the point of wearing silk: to show that one participated in the culture of gentility and that one was entitled to a share of status, to the respect of others, and to self-esteem. It is almost certainly true that in the late seventeenth and eighteenth centuries, more people than ever before found themselves wanting to participate, which in turn was probably due to a rise in and broader distribution of incomes as well as to the availability of new fabrics that could be effectively used as substitute status goods. But the motivations behind the fashion for calicoes were individual ones, not "class" attitudes derived from the aspirations of people who thought of themselves primarily as members of particular social strata in a clearly articulated hierarchy.

This is not to say that the widespread wearing of calicoes was without social implications or that the cultural changes with which cottons were associated were without social effects. Many eighteenth-century commentators noted with great disapproval the fact that people at middling levels of income and status had taken to wearing printed Asian fabrics, and that even people of conventionally low status (especially servants) had done so as well.[101] The fact that wearing calicoes was a statement of participation in gentility, to some degree at least, was well understood and was often presented as a danger to the social order. The crux of the matter was that the traditional foundation of gentility was birth. Vagueness around the edges of the concept, a more complex social reality than theory allowed, had always been part of the context of gentility. But the combination of a fashion item that met all the requirements for status and that could be supplied in large quantities, in ever changing varieties, and at prices that were neither prohibitively high nor unfashionably low, with a desire for signification of status by many people who could not readily claim gentle birth, could be taken as a threat to the notion of inherited gentility as the framework of meaning for social hierarchy. At the very least, this combination threatened either to legitimate cultural plurality in defining status or to inaugurate a reconstruction of the context of gentility itself. Such perceived threats help to explain the bitterness of the debates over calico restriction as well as the modes of argumentation of many of the debaters. The tendency to interpret the fashion for calicoes in terms of classes and potential class conflict was thus more a construction of the opponents of calicoes than it was a reflection of the aims of the people who actually wore them.

The characteristics of calico as a substitute status good also help to explain why legal prohibition did not destroy the calico business in Great Britain. Calicoes were a convenient and attractive means by which a wide variety of people could attempt to participate in the context of gentility. Such people included not just the "lower" orders, but persons of moderate or even high income who had better uses for their money than to buy only the most expensive materials for dress and furnishings. This ensured that people of good standing would continue to buy and wear calicoes and that law enforcement authorities, whose ability to perform their tasks depended on the cooperation of just such people, would often ignore the Calico Acts. It was not wise to wear garments made of printed textiles in the immediate vicinity of Spitalfields because silk-weavers had a tendency to take the law into their own hands, but elsewhere, statute or no statute, it appears to have been safe enough.[102] The East India Company had to be careful, but its calico cargoes were generally as large as before. (See table 2, page 300.) The company imported printed fabrics for reexport (in addition to its legal importation of white cottons for domestic use) in the full knowledge that smugglers would immediately bring them back to England. Like the company, individual British merchants engaged in a complex international trade in calicoes—among other things, encouraging the creation of an effective European calico-printing industry—that allowed them to get around the Calico Act.[103]

It is tempting to jump from the 1721 Calico Act to the Industrial Revolution by arguing that the act left an unsatisfied demand in England so large that smuggling could not keep up with it, so technological innovation was the only way to meet it.[104] Reality was more complex. In fact, the part of the English textile industry disadvantaged by the Calico Act responded to it by expanding its production of *mixed* fabrics, especially fustian, a textile with a linen warp and a cotton weft.[105] The linen component made the fabric stronger than any English-woven pure cotton produced before the mid-eighteenth century. When English printers developed new techniques for affixing better and more lasting designs to the mixed cloth in the 1730s, Parliament granted an exemption from the 1721 act.[106] These mixed "calicoes," supplemented by real calicoes smuggled from India, not only maintained supply at earlier levels but apparently, until the second half of the eighteenth century, met a growing demand for materials for dress and furnishings, both in Britain and abroad. The demand appears to have arisen to a large extent from a continuation of the consumption pattern we have been discussing, from purchases by people of a widening variety of social backgrounds who wanted to take part in the culture of gentility.

Two questions present themselves: If mixed textiles could substitute for pure-cotton calicoes, why was there a revolution in the English *cotton* industry in the last third of the eighteenth century? And if calicoes or near-calicoes could be worn by such a wide range of people, why did they not lose their value as status markers?

The simple answers to these questions are that there were serious technical limits to the expansiveness and the flexibility of mixed-fabric production, and that the context of gentility itself underwent a substantial change, especially in the late eighteenth century with the formation of the culture of respectability. But neither of these answers can be given in terms of calicoes alone or in terms of the context of gentility by itself. The reason for this is that the purchase of fully printed cloth for outer dress or house furnishings accounted for only a part of cotton and mixed-fabric consumption in the second half of the eighteenth century. A substantial proportion of demand was for white, checked, and simple striped cloth—especially the first.[107]

(See table 3, page 301.) This demand derived mainly from an intersection between the context of gentility and the contexts of luxury and virtue, which we shall examine in chapters 3 and 4. We can obtain a suggestion of how the relationship worked by focusing on underwear.

UNDERCLOTHING

Europeans had worn underclothing (that is, garments beneath their outer and intermediate layers of clothing) all through the Middle Ages and early modern period, unless they were too poor to afford it. For much of that time, fashionable men and women had periodically followed modes in which some portion of their underclothing was visible, usually at the collar, sleeves, or hem. "Underclothing" in this sense included shirts and hose for men and underblouses and underskirts for women. In the seventeenth century, western European fashions changed in such a way as to reveal an unusually large amount of underclothing. Outer garments were redesigned in order to achieve that effect.[108] This was especially true of men's styles: slashed doublets, wide-cuffed sleeves, open-fronted coats—the last of which made a place for profuse neckware in place of ruffs or simple collars and for waistcoat and shirt.

It is not entirely clear why this fashion change occurred. Presumably, the people who adopted it wanted to let others know that they were *wearing* undergarments. It is not unlikely that they wanted to display the quality and cost of their shirts and the like, and possibly also the fact that those garments were either new or clean. Such motives could be readily associated with gentility in the form of conspicuous consumption, especially if the garments displayed were made of silk or silk and linen mixtures. They could also be connected to courtesy: clean undergarments as a sign of refinement. Even cleanliness could be associated with status display: it showed that the wearer had servants to keep his or her underwear in order.

Whatever the immediate reason for the change, the fashion stuck—not only into the eighteenth century, but, with respect to men's formal clothing, down to the present.[109] Beverly Lemire has shown that, in the last quarter of the seventeenth century in England, white cottons and fustians from India were being used for shirts and other undergarments in place of the expensive silks and cambrics that the truly wealthy wore. By the middle of the eighteenth century, seafarers (not just officers, but simple seamen) and many other working people regularly wore cotton shirts, whereas many of their predecessors in the previous century would probably not have owned a shirt in their entire lives.[110] Linen was still the favored material for shirting, and until the mid-eighteenth century it was cheaper than high-quality cotton. But then the situation changed. The price of good linen began to rise relative to cotton, while the quality of English-made pure cottons, which had been improving for some time, took a major leap forward with the introduction of the new spinning technologies of the 1760s and 1770s. British manufacturers could now produce strong cotton warps for all weights of fabric, so that all-cotton garments could serve a wider variety of needs than those made of any other material. In the last years of the eighteenth century, cotton moved strongly to replace linens and mixed textiles as the favored material for shirts and undergarments at almost every income level in Europe and America.[111]

Obviously, technological advances played a large part in the change, to some extent unintentionally. In the years following the 1721 act, the cotton industry had turned already-existing mixed fabrics into reasonable substitutes for calicoes. The industry had developed new dyeing techniques and new looms so as to increase both productivity and evenness of quality—all as ways of meeting demand for calico.[112] Buyers of whites and checks had been the secondary beneficiaries of these improvements. The spinning innovators after midcentury were probably still thinking mainly in terms of imitating Indian calicoes, but they discovered major opportunities in undergarments as well. The supply of linen had proved inelastic, and linen production did not submit to technical improvement in either quantity or quality the way cotton did.[113] There can be no doubt that the "revolution" in cotton technology associated with the names of Hargreaves, Crompton, and Arkwright made it possible for cotton to become the primary material, not just for outerwear, but also for shirts and underclothing in the last quarter of the eighteenth century, which contributed to the immense expansion of British cotton production during that period.

Technology was, however, not the only factor involved. Calico demand, the initial driving force behind innovation, derived from a continuation of fashionable purchasing that extended far beyond the boundaries of the elite and near-elite. The even more expansionary demand for white and checked cotton arose from all classes of the population.[114] Showing clean, white shirts and underblouses no longer suggested gentility in any traditional meaning of the word (that is, hereditary status and its accompanying lifestyles). The self-consciously genteel did it, but so did many others, and the custom did not change with fashion. Consumption framed by the seventeenth-century context of gentility had been transformed into consumption based on several cultural contexts linked to each other within the larger framework of respectability. People could still distinguish themselves as putatively "genteel" by staying at the leading edge of fashion in outerwear (much facilitated by the flexibility of the new cotton fabrics in carrying prints and colors) and by displaying undergarments (or at least their edges) made of expensive materials. But by adopting current fashions in standard cottons and by wearing cotton versions of undergarments, people could also show that they deserved esteem on account of their respectability. Undergarments were especially important in the latter regard because they proclaimed the cleanliness of the wearer. This no longer denoted primarily the wearer's income, but rather his or her attention to the material manifestations of virtue—that is, qualification for esteem as judged according to standards derived from the context of virtue that we shall discuss in chapter 4. And apart from considerations of status and virtue, clean cotton garments were convenient (with regard to washing) and comfortable. Comfort and convenience had become legitimate, meaningful objectives of consumer behavior within another cultural context: the altered context of luxury. We turn to this context in the next chapter.

3

L U X U R Y

Luxury is a very difficult topic for historical study in Western society because, as a word, a concept, and a set of cultural practices, it has always had multiple meanings, few of which have been stable over time or unambiguous. It has often been closely connected to the cultural aspects of status—as, for instance, when a contemporary advertisement refers to a "luxury automobile" with the clear implication that if you own such a thing, you will be considered a member of the social elite. At the same time, the connection to status has seldom been definitive. What makes a luxury automobile luxurious is mainly the pleasure it is supposed to give the owner. Part of the pleasure, to be sure, derives from making other people think that you are better than they, but the primary images of luxury car ads are sensual, and often overtly sexual. Or consider the contemporary distinction between a "luxury" and a "necessity": things that it would be nice but not necessary to have, as opposed to things you really must have. Again, while it is true that the poorer (and thus, perhaps, lower in status) you are, the more you must forego luxuries and concentrate on necessities, the essence of the distinction does not reside in status. It has something to do with pleasure ("nice to have"), but not necessarily in the same way that the car advertisement suggests sensuality. Also, hanging over the luxury/necessity distinction and other uses of *luxury* is a hint of moral disapprobation that has little to do directly with status. If a person spends excessively on "luxuries," it may be an indication of a deficient moral character, perhaps because the money could have been spent on worthier things, perhaps because the pleasures one obtains from luxuries are unworthy in themselves. The moral formulation of luxury has a very long history. For much of the last two thousand years, people in the West who used the word *luxury* (*luxuria*, *luxe*) have generally intended it to be understood in this sense.[1]

Despite the difficulty of making historical sense of luxury, it is necessary to try to do so. Luxury is closely connected with the consumption of commodities. Recent historians of early European consumption have emphasized the pursuit of luxury by large and increasing numbers of people as a significant factor leading to economic change in the eighteenth century. Several scholars have also focused on a major eighteenth-century debate about luxury as an event that helped to reshape economic consciousness. The basic question under debate was whether luxury, as a sin and a drain on scarce resources, ought to be restrained by state prohibitions or, as an expansive economic force, countenanced and even encouraged regardless of its moral implications. Most of the scholars who have studied the controversy regard it as having been "won" by the side that argued that selfishness and desire for luxury on the part of individuals are necessary for material prosperity and economic expansion at the level of the nation. Traditional morality was thus separated from "objective" understanding of social reality, and new uses of the word *luxury* became possible.[2] However, the fact that luxury retained a hint of moral opprobrium throughout the nineteenth and twentieth centuries suggests that, as far as popular consciousness was concerned, the victory was far from complete. In any event, luxury is clearly a subject that has to be considered here.

Several relatively distinct approaches to luxury and its relationship to early modern consumption have appeared in recent (and not so recent) studies. John Sekora and Christopher Berry have looked at the long history of concepts of luxury in the West, from ancient times to the eighteenth century. Sekora makes the useful point that *luxury* has always had a wide range of meanings (usually, before the eighteenth century, negative) and that people have tended in any era to use the word to describe forms of behavior they disliked because they deemed them "excessive."[3] Berry attempts to give a theoretical description of luxury that can be applied across cultures and time.[4] Both emphasize the conceptual change that took place in the eighteenth century, but neither is wholly successful at getting beyond the boundaries of the intellectual debate over luxury and into the wider fields of practice and consumer behavior.

Other scholars have had more success in investigating the broader frameworks within which luxury had meaning in the seventeenth and eighteenth centuries. In particular, Maxine Berg, John Brewer, and others have related the changing meanings of luxury in Europe to the emergence of a "middle" range of manufactured commodities (in terms of quality and price) that appealed to the middle classes. "Luxury," in this sense, refers to pleasures previously restricted mainly to the upper classes that became available to a middle class expanding in size and importance in the eighteenth century. Many, although not all, of these pleasures (intellectual and aesthetic as well as overtly sensual) were afforded through commodities—at first mainly imports from outside Europe, which were later replicated in the factories of the Industrial Revolution.[5]

This kind of approach has given us a much greater understanding of the social, cultural, and economic contexts of early modern luxury than we have had in the past. There are some problems with it, however. Even though neither Brewer nor Berg assumes that simple emulation of social superiors was the primary motive of people seeking luxury through consumption, their arguments are still constructed primarily around an explanation of behavior based on social classes, in which the expansion of the middle class is the main cause of change. Not only does this implicitly subsume any explanation for cultural change within a determinative pattern of socioeconomic modernization, but it also tends to subordinate the phenomena associated with luxury to considerations of status—to present luxury as a kind of extension of gentility. This is not necessarily a false trail, but because luxury and status are not the same, it obscures some extremely important factors affecting changes in consumption.

Yet another approach focuses on the affective aspects of commodities and how those are culturally constructed. Colin Campbell has demonstrated the vital importance of sensuality to any discussion of luxury. He has suggested that nineteenth-century Romanticism created a way to incorporate sensuality as well as consumption of luxuries into capitalist culture, as a necessary counterweight to the production-oriented "Protestant Ethic" of self-denial described by Max Weber.[6] Recently, John Crowley has described the way in which the idea of moderate sensual pleasure was converted in eighteenth-century Britain into the concept of "comfort," which helped to legitimate the consumption of luxury products.[7] Simon Schama, writing of the ways in which the culture of the seventeenth-century Netherlands accommodated itself to the presence of great wealth, shows how the Dutch developed a distinctive set of cultural traits that justified the abundant possession of enjoyable commodities as something other than "luxury."[8]

Werner Sombart preceded Campbell and Crowley by many decades in emphasizing the sensuality at the core of the cultural meaning of luxury. In 1922, Sombart argued that luxury—which he defined as substantial expenditure on fashionable clothing and other material objects—was based mainly on sexual desire and sexual imagination.[9] One of his most interesting arguments was that luxury was the center of a set of cultural practices developed in the courts of late-medieval and Renaissance Europe. Unlike Norbert Elias, who presented the courts as centers for the construction and dissemination of the culture of courtesy (that is, of male self-restraint and control of the passions), Sombart saw them as places where "courtesans"— women of uncertain social and moral standing—constructed a culture of luxury centering around sensuality and stylized sexual competition. According to Sombart, the courtesans seized control of fashion from upper-class men and created a framework of images that connected fashion, female sexual attractiveness, a positive valuation of sensual pleasure in general, and material representations of all these things. By establishing a part-fantasy world of sensuality in which they were the centers of attention and of which fashionable clothing, food, and manners were the material manifestations, women capable of taking part in the culture of luxury delimited an area of life in which they could make decisions (especially about fashions) and lead physically more comfortable lives than other women. The sensual appeal that pervaded the culture of luxury attracted men and led them to defer, in some respects, to women. Although the original creators of the culture of luxury were courtesans, Sombart claims that in the sixteenth and seventeenth centuries it was adopted as part of the framework of behavior for women (and men) throughout the upper classes of western Europe. Thus, women as a group acquired status within the elite through the development of luxury.[10]

Sombart's discussion of luxury has many faults, with regard both to attitude and to evidence. His definition of *luxury* itself is narrow and not very helpful. But his focus on sensuality as the affective characteristic of the cultural framework that gave luxury meaning in early modern Europe is, like Campbell's, enormously important. It allows us to examine that framework in something like its own terms, not ignoring its connection to social structure but not submerging it in class considerations either.

In this chapter, the word *luxury* will be used to refer to a distinct cultural context in seventeenth- and eighteenth-century Europe, a context that intersected significantly with gentility but was fundamentally autonomous, following its own internal dynamic. Like gentility, it had a long history in Western societies. Like analogous constructs in the Western past and in most non-European societies, it incorporated a set of customs and practices according to which sensual pleasures were identified, understood, sought, obtained, and legitimated, in terms both of actual experience and of imagination. Among other things, it was the cultural framework within which the word *luxury* possessed its many meanings, but it ranged even more widely than the uses of the word indicated. Indeed, an interesting problem arises from the fact that before the eighteenth century, as we have seen, the word *luxury* was used most often to condemn the very activities—the culturally defined experience and cognition of pleasure—that were the most obvious features of the context. If the negative valuations of *luxury* were excluded from the context, that would place much of the context outside the then standard usage of the word. In fact, however, the context of luxury is best understood as including both a set of morally problematical behaviors and the cognitive and linguistic frameworks within which people attempted to deal with the problems posed by those behaviors—but excluding solutions that called for doing without pleasant sensual experiences altogether.

Cultural contexts incorporate not only inconsistencies, but often whole discourses in which elements of the context are placed in standard forms of opposition to one another. This was noted in the previous chapter with regard to the antagonistic relationship between magistracy and honorable extravagance within the context of gentility. The present chapter will argue that the European context of luxury was a major locus for cultural dynamism in the seventeenth and eighteenth centuries not only because of its relationship to status and class, but also (and especially) because the discourses and the cognitive patterns that had previously allowed certain forms of sensual behavior to be both practiced and morally condemned had come apart. Many intellectually inclined people perceived that the vital task of managing the dissonance between hedonistic behavior and traditional moral views of luxury was not being accomplished and that new ways of framing sensuality had to be constructed—hence the importance accorded to the eighteenth-century debate over luxury.[11] But apart from that, Europeans at all levels of society (except perhaps the lowest) had to work out, in their daily lives, ways of navigating the dangerous waters around sensuality. In part, they had to do so because commodities associated with sensuality were available in larger numbers and in greater variety to broader segments of the European population than ever before. This working-out was a complex process, involving intersections between the context of luxury and several others. It produced at least three major cultural innovations in the eighteenth century. One of these was the previously mentioned concept of a luxury separated from traditional morality that was accepted into classical economics as an "objective" representation of consumer behavior.[12] The present chapter will pay more attention to the other two: the shaping of "taste" as a mode of intellectually constructing a new relationship between luxury and gentility, and the development of the related ideas of "comfort" and "convenience" as ways of simultaneously understanding, legitimating, and morally limiting sensual experience. The latter development was closely related to the emergence of the context of virtue discussed in chapter 4.

By the end of the eighteenth century, these and other successful constructions of sensuality had been linked together and formed into a relatively coherent cultural context with sufficient continuities with its predecessor that it is reasonable to treat it as a heavily modified version of the early modern context of luxury. Much of the modified context of luxury was subsumed within the broader culture of respectability. At the same time, most respectable people in the Western world came to experience and understand sensuality primarily through commodities and through commodified rituals such as commercial public entertainments.

It would lead too far beyond the limits of the present book to discuss the full commodification of respectable luxury and the emergence of alternatives to it. Although the trends are observable in the eighteenth century, their full impact was not felt until the nineteenth. This chapter will deal with some of the factors leading to the partial breakdown of the early modern context of luxury and to its reconfiguration in the eighteenth century as part of the culture of respectability. It will first discuss these matters in general terms and then focus more specifically on their effects on the consumption of spices, pepper, and sugar between 1600 and 1800.

As a point of entry into the discussion, let us return to the subject of demand for cotton textiles where we left it at the end of chapter 2. In the light of what has just been said, it is not difficult to suggest an additional reason for the large growth in consumption of white cottons in the eighteenth century: the emergence of comfort and convenience as cognitive categories and as legitimate goals of individual action. Cotton and cotton-linen underwear was comfortable. People of different income levels (high, middle, even low) could afford cotton because, by the last quarter of the century, it was relatively cheap. They could enjoy doing so without feeling guilt or being accused of sinful behavior because the pleasure, or at least the relief from physical irritation, provided by clean, soft underwear was acceptable as a comfort connected to respectability. It did not connote excess or moral weakness. In addition, white cotton underwear, shirts, and so forth were convenient. They could be washed frequently and more easily than other white fabrics, which was, as we shall see in chapter 4, essential to the function of clean underwear as a sign of virtue. Time and money saved because cottons were easier to wash were time and money not wasted. The categories of cleanliness and convenience, which had not existed in anything like their modern forms in the seventeenth century, were by the end of the eighteenth integral parts of the context of luxury and of respectability, and as such they exerted a substantial influence on consumer behavior.

THE CONTEXT OF LUXURY IN EARLY MODERN EUROPE

At no time between the sixteenth and the eighteenth centuries was the European context of luxury stable, although decisive changes occurred more toward the end of the period than the beginning. The sources of instability were many—too many for all of them to be discussed here. Some of the instability can be represented in structural terms, as arising in the connections between luxury and the social order and between luxury and commerce.

Certain connections between luxury and early modern social structure are obvious: elites usually had more of the means to purchase luxury goods (that is, commodities desired for the sensual pleasure they produced or suggested) than did other people, and many luxury goods, because expensive, were also status commodities. To some extent, then, luxury consumption followed patterns similar to consumption in support of gentility. There were vital differences, however. Consumption intended to convey or support genteel status could not be easily separated from other considerations, especially family honor. In the seventeenth century, the same expenditure on, say, fashionable clothing could not have the same status meaning for an untitled merchant that it did for a nobleman (except perhaps in the Netherlands).[13] In terms of sensual experience, however, the difference was less apparent. Under circumstances in which fashionable clothing was intended to attract sexual attention or to gain entry into places where pleasure (of whatever kind) was available, the personal and family status implications of the clothing were much less important, although not completely meaningless. The extent to which sensual experience could be obtained through commodities, and the variety of experiences thus obtained, depended much more on a person's wealth than on his or her gentility. In a sense, as Sombart suggests, the culture of luxury was by nature more closely related to markets than were traditional European cultures of status, and more clearly represented by commodities. It was therefore more readily affected by changes in markets than was gentility, and thus, in an era of major commercial change, more unstable.

Sombart's thesis about the origins of luxury illustrates another range of complexities in the relationship between luxury and gentility. The field on which the status games we observed in chapter 2 were played was primarily marked out in accordance with the rules of gentility. However, intersections of gentility and luxury (for example, the cultural ethos the creation of which Sombart ascribes to Renaissance courtesans) could create a more complicated playing surface—more like three-dimensional chess, to change the metaphor slightly. Individuals without genteel status could sometimes, through supplying sensual experiences (as courtesans did) or providing access to commodities or rituals that excited sensual fantasies (as East India merchants did), execute a gambit that brought them higher status than they would otherwise have been able to achieve. It was, however, typically a form of status considered to be morally problematical and, quite apart from morality, less than fully honorable or genteel. (In Restoration England, the king's mistresses and the East India Company possessed considerable status and influence but were not accepted as entirely legitimate, possibly one reason the mistresses sought noble marriages and the company insisted on calling itself "honorable".)[14]

Partly because luxury goods were often also status goods, many of them were subject to sumptuary regulations in most parts of Europe in the sixteenth and seventeenth centuries. This, too, suggests the complexities and tensions in the relationship between luxury and gentility, because makers of sumptuary legislation usually had other, if secondary, motives besides the desire to maintain social subordination. They aimed also at curtailing waste and controlling immoral behavior, especially by the governing classes and the wealthy. This can be understood in part as an effort to enforce what was called "magistracy" in chapter 2, and perhaps as an extension of the courtly "civilizing" process postulated by Elias, but it can also be seen as a conscious manifestation of cultural management of the contradictions inherent in luxurious behavior. Sumptuary laws, by attempting to restrain elite expenditure on such items as exotic foods, clothing made of soft or expensive fabrics, and (as we shall see later in this chapter) spices from Asia, in essence recognized that upper-class people would buy these things anyway, and, furthermore, that their consumption conveyed a distinction that was useful for protecting the social order. At the same time, luxury goods were dangerous: they could encourage excessive sensuality, waste resources, create envy on the part of the less privileged, and motivate people outside the aristocracy to challenge the established hierarchy of classes so as to have greater access to commodified sensual experiences. Sumptuary laws reminded everybody that only the aristocracy could be trusted with substantial amounts of luxury goods, and even aristocrats had to be watched (or watch themselves, for sumptuary laws were difficult to enforce among the gentry).[15]

A second structural feature of early modern Europe connected with luxury and its discontents was organized, large-scale commerce, especially the great overseas trading companies and the growing network of mercantile and financial houses to which they were linked. Directors, supporters, and critics of the companies all agreed that the companies were mainly in the business of supplying Europeans with status and luxury goods.[16] Not surprisingly, they sometimes confused the status and luxury functions of particular commodities, but on the whole, company personnel and merchants who dealt in overseas goods were quite aware of the distinction and its implications for marketing.[17] As we shall see later in this chapter, the companies tended to change the emphasis of their marketing strategies from a focus on gentility in the seventeenth century to a balance between luxury and status concerns in the eighteenth.

This change reflected an important phenomenon of the latter century: the expansion of commercial access to the context of luxury beyond the limits of the European upper classes. Possibly because of changes in the distribution and level of income in western Europe, but certainly because of the unanticipated expansion of the production, purchasing, and carrying capacities of European overseas commerce, a greater amount and variety of luxury goods became available in Europe at lower prices than ever before. We have seen some of the consequences of this development for the area of social and cultural life framed by gentility. It had even more impact on the context of luxury, because it threatened to undermine the always unstable means through which Europeans attempted to manage sensuality. For one thing, by making goods like exotic foods and spices available on a very wide basis and by creating, in the East Indies companies and the trading elites of cities such as London and Amsterdam, a powerful, organized force interested in building demand for those goods, the new structures of commerce made nonsense of the inherent rationale for sumptuary laws. In a world in which luxuries could not even notionally be limited to the aristocracy (and in which states attempted to make the growing revenue burden fall on nonaristocratic classes by taxing luxury consumption), it was pointless to rely on the distinction between the gentry and the rest as a basis for managing sensuality.[18]

Other sources of instability in the seventeenth-century European context of luxury were more cognitive in nature than structural. The central cognitive fact about luxury goods is that they, and mental images that they stimulate, are very important for the ways people construct the fantasies that make up a large part of their psychic lives. Consumers respond not only to the inherent physical qualities of goods through their senses, but also, through intellectual activity and imagination, to possibilities and suggestions that arise from the places of particular material objects in various cognitive frameworks. Recognizing the cognitive element in consumer appetites, and recognizing further that this element is strongly influenced by society and culture, is the foundation of modern advertising.[19] The fact that even the sensual experience of goods is in part socially and culturally constructed creates opportunities for influencing consumer behavior. Of the products with which this study is primarily concerned, only sugar has a claim to being universally desired—regardless of culture—by people who have tried it, and even sugar consumption responds to cultural differences. (The British consume much more sugar per capita than the French; in the eighteenth century, it was estimated that they consumed eight to ten times as much.)[20]

The sensual fantasies we create (or borrow) are, of course, frequently linked to contexts other than ones that overtly focus on sensuality. For example, in its advertising, the American automobile industry traditionally joins together images of status, the fashionability of new car models, and suggestions of sensual (especially sexual) pleasure. In the sixteenth and seventeenth centuries, part of the "medical" appeal of a great many of the exotic consumables imported from overseas was their supposed aphrodisiac qualities, while they also, at least for a while, functioned as symbols of gentility.[21] From the early seventeenth century at the latest, European retailers of imports exploited the capacity of luxury to link other contexts together—thus adding to tensions within the context of luxury and helping to bring about its reconstruction in the eighteenth century.

Of course, cultural construction does not explain everything. Many consumables simply feel good, especially in comparison to alternatives: silk, linen, or cotton undergarments as opposed to woolen ones; spiced food as opposed to bland food; and so on. It is not necessary to insist that conscious or implied meaning is *always* present in the motivation behind consumption, but only that meaning *often* shapes consumption and that consumption deriving from pleasurable sensation frequently leads to cognition—especially to rationalizations that reconcile such consumption with other parts of the consumer's culture.

In recent years, the crucial importance of fantasizing, as a culturally constructed mental operation, has been recognized by historians of consumption.[22] It is now generally agreed that in the past, as at present, individuals employed goods or the mental images of goods in order to construct pleasurable fantasies, not only for their own enjoyment but also to induce other people to buy (sometimes quite literally) into the fantasies. People who successfully projected a fantasy could achieve a wide range of personal goals, not all of which can be understood in terms of conventional status considerations. We can agree with Karl Marx that commodities are objects of fetishes, but we must go considerably beyond Marx's observation if we want to understand the uses to which commodified fetishes could be put.[23]

The history of fashions in European clothing provides endless examples of the role of fantasy in luxury. Sexual suggestion is presumed, on strong evidence, to have been part of the motivation behind many of the innovations in men's clothing fashions in the late Middle Ages—especially the custom of wearing uncovered, close-fitting stockings, which started in Italy and created a major industry all over Europe.[24] Stockings were originally, in northwestern Europe at least, an aristocratic fashion, and even then, for only a portion of the male elite. They were considered unseemly for merchants, town councillors, judges—people who were supposed to embody justice and magistracy in their behavior and who continued to wear full-length gowns in public. The wearing of stockings had spread to nonelite males by the fifteenth century, possibly through their adoption by soldiers, who were major disseminators of early modern fashions. Breughel's sixteenth-century soldiers and well-to-do peasants wear them, often in situations that suggest aggressive male sexuality.[25] Apart from their apparent practical function of showing off, as it were, the sexual merchandise of the wearer, hosiery presumably connected with male fantasies of sex, potency in all of its meanings, and violence, to varying degrees indicated by the relative loudness of color and pattern. They would thus have been consistent with Norbert Elias's view of the violent element in early modern society that so urgently required "civilizing."

By the late sixteenth and early seventeenth centuries, civilizing agents were at hand (at least with regard to consumption). Among these were fashionable women, both aristocrats and those whose husbands belonged to the urban mercantile and professional elites or to the upper-middle apparatus of the state. We saw in the previous chapter that such women created in the Parisian salon the archetypal setting for fashion competition in the context of status, and also that the salons provided a vital nexus in the new business of fashion marketing. They did more than that, as we can see if we ask ourselves what the women who established the salon culture of Paris, and the women who imitated them throughout Europe, thought they were doing.[26]

Clearly, part of what they were doing was playing the game of status, turning themselves into the arbiters of gentility and advancing the honor of their husbands and families through the reputations they acquired. But they were also laying out the rules of another game, a game in which the object was to acquire influence and reputations for *themselves* and a certain amount of control over the world around them. In many respects, they were simply employing strategies that had been practiced by women at courts for centuries—including reigning monarchs such as Elizabeth I of England. But they were not at court, at least not usually, and the game they played was far more varied and open than was possible at court. The salons in Paris and other networks and gatherings elsewhere (such as the ones Pepys occasionally penetrated in London) had different orientations depending on the interests of the ladies who presided over them. The famous circle of Madame de Sèvignè (1626–1696), for example, featured some of the leading writers and intellectuals of the mid-seventeenth century, although it was also noted for lighter matters and a fair amount of flirtation—poetically expressed, of course.[27] Others were less mentally rigorous. But practically all salons shared a concern with fashion, with sensuality, and with sex, not as sites for excess, but as places where rules governing such activities and the fantasies associated with them could be worked out within a culture of luxury—worked out mainly by women.

Fashion and sexual fantasy had been part of a pattern of gallantry and formalized flirting in courts throughout Europe in the sixteenth century, for which the sexual suggestiveness of court costume was presumably a support.[28] In the seventeenth century, at court and especially in salon society, this pattern of behavior was modified to make it more overtly respectful of the women who were the objects of gallantry and male competition, and more decorous in regard to what came to be assumed to be ladies' refined natures. In France, the rather direct approach to sex in court circles in the Valois and early Bourbon eras gave way to the more restrained, more heavily verbalized and fantasized sexuality of polite society in the reign of Louis XIV. This does not necessarily mean that there was less actual sexual activity or promiscuity among the French elite during the latter period, but rather that the behavior surrounding it was more formal and elliptical, less aggressive on the part of men and more controllable by women. Men and women ritually sought to form friendships, which might or might not incorporate physical sex but were politely assumed not to do so in the absence of marriage or strong evidence to the contrary.[29] Male costume changed accordingly. Just as, in the sixteenth century, full-length stockings with codpiece were replaced by thigh-length stockings with short trousers, these gave way in the seventeenth century to more subtly suggestive garments: stockings and knee breeches, which still showed off a good leg but did so more decorously. Women adopted dress styles that were on the whole more, rather than less, suggestive, indicating that sexual fantasy had become like sex itself—a game for two.[30] It may have been, as Sombart claims, that suggestiveness in female dress among the well-to-do derived from the dress of prostitutes and royal mistresses in the previous century, but if so, it was part of a different, more complicated way of playing on male fantasies than was traditionally practiced by courtesans.[31]

Another aspect of the fantasy element of the context of luxury was a fascination with the exotic. As we saw in the previous chapter, it was not just the relative rarity of overseas commodities that rendered them desirable as consumer goods, but also the very fact that they came from places that were interesting because they were outside Europe, and by extension outside European norms.

A great deal has been written in recent years about the cultural construction of the "other" by westerners in the course of European overseas expansion.[32] The construction of "others" appears to be a normal part of the process of human social cognition, and it can take many forms. We often identify and value our own institutions, behaviors, and systems of meanings by contrasting them with others. We construct images of "others," including individuals of our own acquaintance, in attempting to "understand" them—which generally means predicting how they will behave, prescribing how we think they ought to behave, or justifying our actions with regard to them on the basis of our predictions and prescriptions.[33] We also construct "others" in such a way as to point up deficiencies in "us." (For example, Eastern spirituality, which supposedly demonstrates what is wrong with "our" Western materialism; Western empiricism, which displays to many Asians the "weakness" of Asian traditionalism.) The construction of "others" in these senses obviously has its dangers, as it often produces both error and bad behavior, but it is natural and frequently useful. One further construction of "others"—exoticism in taste—is crucial to explaining consumption in the early modern European context of luxury.

Things that are unusual, that come from a great distance away or that one does not see every day, are interesting in themselves. In the early modern era, Europeans of all social classes and all countries had a vast appetite for new and unusual sights and tastes, sharpened perhaps because they had become aware through printed books of the existence of so many things in the world, but could still rarely experience them directly.[34] Thus objects from the other ends of the earth had a market that arose just out of curiosity. This, however, cannot explain the depth and breadth of European desire for the exotic in the seventeenth and eighteenth centuries; that desire manifested itself in the *continued* consumption of products that, although exotic in origin and character, rapidly ceased to be unusual—thanks to the un-. precedented capacity of European commerce to procure them on a large scale and a regular basis. A wide range of exotic herbs and spices, potables such as coffee, tea, and chocolate, textiles such as calicoes—all remained luxury commodities for a long time after their widespread introduction; that is, they were used, discussed, and desired in large part because they came from overseas, and they were employed in patterns of consumption that emphasized that fact. Tea, for instance, was taken in Europe for almost the entire second half of the seventeenth century using Chinese teaware and in a manner that deliberately (although somewhat lamely) attempted to reproduce Chinese tea ceremonies.[35] Only at the beginning of the eighteenth century was tea culturally "domesticated" through the development of self-consciously European patterns of imbibing it, and even then, the Chinese aspect did not disappear. Most of the other products followed similar careers—a lengthy period of exoticism before Europeanization, too long for novelty by itself to have been at work.

One feature of early modern European exoticism that helps to account for its staying power in particular cases has been examined recently by historians: the emergence in the seventeenth century of "virtuosity," a kind of secular expertise that emphasized education, knowledge of a wide range of nonstandard subjects, curiosity about the physical world, and refinement of tastes.[36] Virtuosity clearly influenced consumption patterns, shaping the demand for exotic products (especially ones of scientific interest) from around the globe. In chapter 5, we will see that French and English *virtuosi* helped to create the culture of the coffeehouse in the third quarter of the seventeenth century and thus contributed significantly to the fashion for coffee and tea. *Virtuosi* tried to stake out a cultural claim to genteel status on the basis of knowledge, taste, and breadth of interest, but they also emphasized the pleasure of experiencing, or at least knowing about, the exotic for its own sake. But although virtuosity had a strong effect on the creation of cultural modernity and a not insignificant influence on respectability, it was not the most general manifestation of exoticism within the context of luxury.

The essence of exoticism as an aspect of luxury appears to have been the use of imported commodities as foci for fantasies that suggested violation, or at least attenuation, of familiar cultural patterns—especially moral norms. Naturally enough, sexual norms were common objects of such imagined violation. People often believe that members of other cultures have better sex than they—not necessarily that the others have greater capacity in this regard, but that they have fewer social or cultural inhibitions on employing it.[37] Differences in behavior between peoples (real or imagined) are construed so as to make the "other" out to be able to do things prohibited or frowned upon in one's own society that one thinks might nevertheless be pleasurable. Like much of the travel literature of the seventeenth and eighteenth centuries, exotic imports served as tokens of the excitement supposedly available in the lands they came from. Thus, the pleasant feeling of soft fabrics such as silk and fine cotton was desirable not only in its own right, but also because it suggested images of Eastern lands where sexual activity supposedly took place with more variety and style than in Europe, and amid a profusion of soft textiles.

Exotic goods presumably stimulated other fantasies, including ones that took the form of individual wish-fulfillment. A European man could not actually *be* an "oriental despot," but he could, by wearing Indian dressing gowns and smoking a hookah, *pretend* in a harmless way that he was one.

Men and women sensible of homosexual inclinations but unwilling to risk the dangers of contravening the heterosexual order of their own society might fantasize about others in which such distinctions were less clear. This may explain the eighteenth-century fashion in European women's dress for what was taken to be the habit of denizens of Ottoman harems.[38]

The existence of such motives for consumption is supported by a fair amount of evidence from descriptions of fashionable life and from published sermons and diatribes against "luxury" that concentrated on the role of commodities in stimulating sinful fantasies that, in turn, might lead to sinful actions.[39] We know from the role played by fantasy-stimulation in modern advertising that it is a major economic factor today, and we can safely assume a similar psychological influence on buyer behavior in early modern Europe.

We now have an idea of some of the structural and cognitive contours of the early modern European context of luxury and of some of the sources of tension within it. We have also seen that pleasurability and fantasy were both regarded as at least potentially dangerous, even by people who themselves participated in luxurious living. This belief, together with a growing perception that existing modes of dealing with the danger were inadequate, was a major reason for the dynamism of the context of luxury in the seventeenth and eighteenth centuries. It helped to motivate the construction of a new moral discourse and a pattern of legitimate consumer behavior that could accommodate luxury to broader changes in Western culture, social organization, and economic life. In turn, the new discourse and the new behavior patterns, closely linked to other contexts that comprised respectability, became central to the formation of the "global economy" of the nineteenth and twentieth centuries.

One way of dealing with the dangers of luxury is to ban its offending aspects altogether.[40] The problem is that the approach seldom works for long even on the rare occasions on which it is seriously adopted. It is difficult to get people to give up luxury—pleasurable sensuality, fantasy, and exoticism—and the material items that go with it, if they can afford them. It is equally difficult to persuade people to refrain from using luxury to affect the behavior of others. Early modern Europe did not lack advocates of voluntary or forcible renunciation of the pleasures of the flesh: moralists who argued against luxury and other sins from the standpoint of Christianity (Catholic or Protestant) and, from the late seventeenth century onward, from other moral perspectives as well.[41] They did not succeed in rooting out luxury in any of its meanings, but they did identify the points where sensuality, fantasy, and exoticism (often linked with status consumption) created dissonance with the moral and political order.

One danger they often emphasized was that the wrong people could pretend to luxury—that is, either the truly common people, who would see access to luxury goods as the equivalent to access to some degree of power and an invitation to impertinence toward their betters, or the well-to-do among the nongenteel.[42] In the latter case, the result might be political confusion and a decline in the seriousness and sobriety of the classes whose main task was to manage the world so as to support the elite—senior servants, retail merchants, and the like. In other words, the ruling class—the gentry broadly defined—should have a monopoly on practicing luxury, because they were the only class that could do so without endangering the social order and the common welfare.

Erasmus Jones, English author of a violent attack on "luxury" in the early eighteenth century, expressed this kind of view in vivid prose: "Can there be a more provoking Sight in the Streets of a rich Trading City, than for a little Quill-pushing fellow, with a Salary of fifty Pounds a Year, a laced Hat, a yard of Steel at his A—e, and perhaps a Cl—p into the bargain, to take the Wall of an eminent Merchant?"[43] Jones immediately moves to a connection between inappropriate behavior in dress and consumption and inappropriate claims to political participation. "It is astonishing, that in a great trading City, where Labour, Industry and frugality should be the only prevailing Motives or considerations," [people dispute violently over elections to the Common Council]."[44] Apparently, politics are inappropriate in a business community and should be left to gentlemen.

There was disagreement among moral and social commentators about whether or not genteel people *themselves* should abstain from luxury. Some who identified themselves with the aristocracy argued that it was actually the gentry's duty to live luxuriously, just as it was their duty to consume conspicuously. Conspicuousness they owed to their honor and the need to reproduce the social hierarchy; living luxuriously they owed to all the people who would be unemployed if they didn't: valets, hairdressers, manufacturers of perfume, merchants dealing in luxury goods, East India companies. If this view was a bit self-serving, in the world of seventeenth- and early-eighteenth-century Europe it possessed a modicum of economic truth that disturbed moralists. As Bernard Mandeville ironically put it in "The Grumbling Hive," the poetical predecessor to *The Fable of the Bees*,

> The Root of evil Avarice,
> That damn'd ill-natur'd baneful Vice,
> Was Slave to Prodigality,
> That Noble Sin; whilst Luxury
> Employ'd a Million of the Poor,
> And odious Pride a Million more.[45]

But the notion that luxury was the right and/or the responsibility of the hereditary upper classes in fact ran counter (or at least at an angle) to several important tendencies in early modern European thought and practice, especially among the aristocracy itself. The most important of these tendencies arose from religion. The great reformations of Christianity in the sixteenth and seventeenth centuries comprised a great many cultural changes, many of which reflected alterations in emphasis and seriousness rather than full-scale innovations. Some of these alterations, which found echoes across the Protestant-Catholic divide, had to do with luxury.

The ambiguities inherent in elite luxury—for example, that high-ranking people were expected to live luxuriously and consume conspicuously, while at the same time accepting a religious tradition that portrayed luxury as at least potentially sinful—led to considerable soul-searching among Protestant reformers and Catholic counter-reformers.[46] The latter, of course, still had access to the device of absolution to deal with the paradox in specific cases, but the general problem still remained. Because Calvinists developed the most considerable body of writing concerning luxury, we can refer to the "Calvinist" position on the subject, but in fact quite similar views were found among many upper-class Catholics and non-Calvinist Protestants. On the whole, aristocratic Calvinists did not object to conspicuous consumption, to obeying status-based rules of behavior and dress, or even to following fashion—as long as these activities were kept within the limits of good sense.[47] Such limits were a bit vague, but in general they consisted of not spending more on consumption than was needed for social effect and not following short-term, extreme fashions, hewing instead to modes that people of quality found appropriate after due consideration. It was "luxury" that Calvinist gentry found problematical, luxury in terms both of gross waste and of conscious pursuit of sensual pleasure. Even in this, however, the key to the "Calvinist" position was good judgment. God gave humans senses and the ability to distinguish among degrees of pleasure and pain, and there was nothing inherently wrong with exercising those capacities within limits. Indeed, one of the many things Calvinists derided in the practice of Catholicism was deliberate mortification of the flesh. But too much sensuality—especially, but not exclusively, in the area of sexual activity—was sinful or could lead to sin. If one got used to eating more or richer food than was necessary merely to obtain a modest amount of pleasure, one might easily move on to something worse.[48] Along more strictly Calvinist lines, commentators could also argue that it was the duty of the elect—whom Calvinist aristocrats tended to identify as themselves—to maintain their moral standing in order to serve as magistrates. Luxury threatened magistracy, as it threatened godliness, by tempting the upright to put personal pleasure before God and duty. Also, it set a bad example. Not only merchants but also landed aristocrats of a reforming persuasion often rejected the argument that luxury was necessary in order to create employment. Beyond a certain point, the money spent on luxury could be better directed toward commercial investments or agricultural improvements that would create jobs and meaningful wealth (and yield a profit for the investor rather than for the people who sold him luxuries).[49] Luxurious living by the elite caused members of the inferior classes to imitate them, which reduced the capacities of the workforce and might lead to social indiscipline.

Not all religious reformers agreed with the mainline "Calvinist" position on luxury. Many Protestant and Catholic conservative reformers, although often in favor of personal abstemiousness, believed that maintaining religious allegiance required at least an artistically sensuous presentation of religion and that civil order necessitated luxurious grandeur on the part of the state and the nobility. This view was one of the bases of the Baroque aesthetic of the seventeenth century.[50] On the other hand, extreme Protestant radicals tended to regard the "Calvinist" position as too much of a compromise with sin. Some attacked all decoration in dress, all fanciness in cooking, and all sexual suggestiveness in anything whatsoever.[51] Quakers, Mennonites, and any number of smaller sects throughout Protestant Europe took this position, thus (as in other respects) opting out of the mainstream of European society and Western cultural history. But certainly by the second half of the seventeenth century, most Calvinists of upper and middling status were not interested in opting out. They were rather inclined (after decades of struggle) to seek modes of accommodation rather than grounds for conflict with social peers of differing religious orientation, among whom similar desires for compromise had also appeared. Within many countries, Lutherans, Calvinists, Arminians, crypto-Catholics, and overt Catholics had come to the conclusion that order had a higher priority than narrow orthodoxy and that the state had to promote and reflect accommodation at least among the ruling classes. Thus in England after 1660, gentry of Puritan background greatly lessened their demands for strict moral regulation of behavior, while their former antagonists tended, especially after widespread popular revulsion against the "lewdness" of the early Restoration, to see the virtues of virtue and to search for consensus on matters such as luxury. The vogue for Jansenism among aristocratic French Catholics in the mid-seventeenth century arose in part from similar motives.

The search for accommodation incorporated many specific efforts, some of them political. With regard to the issues that surrounded luxury, one of the most important cultural approaches to accommodation was the development in the late seventeenth and eighteenth centuries of the concept of *taste*, which eventually became one of the principal cognitive and behavioral components of respectability and an immensely important influence on consumption.

TASTE

Several of the features of the concept of aesthetic taste—for instance, the belief that there are only a few right ways and a great many wrong ways to appreciate beauty and to incorporate it into the practice of living, or the assumption that correctness in appreciation bespeaks the quality of the appreciator—have deep roots in Western cultural history.[52] But the concept itself and the behaviors conventionally attached to it were products of the late seventeenth century. Taste responded directly to the problematical aspects of luxury that were noted previously. To satisfy the "Calvinist" critique of luxury, the rules of taste provided a set of limits to exuberance and sensuality. The limits were formulated in terms of an aesthetic of balance and order; they were consciously tied to a notion of moral limit and to a standard of public acceptance. The rules were set by consensus within polite society, influenced by opinion leaders and the mechanisms of fashion, but on the understanding that extremes of fashion were to be avoided by people with good taste.[53] With regard to the social defense of luxury (that is, that it provided economic benefits to society as a whole), taste did not require that luxury be given up, only that it be aesthetically restrained. Tasteful expenditure on luxury continued to create employment for the nongenteel, but the effect that was sought was richness in quality and fineness in form, not simple abundance. And in terms of the social critique of luxury (that it might encourage laziness, impudence, or political unrest among the lower or middling classes), the point about taste was that it was something that required breeding and years of practice to develop. For the most part, only people of gentle birth or those from families of sufficient means to afford the appropriate education (both in book knowledge and in manners) could hope to display the kind of taste that was needed for acceptance in genteel society—and thus for penetrating the corridors of power.[54] Simply putting on the right kind of clothing or imitating genteel fashions and rituals would not do the trick. People outside the aristocracy with money and ambition would be forced to seek advancement for their children rather than themselves, and to do so by educating their sons to be gentlemen and their daughters to marry gentlemen, thereby coopting a potentially dangerous element in society. People without sufficient money or breeding—tradespersons, servants, and the like—could do their poor best to dress and act better than they were. All they would end up doing was providing their betters with sources of amusement through their gaucherie.

Thus taste had implications for gentility as well as the context of luxury, even though it developed as a cultural phenomenon primarily in response to the problems posed by luxury. It also provided much of the impetus to the emergence of aesthetic theory in the arts and to a vast expansion of the market for paintings and sculpture that met the requirements of theory.[55] The dominant aesthetic motifs of the eighteenth century, rococo followed by severe classicism, were constructed consciously around generalized notions of taste that were intended, in part, to define legitimate luxury.[56] Consumption in a wide variety of areas responded to changes in taste that were often expressed in quite sophisticated terms as general aesthetic standards. To take a single instance, patterns of printed cotton and silk cloth became considerably more subdued in the second half of the eighteenth century than they had been earlier, a change corresponding to the supersession of rococo by classicism. Fascination with the exotic, although still very strong in motivating textile buying, manifested itself in more balanced, more subtle suggestions.[57] In some degree, taste domesticated the foreign and unusual.

Although in the late seventeenth and throughout most of the eighteenth century, taste was a blatantly aristocratic cultural phenomenon and although it developed within cultural contexts dominated by luxury and gentility, it implied the possibility of changes in the ways Europeans thought not only about luxury (which we have seen), but also about aristocracy and gentility. This was due in part to the inherent logic of the concept, and in part to its connections to significant intellectual developments of the period. In the cognitive world laid out by John Locke and the earl of Shaftesbury, claims for the monopoly of taste over aesthetic judgment had to be formulated in terms of human sensibility rather than impersonal "laws."[58] If taste represented a refinement of sensibility, and sensibility was something for which essentially everyone had the capacity, then it was theoretically possible for anyone, regardless of social standing, to display taste. A similar implication lay in the notion that taste was something one acquired—through effort as well as experience—for purposes of demonstrating one's fitness for genteel society. This was more or less how Lord Chesterfield presented the matter to his son—his illegitimate son, who would have been particularly susceptible to the imputation of not being a real gentleman if gentility were entirely an attribute of birth.[59] If taste could be acquired, its connection to gentle birth derived not from necessity or even convention, but merely from the supposition that in the large majority of cases, only people who were born into genteel families were likely to be able to acquire it. It was not impossible for someone outside the aristocracy of birth to do so. Even more insidious was the corollary: if taste was the mark of a gentleman or lady, and taste could be acquired by someone not born to gentility, then gentility itself did not depend upon birth. By itself, this was not the stuff of revolutions. Few political upheavals have originated with logic derived from aesthetics. But when it was connected with revisions to the *moral* implications of gentility, that was a different matter altogether.

Moral and political implications were not far distant. Luxurious consumption conducted according to neoclassical standards of taste presented, by its very nature, the appearance of balance and order, which were, in the classical tradition, qualities associated with justice and good behavior. A characteristic position of the eighteenth-century advocates of good taste (Lord Chesterfield, for instance) was closely linked to the new doctrine of "politeness": that what is important in life (especially in society and politics) is how you appear to other people, and an important part of appearing well to others is behaving politely and tastefully in every public circumstance—not only as a sign of good breeding, but because of the implication of probity and worthiness that went with it.[60]

Not everyone bought Chesterfield's position. Critics such as Samuel Johnson complained that it condoned hypocrisy and permitted, even encouraged, a social arrangement in which people with low moral standards could, by showing taste, be accorded the approbation that ought to go to those of proven virtue. Johnson reportedly claimed that following Chesterfield's advice meant adopting "the manners of a dancing-master and the morals of a whore."[61] Chesterfield would have denied this, saying that of course one should be virtuous, but the way of the world was such that it availed neither oneself nor anybody else to possess ever so many virtues if one appeared a figure of ridicule in public. This may be regarded as the wise advice of a realist, but the whole subject of taste—its aristocratic assumptions, its emphasis on appearance—made some moralists justifiably uneasy. From the standpoint of gentry trying to use aesthetics to formulate a convergence between luxury and morality, taste provided a reasonably satisfactory framework for discourse and behavior. This was probably one of the reasons that the words *luxury* and *luxe* were increasingly used nonpejoratively in England and France as the eighteenth century continued. But there were other perspectives that had to be taken into account. Novelists and philosophers (especially Rousseau) mercilessly attacked the moral presumptions of taste as Samuel Johnson had done.[62] By itself, taste was not enough, although it was a start.

COMFORT AND CONVENIENCE

In a recent article, John E. Crowley has suggested that the modern concept of *comfort* was invented in eighteenth-century Britain.[63] One might quibble that perhaps the Netherlands preceded Britain in this area of innovation, but the fundamental observation Crowley makes is extremely important.[64] "Comfort" is not the same thing as pleasurable experience in itself. It is a particular cognitive framework that sets the terms under which physical pleasure can be perceived as a morally acceptable experience—a framework that includes limits to sensations, typologies of their stimuli, and a notion of the environments within which the pursuit of pleasure is morally viable. As we shall see in chapters 4 and 6, the construction of comfort as a cognitive entity can be explained as a conscious linking of cultural contexts. Just as we have interpreted the origins of "taste" partly in terms of an intersection between luxury and gentility, so we can view "comfort" as the result of interaction between luxury and what we will call in the next chapter the "context of virtue." Benjamin Franklin, who will be one of the main characters in our discussion of the context of virtue, contributed greatly to the delineation of comfort as a legitimate behavioral aim, as a motive for invention, and, indeed, as a criterion of level of civilization.[65]

Comfort responded to the moral problems of sensual experience through consumption in a way that taste, by itself, could not. Comfort was not a matter of appearance, but of sensibility and feeling. Sitting comfortably around a fireplace of an evening, smoking and talking companionably with family or friends—this was comfort. The circumstances (hearth, perhaps home, friends and family, tobacco) framed the pleasurable experience in meanings: the genuine benevolence of friendship, the moral centrality of family and home, the association of tobacco with an even temperament and balance between reason and sensibility. The pleasure one felt was innocent and wholly moral, and the (supposedly) modest expenditure involved in the consumption activities related to the pleasure could not be sinful or immoral in the traditional sense of luxury. Wearing comfortable clothing meant that one was not experiencing pain for the purpose of outward show or was not unduly permitting fashion to interfere with the fluidity of motion needed to perform physical tasks properly.

The idea that substantial amounts of consumption for pleasure or for the avoidance of pain could be consistent with morality was quite novel in the eighteenth century. It was clearly connected with the sentimentalist trend in Enlightenment philosophy, which provided intellectual legitimation in the rare cases in which that was necessary, and with sentimentalism in fictional literature, which swept the entire continent of Europe in the second half of the century and which made great play with images of comfort such as those noted above.[66] It also had an impact on demand for manufactured commodities, as we saw in the example of cotton underclothing earlier in this chapter.

As we saw in the same example, however, comfort was not all there was to it. Cotton underclothing was also convenient. Although the notion of convenience probably had different historical roots from those of comfort, the two ideas developed in parallel fashion in the eighteenth century and performed parallel, closely linked roles in modifying the context of luxury. Benjamin Franklin helped to define both comfort and convenience in practical terms and regularly presented them within the same frameworks.[67] Convenience referred, in its most general sense, to ease of doing something— not simply the rational adjustment of means to ends so as to economize on input, but the avoidance of unnecessary pain or other obstacles sensible to humans and the saving of time that might (notionally, at least) be devoted to more useful purposes. These other purposes might be efforts devoted to material production or intellectual improvement, but they might also include moderate, virtuous pleasure and rest, which were of course necessary in order to work effectively at other times. ("All work and no play . . . ") As a cognitive and discursive construction, convenience had a great many uses, but one of its most important was in reconciling certain pleasurable experiences—especially ones that could be represented as absences of unpleasant experiences—with moral and social order. Commodities like washable cotton shirts, blouses, and underclothing provided comfort and convenience simultaneously.

Taste and the complex of notions associated with comfort and convenience, together with the construction of a pattern of social thinking and argumentation that claimed to separate considerations of morality from descriptions of human economic behavior, constituted the major cognitive and discursive modifications in the context of luxury in the eighteenth century. They possessed many different sources, some of them common to all, some of them not. They were developed in response to a great many stimuli by people with quite different motives. In each case, they connected luxury to other cultural contexts, although not always to the same ones and not always in the same ways. They shared at least one primary characteristic: taken together, they afforded a framework within which sensual experiences provided or suggested by commodities of bewildering variety and unprecedented availability could be enjoyed without appearing to threaten anything of significance. They also, therefore, created a framework within which sales of such commodities could be deliberately expanded. There were major inconsistencies among the elements of the modified context of luxury, most evidently between taste, comfort, and convenience, all of which had explicit moral content, and the "objective" model of "economic man," which pretended to isolate moral factors from behavioral description. Nevertheless, the new version of luxury was an extraordinarily powerful cultural construct, especially when it became, in the late eighteenth century, an integral part of the culture of respectability.

Let us now look at specific changes in material and behavioral aspects of the context of luxury in the seventeenth and eighteenth centuries. We can do this by examining alterations that occurred in those centuries in European consumption of sugar, pepper, and Asian spices.

SPICES OF LIFE

Asian spices and pepper had been imported into Europe for many centuries before the early modern period. They were the staples of the pre-Portuguese trade between Europe and East Asia, and the Portuguese did very little to change the situation.[68] The founders of the VOC and the English East India Company at the start of the seventeenth century believed that their profits would primarily come from wresting the spice and pepper trades from the Portuguese and from the chain of carriers on the traditional Indian Ocean spice route, which started in Indonesia and ended in Italy.[69] The two companies did not succeed in completely eliminating the Portuguese, but they quickly reduced the Portuguese share of the spice trade to minor proportions. The English, in alliance with Persia, captured the port of Hormuz from Portugal in 1622, thereby not only neutralizing the main point at which the Portuguese had been able to extort a profit from the traditional traders, but in effect putting an end to the traditional trade altogether.[70] It was, however, the Dutch company that soon came to dominate the spice trade by gaining effective military hegemony over the Spice Islands from their main base at Batavia in Java. We saw in the previous chapter that the Dutch unceremoniously shouldered the English aside in the process and cemented the welfare of the VOC to the fortunes of the spice and pepper trades. For most of the seventeenth century, it seemed a good decision. Thereafter, it helped to ensure that the VOC would fall behind the English company as the leading force in Eurasian commerce. The primary reason for this change lay in the nature of demand for pepper and spices in Europe, but in order to understand what happened, it is necessary to look first at the structure of commerce in Asian condiments in the seventeenth century.

At the beginning and as late as the middle of that century, pepper was the most important consumer product being brought into Europe from overseas, followed closely by the three major Asian spices: cloves, cinnamon, and nutmeg. Together, they outranked all other overseas imports into Europe except silver in value and derived income and as objects of interest on the part of governments, merchants, and expansion-minded publicists in northwestern Europe.[71] All four commodities shared essentially the same transportation and distribution systems, both outside and within Europe— although they were produced in different places in Asia. Most spices came from what is now Indonesia, whereas pepper originated in a wide variety of areas, especially on the coasts of India.

By 1600 (even before the formation of the VOC), Amsterdam had replaced Antwerp as the primary center of pepper and spice distribution in Europe—and also as the center of the woolen cloth trade.[72] The proximate reason for the change was the migration of business networks, capital, and merchants from Antwerp to the United Netherlands as a result of the Dutch revolt and the retention of Antwerp by the Habsburgs in the 1580s. Just as Antwerp's sixteenth-century primacy in the Asian trade had been built on the structures and capital of the woolen trade, so, too, in Amsterdam, commerce in pepper and spices was closely connected to the growing northern Netherlands textile business and to Amsterdam's particular specialty: the Baltic grain trade. The peculiar structure of Amsterdam's commerce constituted a large part of the framework around which the European side of the VOC's business was built. Amsterdam capital usually called the shots in the VOC directorate, and the company fed its products into an Amsterdam-centered structure of marketing and distribution.[73]

These structural circumstances had important implications for the VOC's understanding of the nature of demand for its products. During the first half of the seventeenth century, for example, Dutch grain merchants purchased large amounts of pepper and spices and actively worked at developing a market for them in Poland and in other Baltic regions. Making a large profit from the sale of Asian commodities was not their primary objective; rather, they hoped to use pepper and spices as an alternative to silver in paying for Baltic grain and making up the consistently unfavorable balance of payments between the Netherlands and the Baltic. The VOC was particularly responsive to Baltic grain traders; many of the VOC's directors were Baltic merchants in their private capacities, and, in any event, the grain trade was economically more important to the Netherlands than all of its extra-European commerce added together. Several other groups of merchants who were engaged in less prominent sectors of Dutch commerce employed spices in similar ways. This helps to explain why the VOC maintained its focus on spices and pepper for much longer than was healthy for the company as an organization, and it also partly accounts for some of the peculiarities of the VOC's supply, marketing, and pricing policies.[74]

The volume of the pepper and spice trade with Asia fluctuated considerably (sometimes wildly) throughout much of the seventeenth century, as did the prices of individual commodities. The period from the 1630s to the 1670s is famous in Dutch commercial history for its speculative booms and busts, of which the tulip craze of the 1630s is the best known but which also frequently involved the Asian condiments.[75] Purchase prices in Asia also showed wide and unpredictable changes. The VOC worked at great expense in company money and Asian blood to try to gain a degree of monopolistic control over pepper and all the major spices. Toward the end of the century, it came close to success with respect to spices. Although pepper was so widely grown and so many substitutes were available that no one could have a complete monopoly on it, the VOC did take over the lion's share of that market as well (see table 4, page 302). The VOC's control over spices was due, among other things, to its ruthlessness in dealing with East Indian rulers and peoples who dared to sell to anyone else. In the 1620s, for example, the VOC leadership in Europe agreed with its agents in Batavia that too many cloves were being grown at their primary source, the Banda Islands— too many cloves for the VOC to control, and far too many for the company to buy itself. Accordingly, VOC military expeditions attacked the islands, destroyed the crops, and killed or enslaved the growers.[76]

Contrary to what one might expect, the main reason for the VOC's expensive monopolistic spice program was not actually to drive up European spice prices as much as possible or to flood the market, but rather to create long-term price stability, a direct consequence of the fact that spices were a vital medium of exchange in other significant areas of commerce.[77] If the VOC could, by controlling the flow of spices into Europe, maintain the stability of their prices, they would in effect create a situation of great security and predictability in markets in which spices played a major role as exchange media. They could do with spices what no European government (even the Dutch) could do with regard to silver and gold: keep its value constant. As a monopolist (or at least as the largest of the oligopolists), the VOC ought to have been able to ensure that prices were stabilized at a high enough level to bring profits to the company. As the possessor of the world's greatest commercial bureaucracy, it was in a position to establish and carry out policies on a global scale—the only way price stability could be realized. And located as it was at the hub of Europe's information network, the VOC could forecast short-term continent-wide demand for spices with reasonable accuracy and increase or decrease its offerings on the market accordingly. When seen in this light, the VOC's adherence to its policy of focusing on spices and maintaining its partial monopoly at all costs (or at least at very high costs) makes a good deal of sense.

Because of the VOC's efforts, the prices of the traditional spices remained extraordinarily stable in the first part of the eighteenth century (see table 5, page 303). The amount of imports increased, but overall only in direct proportion to population growth.[78] Because the VOC never acquired the same degree of control over pepper, pepper prices continued to fluctuate, but not as widely as early in the seventeenth century. Demand for pepper also grew overall only at about the same rate as population from the late seventeenth to the late eighteenth century.[79]

The problem for the VOC was that while it was bearing a huge overhead to maintain hegemony over the spice trade, its competitors moved perforce into more dynamic areas of overseas commerce such as the marketing of Asian textiles and tea. The VOC was also active in these areas but could not direct its full attention and resources to them.[80] Also, because of the overhead, the VOC could not produce the net profits that the British East India Company and a host of smaller competitors and interlopers could. Things would undoubtedly have been better if demand for spices and pepper had remained as buoyant in the eighteenth century as it had been in the sixteenth and most of the seventeenth. The VOC could have, as we have seen, maintained steady prices while making an equally steady profit. But in fact, demand growth was sluggish from the late seventeenth century on. Those among the *bewindhebber* (directors) of the VOC who argued for a radical change of policy—men such as the polymath Johannes Hudde and the long-time company advocate (attorney) Pieter van Dam—believed that the European market was saturated and that the only ways to expand sales were to lower prices in Europe, push pepper and spices at the geographical margins of the European economy, or increase the company's intra-Asian pepper trade. Otherwise, the company needed to use its monopolistic position to raise prices, on the assumption that demand would not be greatly affected and profits would rise.[81] Dutch merchants dealing in spices attempted with some success in the early eighteenth century to focus on markets in Eastern Europe and America, and the VOC made considerable efforts—not wholly successful—to increase Asian markets, but it was not enough to offset the lack of dynamism in European demand. The VOC, however, remained committed to its previous pricing policy, mainly because its personnel continued to think of pepper and spices in terms of their traditional role in Dutch trade and finance rather than as consumer products sold directly by the company. For this reason (and many others), the VOC suffered a relative decline in the eighteenth century.[82]

The significant question for us is *why* per capita European demand growth for spices and pepper slowed in the latter part of the seventeenth century and in the eighteenth. Even if we were to accept the saturation argument of Hudde and van Dam, it is by no means clear what "saturation" meant. It surely did not rest on physiological limitations. Condiments make up at most a tiny fraction of individuals' food intake, not enough for processes of physical rejection to operate. Apparently, Europeans simply did not desire more pepper and spices. Had they wanted more, the production and transportation capabilities for filling the demand were certainly present. Cost would not have been a major impediment. In the face of substantial, continually rising demand, it is not likely that even the VOC could have resisted the temptation to satisfy the demand and reap large profits. Given the absence of evidence of a fall in average income in northwestern Europe in the late seventeenth and eighteenth centuries, it seems clear that people decided to spend their money on other goods besides pepper and spices.

SUGAR

A major candidate for one of the "other" goods was sugar. Cane sugar, which appears to have originated in India and which may have been imported into Europe in Roman times, was a not-insignificant item of elite consumption and of intercontinental trade in the late Middle Ages.[83] By the fifteenth century, it was being grown on islands in the eastern Mediterranean subject to Venetian rule and imported into Europe proper in respectable quantities. Sugar often appeared as a medicinal product when it was mentioned in European publications, although probably its appeal had more to do with its taste than with anything else.[84] The growing of sugar was introduced into the Atlantic islands occupied by the Portuguese in the fifteenth century. It was in those islands that the system of plantation production of sugar with slave labor developed, the system later exported to the Americas. Although unsuccessful attempts were made on numerous occasions during the next three centuries to produce sugar using free (or at least nonslave) labor, from the fifteenth century until the nineteenth century sugar, slavery, and the commercial plantation were closely linked.

In Portuguese Brazil and in various places in Spanish America in the sixteenth century, the plantation production of sugar became a moderately substantial business. However, the full transformation of sugar into a major force in world history did not really begin until the countries of northwestern Europe began to set up permanent colonies on West Indian islands. English settlers began growing sugar in Barbados sometime in the 1620s, although indigo remained for years the primary crop there. Cromwell's "Western Design" of the mid-1650s, which led to the conquest of Jamaica and a government-sponsored project to expand production on Barbados, was a major turning point. National prestige was at stake. Early experiments in settlement by white farmers on small plantations and in multicrop agriculture failed, so state policy moved in the 1660s and 1670s to an almost exclusive focus on sugar and on plantations worked by African slaves, which prospered and expanded mightily.[85] The Jamaican-Barbadian plantation economy became closely connected to major sources of capital in England, which created an economic nexus that drew in other English colonies in the West Indies and ultimately the colonies in North America as well. French and Dutch settlements followed suit; the period of their greatest development came in the eighteenth century when the French outstripped the British in sugar production and in sugar imports into Europe. (Although not in consumption. The majority of the French sugar trade was for reexport.)[86] All in all, the sugar trade (with the slave trade that made it possible) was the axis around which the Atlantic economy of the eighteenth century revolved.

The vast expansion of West Indian sugar production in the last third of the seventeenth and the first half of the eighteenth centuries (see table 6, page 304) was the result of a number of factors, including government policy in Britain and France, the availability of capital and the existence of structures that permitted its successful investment, and the supply of cheap and effective labor through the West African slave trade. But such expansion also required a basis on the demand side in Europe: a continually expanding consumption of sugar by Europeans, which cannot be explained solely by reference to the productive capacities of the West Indian plantations and their effects on prices. This was precisely the difference between sugar and the pepper-spice ensemble. Per capita demand for sugar increased; per capita demand for pepper and spices did not.[87]

Until recently, many historians apparently assumed that sugar in essence created its own market and that the population of Europe consumed as much sugar as was available because of a natural craving for it.[88] But as we saw from the example of the difference between per capita French and British sugar consumption, this assumption is not correct in the terms in which it is stated. It is quite possible for groups of people to limit their intake of sugar, to allocate their discretionary income in other ways, and to build their decisions into their culture. That *some* sugar will be consumed if available, and that, in most societies, if sugar is cheap enough, a great deal will be used, are propositions to which we can agree without difficulty. But that is different from simply assuming that the specific nature of positive demand for sugar is a matter of little importance.[89]

To reinforce the point, we should note that most of the ways in which sugar is employed in cooking—especially in making sweet desserts—were developed in France in the seventeenth century. At that time, France was at the center of European sugar consumption, at least as far as interest in the ways in which sugar could be used was concerned. But although France remains a center of fancy sugarbaking to this day, the fascination of the French with sugar did not outlive the seventeenth century. This was not due to changes in price or availability. French duties on sugar were high, but high tariffs were easily evaded by smuggling in the eighteenth century if the demand was there—as was demonstrated by tea in Britain and by Asian textiles in France. As we have seen, France became the primary supplier of West Indian sugar to the rest of continental Europe in the late eighteenth century. But sugar played no important role in French culture as it did in Britain and the Netherlands.[90]

There was evidently a complicated process at work to shape demand for sugar, spices, and pepper. By the eighteenth century, it had produced quite different results for sugar as opposed to the other commodities. The physical nature of the products and state policies toward them had something to do with the difference, but not everything. Cultural contexts help to explain the rest of the process and its varied consequences.

THE CONTEXTS OF CONDIMENT CONSUMPTION

The principal contexts that appear to have framed the consumption of pepper, spice, and sugar in early modern Europe were those of gentility and luxury, together with the context of virtue that will be discussed in chapter 4. As we have seen, the last context influenced the construction of comfort, which plays a part in our consideration of condiments. It also incorporated notions about the pursuit of physical health as a sign of virtue. For the moment, however, we will concentrate on luxury and gentility. It is enough at present to note that pepper, sugar, and all the major spices were held, at one time or another, to have had medicinal properties and that part of the demand for them was for use in maintaining or restoring health.[91] It seems fairly clear that this was not the primary reason for their consumption, although the fact that they might be perceived in a health-giving context was a subsidiary source of appeal and could be employed to offset qualms arising from luxury consumption. (In other words, you could make your conscience easier about eating a great deal of sugar, which you enjoyed but which worried you for various reasons, if you could convince yourself that sugar was also good for you.)

Throughout most of the Middle Ages, spices, pepper, and sugar were all status commodities in Europe, especially the first. All were extremely expensive; quite small amounts of cinnamon, nutmeg, cloves, ginger, and so forth were sometimes included as specific bequests in the wills of significant persons.[92] In the late Middle Ages, from the fourteenth century to the sixteenth, pepper and sugar became increasingly available because of the expansion of the traditional trade with Asia, as did some of the spices. Until the entry of the Portuguese into the Indian Ocean at the end of the fifteenth and beginning of the sixteenth centuries, however, the prices of all these goods were sufficiently high that they could only be afforded by the European elite—wealthier nobles, the upper clergy, and merchants—and municipal corporations and monasteries for particularly sumptuous feasts. It appears from court records and fifteenth-century cookbooks that even for the people who could afford spices as condiments, they were not regular items of consumption but rather items for special, usually public, occasions. In other words, they fit the general pattern of status goods quite well: they were rare, expensive, and suitable for conspicuous consumption in support of gentility.[93]

They also, of course, imparted flavor, thereby making the process of eating more enjoyable than it would otherwise have been and providing a range of variation in taste sensations. Without pepper and the Asian spices, artistic cookery would never have developed as it did in Italy in the late Middle Ages. A large proportion of the recipes for special dishes (that is, meals for feasts for the upper classes) that have come down to us use pepper, spices, and sugar as the primary means of giving distinction to the cook's creation.[94]

Spices, pepper, and sugar fit into the context of luxury not only because their sensual qualities provided a variety of delightful tastes, but also because they came from the mysterious East. The very trade that brought them also brought the tales of distant places (some accurate, most inaccurate, many completely absurd) that were a staple of "popular" literature in the late Middle Ages. When one consumed nutmeg, one could enjoy not just the taste of the spice itself but also the thought that it might have been harvested by someone whose anatomy placed his external members in different relation to one another than was the norm for Europeans. And, of course, some spices were reputed to have aphrodisiac qualities. Even if the physical bases of such reputations were imaginary, imagination presumably counted for a great deal if the items in question were consumed in the appropriate manner and setting.[95]

Let us now dispose of a "fact" most of us learned in school when we first studied the spice trade, just before we heard the equally spurious "fact" that the Portuguese were impelled to seek a sea route to India in the late fifteenth century because of the Turkish conquest of Constantinople in 1453. This is the notion that spices and pepper were a "necessity" in late medieval and early modern Europe for disguising the taste of rotten meat in the winter, while sugar and cloves were "essential" for preserving foods.[96]

It is of course true that sugar and cloves are preservatives and that heavy spices and peppers can disguise spoiled meat. It is also true, however, that the costs of these commodities until well into the sixteenth century were so high that only a tiny proportion of the things that needed to be preserved or disguised could have been treated with them. There were plenty of domestic European substitutes, if such were needed: horseradish, for example, and salt. There was no "necessity" involved in the demand for spices, pepper, and sugar.[97] One also wonders, given the preference of Europeans until very recently for "ripened" meat, whether the notion of a disguise for spoiled meat really makes much sense. If meat were so spoiled that medieval (or nineteenth-century) Europeans found it unpalatable, it is unlikely that any spice or pepper from Asia could have disguised it. In other words, the wealthy might choose to employ products imported at great expense from Asia to preserve foods and to impart a better flavor to meat, but they were under no necessity of doing so—and their reasons for choosing to do it are probably best explained in terms of flavor (luxury) and conspicuous consumption (gentility).

If spices, pepper, and sugar were consumed within essentially the same contexts and in much the same ways through the sixteenth century, what happened after that to give them different economic trajectories? For one thing, largely because of the wide availability and use of all three sets of products, they had lost most of their traditional value as status commodities by the middle of the seventeenth century, which meant that they were left mainly as luxury goods. This change in turn meant that the different ways in which pepper and spices on the one hand and sugar on the other acted as luxuries led them to experience quite different patterns of demand. Before the seventeenth century, already existing differences in luxury consumption had been counterbalanced by similarities in the modes in which the two groups of condiments were consumed as status goods, but in the seventeenth century the balance was upset. Differences were accentuated even more by changes in the ways in which the context of luxury came to be framed in the late seventeenth and eighteenth centuries—particularly with respect to the rise of taste.

First, pepper and the spices. Pepper became available in such large quantities by the second quarter of the seventeenth century—not only because of the capacities of the East India companies, but also because of gluts produced by speculation—that it could usually be afforded regularly by people who were not members of the social elite.[98] It did not become cheap, exactly, but it was within the grasp of families with moderate amounts of disposable income. Throughout the seventeenth century, such families bought considerable amounts of pepper. Apart from occasional changes in fashions for highly peppered foods and a rather lengthy vogue for white pepper around the turn of the seventeenth and eighteenth centuries, there was nothing modish about cooking with pepper in western Europe. It was not expensive enough to signify as conspicuous consumption in any meaningful way.

The histories of the spices (as opposed to pepper) were a bit more varied in the seventeenth century, and some of the minor ones were occasionally rare and fashionable. In general, however, the same thing seems to have happened to cloves, cinnamon, nutmeg, and mace, a nutmeg by-product, as happened to pepper. They were thought of as being special. Family rituals developed around them (such as the custom of putting cloves in a piece of fruit one Christmas and eating the fruit at the next Christmas, which persisted in Britain down to the twentieth century). They were widely recommended for seasoning all sorts of foods in the increasingly numerous cookery books of the late seventeenth and eighteenth centuries—books that were no longer presented as guides to the preparation of elaborate feasts, but rather as resources for the household. But using spices and pepper did not imply genteel status. They had become luxury goods, pure and simple.[99]

The VOC leadership took some time to understand this change, mainly because of the company's emphasis on pepper and spices as media within larger systems of commerce. VOC directors continued into the eighteenth century to think of eastern Europe as the primary area for expanding spice and pepper demand, and they believed that their main consumers in this area were the Polish, Prussian, Lithuanian, and Russian nobles who controlled the production of grain.[100] These aristocrats were thought (with good reason) to be major purchasers of fashionable western European goods for purposes of status competition. Whether or not this was true of imported Asian condiments is unclear, but certainly the VOC leaders *believed* that the status and fashion model of marketing was still applicable in a region that was particularly important in their scheme of things. This belief did not serve the long-run interests of the company very well.

The demand for pepper and Asian spices in western Europe appears to have been based almost entirely on luxury consumption (as we have defined it) from the late seventeenth century into the nineteenth, although some elements of luxury demand disappeared over time. Standard black pepper lost any trace of exoticism quite early. Other peppers, however, retained that characteristic—especially the hotter red and yellow peppers from Africa and America. White pepper (which was simply Indian or Indonesian black pepper processed in Asia to make it white) appears to have been in demand because of some sort of exotic appeal.[101] But the main appeal of pepper and spices was clearly sensual: it added zest to a wide variety of foods, and it did so for a wide variety of Europeans. This, then, was the situation at the end of the seventeenth and the beginning of the eighteenth century, when (despite occasional fluctuations in price due largely to wars and inadvertent overstocking) average European demand for pepper and the major spices had clearly leveled off, to grow thereafter approximately at the pace of population increase (see table 4, page 302).

Of course, demand for luxuries can lead to profits even if they are not status goods. If per capita consumption of pepper and spices did not rise in the eighteenth century, it did not fall either, and while the VOC's malaise probably resulted in part from spending too much effort on them and too little on developing other lines of trade, the company was still a large, prosperous, and growing concern throughout the eighteenth century. It is true that there was no cyclical fashion process in the eighteenth century that would regularly heighten demand for particular condiments—unlike the case with silks and cottons. Cloves were not the rage one year, to be replaced by nutmeg the next. But the spices played an important role in the process by which the aesthetics of taste came to govern European cuisine in the eighteenth century. This ensured continuing demand, but it also carried with it an inherent brake on demand expansion, because the essence of taste was restraint and balance.

In his comparative history of French and English cooking, Stephen Mennell brilliantly demonstrates how aesthetic taste came to frame haute cuisine in the late seventeenth and eighteenth centuries (especially in France, but also in England).[102] Pepper and spices played vital roles in this process. According to Mennell, until the seventeenth century, both luxury and genteel status in elite dining derived much more from the amount of food served at meals and from the variety of courses than from the quality of the taste. Sumptuary laws reflected traditional concern with this aspect of luxury. Condiments were used in heavy doses when they were used at all, apparently so as to make it completely clear what spices, and how much of them, one was consuming—which was consistent with the general theory of cookery at the time. It is not surprising, under these circumstances, that pepper should have been far and away the most widely cited condiment in the cookbooks of the sixteenth century.[103] Laid on heavily, the various types of pepper were unmistakable and could be used quite liberally. In terms of flavor, the rest of the dish acted to a large extent as a platform for their conveyance.

In the late sixteenth and seventeenth centuries, with the spread of fashionable and professional cookery on the Franco-Italian model to the rest of Europe, a variation on the "more is better" approach arose: the custom of creating new flavors by mixing very different seasonings together.[104] Again, the flavor of the seasonings was supposed to be the primary experience, to be savored alongside, but not really as part of, the flavor of the item that was seasoned. The ability to create such mixtures that were palatable in themselves and did not counter or detract from the flavors of the foods with which they were served constituted a large part of the cook's art in the seventeenth century, something that the authors of the burgeoning literature of cookery attempted to convey to their readers. This fashion of cooking and its increasing adoption for larger numbers of meals by larger numbers of people of the middling as well as upper sort was probably an important part of the reason for the expansiveness of demand for pepper and spices in the seventeenth century, just as its development and attractiveness were made possible by the ability of the VOC to supply the desired amount of Asian condiments at reasonable prices.

The application of the principles of taste to western European cooking in the late seventeenth and the eighteenth centuries changed the situation substantially.[105] Along with the emphasis on restraint that was so central an aspect of taste and that had a notable effect on the amount of seasoning employed in cooking, taste also aimed at harmony and balance. In cooking, the key to taste was the use of seasonings to mingle with, complement, and enhance the flavors of the foods seasoned, not to have a separate existence. (That is, technically they became seasonings rather than condiments.) This remains the ideal of modern Western cuisine. Moreover, "taste" in cooking emphasized subtlety (at least in comparison to its predecessors) and occasionally even understatement. Thus, from the eighteenth century on, the consumption of pepper and spices in the Western world depended on culinary practices that embodied a culture of limitation that emphasized quality of product and experience rather than quantity of either. There was no other significant source of demand for pepper or the major spices, as the gentility context had long been irrelevant and the literature of health no longer put much emphasis on the relationship between spices and physical well-being. So, due in large measure to an alteration in the cultural context of luxury in the European world (the advent of taste), the market for pepper and spices had to conform to a pattern that afforded only limited increases in demand. In the nineteenth century, as people at the lower end of the Western social order admitted themselves to a cultural context—the culture of respectability—that incorporated principles of taste, and as many of those people acquired additional discretionary income, there appears to have been another surge of demand for spices.[106] This was not enough, however, to lend the spice trade more than a shadow of its former glory in relation to other sectors of the global economy, and the fashion did not sustain itself.

But what about sugar? Sugar as a commodity in itself had ceased to be a status good (at least with regard to gentility) by the beginning of the seventeenth century, remaining primarily a luxury. Unlike the other condiments, however, sugar became in the late sixteenth and early seventeenth centuries the central ingredient of an array of products that did retain their places in the context of gentility for a very long time. These were the sugar-based confections created by the new profession of sugarbaking.[107] The standard confections, the standard methods of making them, and the profession itself were all French in origin. Sugarbaking may in fact have been the first instance of a French culinary fashion passing into general European use while still retaining its reputation for being French. In the seventeenth century, not only the fashion but a great many sugarbakers emigrated from France to the Netherlands with the Huguenot diaspora. They went particularly to Amsterdam because that city had become a major center for the sugar trade, and also because sugarbaking had developed a much broader clientele there than it had in the French cities—in other words, not just customers who bought confections for fancy display, but customers at the middling level of society who developed their own rituals for consuming and exchanging small confections as part of the protocol for family events, visits, and the like.[108] Confectionary on a grand scale for conspicuous consumption continued to be practiced, especially in France and England. This included the creation of "sugar courses" for banquets: whole courses, usually on the table when the guests arrived, that consisted entirely of sugar replicas of the items that would be served in the later courses, and sometimes of the plates as well. After marveling at the ingenuity of the sugarbaker and the wealth of the host, guests could either eat the confections or not, as they chose. The course would then be cleared and the real meal would begin.[109]

By the end of the seventeenth century, however, the status consumption of confections had fallen as their more egregious forms came to be considered to be in questionable taste. Confectionary thus became primarily a luxury good like the other forms of sugar. As we saw with pepper and spice, it is not necessarily a bad thing to have a luxury good to market, as long as supply is sufficiently elastic to respond to expanding demand without unduly raising prices and causing customers to find substitutes—and as long as consumers have discretionary income. The burgeoning West Indian plantation economy of the second half of the seventeenth century provided the elasticity. The sources of the discretionary income are much more complicated and have been the subject of considerable dispute among economic historians. But regardless of the outcome (if there ever is one) of the debate about whether, and whose, incomes rose or fell in the seventeenth and/or eighteenth centuries, it is certainly clear that increasingly large proportions of the population of northwestern Europe lived in towns and cities, bought and sold in markets with money, depended on money incomes for at least part of their subsistence, and internalized the developing cultures of the market economy.[110] All these things meant that a growing pool of disposable income was available. Whether or not real standards of living for particular sectors of society in particular places improved or declined, and whether or not the nominal wage for a day's work in a particular trade or the market price for a quintal of wheat in a particular area rose or fell, discretionary income was still in the hands of a large and increasing number of people in early modern Europe—at least in France, the Netherlands, England, and probably most of Germany—simply because incomes were increasingly realized in money.

By definition, discretionary income can be spent in a variety of ways according to the choices of the spender. If a person of small means wanted to spend some money on sugar rather than bread, he or she could do so. In terms of calories, it might or might not have been a reasonable decision, but it is unlikely that comparative nutritional content would have had much to do with it. Early modern pamphlet literature (like its modern equivalents) is full of attacks on the "profligate" buying habits of the lower orders because they did just that—used the discretion that their income allowed them in the market.[111] Of course, the less income you had, the less choice you had, but there does not seem to have been a clearly understood "subsistence level" at which all money *had* to go for certain "necessities." All this is simply to say that the question of where the demand for sugar or anything else in early modern Europe came from is a very complex one that has as much to do with the structure of the economy and with the social and cultural factors that framed the options for making purchases as it does with the relatively abstract notions of average income and standard of living.

This is significant for explaining the career of sugar because sugar clearly became a customary luxury for a very great number of Europeans on a much larger scale than did pepper and spice. This was especially true in Britain and the Netherlands and in urban areas. By the latter part of the seventeenth century (and perhaps before), people at the middle levels of society in those places regularly consumed substantial amounts of sugar. By the eighteenth century, this probably included not only people with fair amounts of discretionary income, but some at the margins of the middle range or below—people who had to make fairly rigorous choices and could not afford a wide range of luxuries. Sugar was apparently one of the luxuries that was generally chosen.[112]

Why? Part of the reason, of course, is that most people like sweet-tasting things, and cane sugar is one of the most concentrated forms of sweetness that is readily available. Not everyone in any given population enjoys sweetness, and even among those who enjoy some forms of sweetness, not everyone likes cane sugar. Nevertheless, a liking for sweetness is one of the most common tastes in the world, even though it can be strongly influenced and modified by particular cultures.[113]

This does not, however, get us very far. Given the fact that sugar was one of a number of luxury options for consumers in the seventeenth century (including some, such as honey and Mediterranean oranges, that are also sweet), we need an idea of why it was that sugar was so popular in comparison to other luxuries—especially spices and pepper, which were considered to belong to the same category as sugar right up to the eighteenth century.

One reason, in the seventeenth century at any rate, was that sugar was ideally suited to the notions of cooking that dominated the period. If one compares popular cookery books of the late sixteenth century with their successors of the second half of the seventeenth, one finds a remarkable change with regard to the use of condiments and seasonings. In the leading cheap German cookbook of the late sixteenth century, the *Koch und Kellermeisterey* of "Master Sebastian" (1581), fewer than half of the recipes for meat and fish and only a small fraction of the recipes for vegetables, sauces, and desserts contain any reference to imported condiments of any kind, and by far the most frequently mentioned of them is pepper.[114] It is not that Sebastian is unacquainted with sugar. He goes on at some length about ways of improving the taste of old wine by putting candy sugar in it. (In fact, sweetening wine appears to have been at that time and for several decades of the seventeenth century one of the major uses of sugar in Europe.) And in his chapter on confitures and preserves he gives pride of place to sugar, explaining why sugar is better and healthier to use than honey.[115] But in general, Sebastian, like most of his contemporaries among cookbook writers, did not use much sugar in his cooking. Less than one hundred years later, it was very difficult to find a cookery book that did not recommend sugar glazes for practically all meats, sugar bases for sauces, sugar for all forms of baked goods, and so forth. (There were a few exceptions. "Sugar," wrote one author, "is temperate, although somewhat inclining to hot, and is good for all sort of Food, except in Tripes; for being put thereon, it makes them stink like the Dung of an Ox newly made.")[116] By contemporary standards in the United States, the use of sugar prescribed in these books is sickeningly heavy, and Americans consume a great deal of sugar.[117] And late-seventeenth-century Europeans were still sugaring wine. The same cookbooks also prescribe much more spice than their sixteenth-century predecessors, but the prevalence of sugar in the later books is the most noticeable difference between them.

The point of this seventeenth-century approach to cooking is the one we have discussed previously: the various foods cooked or served with sugar are essentially platforms for the sugar (as spiced foods were platforms for spice). The issue of whether sugar "goes with" the food hardly arises. The tastes are essentially separate. Sugar lends itself to this kind of cooking because its taste is unmistakable and essentially uniform. Sugar cooked with many of the foods suggested in the seventeenth-century cookbooks would certainly have produced unusual arrays of flavors.

From this standpoint, the application of "good taste" to cooking at the end of the seventeenth and in the eighteenth centuries ought to have had a devastating effect on the demand for sugar. Eighteenth-century cookbooks show a substantial decline in the number of items for which sugar is suggested and a reduction in the amount of sugar prescribed for most recipes.[118] Moreover, the sugaring of wine largely ceased, or at least was reduced to such an extent that one hardly finds references to it in western Europe after the beginning of the eighteenth century.

In fact, however, at no point in the late seventeenth and eighteenth centuries did West Indian or Brazilian cane sugar suffer from anything that can be read from the economic record as a sustained decline in demand (see table 6, page 304). One of the reasons for this was that, as Sidney Mintz emphasizes in his major study of sugar in world history, sugar performs many different functions and has many different uses in various societies.[119] In the period with which we are concerned, consumption of sugar for some of these other functions and uses appears to have expanded at the time that its use in cooking declined. Most of these alternatives were forms of luxury consumption.

Although fancy sugarbaking for the elite no longer played a significant status role in the eighteenth century, the making of small sugar confections (sugar biscuits, cakes, and so on) appears to have expanded, serving a broad market made up of people from every social level, at least in urban areas of France, the Low Countries, Britain, and Germany.[120] Equally important was sugar candy. Sticks of sugar had been eaten or sucked, especially by children, since the sixteenth century. In the seventeenth and eighteenth centuries, the typical (although not the only) form for this kind of consumption was a triangular wedge of hard sugar, sold and held in a paper wrapper. These were called "candies," a name that came from the sugar the VOC imported from Kandy, in Ceylon. "Candy" originally referred to the shape in which this hard sugar was transported: it was molded into oblongs that were wide at the base, triangular along the sides, and pointed at the top. The habit of breaking off the point for licking before melting the rest of the oblong down for use in confection or cooking led to a regular industry in the Netherlands, whereby all large pieces of candy sugar had their points broken off for sale.[121] In the eighteenth century, sugar candy was produced deliberately in a variety of shapes, but the traditional pointed wedge remained popular for many years. Sugar was the ideal base for a luxury of this sort because of the intensity of its sweetness and the simplicity and potential large scale of its transformation into candies. Spices could be used to give sugar candies distinctive flavors, but sugar was the essence of the candy business. It thus found a new kind of large-scale luxury market—a market for a habit-forming, nonmealtime ingestible, completely beyond the deadening reach of "good taste." Sugar was truly a "comfort" food—as it remains.

Sugar found other expanding uses in Europe in the late seventeenth and eighteenth centuries. Fruit preserves had been prepared with sugar for centuries, but the ready availability of sugar and the increasing availability of suitable, cheap ceramic and glass vessels made an expansion of the practice possible. The widespread adoption of breakfast and a late afternoon meal provided a reason to take advantage of the possibility, to add a touch of slightly exotic (and sweet) luxury to the various breads that were the staples of the meals.[122]

There were thus important reasons for the very different history of sugar as opposed to the spices and pepper in early modern Europe, reasons that had a great deal to do with modes of supply and with intrinsic properties of the commodities, but that also derived from the roles of particular condiments in the changing context of luxury. However, even this is not the whole story. Three factors of crucial importance have been left out of the discussion of sugar thus far.

In the first place, sugar came under increasingly harsh medical criticism in the late seventeenth and especially in the eighteenth century. Earlier, all the condiments had generally been regarded as conducive to health in various ways—sugar and certain spices such as ginger in particular.[123] Few objections were ever advanced against the spices and pepper (except for very hot peppers), even though their positive medicinal qualities were increasingly downplayed in the eighteenth century. But sugar became the object of outright attack as something deleterious to health—for reasons real and imagined. There were medical defenders of sugar in the eighteenth century in Britain and France (the industry was too rich and too powerful not to be able to rally support), but at best they were able to restrain, not to turn aside, the violence of the assault.[124]

Second, and as we shall see, closely related to the first, was the association of sugar with slavery. The association was an undoubted fact from the second quarter of the seventeenth century, but it came to be regarded by at least a few people as something problematical toward the end of that century. By the 1770s and 1780s, it was a major moral, economic, and political issue in both Britain and France that had significant implications for the consumption of sugar.[125]

The third factor was a circumstance noted by most commentators on the sugar industry in the eighteenth century: by far the most important use of sugar, the foundation of its demand, was its consumption with tea and coffee, particularly the former. Both luxury and gentility had a great deal to do with the emergence of this practice. In Britain particularly, a nice cup of tea with sugar became by the nineteenth century the prime archetype of comfort—as it remains. However, the transformation of the practice into a major fact of economic, social, and political life must be understood primarily with reference to yet another context: the context of virtue, which is the subject of the next chapter.

4

VIRTUE

The early modern contexts of gentility and luxury had deep historical roots. The context that will be examined next also contained some factors of great antiquity, but as a cultural construct it was quite new. It was put together in the seventeenth and eighteenth centuries, as were the most important of the elements of which it was composed. To a greater extent than any of the other cultural phenomena discussed in this book, the context of virtue was the glue that made respectability coherent and gave it its distinctive moral character. The nature of the context can be explored by focusing on two of its constituent behavior patterns: consciously promoting one's health through careful attention to diet and exercise, and keeping oneself and one's family clean in clothing and body.

DR. BLANKAART'S PRESCRIPTION FOR HEALTHY LIVING

Among the many books on health and diet published in the late seventeenth century, one of the best was *De Borgerlyke Tafel: Om lang gesond sonder ziekten te leven* ("the bourgeois table: how to live long and healthily without sickness"). *De Borgerlyke Tafel* was written by Steven Blankaart, M.D., a physician of Amsterdam, and published in 1683.[1] It is a model health book, forcefully written in plain language with little recourse to technical jargon, consistent with the accepted medical theories of the era but firmly grounded in the author's empirical observations. Blankaart's personality, undisguised by the Baroque formality that embellishes so much of the other pamphlet literature of the period, comes through strongly: his commonsense approach to medical issues, his grumpiness about the foibles of his contemporaries.

Blankaart discusses many imported consumables: sugar, tea, coffee, and tobacco. (He favors the last three as supports to physical and mental health, but strongly disapproves of the first.)[2] What is important for our purposes is that he frames the discussion of these products, as he does the whole of his subject, within a distinct public discourse, one that had been forming for about a century and had attained, by Blankaart's time, a shape that can be readily recognized in the contemporary world. The focus of this discourse is physical health and its relationship to virtue and society.

"'Tis certain that the health of the body is the greatest treasure men can have on earth."[3] Blankaart's formula does not rule out posthumous treasures in heaven, but his focus clearly rests on the here and now—as is appropriate for a physician. His book is suffused with materialism; it makes practically no reference to religion, God, spirituality, or belief. But qualities such as virtue and morality are not absent. Blankaart does not, for example, so much oppose the consumption of sugar as the tendency to consume too much of it—a tendency partly grounded in the addictive nature of sugar itself, and partly in the moral weakness of people who use it. Balance and measure must be applied to eating and drinking in order to maintain health. On the other hand, Blankaart follows (at a distance) his contemporary, the Dutch "tea doctor" Cornelis Bontekoe, in stating that tea can be taken in large quantities, twelve or twenty cups a day, without ill effects and with positive benefits for the body.[4] Blankaart's animus against sugar rests partly on the empirical observation that sugar appears to lead to corpulence, tooth decay, and other maladies, but he does not seem to recognize the uncomfortable effects of drinking large amounts of tea. He refers to the theory of humors, which allows him to blame sugar for generating excessive choler. But other writers on health used the same theory to attack tea and to praise sugar.[5] Something else leads Blankaart to warn against excessive sugaring while favoring what seems to us excessive tea drinking: sugar is *morally* suspect; tea is not.

The idea of morally devaluing sugar consumption was not new. Even in the first quarter of the seventeenth century, at a time when the use of sugar was spreading rapidly and when most publications on health treated sugar favorably, the Amsterdam municipal authorities more than once passed ordinances banning the sale of marzipan figures in the shape of humans and other of God's creatures.[6] The ordinances seem to have had little effect, but they reveal an attitude that ran much deeper than religious scruples about culinary anthropomorphism. It may have represented distress about the status implications of the ready availability of a commodity (marzipan) that was in the not too distant past consumed in quantity only by the elite, and also about the potentially sinful self-indulgence inherent in satisfying a craving for sugar—distress articulated, in other words, in terms of gentility and luxury.[7] This is not, however, true of Blankaart's critique of sugar.

Blankaart focuses on the implications of excessive consumption of sugar, and of inattention to dietary discipline in general, on the part of the individual citizen—implications that have little to do with conceptions of luxury as the road to sin or with the social dangers inherent in luxury practiced by the wrong people. Excessive self-indulgence and lack of proper concern for one's own health is evidence of a lack of virtue that may also be displayed in public life. If a man can't control himself in his own interest when eating and drinking, how can he control himself when he is supposed to be acting for the common good?

Blankaart emphasizes balance in diet, moderation and self-discipline in behavior, and simplicity in taste throughout his book. He grumbles that he has had to add the customary section on table manners at the insistence of his publisher, but implies that such matters are really superfluous and have nothing to do with the seriousness of his work. He addresses himself to urbanites (his fellow citizens of Amsterdam), who need his advice badly. Country people, he says, unwittingly follow the example of the ancients by eating healthy foods and maintaining proper diets, whereas contemporary city-dwellers pay more attention to flavor than to content in their meals.[8] City people are guilty of excess: they eat too many soft foods, too much salt, and far too much sugar, and therefore they live shorter and less healthy lives. They need balance in diet, as in other things.

People who follow fashion are, according to Blankaart, the people most likely to display imbalance and excess in eating and thereby to reveal their moral weakness. Such people, for example, quickly adopted tea as a fashion when it appeared at midcentury. They made tea popular, but then dropped it when they discovered that others were drinking it as well.[9] This was unwise, because tea is the healthiest of all drinks. Blankaart does not necessarily equate the wealthy and powerful with the fashionable. Anyone with means can be fashionable if he or she is weak and foolish, although it is the upper classes that adopt fashions most readily.

Blankaart is thus explicitly attacking what we have described as status behavior and luxurious behavior, but he is not doing so according to the modes of criticism that were normally part of the contexts of gentility and luxury. His critique and his positive recommendations are conceived in quite a different context, one that features a strong materialist orientation, a focus on individual behavior, and a peculiar way of associating virtue and worthiness for community service with balance, moderation, and self-restraint in achieving individual well-being. In Blankaart's case, the last is framed in terms of physical health. He does not mention cleanliness. Seventeenth-century Europeans had no reason to think that cleanliness and health were related in a direct, causal way, and Blankaart is writing about health.[10] Nevertheless, cleanliness is also part of the context that informs Blankaart's book because, as we shall see, being clean and working to be healthy are both signs of the same kind of virtue.

THE DISCOURSE OF VIRTUE

Blankaart touches on some of the central concepts of the wider context of virtue, but he was not writing directly about them; he was writing a handbook on diet. Two or three generations later, Benjamin Franklin described that wider context very explicitly.

In two famous passages in his *Autobiography*, Franklin describes how, as a young man in the late 1720s, he developed a method by which he sought to achieve moral perfection.[11] He did not, he admits, attain his goal, but he managed at least to improve himself and he retained the list of basic principles he made up at the time for the rest of his life. There is some humorous self-deprecation in the two passages, but not much. Franklin seems to have been serious about the main elements of his moral strategy, at least as he presented them when writing forty-three and fifty-six years later. Indeed, Franklin appears to see the moral perfection episode as the foundation of his achievements in life, and so it was treated in American schoolbooks well into the twentieth century.[12] Historical research has made it clear that Franklin was a great deal more complex and "imperfect" than the *Autobiography* portrays him, but that is largely irrelevant for present purposes.[13] In the *Autobiography*, Franklin is selectively narrating parts of his life so as to give them meaning—for his readers and (presumably) for himself. His text must distribute his memories around a framework that he thinks he and his readers share, and he must use a form of discourse that his readers will understand. That we still easily understand him is a measure not only of his success as a writer but also of the continuing viability of the framework he selected.

It is worth quoting a large part of what Franklin says about his strategy, despite its familiarity:

> I concluded at length, that the mere speculative Conviction that it was in our Interest to be compleatly virtuous, was not sufficient to prevent our Slipping, and that the contrary Habits must be broken and good ones acquired and established, before we can have any Dependance on a steady uniform Rectitude of Conduct. For this purpose I therefore contriv'd the following Method. . . . [His method was to list principles

of good moral behavior selected from various sources and use the list as the basis of a repeating, self-conducted course of moral improvement.]

. . . I included under Thirteen Names of Virtues all that at that time occurr'd to me as necessary or desirable, and annex'd to each a short Precept, which fully express'd the Extent I gave to its Meaning.

These Names of Virtues with their Precepts were

1. TEMPERANCE

Eat not to Dulness.
Drink not to Elevation.

2. SILENCE

Speak not but what may benefit others or yourself. Avoid trifling Conversation.

3. ORDER

Let all your Things have their Places. Let each Part of your Business have its Time.

4. RESOLUTION

Resolve to perform what you ought. Perform without fail what you resolve.

5. FRUGALITY

Make no Expence but to do good to others or yourself: i.e. Waste nothing.

6. INDUSTRY

Lose no Time. Be always employ'd in something useful. Cut off all unnecessary Actions.

7. SINCERITY

Use no hurtful Deceit.
Think innocently and justly; and, if you speak, speak accordingly.

8. JUSTICE

Wrong none, by doing Injuries or omitting the Benefits that are your Duty.

9. MODERATION

Avoid Extreams. Forbear resenting Injuries so much as you think they deserve.

10. CLEANLINESS

Tolerate no Uncleanness in Body, Cloaths or Habitation.

11. TRANQUILITY

Be not disturbed at Trifles, or at Accidents common or unavoidable.

12. CHASTITY

Rarely use Venery but for Health or Offspring; Never to Dulness, Weakness, or the Injury of your own or another's Peace or Reputation.

13. HUMILITY

Imitate Jesus and Socrates.[14]

This list is the part of the *Autobiography* that made D. H. Lawrence most furious—point 12 particularly, which seemed to him to reduce sex and love to mere selfish calculation rather than natural expression.[15] From another perspective, it is possible to suspect Franklin of trying to be humorous, especially in points 12 and 13. At least with respect to 12, the suspicion would be incorrect, just as Lawrence's complaint is somewhat, although not entirely, misdirected. Franklin's resolution about chastity (which he does not discuss further in the book) is a straightforward moral inference from what was then accepted medical "knowledge": that health required a balance of the body's humors. The health of an adult male depended on balance maintained, among other ways, through ejaculation and intercourse at appropriate intervals. The health of an adult female also depended on regular intercourse, which provided the occasion for the mixing of male and female "sperm" in the uterus—a peculiar requisite for humoral balance in a woman's body. Intercourse was obviously also required for procreation, which was believed to have a positive effect on women's health (despite the high actual frequency of death in childbirth).[16] Franklin is not implying that he is only interested in the effects of sexual intercourse on himself; the last part of the explication obviously belies that notion, but so actually does the first. "Venery" is necessary for the health of *both* partners. Franklin does not say that one shouldn't enjoy sex. He takes it for granted that people will naturally do so, and he assumes that his readers share with him the common early modern understanding that orgasm is part of what makes intercourse physically healthy. Like most of his contemporaries, he believes that both sex and affection between partners are essential to a stable marriage, which in turn is one foundation of a stable society. He is at some pains in the *Autobiography* to assert the affective character, the propriety, and the success of his own marriage, which was in fact entirely "natural," never having been officially sanctioned because of his wife's previous marriage.[17] However, he never describes an overpowering, passionate love for his wife or anyone else. He hints that he was overpowered by *lust* at various times in his youth; he treats these instances as mistakes, not sins.[18] What he is most concerned about is the exercise of moderation and restraint, in these as in other matters.

What we have in Franklin's approach to chastity as a virtue is thus a self-imposed dictum regarding his personal behavior, framed in the first instance in terms of the physical health of his own and his partner's bodies, second in terms of procreation (which he appears to regard as an option, not a requirement), third in terms of his and his partner's reputations and mental well-being. Because the dictum and its explication are framed within a discourse of "virtue" and (notionally, at least) "perfection," we can assume that the behavior he advocates is supposed to lead to "good," while contrary behavior or behavior explicitly rejected is "bad." Franklin does not employ, or even hint at, concepts such as "evil," "sin," "damnation," or "corruption"; good is to be striven for in behavior, and failure to achieve it is an indication that one should try harder. Good and bad (the latter implicitly defined as deviation from good, or error) seem to be the main constituents of his moral system as well as the limits of his moral discourse. Bodily health is, to Franklin, an important element of the good to which moral behavior is to lead, and actions that support the maintenance of physical health are like-wise good actions. Health, as an aspect of good, is an end in itself—one of several, to be sure, but defined separately from the others, noncontingently and noninstrumentally. Health isn't good primarily because it leads to something else; it's just good. This appears to be a more unqualified version of Blankaart's "greatest treasure men can have on earth."

But although health is an end, one formulated in terms of the individual who is or would be healthy, it is not without implications for other people or for the community as a whole. The implications of Franklin's dictums about chastity for a person's sexual partner are obvious (or were, to someone with an everyday understanding of early modern medical theory and the mechanics of reputation). With regard to the community, the consequences of looking after one's own health are not so obvious. The "dullness" that is to be avoided by moderation in sex (and eating, under "temperance") suggests that one might be a better community member or business associate if one practiced these virtues.[19] To go beyond that, it is necessary to look at another aspect of Franklin's scheme of virtue.

Franklin states that his concern for perfecting himself arose from his belief that it is in each person's "interest" to be virtuous.[20] Interest appears to lie close to the heart of Franklin's concerns—as it does among other thinkers of the seventeenth and eighteenth centuries, who often juxtapose, as Franklin implicitly does, interest to passion.[21] So what is "interest"? In one sense, interest is the array of things present in a person's situation that are or may be of benefit to him or her. However, early modern writers on the subject also generally assumed that among the interests individuals possess, many are necessarily embodied in collectivities of people—both in the form of anticipated benefits to be obtained vis-à-vis other people that depend on the actions of the collectivity (for example, Franklin's desire for political office in competition with others), and in the form of an interest shared with other members in the fortunes of the collectivity as a whole (Franklin's interest, as a Pennsylvanian, in the outcome of the colony's disputes with its proprietors).[22] The general frame of the discourse of interest appears to have been taken originally from mercantile practice—for example, from the relationships of stockholders and companies. Well before Franklin's time, however, the discourse had generalized and was widely employed in discussions of politics and the social order. Other perspectives on interest were also possible, again for the most part derived from commerce. There was, for example, the "interest" one received on a loan—the reward for productive use of one's resources and for the risk one took, in which the interests (in the previous sense) of the debtor and the creditor were both served by the success of the former. And there was the murkier but still very important idea of interest as organized influence—as in the "Quaker interest" in the politics of Franklin's Philadelphia or the Baltic trading interest in the management of the VOC.

All these uses of the word *interest* shared an implied reference to the image of a person rationally assessing his or her circumstances, deciding what would be required to improve or protect those circumstances, and weighing the risks and benefits of various possible courses of action.[23] *Interest* in the first sense noted in the previous paragraph (benefit analysis) refers to the assessment and decision process; in the second (the loan), to actions and their results that afford improvement; and in the third (political interest), to contexts within which one can rationally predict how people will behave in pursuit of their own interests. This is, in other words, the framework of a whole discursive and predictive world, and it is a significant part of the cultural context within which Franklin is writing.

We can now return to Franklin's list and to his virtue of temperance. Where does the interest lie in eating not to dullness and drinking not to elevation? Clearly, as with chastity, there is an interest with respect to one's own health. There was nothing new in Franklin's idea that moderation in eating and drinking can promote physical well-being. It was a central concept of ancient Greek as well as medieval and early modern European medicine.[24] But was it traditionally a *virtue*? Not as Franklin defines it. Gluttony was a sin to Christians, a significant part of the broader, murkier evil of luxury. The classical and Christian virtue that was juxtaposed to gluttony and to luxury in general was called "temperance," but this referred to moderation and balance in all forms of behavior, not particularly to the intake of food and drink.[25] Indeed, in the medieval Christian moral scheme it was fasting, not moderation in consumption, that was morally significant, and it bore no relation to physical health. Franklin uses the traditional word *temperance* for the first item in his list, but explains that it means so many different things to different authors that he will restrict himself to its most basic and important definition.[26] He appears, therefore, to have redefined the term *temperance* to refer, not to a universal form or idea, but literally to moderation in support of the body's health. "To *Temperance* he [the author, in the mode of an ancestor addressing his posterity] ascribes his long-continu'd Health, and what is still left to him of a good Constitution."[27] Franklin's temperance is a virtue, but in a moral system in which the interest in being temperate seems to be largely physical.

But that is not all there is to it. Franklin's explication of temperance refers directly to "dullness" and "elevation." These are more than symptoms of unhealthy excess in an individual. They also refer to sources of disability in interacting with other people. A dull or inebriated young man would not, for example, have been able to hold up his end at a meeting of one of Franklin's discussion groups. The *Autobiography* has many references to contemporaries who never fulfilled the promise of their intellects because of drink— men who Franklin claims, in some cases, were naturally more gifted than he.[28] But Franklin was more virtuous and therefore more successful at his calling and was able, in the fullness of time, to render important services to the public. Moreover, Franklin points out that his contributions to science and to the public weal began in his middle age, after he had retired from business with a sufficient fortune, and he implies that had he not followed an abstemious personal regimen, he probably would not have lived to make such contributions.[29] There are, in other words, substantial consequences for the community in a person's being virtuously temperate in Franklin's sense: a man's health is one foundation of the personal success that can allow him, both in his calling and in his public service, to be of use to his fellows, and the state of his mental faculties, which is grounded in part on action to maintain physical health, is one of the factors that determine how successful and useful he can be. Although Franklin does not discuss the roles of women specifically, a similar argument could be made with respect to raising a family, managing a household, and helping with a business, all of which Franklin praises his wife, Deborah, for doing well and virtuously (in the very small part of the *Autobiography* in which he refers to her at all).[30]

To summarize: by practicing virtues, one strives after perfection in order to achieve a number of goods, in each of which one has an interest. Actual perfection is probably unattainable, but seriously working toward it makes virtuous behavior habitual, which maximizes the return of good attained for effort expended. The virtues of temperance and chastity (both defined in Franklin's way) allow one to achieve various goods: physical health, worldly success, and the ability to play a useful role in the community. All three of these are goods in themselves—the first two obviously so, the third apparently because of the satisfaction it brings and because community well-being serves to protect and advance the goods of its members. But the goods are also connected: health makes success possible, while success brings reputation that makes one eligible for public service. In theory, health, success, and public service could be connected in various ways. (For example, as Franklin's actual career amply demonstrates, public service can contribute to private success.) But Franklin assumes a linear progression of health to success to service. This would appear to represent a basic order in Franklin's moral world, including its social and political aspects: the individual, then the private calling or business, and then the public. This does not necessarily mean that individual or private interests are more important than public ones. Franklin insists that public service often requires considerable personal and private sacrifice, and that for those whose own houses are in order, public benevolence is a moral duty (although one that should be based on a rational assessment of interest).[31] He wrote the passage we have been discussing shortly after the end of the American Revolution, which he interpreted as a massive sacrifice on the part of individuals, not least of them himself. What the people who made the revolution had done was to recognize that almost every aspect of their interests—individual, family, business, local community, state, and so forth—was affected by a public threat from the British government. The situation required measured, reasoned action in order to maintain the good, and it required that at least some individuals, acting benevolently, take the risk of losing their lives and property in order to protect the public context within which their private interests existed. The key political point was that virtuous persons decided as rational individuals what was needed, what the risks were, and acted accordingly. The individual is thus prior both to his or her business and to the community. Individual reason must precede, although not necessarily supercede, public exercise of reason, and individual virtue must similarly precede public benevolence.

What the ancients had called "temperance," Franklin includes in his list as "moderation": "avoid extreams," maintain balance, act neither too vigorously nor too passively. At the same time, he has inserted the substance of these injunctions into several of his other enumerated virtues: "order" and "resolution," as well as temperance and chastity. In a way, he has altered the arrangement of the four classical cardinal virtues (courage, justice, temperance, and prudence, each equal to the others) by emphasizing the classical temperance (Franklin's "moderation") as a kind of foundation or general virtue.[32] The content of prudence is handled largely through his concept of the "interest" of the individual, but prudence itself is neither named nor listed. He does put justice in his list, but gives it a fairly narrow scope compared, for example, to Plato or Aristotle ("Wrong none, by doing Injuries or omitting the Benefits that are your Duty") and links it to public benevolence. Courage, the classical virtue most closely tied to the traditional concept of male honor, is at most barely suggested; it is certainly not addressed directly or named. This is a morality neither for heroes nor for aristocrats.

Most of the other items in Franklin's inventory of virtues are also significant elements of the context of virtue. "Resolution" gives you a reputation for reliability and induces others to trust you. "Frugality" allows you to accumulate resources for investment, while "industry" leads you to make the best use of them. These are not difficult to interpret. Not so "cleanliness:" "Tolerate no Uncleanness in Body, Cloathes or Habitation." There is no indication that Franklin associates cleanliness with health in a causal fashion, and again, little historical reason that he should. Cleanliness appears to be another self-referential virtue: being clean is good for its own sake. If other people observe that you are clean, they will probably infer that you are virtuous in other respects, but at least in theory the basic reason to be clean is that it is good to be so.

Why? Franklin does not say, apparently assuming that his readers will understand. Any instrumental value of cleanliness for enhancing productivity would seem to be incorporated under "order." The best explanations are likely to be historical ones. For one thing, cleanliness is associated in Western traditions with sanctity: witness the rituals of cleaning the utensils of the Eucharist and the hands that hold them, which were maintained in the Mass and in many Protestant services even through the dirtiest periods of early modern European history.[33] Franklin, in secularizing the holy, may be retaining its outward signs. Equally important is the fact that cleanliness in clothing was a sign of gentility. To qualify for the esteem of others and for public responsibility, according to Franklin, an individual had to show evidence of his or her virtue. Franklin may have transferred a traditional outward emblem of the esteemed and responsible (clean clothes) into the context in which his moral system had meaning.

We now have, thanks to Franklin and Blankaart, a relatively explicit idea of the main elements of the discourse of virtue that composed a substantial part of the context with which we are dealing in this chapter. This discourse incorporates a secular morality—not necessarily an irreligious one, but one in which the central focus is good human behavior and in which religion plays at most a supporting role. Franklin says that, although he belonged to no religious denomination, he respected the tenets of them all "tho' with different degrees of Respect as I found them more or less mix'd with other Articles which without any Tendency to inspire, promote or confirm Morality, served principally to divide us and make us unfriendly to one another."[34] The key to moral behavior is individual self-control and self-direction in pursuit of what is good, which in the first instance is the rationally conceived interest of the individual. Some good things (physical health, for example) are fundamental interests of the individual. Others are somewhat more derivative and instrumental, such as a good reputation among one's associates. But regardless of their status, individual goods and the behaviors (virtues) most suitable for their attainment have public implications. The respect and trust of others, essential to success in business, is built on the inferences derived by those others from a person's virtuous behavior. Success in one's business and community approbation of one's virtues qualify one for public responsibilities. In discharging those responsibilities, one should be benevolent.

From this summary and from the form of the discourse of virtue, we can readily detect many of the likely origins of its major elements. As Max

Weber famously pointed out, one of Franklin's most important sources was a desanctified Calvinism. Practicing virtue will not bring you salvation; it will instead conduct you to the achievement of your interest in this world. But on the basis of your achievement of worldly success, you and others can assess your fundamental worth.[35] Much the same thing can be seen in Blankaart, who was writing for a generally Calvinist audience in late-seventeenth-century Amsterdam.

Another source was the complex of related ideas that we considered under the heading of "magistracy" in chapter 2—a complex related to the notions of "civic humanism" and "republican virtue." Blankaart makes only implicit reference to these ideas; Franklin is concerned with them more directly. But Franklin's approach differs from more traditional and genteel notions of magistracy in that he gives priority to the interests of the *individual*. In the republican scheme of things, the community is prior to the interests of the individual, and the individual shows himself most favorably in the service of the community. Virtue is displayed most fully when it is disinterested.[36] With Franklin, as we have seen, individual interest is logically prior to the community and its interest. It is sometimes necessary to sacrifice personal interest to the community's interest, but the decision to do so is based on a higher consideration of individual interest. Altruistic public behavior arises primarily from the duty of the individual to be benevolent (a duty again arising from a liberal conception of individual interest), not from a postulated superiority of the community. Franklin is sometimes muddled about the limits of benevolence and about the criteria by which we are supposed to decide when our interests as members of the community should lead us to risk our individual well-being for the common good. Nevertheless, his way of approaching these matters became standard for respectable Europeans in the eighteenth and especially the nineteenth century.[37] Despite the influence of the "republican" tradition, Franklin's virtue and the notions of virtue incorporated into respectability were *not* republican virtue.

Another source important for Franklin and especially for Blankaart is a consensus about medicine, physical health, and diet that developed in the seventeenth century from much older constituents. One aspect of the consensus was a new view of the human body as a basic framework for explaining behavior. In his analysis of the discursive reconstruction of sex and gender differences in early modern England, Anthony Fletcher shows that the body ceased to be treated as an object of secondary importance, a conduit through which forces (spiritual and social as well as physical) from the world in general influenced human thought and behavior. It came instead to be regarded as a fundamental causal agent in its own right.[38] Commentators distinguished mental and behavioral characteristics of males from those of females more completely and portrayed them as being derived from absolute physical differences between male and female bodies. The condition of the body acquired increased significance as a source of good or bad behavior and good or bad thinking. This change is consistent with Blankaart's assumptions and with Franklin's ascription of moral meaning to physical health. Its significance will be seen more clearly later in this chapter when the custom of taking tea with sugar is discussed.

There were many other sources for the discourse employed by Franklin and Blankaart, but the bodies of religious, social, and medical thinking we have just examined cover a great deal of the cognitive background to the cultural context in which the discourse was embedded. Let us now look at a structural aspect of the context of virtue—its relationship to the construction of the bourgeoisie—and a behavioral one—its connection to the Western custom of drinking tea and coffee with sugar, which will return us to our discussion of the literature of health and diet represented by Blankaart.

"BOURGEOIS" VIRTUE

One word that immediately presents itself to describe the outlook exemplified by Blankaart and Franklin is *bourgeois*. Apart from any inference we might make from Blankaart's moral attitudes, he entitles his book *The Bourgeois Table* and he makes an explicit statement in the introduction that he is writing for his fellow burgers of Amsterdam.[39] In one sense, he is using *burger* or *borger* (*burgher*, *bourgeois*, *burgess*, and so on) in its traditional, legally-sanctioned meaning to refer to the enfranchised citizens of an incorporated municipality. But Blankaart probably intends more than that. He appears to be writing for well-off (or at least not-poor) urbanites bearing the responsibilities that attend upon possessing some sort of social esteem and with sufficient discretionary income to make varied dietary decisions. There were quite a number of people living in Amsterdam who fit that description without being technically citizens—town-dwelling nobles, Jews, Catholics, people born in other towns but resident in the city, and so forth.[40] But although we can conjure an image of Blankaart's intended audience from his writing, he gives no clear description of it, nor does he define it negatively by contrasting it to other classes (except when he differentiates between "city people" and "country people"). Blankaart does not use the language of gentility, but neither does he reject or criticize the gentry as a class. His strictures against the fashionable are probably directed in part against noblemen and members of the urban aristocracy of Amsterdam, but it is behavior rather than inherited status with which Blankaart is primarily concerned. Neither an active bourgeois class consciousness nor a clear set of bourgeois class antagonisms is evident in Blankaart's book.

Benjamin Franklin has been portrayed as the quintessential exponent of "bourgeois values" and as a prime eighteenth-century representative of the bourgeoisie itself.[41] Franklin does not use the term *bourgeois*, but that does not necessarily discredit the portrayal. Even in France, only around 1792 (two years after Franklin's death) did *bourgeois* begin to refer to a significant national sociopolitical class (the non-noble rich) rather than to enfranchised town citizens with independent incomes.[42] Franklin does use *citizen* to mean much the same thing as *bourgeois* or *burgher* in their technical early modern sense ("citizen of Philadelphia") and, after the American Revolution began, he followed the growing custom of describing himself as a "citizen" of larger polities (Pennsylvania and the United States). But this latter usage refers to membership with others in a common political entity, not to a social class.[43] Franklin does not, in fact, have a name for a class resembling what would later be called the bourgeoisie, and if he possesses a conception of one, it is extremely vague at best. He makes it clear in the *Autobiography* that there *is* a class of gentlemen, and he makes it equally clear that he does not belong to it.[44] Gentlemen are prone to depend too much on birth and a useless education as their means of acquiring the connections necessary to succeed in life, and because of that they often (although not inevitably) fail. Nongentlemen like Franklin are forced by circumstances to find success by developing the appropriate virtues. Franklin perceives status differences among the nongentry, although he does not arrange them so as to create consistent social groupings or categories. He usually prefers to present such differences in terms of degrees of public esteem depending on the community's perception of the manifest virtues (or the lack thereof) of particular individuals and families. He is of course aware of social implications of wealth, but in the *Autobiography* he makes little use even of the categories "rich" and "poor"; religious affiliation is vastly more important as a category for explaining action.[45]

With Franklin, then, we appear to have the prototypical bourgeois without a clear conception of the bourgeoisie as a distinct class—or even of a "middle class."[46] Is Franklin deliberately attempting to disguise social reality? This is doubtful. Why should he have wanted to do so? "False consciousness"? Perhaps—if we restate the old Marxist notion of false consciousness to suggest that the conceptual framework available to Franklin was inadequate for understanding the society in which he lived and that his discourse lacked the capacity for describing it. But in fact, the problem is only compounded by stating the solution in that way. Why should conceptual frameworks and discourse have been so deficient? According to conventional historical metaphor, the bourgeoisie or middle class had been "rising" for one, two, perhaps three centuries by Franklin's time, leavened by the yeast of capitalism. Shouldn't the shape of the loaf have been readily discernible by the mid-eighteenth century?

Perhaps one part of the answer lies in the sphere of politics. It could be argued that only with the revolutions at the end of the eighteenth century was there a need, or at least a set of motives, for a class-based social analysis through which the existence and the pivotal revolutionary role of the bourgeoisie could be perceived. As we have seen, there is good reason to think that the French Revolution was the occasion for the conceptual debut of the bourgeoisie.[47] But why should the French Revolution have had this effect, and not the American Revolution or even the English Glorious Revolution of the late seventeenth century? Franklin clearly experienced a paradigm shift at the time of the American Revolution, but as we saw with his changing use of *citizen*, it did not result in a new class consciousness.

Late-twentieth-century research on the French Revolution, while it did not produce consensus about causes and process, at least dissolved the older view that the revolution was a seizure of power by the bourgeoisie. It also opened the door to questions about the nature of the eighteenth-century bourgeoisie, and even about the utility of the concepts of "bourgeoisie" and "class" as bequeathed to us by Marx.[48] It is now possible to question whether the bourgeoisie as historians have claimed to understand it even *existed* prior to its discursive construction in revolutionary polemics at the end of the eighteenth century, and if it did exist, to ask what forms its existence took. It is no longer assumed uncritically that the formation of capital as a means of production directly created a social class, the bourgeoisie, whose thought, behavior, politics—in a word, whose *culture*—were defined primarily by ownership of capital.

At the very least, this means that one should ask not how the formation of the bourgeoisie as a social class affected consciousness and behavior, but rather how the modern bourgeoisie, as a sociocultural entity with complex, interacting structural, behavioral, cognitive, and material aspects, came into being—whether prior to or simultaneously with the political events that caused it to be named. It means, for instance, that one should refrain from describing Franklin and Blankaart as "bourgeois" or even "middle class" simply because they were neither aristocrats nor members of the lowest classes, and also from inferring that their choice of discourse arose primarily out of a particular kind of relationship to capital that bourgeois persons are presumed to possess. Instead, the question should be what they and others like them contributed to the construction of the bourgeoisie—what their contributions tell us about the nature of the bourgeoisie and its connections with such other historical phenomena as capitalism.

The present study suggests that the culture of respectability was one of the main constituent elements of the bourgeoisie. Respectability was obviously not the only such element, nor was respectability as a cultural phenomenon ever limited just to people who thought of themselves as or could reasonably be called bourgeois or middle class. Nevertheless, respectability serves in essence as a compendium of most of the accepted behavioral and cognitive markers of the bourgeoisie—and, as we shall see, of many of its material and structural markers as well. We should not view respectability as a product of the prior emergence of the bourgeoisie, but rather as something the formation of which contributed to shaping the bourgeoisie itself. Of all the contexts that were connected together in the eighteenth century to form respectability, that of virtue appears to have been the most important for the self-definition of the bourgeoisie. So in their own ways, Franklin and Blankaart, by engaging in the discourse of virtue and interpreting the context in which the discourse was embedded, may have been helping to create the bourgeoisie.

TEA, COFFEE, AND SUGAR

By the second quarter of the eighteenth century, tea and coffee were normally consumed in many parts of northwestern Europe (especially Britain) with large amounts of sugar.[49] The adoption of this custom as a regular, continuous practice had enormous consequences. It ensured that any increase in consumption of tea or coffee led to an increase in demand for sugar. It helped to maintain the viability of the British East India Company in Asia and the plantation slavery system in the West Indies. In the nineteenth century, tea with sugar became an important part of the British working-class diet.[50] What is not clear in the historical literature is when and why the custom of taking tea and coffee with sugar arose. With regard to *when*, it is clear that the custom was not imported with tea from China, and although the sugaring of coffee was certainly practiced in the Near East in the sixteenth and seventeenth centuries, it does not appear to have been standard in northern Europe at the time that coffee first became fashionable there in the 1640s and 1650s.[51] Sidney Mintz, in his admirable interpretation of the role of sugar in world history, says only that "documentation for the custom of adding sugar to these beverages [tea, coffee, and chocolate] during the early period of their use in the United Kingdom is almost non-existent."[52] There is, however, evidence on which to base an informed guess. With regard to *why*, the formation of the context of virtue provides a large part of the answer.

As we saw in the previous chapter, sugar was the object of a sustained vogue in northern Europe in the sixteenth and seventeenth centuries. Tea was a recent import from the Far East, practically unknown in Europe until the mid-seventeenth century and then a drink of fashion in the 1650s and 1660s. In France, the fashion faded rather quickly, to be periodically reawakened in the eighteenth century. In the Netherlands and England there was a delay between the initial period of fashionability and a substantial expansion of tea drinking (this time with sugar) around 1700. Coffee became fashionable in France, England, the Netherlands, and Germany at about the same time as tea and went through similar alternations in vogue until the early eighteenth century.[53]

Mintz cites a book by John Chamberlain as evidence that, by the time the book was published in 1685, sugar was already being added in England to coffee, tea, and chocolate.[54] In fact, Chamberlain's book—a compilation of continental sources on those commodities—does not quite say that. The section on coffee states that a little sugar is sometimes put in coffee in the Near East for medicinal purposes.[55] Most of the section on tea comes from a treatise published by Dr. Nicholas Tulp, physician of Amsterdam, in 1675. It concentrates on tea's medicinal properties and mentions sugar only when it says that the Chinese, unlike the Japanese, add "a few graines either of Salt, or Sugar" to tea while it is boiling.[56] So while Chamberlain's book does not prove that Europeans were not sugaring their tea and coffee in 1685, it also gives no evidence that they were doing so in a regular or customary way.

Sugar is not mentioned in connection with tea in the best-known reports of its initial fashionable use in the 1650s and 1660s, although Thomas Garway, founder of one of the most famous London coffeehouses, recommended sweetening tea with honey in the 1650s.[57] Cornelis Bontekoe, the "tea-doctor" who was the most notorious advocate of heavy tea drinking, does warn against taking sugar with tea in a pamphlet published in 1678. This may indicate that at least some people were doing it at that time, but the warning is buried at the back of the pamphlet and is made only in passing.[58] It is more likely to represent growing medical distrust of heavy sugaring in general. Steven Blankaart writes in 1683 that putting herbs and spices in tea gives it a good taste. He does not mention adding sugar to tea or coffee, and the vigor with which Blankaart condemns the sugaring of other foods and drinks makes it almost certain that he would have done so had the practice been at all common.[59]

Thus, although tea and coffee were undoubtedly taken with sugar in the Netherlands and England by some of the more gastronomically adventurous before about 1685, there is no sign of a general fashion for doing so. By 1710 at the latest, however, there are clear indications of the prevalence of the practice in Britain, and by the 1720s and 1730s, it had become quite general in other countries as well.[60] The years between about 1685 and just after 1700, therefore, appear to be the key period.[61] Probably not coincidentally, the period immediately after 1700 also saw immense increases in the importation of tea, coffee, and sugar into Europe.[62]

This should remind us that, in the eighteenth century, Europeans did not simply consume large amounts of coffee or tea or sugar as separate commodities. They consumed them *together*, tea or coffee with sugar (and milk), and tea and coffee as substitutes for each other according to taste, circumstances, or time of day. They did so to a large extent in particular cultural settings: in the performance of daily rituals in the home and in the public, commercial setting of the coffeehouse.[63] If we were to focus just on the individual products coffee and tea, we might be led to adopt the simplest form of explanation for the growth in their demand by saying that they were introduced from abroad as novelties and "caught on"—that is, generated their own demand. But when we confront the actual mode in which coffee and tea were taken after about 1700, as part of an ensemble including sugar, milk, and porcelain or silver services, in particular social settings, we cannot take the simplest explanatory route. Although some of these practices (tea drunk from porcelain cups, for instance) were suggested by non-European models, the ensemble was European and must be interpreted in terms of European contexts in existence at the time the ensemble was formed.

Obvious candidates were discussed in the two previous chapters: gentility and luxury. The initial introduction of tea and coffee into Europe as significant consumer items in the mid-seventeenth century can be readily explained in terms of status and fashion. Both items became fashionable among the French and English aristocracy and the Dutch intellectual and political elite, and the vogue spread to a wider public by means of coffeehouses in the 1660s and 1670s and because (in the case of tea) of a general fad for things Chinese (*chinoiserie*).[64] But why did the fashion not pass? (For evidence of the extraordinary increase in tea consumption after 1700, see table 6, page 304.) The very popularity of tea-taking and coffee drinking should, according to Simmel's theory of fashion, have discredited those practices among the elite, which should have gone on to other status-bearing activities. Nonelite imitators of upper-class fashions should have followed the same course somewhat later. Why did this not happen?

Actually, as we have seen, there is evidence that, with respect to the individual products coffee and tea, something of the sort did occur in the 1670s and 1680s. Contemporary observers remarked that the vogue for tea had retreated among the aristocracy.[65] The practice of drinking tea Chinese-style declined with the passing of the *chinoiserie* fad. The resurgence of demand for coffee and especially tea around 1700 was tied to a new consumption practice that involved the *sugaring* of tea and coffee. This practice may well have begun as another aristocratic fashion. We have no specific evidence of this, but it is a reasonable conjecture. There is anecdotal evidence that the custom of putting milk in tea originated in particular French aristocratic circles around 1690.[66] But this leaves us with the same question. Why did the fashion for mixing certain substances in coffee and tea not pass after it had become widely popular, to be replaced by some other vogue? Reasoning within the framework of gentility gives us no clear explanation.

One approach to the question is to focus on the main additive, sugar, rather than on tea and coffee. We have seen that the practice of sugaring foods and drinks had become widespread in the seventeenth century—too widespread to be considered an elite fashion. Also, in the late seventeenth and early eighteenth centuries there seems to have been something of a revulsion against sugaring, perhaps in part a result of elite emphasis on refinement in tastes. It is therefore unlikely that status considerations framed in terms of gentility had a great deal to do with the persistence of the practice of sugaring tea and coffee after the beginning of the eighteenth century.

But as we saw in chapter 3, well before the end of the seventeenth century the meaning of sugaring was defined much more in terms of luxury than of gentility. Tea and coffee could also be interpreted as items of luxury consumption because of their exotic character. But why should people *combine* sugar and coffee or tea? Possibly, because in the course of sugaring a wide variety of food products, some people inevitably tried sugar with coffee and tea, and liked it. They may simply have liked the mixture of bitterness and sweetness, which satisfied an elementary sensual desire, or they may have regarded the combination of sensually gratifying, exotic consumables as an especially luxurious experience. But as individual tastes vary in these respects, while the custom of sugaring became general in much of Europe (essentially universal in Britain, considerably less so in France), it would appear that there were other cultural factors involved in the practice of combining tea and coffee with sugar. These are most readily explained by reference to the context of virtue.

One of the main sources of evidence we have for linking the tea-and-sugar and coffee-and-sugar customs to the formation of the context of virtue is the large body of literature on health, medicine, and diet that became a staple of the western European publishing trade in the seventeenth century. The books of Blankaart and Bontekoe are prime examples of this genre. Such books were not new, but their number, variety, and market appear to have expanded enormously during the century.[67] The literature on health was closely related to other popular genres (self-improvement books, cookery books, books on family management, and so on) that dealt with subjects of significance to people at all but the lowest levels of society. Cookbooks, for example, not only contained recipes and advice on table manners and on staging banquets, but also commentaries on the implications of various foods for health. Important elements of the traditional literature of piety and good behavior found their way into the health literature, helping to define a discourse that related physical health to morality and social values—a relationship that we saw in Franklin's moral writings. Franklin himself, as the publisher of *Poor Richard's Almanac*, was a leading contributor to the eighteenth-century continuation of the general literary type to which the health literature belonged.

In medical treatises and books on diet and health in the sixteenth and early seventeenth centuries, sugar was usually treated as a drug that could alter the balance of the humors of the body by generating choler (the hot humor) or that could improve the efficacy of other drugs.[68] Early on, most commentary was favorable. In the late seventeenth century, however, much of the popular medical literature turned against sugar—or at least against its overuse. We have discussed Blankaart's attack on excessive sugar-taking. Blankaart gives some of his reasons in terms of current medical theory, but his argument is based primarily on empirical observation: diets with large amounts of sugar appear to be correlated with tooth decay, corpulence, gout, and other health disorders. Many other important medical writers began to oppose excessive sugaring at about the same time, and although sugar had its defenders (not least among people with an economic interest in the West Indies), the effects of the change can be seen in the greater moderation with which sugaring is recommended in books on health and cooking after about 1700.[69]

Medical writings on tea and coffee were quite extensive, and unlike the equivalent material on sugar, they tended to be favorable until well into the eighteenth century (except for a brief period during the 1660s and 1670s). These publications ranged from sober evaluations of the properties of tea by physicians to what amounted to outright advertising of the medicinal qualities of the two commodities, with most falling somewhere in between.[70] It is tempting to explain them as a cynical marketing technique of the Indies companies or big merchants. Nicholas Tulp was a director of the Dutch East India Company, and C. R. Boxer reports a rumor that Bontekoe was in the company's pay.[71] But for most writers on health, other motives were apparently at work. Many were presumably paid by publishers interested in sales. For physicians, alignment in the public mind with a fashionable drug could enhance reputations and expand clientele. Although Bontekoe was widely ridiculed, his writings on tea made his fortune.[72]

We have seen how writers such as Blankaart framed their comments on the healthy or unhealthy properties of foods such as sugar, tea, and coffee within a structure of argumentation that associated consumption with an individual's moral and community standing. To Blankaart, sugar, although highly popular and widely used, was suspect because of its deleterious effects on physical health, because of its association with luxury and fashion, and because of what excessive use of sugar said about a person's self-control. Tea and coffee, on the other hand, were good for a person's health—in large part because they balanced other kinds of food and helped to maintain the equilibrium of the body. Along the same lines, although tea and coffee provided a range of physical and mental benefits in themselves, one of their main values lay in their ability to correct the effects of excessive ingestion of something else. Tea and coffee were not luxuries to Blankaart; in some sense, they physically offset luxury consumption. Thus, by regularly consuming tea or coffee, a person was implicitly displaying self-control and a proper interest in physical health. Neither Blankaart nor Bontekoe specifically advocated the mixing of tea or coffee with sugar for swallowing at the same time (indeed, Bontekoe specifically cautions against it), but the outlines of a frame in which it would make sense to do so are apparent in their writings.

The frame is even clearer in the books and pamphlets of Thomas Tryon. Tryon (1634–1703) was one of the most popular English writers of "how-to" books in the late seventeenth century. He was best known as the proponent of his own religion that featured the adoption of a "clean" (vegetarian) diet, but he also wrote for readers who did not care to adopt his whole program.[73] Benjamin Franklin followed Tryon's dietary theories in his youth, and although he dropped strict vegetarianism, he continued to share some of Tryon's materialist approach to virtue.[74]

Tryon wrote extensively on the subject of ingestible liquids. He particularly opposed the drinking of spiritous liquors, partly because drunkenness was morally repulsive and socially dangerous, but also because "fierce, strong, burning" spirits were bad for physical health.[75] He suggested a variety of healthier alternatives: beer made without hops, nonalcoholic fruit punches, and so forth. Most important, Tryon touted drinks made by infusing water with health-giving herbs—thus anticipating the eighteenth-century portrayal of tea as a healthy herbal infusion and as an alternative to alcohol.[76] Tryon was especially concerned about sugar. He may at one time have been a sugar merchant, although hats were his main stock in trade. At any rate, Tryon had visited the West Indies and had been disgusted by plantation slavery. He did not explicitly condemn slavery or the sugar trade, but he believed that slavery's ferocious manifestation in the Caribbean was immoral and was due directly to the conditions of sugar production. Tryon argued strongly for the introduction of textile manufacturing into the West Indies to replace sugar growing.[77] At least by implication, Tryon saw sugar as a morally suspect commodity.

On the other hand, Tryon believed that many of sugar's effects on the body were by themselves healthy and desirable. To Tryon, taste is the most important of the senses because it gives direct access to the fundamental properties of matter. Through taste, these properties can be classified into three categories: salty, bitter, and sweet. Each property has, by itself, good effects on the human body. The delight people take in sweet foods is a sign of the fundamentally healthy and necessary character of sweetness. Sugar is the most concentrated form in which sweetness can be ingested, and therefore, taken in small quantities, it is a wholly acceptable element of diet.[78] But in large quantities or in solid foods, when taken together with fatty substances, or when turned into spirits, sugar becomes a danger to life:

> let them refrain All or most sorts of Food made sweet with Sugar, for the frequent use of such Meats and Drinks do prove very prejudicial to most Peoples health, but most especially such as are subject to the forementioned Diseases [stone and gravel]; for over-sweetness in Foods and Drinks, does not only thicken the Blood, and hinder its free Circulation, but it indues it with a watery phlegmatick quality, and turns the Humours to the highest degree of souerness, most especially if fats and sweetness be compounded together, as they are for the most part (as the sweetest Wines make the sharpest Vinegar) which immediately tends toward Putrifaction, whence proceeds various Diseases, according to each mans Constitution and Complexion, viz. Scabs, Boyls, Leprosies, Consumptions, Gout and Stone, all Stoppages of the Breast, ill Digestion, Nautiousness, rotten Teeth, offensive Breath, all which distempers have of late years been more brief and frequent, since the common eating of sugared Foods and Drinks.[79]

Tryon's solution to the problem of obtaining the sweetness of sugar without its dangers is the preparation of healthy nonalcoholic drinks in which a modest amount of sugar is supplemented by naturally sweet fruits and in which herbs are infused. The herbs counter the effects of the sugar through their own (healthy) bitterness, and any excessive bitterness in the herbs is offset by the sugar.[80] Tryon does not specifically refer to tea in this context, but tea drinks with sugar (and a slice of lemon) fill Tryon's prescription almost exactly.

The publication of Tryon's most popular works on food and health in the late 1680s and 1690s is consistent with the timing of the appearance of the tea-and-sugar custom, but the fact that he does not specifically advocate the mixing of tea and sugar makes it unlikely that he created it. Rather, what we see in Tryon's and Blankaart's books is the formation of a particular set of concepts that made it reasonable to combine two largely separate practices (sugaring and the taking of tea and coffee) into a new practice that had meaning within the framework of discourse on health—something that might occur to many people independently and then spread by imitation. The physically harmful properties of sugar would be balanced by the properties of tea and coffee without requiring the consumer either to give up sugar altogether or to feel guilty about not doing so. Some of the negative moral implications of sugar might also be offset by taking it with coffee or tea. The status implications of both products would be maintained, although the resulting practice implied a redefinition of what it was that conveyed status: individual virtue and self-discipline rather than wealth or genteel birth, and moderation and balance rather than excess.

We have no specific account of the first time someone in northwestern Europe mixed sugar with coffee or tea and we have no report of an ensuing fad. But the important point is not who did it first, but rather that the practice caught on and became customary—especially, but not exclusively, in Great Britain. And although the initial experiments may well have taken place among the fashionable elite, the fact that the practice became a custom and fell out of the cycle of fashions was probably due much more to the connected roles of coffee, tea, and sugar in the context of virtue than to anything having to do with gentility or luxury. Thus apart from any other significance it might have had, the formation of the context of virtue was a matter of enormous importance for the histories of the plantation system in the Caribbean, Atlantic slavery, and European imperialism in Asia.

Before leaving the literature of health, some attention should be paid to characteristics shared by the writers who have been discussed. Most of them were citizens, or at least residents, of towns and cities and thus "bourgeois" in the archaic technical sense. Three were Dutch physicians, although from quite different status backgrounds. Tulp was a member of Amsterdam's ruling elite and a director of the VOC—an honorific office, not necessarily a sign of mercantile activity on his part.[81] Blankaart's status is unclear, but certainly was not as exalted as Tulp's. Bontekoe was a man on the make, possibly the son of an innkeeper, who rose in the world through linking his professional practice to his notoriety as a publicist.[82] All three would undoubtedly have recognized each other as members of the same profession, but probably not as members of the same class or other status group. Two of the other writers were businesspeople. The Frenchman, P. S. Dufour, an editor of publications on tea, coffee, and chocolate, tells us directly that he is a merchant who deals in (among other things) those three commodities.[83] Tryon was a merchant of London, technically a haberdasher. It is not clear to what extent he traded in the commodities he wrote about, but it appears that his main interest in writing was in propagating his ideas about religion, health, and policy, not in expanding his business. We should probably not, therefore, try to make very much either of these people's shared standing as

"bourgeois" town-dwellers or of common "capitalist" connections to markets. Their actual backgrounds were too diverse to support many inferences
about group motives on those bases.

There *is*, however, one obvious connection among them: they all wrote
for publication to a large audience with the intention of influencing public
opinion. This makes them participants in the "public sphere." In Jürgen
Habermas's view, the public sphere and public opinion are essential features
of bourgeois society and were major products of the emergence of capitalism and the bourgeoisie in early modern Europe.[84] One could therefore
argue that the health and diet writers were "bourgeois" in a very fundamental, significant way because they participated in the public sphere during
what Habermas and others identify as its formative period.

There appear to be at least three connections between the emerging public sphere and the early modern literature of health and diet. First, that literature was one of several discourses carried on within the range of perception
of any person literate in the appropriate vernacular languages to whom printed publications were available, with sufficient means and interest to buy the
publications. Second, although the literature dealt only tangentially with
current political issues, it did suggest, as we have seen, visions of community well-being and implications for policy. In other words, it possessed
moral and ideological content that was, at least implicitly and sometimes
overtly, a subject of controversy. Third, it had obvious connections to the
market economy, mainly because its aims were to shape opinions about
products on sale in markets and to influence the behavior of consumers—
regardless of what the personal interests of the writers in market outcomes
might have been.

It is also important to notice the particular mode of discourse adopted by
the writers as participants in the public sphere. It is essentially the mode analyzed above in the case of Blankaart and connected more generally to the
context of virtue through the example of Franklin. In this discourse, the acts
of ingesting or not ingesting certain items, combining or not combining
them with each other, are presented as means of supporting health and
avoiding illness, which are in turn not simply physically desirable ends but
virtues. The writers suggest that the behavior of consumers has moral implications and consequences, and further that the moral standing of consumers
is connected to how they take care of their health.

Most of the health-and-diet writers make these suggestions with a peculiar kind of authority. It is not the authority of high social status or general
education, as might be advanced by a gentleman discoursing with other gentlemen. It is not religious authority, nor, for the most part, is it buttressed by

classical citations. It is a dual authority: that of men who present themselves as sober, virtuous, moderate citizens willing to lay useful suggestions before the public (and, by implication, to run the risk of public criticism and rejection), and that of professionals. The former is clearly a persona derived from the context of virtue itself. The latter is closely related, although easier to miss. Some of the authors are physicians, writing on the basis of their qualifications and experience.[85] But even the merchants claim professional expertise. Tryon's claims are admittedly weak (travel in the West Indies), but Dufour is quite insistent about the nature and strength of his. Not only does he mention offhand that he has translated a book from Latin, but he also says that the fact that he is a merchant in the Levant trade gives him credibility "especially in this instance, where we are dealing with a drug with which merchants have acquainted us. It is to those who have done business in the Levant to whom we in France owe the discovery of coffee. It is they who furnish us with it. It seems to me that, with regard to a subject of this nature, there are a great number of things about which a merchant may perhaps be better informed than a philosopher."[86] In a sense, Dufour is apologizing for writing a book, but his tone is far from apologetic. In fact, he is vigorously asserting a qualification that a conventionally better-educated writer would probably not possess.

In chapter 5, relationships among the public sphere, the construction of the bourgeoisie, and the cultural contexts from which respectability was formed will be discussed more extensively. For the moment, it is sufficient to note that an analysis of the literature of health and diet suggests that the context of virtue may have been an essential, formative, and possibly definitive feature of both the bourgeoisie and the public sphere.

CLEANLINESS

The tenth item in Franklin's catalogue of virtues was "CLEANLINESS: Tolerate no Uncleanness in Body, Cloaths or Habitation." As we saw earlier, Franklin's virtue of cleanliness has to be understood not as we might view it, as something causally connected to health, but rather as a virtue in itself, parallel in meaning and significance to the virtues that constitute healthy living. There was some thought before the eighteenth century that unclean physical surroundings might contribute to an unhealthy atmosphere, but this had more to do with drainage and the disposal of offal than with keeping households physically clean.[87] We have also seen that the emphasis on cleanliness in clothing may have had a number of sources, including the traditional religious association of holiness with purity, both metaphorical and real, and the presumption that if one wore manifestly clean clothing—

especially clothing on which dirt would have shown easily—one was wealthy enough to afford domestic assistance and several changes of clothes. Although these ideas reappear to some extent in the growing vogue for cleanliness in eighteenth-century Europe, they appear in transmuted form, stated differently and with altered emphasis, within a new cultural framework: the context of virtue.

Clean Bodies

The history of bodily cleanliness in Europe has been difficult to reconstruct, partly because ideas about washing have apparently never been entirely uniform even in the same region and period and partly because washing customs have changed fairly dramatically over time. The High Middle Ages seem to have been a comparatively clean era in western Europe, possibly because of Muslim influence exerted during the Crusades, possibly not.[88] There is also consensus that, on the whole, standards declined markedly in the late fifteenth and sixteenth centuries, not to rise again until well into the seventeenth. This change occurred at all social levels, although there were individual exceptions and brief vogues for bathing, especially at courts.[89] Religious rituals of washing the face, hands, and feet and the social ritual of cleaning hands before and after meals did not disappear. It was rather the practice of washing the rest of the body and the hair that fell out of favor in early modern Europe.[90] The decline of body washing appears to have been connected, not with poor economic conditions, but with the dissemination of a medical opinion that excessive bathing was dangerous to health and with the spread of the idea that communal bathing (the standard form of medieval body cleansing) was dangerous to morals. There was some truth to both notions. Bathing by immersion in badly heated houses in winter is probably not very healthy, and urban communal bathing seems to have been connected to prostitution. (In Shakespeare's time the term for a public bath—stews—also meant "brothel.") But it was probably not just specific evidence of ills arising from bathing that led to its decline, but also the construction of cognitive frameworks within which such ills could be imagined, given meaning, and related to each other. The Reformation probably played a part in this, together with the early stages of the development of the health and diet literature. The latter was built, as we have seen, around a connection between health and morality.[91]

Immersive bathing slowly returned to fashion in western Europe in the course of the seventeenth century, at first among wealthier people. The desire to be clean had little to do with the revival. Rather, it arose initially from changes in medical opinion about the effectiveness of hot and cold immersions for the treatment of a variety of ailments.[92] The preferred locale for such treatments was the natural "bath"—the traditional place where one took the waters. Baths—built around hot springs, cold springs, or sulphur springs, and sometimes all three—had operated since Roman times and had never wholly disappeared, even in the dirty part of the early modern period. They had suffered from some of the same factors that had led to the decline of bathing for cleanliness, but many baths still had visitors right into the seventeenth century, when doctors began prescribing them more frequently to their patients and when the towns in which they were located began to repair them.[93]

What occurred next is complicated and not fully understood. While medicinal bathing at springs continued to rise in popularity throughout the seventeenth and into the eighteenth century, another factor not wholly separate from it entered the picture at about the same time that tea and coffee became fashionable—that is, during the third quarter of the seventeenth century. European merchants and travelers who had been to the Near East brought back (along with coffee) customs they had picked up—one of which was bathing. Hot baths, often advertised as "Turkish" and frequently connected with coffeehouses, appeared in the major western European cities, first in Italy, and then elsewhere.[94] These were widely advertised (like coffee and tea) as supports for health, and they competed with natural baths for medical referrals. But very quickly, perhaps because of associations with the "luxurious" East, their exotic and sensual appeal became at least as important as their image as resorts for health. Nonurban resorts—especially in England—took over some of the same image for themselves. The English Restoration court, after contributing to the fashion for Turkish bathing in London, began to frequent Tunbridge Wells, not mainly for health but for the gambling and other related activities.[95]

Up to about 1700, then, bodily cleanliness was only a by-product of the fashion for immersive bathing, not an objective, and bathing itself was something done away from home on a seasonal or occasional, not a daily or weekly, basis by quite a small number of people. In England particularly, there was a status element involved in bathing: one went to Tunbridge Wells to test the waters of fashion—to be seen, if not to be clean. But even more, patronizing bathhouses was regarded as a form of luxury and was attacked by critics on that basis.[96] It held a place in regimens of health prescribed by physicians, but because bathhouses and natural baths were associated with luxury, they did not immediately become part of the context of virtue in the seventeenth century. Going to a bathhouse, although it might be a sign of concern for one's own health, was not at first the basis for an inference of virtue.

Another factor significant for shaping early modern bathing was odor. The history of smell is even less complete than the history of cleanliness, but it does appear that the seventeenth century witnessed an important, although not completely unprecedented, change in the cultural construction of odor in western Europe.[97] During the first two centuries of the "age of discovery," European travelers had made a decidedly negative olfactory impression practically everywhere they went. Some of them may have noticed this; at any rate, the middle of the seventeenth century saw an increasing concern, especially among the gentry, with not reeking from one's daily labors. It may have been that people who saw themselves as gentlemen and ladies did not want to hint that they *performed* daily labors, which might symbolically derogate their genteel status.[98] Initially, the precaution of choice was perfume. Perfume making became in the seventeenth century a major business, centered in Paris and closely allied to the development of the science of chemistry.[99] But no perfume can do the trick by itself without being so strong as to defeat its own purpose. To present a refined body scent, it is also necessary to keep relatively clean. This does not necessarily mean full-immersion bathing, but it does mean some sort of regular washing of all or most parts of the body. By the beginning of the eighteenth century, it appears that such washing, together with a regular use of scent by both sexes, had become relatively common as a sign of gentility among the elite of much of western Europe.[100]

Gentility and luxury were thus the prevailing contexts for bathing or washing at the beginning of the eighteenth century. They remained valid contexts among some groups and in some places. In Britain, for example, "oriental" bathing in warm water was in fashion at intervals, encouraged by the increasingly large number of people who had been to India and the even larger number whose fantasies were stirred by imagining the mysterious (and supposedly lascivious) East. The Prince of Wales (the later George IV) stimulated the last wave of this kind of fashion with the bathing facilities at his palace at Brighton.[101] In France, a series of technical innovations produced baths and douches that could be used for more effective washing at home; such implements themselves became objects of fashion and status competition.[102]

While the status-luxury-odor line of development continued through the eighteenth century (indeed, through the nineteenth and twentieth centuries as well), a second line also appeared. Like the process we observed with tea, coffee, and sugar, so too with bathing a version of a practice that initially had meaning within the contexts of gentility and luxury was constructed to correspond to the context of virtue. The order of events, probably at the turn of the seventeenth and eighteenth centuries in England, is not clear. Indeed, there may have been no order, as different people made a variety of roughly similar inferences and behavior changes at about the same time. In general, a crucial step was to translate the religious notion of ritual cleansing and metaphorical purity into the idea that being clean in one's whole body was a sign of virtue. Whereas ritual cleaning of the hands was a symbolic act, part of conducting the sacraments, thorough washing on a regular basis was a form of self-discipline. Washing to keep clean had no direct sacerdotal meaning, so it was not objectionable to Calvinists or to those of a secular bent, but it retained a loose identification with godliness, and because it manifested self-discipline and orderly behavior, it suggested virtue. More-over, people who practiced a regimen of daily washing (especially in cold water) schooled themselves in virtuous behavior—a regular reminder of how one should behave.[103] We will see later that this idea of virtuous self-discipline as practice in godly living was significant in the thinking of such eighteenth-century religious reformers as John Wesley, who asserted that "cleanliness is indeed next to godliness."[104]

But why *this* particular form for manifesting virtue? Partly because wash-ing with the aim of regulating body odor had become a means of claiming genteel status. Quite a wide range of people in eighteenth-century Europe who thought well of themselves and wanted others to share their view were unwilling to participate in the scent-and-wash fashion. The emphasis on per-fume, which attracted violent criticism from opponents of sinful forms of luxury, was difficult to square with belief systems that featured restraint in the area of sensuality—systems with adherents at all social levels.[105] Moreover, many men of substance who did not belong to the hereditary gen-try and were unashamedly engaged in trade or a profession probably found the "nonlaboring" implication of scent-and-wash inappropriate for them-selves, if not necessarily for their wives and daughters. The answer was not to reject the fashion altogether, but to modify it: to emphasize the washing rather than the perfume, and to subscribe to the notion that an honest, upright person should smell like a person rather than a flower garden— although not *too* much like a person. Restraint of body odor along these lines required regular washing and general cleanliness, behaviors that possessed a vestigial connection to sanctity and presented an image of self-control. The resulting custom was thus loosely consonant with elements of the context of virtue. Regular washing and moderated body odor constituted a claim to sta-tus, one based not solely on gentility or fashionability but also on evidence of virtue (and, of course, the opportunity to wash).[106]

The custom was rounded out by considerations of health. Immersive bathing, when it returned in the seventeenth century, had as its immediate justification the pursuit of health. Cleanliness was a by-product; being clean did not make you healthy, but seeking health through the action of the water, its temperature, and its mineral content on your body necessarily made you clean (or cleaner, at any rate). Of course, many people who attended the baths probably did so because they enjoyed the way the water felt and because bathing was associated with the exotic and luxurious. But in the eighteenth century, as body washing acquired a justification linked to virtue, it became possible to portray immersive bathing as a way of achieving both health and cleanliness simultaneously.[107] The development of in-home bathing apparatuses facilitated the process by which full or (more often) partial immersion became the standard form of washing. Bathing still conveyed status, but it was status presented in terms both of means and of virtue. Bathing meant that one belonged to the "washed" as opposed to the "unwashed"— in the nineteenth century, a major point of distinction between respectable people and others. Bathing at home still gave one sensual pleasure (if one did not follow John Wesley's advice and the duke of Wellington's practice by taking cold baths), but it was pleasure framed in terms of comfort rather than luxury and therefore compatible with respectability.

So while various bathing practices came and went in the fashionable world during the eighteenth and early nineteenth centuries, practices explicable in terms of older notions of gentility and luxury, the really decisive change came with the construction of a cultural framework for bathing that was consistent with the context of virtue and that could be incorporated into respectability. Consider Jean-Paul Marat in his covered bath in 1793, treating himself for a skin disorder and therefore sufficiently protected from aspersions on his revolutionary virtue to receive Charlotte Corday— although of course his virtue did not protect him from the point of her visit.[108] A decade previously, Benjamin Franklin had adopted in Paris the practice of bathing in a covered tub and had taken to receiving visitors in the bathroom, presumably with more satisfactory results than Marat.[109] Franklin is supposed to have helped introduce the new model of bathtub to the United States; his reputation ensured that bathing was seen as something other than a luxury or an aristocratic fashion—that it was a practice appropriate for people who would eventually be called the respectable bourgeoisie.

One further development lies just beyond the scope of this book: the introduction of mass-produced soap made with vegetable oils, which occurred at the end of the eighteenth century. At first glance, it would appear that this was simply a response to an increased interest in bathing, made possible by the invention of a new process for emulsifying oils in the 1790s. We could interpret it as an economic and technological response to demand generated by the formation of the culture of respectability—an important response, which created both a major industry and the demand for palm oil, the economic basis of European penetration into West Africa in the nineteenth century. In fact, however, this last point suggests a set of very complex relationships among bathing, virtue, respectability and some of the most significant ideologies of the nineteenth century. The discovery that palm oil could be used to make inexpensive soap for bathing provided British abolitionists for the first time, around 1800, with the basis of a convincing argument that ending the West African slave trade would not be an economic disaster.[110] West Africans could turn to a "legitimate" trade: the export of palm oil. This connection of palm oil to bathing remained a significant aspect of abolitionism for many decades in the nineteenth century. As the Evangelical leaders of the anti-slavery movement were among the people who most vigorously propagated the pattern of respectability for all classes of the population and made a special point of emphasizing cleanliness, there is some reason to think that the continued spread of the bathing custom and its achievement of a central role in Western culture were due in part to its peculiar connection, through soap, to abolitionism.

Clean Underwear

We are now in a position to return to the earlier discussion of the cultural construction of textile consumption. As we saw in chapter 2, demand for white cotton cloth grew with unprecedented rapidity in eighteenth-century Britain, making it a major product of the early Industrial Revolution. Some of the cotton was intended for printing and dyeing, but an increasingly large proportion of high-quality white cloth was sold as material for shirts, underskirts, drawers—in a word, underwear. Clearly, the well-known technical improvements in weaving and spinning made this possible. Before Britain's prohibition of calico imports in 1721, only a very small proportion of imported Indian cotton seems to have been used for these purposes anywhere in Europe. Linen was the material of choice for underclothing, but it was not able to keep up with rapidly rising demand after about midcentury, even as a component with cotton in mixed fabrics. The inelasticity of European linen production and the difficulty of increasing linen productivity through machinery meant that linen prices rose in the face of growing demand. The technological revolution in British cotton production, although it was most likely not stimulated by white cotton demand per se, nevertheless had the effect of making high-quality pure-cotton fabrics available to replace linen at cheaper prices.[111]

For our purposes, the key question is why the eighteenth-century expansion in British (and eventually non-British) demand for white cottons occurred. In chapter 2, we saw that part of an explanation involved gentility. Adopting the elite dress styles that became standard in the seventeenth century, which displayed the fact that underclothing was worn, its quality, and the state of its cleanliness, was a way of demonstrating one's status as a member of the gentry. Clean, visible underwear implied that the wearer could afford both the material and the service necessary to clean it. As these implications depended on the wearer's means, the style could be readily adopted by persons of questionable standing or clearly not of gentle birth, and in general by people emulating the aristocracy. Emulation and self-expression by people believing themselves worthy of regard can therefore account for the widespread adoption of forms of dress requiring shirts and petticoats in the late seventeenth and early eighteenth centuries, and thus for some of the demand for those items.[112]

We must, however, also explain the rapidly increasing demand for underwear material in the last three-quarters of the eighteenth century, a phenomenon so persistent and so widespread that it is difficult to ascribe to social emulation alone. It is likely that status consumption was substantially enhanced in this period by consumption that possessed meaning in other contexts: specifically, luxury and virtue. With regard to luxury, the sensual effect of soft fabric next to one's skin had clearly been a motive for wearing underclothing for a very long time, but before the seventeenth century, such materials were very expensive, available mainly to the wealthy and even then of questionable morality. Most people made do with rougher fabrics. Indian cotton and especially cotton and linen mixtures, when they became available in sufficient quantity and at appropriate prices, could provide the desired sensual effect. In the eighteenth century, however, their supply proved insufficient to meet increased demand, much of which was probably generated by the reformulation of luxury to accommodate comfort. This made pleasurable purchases legitimate for a wide variety of nonelite people with discretionary income, as long as the purchases were consistent with domestic use and not overly expensive. The appearance of British-made white cottons for comfortable *nonvisible* underwear thus tapped the growing market for comfort that we discussed in chapter 3.[113]

The context of virtue transformed the meaning of *visible* underwear by giving cleanliness in everyday things a strong moral content with immediate implications for community approbation. The fact that one wore and displayed clean white underclothing testified to one's attention to detail in aspects of dress symbolic of orderliness and moral standing. It showed that one was not only able to afford clean and cleanable clothing but also took the trouble to appear in such clothing.[114] This conveyed status, not just in terms of gentility (which it could if the white cloth were itself expensive, like silk, or set off by other expensive fabrics), but more directly in terms of virtue. In the latter context, wearing expensive or exotic fabrics was less important than wearing shirts, cuffs, collars, and underskirts made of thoroughly washable materials. After the new technologies made good-quality cotton available and cheaper than linen, its ready washability made it highly attractive and probably led many people to adopt the wearing of visible cotton undergarments as signs of virtue, virtuous status, and respectability.[115] People with no claim to hereditary status and without great wealth could still, by wearing clean cotton undergarments, announce that they were respectable and could evaluate other people by the same means. To the extent that respectability was an important part of what it meant to be "bourgeois" in the nineteenth century, one might say that clean, white underwear helped to define the bourgeoisie.

The context of virtue was a major factor in the history of the eighteenth and nineteenth centuries. It informed a substantial part of the impetus to European industrialization. It played a role (as we saw in the discussion of the tea, coffee, and sugar custom) in shaping European imperialism and extending the life of the slave trade, although it also created part of the cultural framework for slave-trade abolition. The context of virtue was also an essential element in the construction of the culture of respectability in the late eighteenth century. It intersected with all the other constituent contexts that comprised respectability: with gentility and luxury, as we have seen, and with the two additional, highly gendered contexts that we will explore in the next two chapters. One might say that, as far as historical interpretation is concerned, the context of virtue is the missing link in discussions of respectability. Its importance as a phenomenon in itself has not been recognized by historians, who have tended to overemphasize the significance of status and class considerations in defining respectability and have therefore missed a vital aspect of the ways in which respectability helped to form the modern world.[116]

5

RATIONAL MASCULINITY

One of the novelties of western European social life in the late seventeenth and eighteenth centuries was the coffeehouse (a general term that covered teahouses and chocolate houses as well as establishments in which coffee was the primary beverage served). Coffeehouses have attracted considerable historical attention in recent years, much of it stimulated by Jürgen Habermas's portrayal of them as prime locations at which the "public sphere" was constructed.[1] Coffeehouses are important to the present study in the first instance because their clientele consumed a large quantity of non-European imports. Even more significant, however, is the fact that they were among the most notable places where a new cultural context was created and articulated: the context we shall call rational masculinity.

Rational masculinity was closely related (although by no means identical) to the "public sphere," and also to a great many of the signature intellectual constructions of the eighteenth century: the Enlightenment, political liberalism, even, to some extent, free-market capitalism. It was also closely connected to the context of virtue described in chapter 4, and it became an important constituent of respectability by the end of the eighteenth century. As an element of respectability, its greatest significance lay in the manner in which it defined male social roles and behavior. Rational masculinity was, as is indicated by the name given to it here, a strongly gendered cultural construction. It linked a wide variety of behaviors, assumed human capacities, and institutions to a particular notion of what it meant to be male—that is, reasonable (at least potentially), capable of dealing intelligently and impersonally with reality and of associating with others for specific purposes, but so prone to violence and selfishness that the positive aspects of masculinity were always in danger of negation if not subjected to appropriate restraint. It was not just the physical setting but the culture of rational masculinity in general that gave meaning to coffee (and tea) consumption in coffeehouses and in certain other more or less public locations, and that therefore influenced demand for those commodities. At the same time, the physical effects that coffee produced and the qualities that people commonly assigned to it contributed in themselves to the formation of a coffeehouse ethos and thus to the creation of rational masculinity. The relationships among coffee, coffeehouses, and rational masculinity offer an excellent example of cultural construction. They also provide a vehicle for exploring links between culture and ideology in the eighteenth century.[2]

In this chapter, we look first at coffee and coffeehouses in early modern western Europe and then build from them a picture of rational masculinity. In the last part of the chapter, we examine the case of another imported commodity—tobacco—from the perspective of rational masculinity.

COFFEEHOUSES

The origins of coffee drinking in western Europe have already been touched on in previous chapters. Coffee, a product of Yemen and Eritrea, became first a fashionable drink and then a permanent feature of life in the Islamic world in the sixteenth century.[3] As an exotic novelty, its use spread to Italy late in the same century. It may have been in imitation of Italian fashions that a few French, Dutch, and English aristocrats began to take coffee in the 1640s, at much the same time that some of their social peers began to experiment with tea. In the 1650s and 1660s, a fashion—indeed, a craze—for coffee swept England, followed by rapid cycles of fashionability in France.[4] None of this was planned or organized by big business. The Dutch and English East Indies companies did not, as corporate entities, import a great deal of coffee into Europe until the last two decades of the seventeenth century. They had, however, from a much earlier period sent ships to Mocha, in Yemen, to bring coffee to Asian markets.[5] When they became certain that coffee was more than a temporary fad in Europe, they were in a position to move vigorously to replace Italian and French merchants trading directly with the Levant as the main suppliers of coffee to northwestern European markets.[6] The companies' entry into the Asia-Europe coffee trade did make it possible for coffee drinking to expand hugely in the eighteenth century (see table six, page 304), and it was the VOC that responded to inelasticities in coffee supply by transplanting the coffee bush to Java and other places.[7] But the great companies were clearly reacting to a demand that had established itself without their initially even recognizing its significance.

Although coffee drinking began in northwestern Europe as a fashion in aristocratic homes, in the 1660s its social incidence widened greatly and its standard venue shifted decisively to coffeehouses, public establishments supposedly modeled on coffee shops in Turkey. England led the way. The first English coffeehouse appeared in Oxford in 1650, the second in London in 1652.[8] By the late 1670s, there existed literally hundreds of coffeehouses in London, Amsterdam, and Paris—possibly thousands, if one counts very small shops that were in business for only a brief time. Many of these doubled as teahouses, distilleries, and liquor stores, bathhouses, even brothels. They quickly attracted unfavorable state attention. The authorities in France and England gave their reasons for their attitudes quite explicitly: people meeting in coffeehouses tended to talk about politics, which was supposedly forbidden in the growing autocracy of Louis XIV and discouraged in the nascent one of Charles II.[9] The authorities were not making this up. Samuel Pepys had gone to meetings of a club headed by James Harrington, the radical political thinker, at a coffeehouse in London as early as 1660, although he had ceased to attend before the club was disbanded by the government.[10] In 1675, Charles II issued a proclamation closing all coffeehouses in England, but the public outcry—apparently from all parts of the political spectrum—was so loud and immediate that the proclamation was quickly withdrawn.[11] The French government considered doing the same thing in 1685, but decided that the move would be too unpopular. It elected instead to tax coffee, which yielded a healthy revenue but did not eliminate coffeehouses, and then in 1692 attempted a state monopoly of the coffee supply. Faced with widespread evasion and a loss of its new revenues, the French government backed down on the monopoly in 1693.[12]

Although neither taxation nor state regulation put an end to the coffeehouse, they did probably encourage the institution to seek its clientele among the relatively well-to-do. By the end of the seventeenth century, coffeehouses had lost their faddish character. Their numbers stabilized in the major cities of northwestern Europe (reportedly at six hundred each for Paris and London), as did their patronage and their internal culture. Most important, they had become, and remained throughout most of the eighteenth century, central features of social, intellectual, economic, and political life.[13]

A great deal of information about the sorts of things that went on in eighteenth-century Dutch, English, and French coffeehouses can be gleaned from their frequent depiction in fictional literature and from diaries, newspapers, and business documents. Some of these activities can be summarized by focusing on one coffeehouse at the very start of the eighteenth century.[14]

Daniel de la Feuille, an Amsterdam businessman of Huguenot origin, published in 1701 *Le Guide d'Amsterdam*, an extremely informative handbook for foreign commercial visitors to "the most mercantile city in the world, the general store of the universe, the seat of opulence, the meeting-place of the riches, the delicacies of nations and the affection of heaven."[15] Part of the book's plan is a tour of the city conducted by de la Feuille. On the second day of the tour, we are to be taken to the Bourse, or exchange, which opens for an hour every day at noon. The Bourse is clearly a place of great importance in the economic life of the universe, but before we go there, we must experience an institution that extends and supports the work of the exchange—and a great deal else. We start the day with a visit to the Caffé François in the Kalverstraat.

> The post from England has arrived, and because someone has sent his employer a letter with the news from London, there are in the main room more than a hundred people who have come to discuss not only this letter, but the news of all the countries represented in the assembly. Many merchants take pleasure in exchanging news, over which the politicians who belong to that numerous company display their penetration of spirit and sharpness of vision. Often you see them firing conjectures at one another, if only to show off the force and the vivacity of their reasoning.[16]

De la Feuille refers to the coffeehouse as "the Academy of Politics, where the scholars do their exercises every day."[17] But other things are done as well. "Here we are, Sir," the author-guide tells us directly. "I have come primarily to bring you, [but] I shall at the same time carry out a commission which I have to purchase coffee, chocolate, tea, and various perfumes wholesale" (in other words, not from the proprietor of the coffeehouse, but from other customers).[18] Apparently, when we attend the Bourse at noon, we will go well informed and with our wits sharpened, and we will have already prepared the ground for the business that will be done there. The author also remembers that he had promised to give a friend particulars of the route to Rome, and he proceeds to do so. Somehow in the midst of all this activity we have presumably found time to drink some coffee.

Clearly, we are dealing with more than just a retail point for imported beverages. This is not exactly a revelation. The French café and the contemporary American coffeehouse both claim descent from a long line of establishments in which coffee has been served as a complement to conversation—intellectual, political, or amatory. London coffeehouses are famous for having been, from Pepys's time down to the last quarter of the eighteenth century, the primary sites of rendezvous for the literary great and the places where they lorded it over coteries of the not-so-great.[19] And while the centrality of the coffeehouse to British public life diminished rapidly at the beginning of the nineteenth century, the café maintained its significance (although with ups and downs) on the continent. At the German National Assembly in Frankfurt during the 1848 revolution, for instance, the various political parties were named after the cafés that the delegates who belonged to them frequented.[20]

But let us return to the Caffé François in Amsterdam at the beginning of the eighteenth century. Although this coffeehouse is obviously important enough to be singled out in de la Feuille's guidebook from the scores of similar cafés in the city, there is no indication that it is a leading center of intellectual or literary life. It is not the Café Procope in eighteenth-century Paris, the unofficial assembly room of the Enlightenment. It is not even the Turk's Head in London, where Samuel Johnson pontificated.[21] Admittedly, 1701 is a relatively early date in the overall history of the coffeehouse (although past the time of the "coffee craze"), and Amsterdam, although full of intellectual activity, is not quite a literary mecca on the scale of Paris or London. Nevertheless, it is probably better to concentrate on a coffeehouse not known for having a Diderot or a Johnson in regular attendance, as such an establishment is, in that respect at least, more likely to be typical.

The coffeehouse has a main room of sufficient size to accommodate over a hundred patrons, perhaps tightly squeezed together but not so tightly that they can't sit, hold cups, bend elbows, or allow waiters to pass among them. There are tables and chairs capable of being moved to fit the differing sizes of groups who come together there, and a bar or large table where the coffee (and tea and chocolate) are prepared and dispensed to waiters. There are a few paintings on the walls, as there are in most Dutch commercial establishments that deal with the public. There may be an array of newspapers on some of the tables, perhaps provided by the management. In 1701, however, they are more likely to have been brought by patrons for exchange and discussion. There are also smaller, more private rooms—in Amsterdam, with its narrow buildings, probably upstairs rather than alongside the main room. These are frequently hired by groups: clubs, committees of businessmen, or trustees of smaller charitable or public organizations not affluent enough to have their own chambers.[22]

If we look around, we see that most of the people present are male, with the exception of one or two ladies accompanying well-dressed men, the women preparing the coffee, and possibly the wife of the proprietor (or the proprietress herself), who is watching to make sure that everything works efficiently. The waiters are men. If you want to find waitresses and barmaids, you should go to a tavern. In Paris, things are a little different. Ladies more often visit fashionable cafés and female employees are more frequently found, but even there, except for brief periods, the clientele is largely male and remains so throughout the eighteenth century.[23]

As to the social status of the patrons, that is a little more difficult if one seeks to be precise about classification and doesn't know anybody personally. A few members of the nobility may be present. (There *is* a Dutch nobility, and although a nobleman's political role is much more circumscribed in Holland than in most other places, it is still fashionable to be one, or at least to be the owner of a property that brings with it the title of "lord.")[24] The nobility are important conduits of fashions arriving in the Netherlands from France, and so some of the other patrons are probably paying close attention to the dress of the aristocrats among them, both to identify fashion trends for themselves and to gather intelligence about what is about to sell in the haberdashery line. Also present are a number of wealthy merchants, the backbone of the Amsterdam economic elite. One or two of these may be "regents," members of the families that supply the political leaders of Amsterdam and Holland.[25] We can guess who these people are from their dress—not so much its up-to-the-minute fashionability as its newness and obvious richness of material, and expensive accessories such as hats, shirts, gloves, and so forth. These men may be attending to the news, reading out letters from their correspondents abroad and occasionally commenting on them, but they are probably not the "politicians" who are holding center stage in the discussions that follow. Rather, they are likely to place themselves at tables, either individually or in groups, to do business.

The other patrons are not easily differentiated. Most are dressed well. They wear three-cornered hats, jackets and waistcoats displaying clean neckstocks and shirts, breeches, stockings, and buckled shoes. Many have wigs. Few of the people present can be clearly identified as "workers" from their appearance. There may be some skilled artisans who are sufficiently literate to fit in and who wear some version of genteel attire—master and journeyman printers, merchants' clerks, and the like, willing to pay the admission fee for the sake of the conversation. But most people like these have other things to do on a weekday morning.[26] On the whole, the patrons are people of some education. Several are speaking French, and most of the rest can probably understand it. It is the language in which they have, most likely, read about the ideas they discuss.[27] Most are probably businessmen, not at the exalted rank of the very wealthy merchants or the regents, but independent and prosperous. They, too, are here to listen, to talk politics, and to do business, as are several lawyers with money to invest for their current clients and a desire to recruit new ones. Various other professionals are present, especially physicians, who make up a significant part of the city's intelligentsia. And there are people like de la Feuille himself, who appears to be a commercial agent and broker as well as a writer and publisher—not, perhaps, a person of exactly equal status to most of the others we have identified (or to ourselves, since he is our guide), but able to interact with them without self-consciousness or excessive deference on his part or condescension on theirs.

Indeed, that is one of the most notable, and presumably useful, characteristics of the ambience of the coffeehouse: its relative informality and social flexibility—not without distinctions among people, but within the outer boundaries created by dress, ability to afford coffee, manners, and education, easily achieved mutual accessibility for people of different backgrounds. A common feature of most of the people who fit within the boundaries of the coffeehouse clientele would appear to be mutual ascription of the status of "gentleman," as indicated by the favored title of address: *Myneer*. But there is not even a pretense that everyone present is a gentleman by birth. The people who are here are gentlemen because they *behave* like gentlemen: they dress, speak, and spend like gentlemen. Their reactions to what is said and done in the coffeehouse are supposed to be sober and balanced, at least in theory. In a tavern, dispute may lead to high words and a fight or a challenge to a duel (although the last is not common in the Netherlands). In a coffeehouse, dispute is not expected to produce any physical reaction, and it would be considered derogation from the status of a gentleman either to say things that would produce a violent reaction or to evince such a reaction itself.[28] Clearly, the notion of gentility applied here is substantially different from most of the ones we discussed in chapter 2. The terms that would probably occur to us today to refer to the patrons of the coffeehouse (besides *male*) are *respectable* and perhaps *bourgeois*, not *genteel*.

Let us pay a little more attention to what the customers are doing. Clearly, they are enjoying themselves, but not in the ways that they might if they were consuming wine, beer, or spirits. Their enjoyment comes from socializing with people. The socializing appears, from de la Feuille's description and many others, to be purposeful—a blend of pleasure and seriousness. The focus of general attention is politics, and presumably many of the side discussions that occur while the general ones are going on and afterward are on the same subject. Part of the pleasure of the discussions, apart from the (possibly illusory) feeling that they may have some effect on public life, arises from the "vivacity of the reasoning," as de la Feuille puts it—from the open cut and thrust of people competing, in a sociable way, to be rational about important subjects.

Rationality is also important in business, and a great deal of business is being done—informally, but not casually. Businesspeople in a wide variety of fields let it be known that they will be at the coffeehouse each day, or on certain days, between certain hours, if someone needs to find them.[29] In Amsterdam as in London, there is already at the turn of the century a tendency for specializations to appear among the coffeehouses, the process that will, for example, eventually turn Lloyd's Coffeehouse in London into the world's largest insurance exchange.[30] There is no obvious specialization at the Caffé François (except possibly a focus on French trade), but one assumes that businessmen who deal with each other frequently will find themselves together at certain coffeehouses more often than at others. De la Feuille is presumably stopping by the tables of one or two of the great merchants to inquire about the availability of the coffee, tea, and so on, for which he has his commission, and perhaps to strike a bargain over a lot or two. He may excuse himself briefly to us as he goes up the street with someone with whom he has made a deal to sign an agreement at a notary's office, or the two may decide to meet later at the Bourse to complete the arrangement.[31] Near us, two wealthier merchants are discussing the latest news about the issue of the succession to the Spanish throne. This is not an abstract problem for them, as is soon made clear. It is an issue over which Louis XIV and the prince of Orange (the latter simultaneously stadholder of Holland and king of England) are at cross purposes, and it may shortly lead to war (as indeed it will). The merchants are attempting to work out the odds that the Asian goods aboard the VOC's next few return fleets will get through unmolested, and what the implications of a war would be for the goods they have stored in warehouses.[32] They may even make a wager on whether or not the war will break out, or when. This is not entirely a pastime, although there is an element of sport to it. Each will bet on an outcome that would be a disadvantage to him, so that if the outcome eventuates, he will have some return. Each will probably engage in this crude form of insurance several times in the next few days.[33]

To summarize, we see the following activities occurring at the Caffé François: friendly but nonalcoholic socializing, exercise in rational discourse, discussions of politics, the conduct of business of various sorts, and the exchange of information. As we know from many sources, other things happened or were talked about at particular coffeehouses in England and France, and probably the Netherlands as well. Montesquieu has one of his characters in the *Persian Letters* complain that a great deal of the conversation in cafés and salons is a waste of intellectual ability, as people talk about frivolous matters such as fashion and scandal and avoid serious subjects like politics.[34] But in the Caffé François, we probably have the essential goings-on at a prosperous coffeehouse in a major eighteenth-century European city.

This is all very interesting, but does it mean much? Jürgen Habermas suggests that it does. He says that coffeehouses were a vital institutional factor in the formation of the "public sphere," which was itself a crucial structural feature in the development of modern bourgeois society.[35] Although historians differ about the exact nature of the public sphere and the relative importance of economic and noneconomic factors in its creation, there is surprisingly little disagreement about its existence or about the importance of coffeehouses in providing sites for its articulation.[36] One way to look at the role of coffeehouses is to see them as points at which a number of intersecting functions were performed, one of the most central of which was affording an open discussion of politics. The aggregation of these functions and the importance of conversation and information exchange to all of them led to the elaboration of a set of discursive practices and behavioral norms that regulated the functions. Functions, practices, and norms, taken together, made up a large part of what is meant by "public sphere."

De la Feuille's description of the Caffé François certainly supports the idea that business, politics, and other interests came together at coffeehouses and that the main activity that tied them all together was the exchange of news—most of it political. We can see what made this significant by examining the early modern coffeehouse as a point of intersection among a number of different networks—that is, structures through which goods, information, ideas, and resources of power and wealth were disseminated. The structural role of the coffeehouse as a shared node in several dynamic, changing networks turned it into a space not only for the formation of Habermas's public sphere, but also for the construction of the cultural context of rational masculinity (and a good deal else). Coffeehouses were not the only such spaces, but they were clearly archetypal ones. The characteristics of the intersecting networks and the nature of the commodities consumed in coffeehouses, together with the behavior of the coffeehouse clientele that we have already surveyed in the Caffé François, help to explain the essential features of rational masculinity and their relationships to the phenomena grouped under the heading "public sphere"—as well as to parallel ideological constructs that we usually refer to as "liberalism."

The most significant of these networks can be described briefly. First, distribution networks. Coffeehouses were retail points in an increasingly complex system of distribution for (mostly) non-European products.[37] Not only did they sell prepared coffee and tea, but most of them also sold ground coffee, coffee beans, packages of tea, and a range of other products that varied from establishment to establishment: juices, tobacco, and (especially in France) spirits. Most coffeehouses bought their merchandise from a variety of legitimate brokers and wholesalers. Many in Britain also had recourse to a network of smugglers who usually bought their stock in trade in the Netherlands.[38] Coffeehouses also provided facilities for retail sales by independent vendors. Just one issue of a London newspaper in 1720 advertised the availability of (among other things) medicines, tooth powders, tickets to a ball, lottery tickets, and West Indian citron water at coffeehouses, tea-houses, and chocolate houses—in addition to weightier items, such as a ship and a large quantity of brandy being sold at auction at Lloyds Coffeehouse.[39] Coffeehouses were thus important elements of the structure that serviced and attempted to shape consumer demand.

Coffeehouses played important roles within commercial and financial networks as well. In their public rooms, contacts were made between large-scale buyers and sellers of trade commodities, consumer goods, futures, ships, and so forth; between insurance underwriters and their clients; between lenders and borrowers. Subscription lists for stock issues, projects, companies, clubs, and charitable organizations were regularly opened and advertised at coffeehouses.[40] In facilitating these activities, coffeehouses supplemented the operations of organized exchanges, but they also afforded services and opportunities not available in, say, the Royal Exchange or the Amsterdam Bourse. One of the main advantages of coffeehouses was their flexibility. Dealing could take as long as necessary and, if desired, in semi-privacy. Other people could be brought into a business discussion by summoning them from across a room. It was difficult to regulate such a system, which was exactly its appeal to many participants. In this sense, the coffee-house (or rather, an aggregation of a large number of coffeehouses) was a better model for an efficient market than was a formal exchange.

Two points need to be made about the relationship between commercial networks and coffeehouses. First, it was not just contacts that were made in coffeehouses, but also decisions. As in an exchange, only more broadly and diffusely, the thousands of bargains struck in coffeehouses represented both individual decisions about the investment of resources and, taken together, market decisions. Decision-making in both respects manifested itself in con-sensus that could be articulated not only in words but in changes in numeri-cal indices that were increasingly calculated in coffeehouses as well as in exchanges, to be published in journals (which were frequently edited in cof-feehouses). The second point, however, is that not all significant business decisions were made in coffeehouses (or alehouses or even exchanges). The managers of the largest commercial and financial institutions—the VOC, for example, or the Bank of England—made their decisions in private. They could be influenced by coffeehouse consensus, but when organizations were big and efficient enough to internalize functions such as information gather-ing, they were not dependent on the networks tied to the coffeehouses. The latter networks were a significant structural part of capitalism, but in terms of fundamental decision-making, probably not the most important part.[41] Inherent in this situation was thus a duality between the "public" or "open" functioning of coffeehouses and exchanges, and the "private" or "closed" functioning of bureaucratically organized corporations. The duality was far from absolute. Company directors, usually in their capacities as private businesspeople, often took an active part in coffeehouse life. Corporations such as the Indies companies that dealt in consumer goods could not insulate themselves completely from the consensus of retailers and small wholesalers (although the VOC certainly tried, as we saw in chapter 3). Nonetheless, the duality was quite real. In eighteenth-century Britain in particular, it influenced the ways in which the complex antagonisms between commercial (and often political) interests were commonly simplified and understood: for example, freedom of business opportunity for all as opposed to closed, secret, and potentially corrupt decision-making by corporations. Reality was considerably more complex, but these images, many of them grounded in the coffeehouse style of business, had a profound effect on the public construction of political economy.

Information networks were obviously crucial to the larger roles of coffeehouses. People had all sorts of reasons for going to coffeehouses on a regular basis, not excluding the desire for a cup of coffee. But apart from any other motive, most of them went there for the news—both general news and information particular to their interests. The "coffee craze" in England in the 1660s and 1670s was clearly as much about people enthusiastically exchanging information and hearing the political news as it was about coffee itself.[42] That was what made coffeehouses exciting (and dangerous, according to the authorities). But it was not all for amusement, because the exchange of information in coffeehouses after 1660 was part of an extensive and growing system of information networks, a system centered in the major trading cities but extending all over Europe and much of the rest of the world. It was a part of the jobs of many people to participate in these networks. Samuel Pepys, for example, before becoming secretary to the Navy Board in 1661, was essentially an information gatherer for the earl of Sandwich. This led him to frequent places where information was exchanged. *Exchanged* is the correct word. Shortly after leaving Sandwich's service, Pepys wrote in his diary: "One thing I must observe here, while I think of it; that I am now become the most negligent man in the world as to matter of newes. Insomuch, that nowadays I neither can tell any nor aske any of others."[43] It is likely that one of the reasons merchants chose initially to go to coffeehouses for business was that they could at the same time exchange information. This did not preclude patrons from enjoying what they were doing, but idle curiosity was not the only or the main reason that many of them were interested in the news.[44]

In the eighteenth century, connections between coffeehouses and the news went beyond the fact that customers discussed current events and expected the proprietors to provide newspapers. In Britain, newspapers and journals were themselves often edited in coffeehouses, where the editors picked up bits of news and solicited contributions from other patrons. In the case of Lloyds, the specialized publication edited on the premises, *Lloyds' Register*, became the center around which that coffeehouse was transformed by its patrons into an insurance exchange.[45] In other words, freedom of discussion at establishments such as coffeehouses and freedom of the press were not entirely separate concepts.

Political networks also intersected with others at coffeehouses, in part because of the availability of news and in part because the conversations at coffeehouses were essential to the formation of public opinion.[46] Like other public establishments such as taverns, coffeehouses served in the late seventeenth and eighteenth centuries as local sites for occasional governmental functions (inquests, low-level trials, and so on) and for partisan politicking. In Britain, their functions in these respects declined from the late eighteenth century onward as local authorities acquired their own spaces and as the political activities of the metropolitan political elite migrated to clubs (many of which were actually former coffeehouses). On the continent, cafés maintained their partisan functions much longer, as we have seen.[47] But whatever their roles in the organization and management of parties, the main impact of coffeehouses appears to have been on public opinion formation.

Much of the apparatus developed in Britain and the Netherlands for influencing opinion on political issues—broadsides, pamphlets, newspapers—was intended not so much for private, individual perusal as for reading before groups, typically in coffeehouses, to be followed by discussion and argument. Successful broadsides were those that generated replies and counter-replies, a process that closely replicated, and probably derived from, the argumentation that took place in coffeehouses. Even the form of argumentation gives the impression of oral presentation before an audience of varied interests and opinions, as one would find at a coffeehouse where speakers tried to make their cases with as strong an appearance of rationality and concern for the public good as possible.[48] While not exactly the same as the economic process of creating market decisions through a multitude of individual agreements, the formation of political opinion in coffeehouses was at least similar and suggestive of parallels. Both in the commercial and in the political arena, there was a tendency to understand alternative forms of decision-making as closed, secret, irrational (at least with regard to the public good) and corrupt. Coffeehouses were appropriate settings for making such arguments: they provided in themselves a model of the connection between rationality and public discussion, an image of human interaction from which could be developed further images of the free market, the open public forum, and the free society.

Coffeehouses are also, of course, famous for their roles in hosting the Enlightenment, for serving as points of connection among networks of literary and intellectual leaders and as locations for dissemination and discussion of new ideas.[49] Only a few favored cafés in the major capitals actually attracted the first-rate literary figures of the eighteenth century (or even the second- or third-rate ones), but the clientele of the less-favored establishments certainly read and discussed the significant books of any particular season.[50] The functions of coffeehouses in these respects resembled their commercial and political roles—indeed, often overlapped with the latter.

It is clear that coffeehouses, by connecting so many dynamic networks in so many ways in early modern Europe, acted as a kind of structural foundation for a great deal of creative cultural, political, and economic activity. But what did *coffee* have to do with any of this? Why did *coffee*houses (together with teahouses and some chocolate houses) perform the functions we have discussed, and not other kinds of establishments? The fact that coffeehouses played such roles generated much of the demand for coffee in the late seventeenth and eighteenth centuries,[51] but did coffee itself, as a consumer product, or some image that coffee possessed, have any influence on the networks that intersected at coffeehouses or on the results of their intersection? The answer to the last question is yes, and in the explanation of the answer, the main elements of the context of rational masculinity can be discerned.

Coffee and the Context of Rational Masculinity

Dr. Thomas Short, writing of tea in the mid-eighteenth century, asks us to "consider how many sober Companies it assembles both in Coffee-houses (which in London only are about six hundred) and private Houses. Observe we further the Business, Conversation, and Intelligence it Promotes, the Expence and Debauchery it prevents."[52] Short's book is primarily about tea, but he says that essentially the same things are true of coffee. Apparently, coffee and tea possess public value because, when taken by people in company under the appropriate circumstances, they encourage imbibers to behave in a desirable way (to do business, hold conversation, and act, or at least speak, intelligently) and not to behave in undesirable ways (spending too much and debauching themselves; it is not clear whether debauchery is the object of the overspending or a parallel activity). Short admits that coffee and tea, while they afford healthy stimulation, are not the specifics against a variety of diseases that they were formerly advertised as being. They do help to clear the head and improve spirits and can be used as a dietary supplement (but not for children).[53] They should be consumed in moderation; Short gives precise descriptions of a caffeine "high" and of caffeine addiction.[54]

Cornelis Bontekoe, the "tea doctor," is not even a memory. There were still proponents of coffee in the early eighteenth century who made broad claims about medicinal effectiveness, such as the author of a book called *The Vertue and Use of Coffee, with Regard to the Plague and Other Infectious Distempers*, which was advertised in a 1721 London newspaper.[55] But the direction taken by Short—emphasizing the social value of coffee and tea and their moderate use as healthy and pleasant dietary supplements—clearly prevailed.

One feature of Short's treatment of tea and coffee that is common to most of the favorable literature on coffee and coffeehouses in the eighteenth century is a comparison with alcoholic beverages. Such a comparison is clearly present in his statement that tea and coffee prevent expense and debauchery—the kinds of things, it is implied, that go on in taverns and alehouses. In addition, while wine, ale, and spirits cloud one's judgment and lead to poor business decisions, mild stimulants like coffee and tea (and tobacco) sharpen wits, encourage the focusing of attention on the matter at hand, and help lead to agreements that are beneficial to all parties. Disagreements that inevitably arise in such dealings are handled soberly and rationally, instead of degenerating into the angry disputes that alcohol incites.

A pamphlet entitled *The Way to Be Wise and Wealthy*, originally published in 1716 and probably written by a person named Sowter, gives another perspective on some of these issues. The pamphlet, one of the attack-on-luxury genre discussed in chapter 3, complains of "the great Expence both of Time and Money at Publick-houses, the Frequenting of which is grown so much beyond the Calls and Dispatch of Business (which was the first Pretence of going thither) that now 'tis the least Occasion of it."[56] It is not specified what kinds of "Publick-house" are meant. They may include coffeehouses, but because these are not mentioned by name, it is more likely that the reference is to alehouses, taverns, grogshops, and the like, which had been the preferred meeting places for businesspeople before the rise of the coffeehouse and were still significant, although declining, in this regard early in the eighteenth century. In any event, although one could as readily accuse people of wasting time at coffeehouses as at alehouses (especially if, apparently like the pamphlet's author, one had no clue about the necessity of information exchange for conducting business), it would have been much easier to defend coffeehouse loitering on the basis that Short suggests: that holding civilized, intelligent conversations about important subjects is not a waste of time. And as to wasting money, it was not so much that the beverages available at either alehouse or coffeehouse were particularly expensive in terms of liquid volume or a single standard draught. Rather, a minor degree of alcoholic inebriation led to more drinking in order to achieve promotion to a major degree—a phenomenon paralleled in coffeehouses only to a very limited extent. Also, the *other* things one could spend one's money on at a "Publick-house" were more likely to cause problems ("debauchery," perhaps, or gambling). Less of that sort of thing went on at coffeehouses.[57]

One might suppose that the main attraction of the beverages of the coffeehouse in comparison with those of the tavern would have been specific and instrumental: coffee and tea were better accompaniments to doing business rationally than was alcohol. But that was certainly not all there was to it. You could order coffee at a tavern if you wanted it. Shops selling both types of beverage could have served a wide range of customers, as they do today. The coffeehouses that survived as public establishments in the late eighteenth and nineteenth centuries did precisely that.[58] In any event, as far as it is possible to tell, few eighteenth-century coffeehouse patrons abstained from alcohol off premises.[59] It would appear, then, that the attraction was to coffee and tea *in the coffeehouse*, as opposed to alcoholic drinks in the places where those were featured.

One of the reasons for this had to do with the kinds of people who were likely to be found at coffeehouses and at taverns. Admission to a coffeehouse often cost something, a penny or two, perhaps enough to discourage casual lower-class visitors but not enough to keep away anyone with a specific interest in being there. Also, apart from income considerations, patrons of coffeehouses presumably wanted *not* to be in the company of people interested primarily in heavy drinking or other activities that went on in alehouses, wineshops, and taverns, regardless of those people's social status. These activities might include loud arguments, singing, various forms of uncouth behavior, violence, and, of course, "debauchery." Such things did not necessarily impede the conduct of specific business, but they might; given an alternative place of rendezvous, a fair number of businesspeople might choose the quieter locale.

Even more significant, coffeehouse patrons were announcing to the world and to themselves that they were the kind of people who deliberately chose to do business and meet company in a coffeehouse. They were suggesting that they valued and possessed the characteristics that coffee and tea were supposed to enhance: sobriety, intelligence, nonboisterous sociability, and so forth. In the seventeenth century, a merchant or broker who announced his hours of attendance at a tavern was conveying merely his availability. By the eighteenth century, a businessman so announcing himself (especially in Britain) was conveying an impression that would probably not promote his enterprise—unless his business were not wholly reputable, perhaps like that of the infamous fence and informer Jonathan Wild.[60] If one is in a business that depends on trust and sobriety, one wants to project an image of trustworthiness and sobriety—hence the attractiveness of an establishment that primarily serves nonalcoholic beverages and yet affords a (more sober) version of the sociability of a tavern.

This may seem an adequate explanation of the replacement (never total) of the tavern by the coffeehouse as a commercial gathering point, but we should keep in mind that there are alternative ways of viewing the desirability of sobriety in business dealings. Alcohol, usually consumed outside the office, plays a considerable and legitimate part in modern Japanese business (in a country where tea is the national drink and where teashops existed long before they did in Europe), supposedly because it promotes closer relations among business associates.[61] This is a cultural difference, not so much between the general values of different societies as between the specific contexts within which certain kinds of business were supposed to take place in early modern Europe and those that inform commerce in contemporary Japan. The contexts are not completely determinative in either case. Many eighteenth- and nineteenth-century Europeans (especially in France) believed that a little alcohol was not out of place in business.[62]

One implication of all this is that commercial activity and coffeehouse behavior in eighteenth-century Europe were jointly informed by particular cultural constructions that emphasized the positive value of sobriety, moderation, rationality, self-discipline, and the negative effects of alcohol and various forms of passion. One of these constructions was surely the context of virtue discussed in chapter 4, but that context is not sufficient by itself to explain what we have observed in the coffeehouse. The peculiar linkage of rationality, sociability, and masculinity that seems to pervade the coffeehouse and that extends, by suggestion at least, to business behavior essentially defines its own cultural context—one closely linked to virtue, but not the same. This is the context of rational masculinity.

A central feature of rational masculinity, obvious in its manifestation or ritual enactment in coffeehouses, is conversation. All the meaningful coffeehouse activities described above involved conversations: general discussions of political news, separate conversations among smaller groups about any of a thousand subjects, business negotiations, and so forth. Any public place can accommodate conversation, but in a coffeehouse it is governed by a code of behavior, not formally articulated but well understood by coffeehouse patrons and capable of being extended to other settings such as clubs, scholarly or scientific societies, small political organizations, or boards of directors.[63] The code enjoins among other things a tolerance of differences of opinion—indeed, a desire to hear and participate in debate, both for the pleasure of doing so and because of an implicit belief that closer approaches to the truth of any issue will come through rational intercourse than by any other means.

There is a corollary to tolerance. Although one is expected to voice objections to what another person says and may do so vigorously, one must not become, or cause anyone else to become, angry to the point of losing self-control. This is more or less what we have come to call "civility." It is not dissimilar to the eighteenth-century idea of "politeness" that we discussed in chapter 2 in connection with gentility. The imagined settings and the cognitive frameworks of the two are, however, quite different. The setting typically associated with politeness is a social gathering attended by well-bred persons of both sexes who display appropriately genteel manners. The conscious object of polite conversation, according to Lord Chesterfield, is to be agreeable—especially but not exclusively to ladies.[64] This means not insulting or upsetting anyone—which is really an object in itself, not an overt means to some further general end apart from maintaining one's social position. It is possible to derive a larger social vision from this notion of politeness, but it is a notion clearly framed by the context of gentility and constantly threatened by its practitioners' suspicions of its superficiality.[65] Good manners in a coffeehouse conversation, tolerance and self-control in any space framed by rational masculinity, are governed by consciousness of a different goal: that of making it possible to have a rational discussion that may eventuate in a sensible decision or a reasonable consensus. Manners themselves are much less elaborate than in a setting in which politeness prevails; again, they are a means to a general end, not an end in themselves.

The rules of idealized coffeehouse conversation, to the extent that they are an application of moderation and good sense to the discussion of serious issues, are also related to the aspect of gentility we called "magistracy" in chapter 2 (and perhaps in some ways to the "republican tradition"). The obvious difference is again the imagined setting: relatively open discussion among the company of a coffeehouse or a voluntary association, as opposed to a closed discussion among people in authority, notionally sitting in judgment. The context for which the coffeehouse is the functional model is a culture of the public sphere, not of an oligarchical elite. The boundary between the contexts is not always clear, but it exists, and it can be recognized in practice by imagining scenes of conversations on either side of it. Eighteenth-century Britons can, for example, visualize the difference between, on the one hand, a political discussion in the cabinet or in the House of Commons (as they are supposed to be, not necessarily as they are), and on the other, discussions of the same issues in hundreds of coffeehouses. In the first case, formally designated authorities debate (with appropriate good sense and moderation) behind closed doors or before a limited, non-participating audience without an official record of what is said. In the second, anyone to whom the company of a coffeehouse is willing to listen can speak, but in accordance with an informal code of manners and discourse that (again, as an ideal) emphasizes self-control, a degree of toleration, and rational argumentation.

This code of behavior is particularly interesting because it is supposed to be largely self-enforcing. It depends on internalized norms and on peer pressure in settings such as coffeehouses. Of course, the management can eject an unruly patron from a coffeehouse or a club can expel a member. But usually, it is expected that the simple process of bringing a violation to the attention of the violator will be sufficient to uphold the code.

How is this self-regulation possible? At least three factors seem to be at work. The first, as we have seen, is that the material elements of the setting (especially, in coffeehouses, the beverages themselves) promote it. The second is that proper coffeehouse behavior gives at least local status and a positive moral valuation to people able to adhere to the informal code. Such people, by behaving appropriately, are considered to be *gentlemen*—as the term is defined in the context of the coffeehouse and in other voluntary associations featuring similar behavioral norms and cognitive patterns.[66] To some extent, coffeehouses impress such norms and patterns on their clientele, in essence creating replicas of the ideal coffeehouse participant. The third factor is perhaps the most significant: the coffeehouse setting, although more open and public than others, is by no means fully open to everyone. It is even less open when it is replicated in other voluntary associations such as clubs.

A coffeehouse may or may not charge admission. It may or may not keep out anyone not properly dressed. It may or may not formally exclude women. But the management and especially the clientele will make someone who does not "fit" aware of that fact. As we have seen, quite a wide range of people do actually fit. Social status plays an informal role in selection, but it is subsumed within a more functional set of criteria. The principle is that people who cannot contribute effectively to the discourse or benefit from it ought to keep away, or, if necessary, be kept away. People whose views on certain matters (politics, for instance) are so different from those of the majority of patrons that rational, unheated dialogue with them is impossible should exclude themselves and engage with more compatible groups—perhaps at a different coffeehouse. People whose dress and manners suggest that they do not have the education or the standing to be able to participate ought also to be excluded. Women are discouraged from patronizing the more serious coffeehouses, or at least from attending significant discussions there, for similar reasons.[67] Women, even if they display appropriate social standing, are assumed not to possess the education or the faculty of rationality to a sufficient degree to make a contribution, and their presence, regardless of what they might actually say or do, is believed to have the effect of diverting discussion along superficial, trivial, or, at best, sentimental lines. Such discussions are more appropriate for mixed gatherings at other places—for example, the pleasure gardens at Vauxhall and Ranelagh, near London.[68]

By attending to the goings-on at coffeehouses and pursuing their connections to a range of social and cultural phenomena, we have identified the outlines of the context of rational masculinity. The name that has been given to it here indicates two of its most notable features: an emphasis on rationality as an object to be promoted, a criterion of value, and a means to desirable ends, and its peculiar form of selectivity (especially, but not exclusively, gender specificity). The emphasis on rationality was neither total nor simple. It was built around a set of visual images, not a rigorous analysis of human rationality in relation to society (although the context certainly supported and was generally consistent with the various attempts at such analysis for which the eighteenth century is famous). The central image was of a conversation among the clientele of a coffeehouse or some similar establishment, or of a voluntary association. Sentiment, feeling, even passion are not absent, but they are kept under control. They may in fact motivate the positions on issues taken by discussants, but by convention it is not the evidence of a person's deep feelings that is supposed to convince others, but rather the reasonableness of his arguments and the extent to which they successfully invoke the common good. The sentiments that are legitimately present are benevolence (in one sense, the positive feelings that are supposed to be generated by acting, or at least thinking, in terms of the common good) and a kind of fraternal sociability. The selectivity inherent in the context is also suggested by the central image: heterosexual men trying to be rational, to control their passions, and to feel brotherly affection toward one another would have a hard time succeeding in these endeavors if there were women present—at least the sort of women to whom they would feel obliged to accord deference. They would have a difficult time also if men of insufficient education, experience of the world, or self-control tried to participate.

These primary features of rational masculinity were, like the cognitive aspects of most cultural contexts, full of contradictions and depended at critical points on the use of images and sensual cues rather than consistent reasoning and careful definition. For example, the assumption that men are inherently more capable of rationality than women and that this justifies the exclusion of the latter (not only from coffeehouse conversations but from any larger civil society informed in substantial part by rational masculinity) was based on recently constructed images of ideal-typical males and females. The way in which they were constructed betrays inherent uncertainty about their accuracy. By creating an image of a special environment that encouraged men to behave rationally and with self-control, the constructors were essentially recognizing that under other circumstances men often behaved quite differently. The "naturally" rational man of the coffeehouse conversation could emerge only under carefully arranged circumstances, which at the very least cast doubt on his inherent naturalness. The construction of the corresponding "natural" woman, who was to be excluded from the central conversation so as to enable it to take place and whose major job was to modify and limit male behavior, similarly reflected doubt about the naturalness of both the male and the female construct and a determination to treat them as real regardless of misgivings.

Other notable features of the context of rational masculinity also center around the image of rational conversation: self-control in debate and similar activities, toleration of diversity of opinion, and the importance assigned to the availability and critical analysis of information in the conduct of discussion. These may be regarded as behavioral modes in support of purposeful, effective conversation. Also significant is a crucial assumption inherent in both the informal code and the actual practice of conversation: that each participant in a discussion possesses his own interests but is enjoined to argue logically and evidentially that the position he favors will, if adopted, result in a higher common good than just the satisfaction of his interest. As we saw in chapter 4, this convention was not unique to rational masculinity, but it was distinctly different from the convention (associated with, among other things, classical "republican" discourse) that interest and common good are incompatible. The whole point of a culture revolving around conversation at the point of intersection among the kinds of networks we have discussed is that interests can be accommodated to each other and that in the process, in the right environment and among rational, well-informed men who exchange ideas and information freely, an accurate consensus about the common good will emerge. This is one of the most questionable and easily subverted aspects of rational masculinity, but it is also its most influential and appealing. As a part of the context as a whole, it was readily transferred to settings other than the coffeehouse or club. One could argue, indeed, that it became an essential part of the cultural foundation of liberal society in the eighteenth and nineteenth centuries.

The last point suggests that there are some serious implications with regard to historical interpretation in recognizing the existence and nature of the context of rational masculinity. The context not only informed a considerable amount of Western consumption of overseas products in the eighteenth century (coffee and tea and, as we shall see later in the present chapter, tobacco)—a matter of great importance for the history of imperialism and the expansion of the global economy—but it also played a vital role in shaping what became the dominant European and American conceptions of civil society. It also strongly affected the construction of gender relations. This is not the place to pursue either of the latter implications very far, but they cannot be allowed to pass without some comment.

With regard to civil society, we have seen that rational masculinity can be viewed as a cultural counterpart to Habermas's public sphere. It was the set of characteristic practices, attitudes, discursive conventions, and images that was assembled in and around the institutions and spaces that Habermas has identified as the structural matrix of the public sphere—especially, but not exclusively, the coffeehouse. As such, rational masculinity was necessarily connected to the development of the ideological tendencies that were first articulated in something like their modern form in the late-seventeenth- and eighteenth-century public sphere: the tendencies that we collectively call "liberalism." Rational masculinity was not an ideology and still less did it encompass a body of political or economic theory, but its history was closely connected with liberalism. In the kinds of patterned interaction that occurred in coffeehouses, in the exchanges of information, in the virtual exchange of goods and resources that took place in the various sites of action in the public sphere, the terms of abstract theory acquired concreteness and detailed meanings that were often not fully articulated in formal discourse. If one wanted clear proof that individuals with interests and passions could, through a process of open, informed discussion, arrive at a rational consensus and proceed to decisions that took full account of the common good, one needed only to look at what went on in a coffeehouse—both real coffeehouses and the imaginary, ideal ones that provided much of the imagery for the context of rational masculinity. The overlap between the real and the ideal was sufficient to create conviction. Or if one wanted an idea of what Locke *really* meant by civil society or by the People, one could do worse than to visualize the culture of coffeehouse discussion and the kinds of people who were likely to take part in it.

Uday S. Mehta, in an exposition of exclusionary tendencies in liberalism, explains:

> Terms such as "English gentry," "breeding," "gentleman," "honor," "discretion," "inheritance," and "servant" derive their meaning and significance from a specific set of cultural norms. They refer to a constellation of social practices riddled with hierarchical and exclusionary density. They draw on and encourage conceptions of human beings that are far from abstract and universal and in which the anthropological minimum is buried under a thick set of social inscriptions and signals.

... In this, they circumscribe and order the particular form that the universalistic functions of Lockean liberalism assume.[69]

The "cultural norms" and the "constellation of social practices" to which Mehta refers are, of course, complex and contradictory in any society, but they are not completely unordered. They exist in (among other formats) the kind of array that we have been calling "cultural contexts." In the cases of people attempting to interpret Locke in the late seventeenth and eighteenth centuries (and presumably in the case of Locke himself), probably the most immediate and relevant context was rational masculinity.

There were other ways in which rational masculinity may have affected the liberal political tradition. Some of the distinction between "public" and "private" within that tradition refers to the difference between conversations in public places (for example, coffeehouses) and private ones. The enormously important role of voluntary associations in liberal practice and political culture (a role that has almost no place in classic formulations of liberal theory before the nineteenth century)[70] may also have arisen because of the significance they held for rational masculinity—especially when limited-membership clubs began in the second half of the eighteenth century to replace the coffeehouses and similar institutions that had originally hosted them.

The context of rational masculinity also had a profound effect on the redefinition of gender in the West that was one of the most notable products of the seventeenth and eighteenth centuries. The belief that men were inherently rational creatures, but subject to all sorts of interference with the exercise of their rationality, was clearly a constituent part of the context. Some important implications of this aspect of rational masculinity will be pursued in the discussion of tobacco below. The notion that women were inherently less rational than men but possessed other desirable characteristics (especially sentimentality), and that this difference created a need for "separate spheres" for men and women in society, will be discussed in chapter 6. The significant point to be made here is that the "separate spheres" doctrine was not the essential feature of the context of domestic femininity that we will explore in that chapter. The doctrine was much more a product of thinking within the framework of rational masculinity, which was employed (without complete success) to shape the behavior of women to correspond to roles consistent with rational masculinity. As such, "separate spheres" had a substantial impact on the articulation of domestic femininity. (In our terms, it formed a major area of intersection between the two contexts.) It did not, however, as Amanda Vickery and others have recently demonstrated, carry the day in the sense of defining the cultural basis of respectable femininity.[71]

Before we turn our attention further toward the construction of femininity, let us look at the subject of gender in connection with rational masculinity from a somewhat different perspective. To do this, we will focus on yet another overseas product in heavy demand in early modern Europe: tobacco.

TOBACCO

The consumption of tobacco in early modern Europe was influenced by a large number of cultural factors, including all of the contexts discussed in this study. Rational masculinity was, however, probably the most significant in this respect, at least in the eighteenth century. Tobacco, in turn, had a considerable impact on the construction of rational masculinity. As we shall see, the peculiar attachment of tobacco to rational masculinity also implied a role for domestic femininity as the most important limit to tobacco consumption in Western society before the twentieth century: respectable women were not supposed to smoke.

Tobacco was one of the first commodities produced in the Americas that became a significant consumer good in the Old World in the wake of the Spanish conquests. Tobacco was transplanted to Europe and in the seventeenth century was grown in some quantity in, among many other places, southwestern England. However, high-quality broadleaf tobacco flourished best in the warmer areas of the New World.[72] Also, because imperial states— especially Spain, France, and England—could generally derive higher revenues from the importation of American tobacco than from the locally grown item, they tended to discourage domestic production, sometimes by quite drastic means.[73] All through the early modern period, tobacco used in Europe was grown primarily in America.

A fashion for tobacco smoking developed first in the Iberian countries in the sixteenth century and spread quickly through the Mediterranean. Its adoption in the Islamic Near East coincided with the rapid development of the taste for coffee in the same area. Both were stimulants arguably not forbidden by Islamic law, and both came to be consumed together in the Turkish and Greek forerunners of the coffeehouse.[74] In the second half of the seventeenth century, with the development of the coffeehouse in northwestern Europe, the Near Eastern connection between tobacco and coffee reasserted itself in the new locale. By that time, however, tobacco smoking had long been fashionable on its own in the region and possessed a distinct cultural identity.

Part of tobacco's identity arose from the popular images of the people who introduced it into northwestern Europe.[75] These included soldiers— especially of the Spanish army that served in Flanders from the 1560s onward, who may have been imitated by soldiers of the other armies engaged in the wars of the Low Countries, including the English one. Adventurers and sailors who had been to the New World (or at least to the Mediterranean) also brought back tobacco and the fashion for using it. Sir Walter Raleigh raised the social status of the fashion in England by deliberately adopting it in the 1580s and 1590s as a means of publicizing his colonial ventures in North America and his schemes for Guiana (although in neither place did he plan for commercial production of tobacco to play much of a role).[76]

Thus, by the early seventeenth century, tobacco's image as a consumer product in northwestern Europe was connected to adventurous, dangerous, and *manly* activities—in an era in which masculinity, risk-taking, violence, and sexual performance tended to be connected to each other and heavily emphasized in portraying the characteristics of the gentleman. It was also an era in which the challenge of aggressive women to the "proper" roles of men and to definitions of masculinity weighed especially heavily on European mens' minds.[77] This may have created a market for new symbols of manliness—especially ones that were legitimated by connections to important national enterprises such as war and imperialism. In England, Raleigh's public relations strategy particularly associated tobacco with the imagery, and thus the ideology, of expansionary Elizabethan nationalism. However, regardless of tobacco's roles as a fashion, as a symbol of male genteel status, and perhaps as an exotic luxury, the early European literature devoted to tobacco treated it primarily as a drug.[78] It was, in fact, one of the most controversial subjects in the discourse of health and diet at the beginning of the seventeenth century. According to some medical authorities, tobacco offered an effective means of dealing with psychic and mood disorders. It was a specific against headaches, had a calming effect when taken under the proper circumstances, and could in general hold off melancholy, or depression. These claims were at least founded on accurately observed (if probably overstated) properties of nicotine. The same literature included much more fanciful ones that portrayed tobacco as a cure for a whole raft of diseases, especially syphilis. Sugar, coffee, tea, indeed almost every exotic ingestible received similar treatment at some point, although the claims made for tobacco in the early seventeenth century seem to have been unusually broad.[79] But tobacco also attracted unusually severe criticism, on medical grounds as well as others. The most famous and one of the most comprehensive of these attacks was a tract entitled *A Counter-Blaste to Tobacco*, written by King James I of England and published "anonymously" by him in 1604.[80]

In his pamphlet, James advances a wide range of objections to tobacco. He presents the medical ones as contradictions of arguments used by advocates of tobacco. To the notion that tobacco smoke, being hot and dry, is good for the brains because the latter are cold and wet, James responds with what would become a standard pattern of health-literature argumentation: the human microcosm is naturally in balance, with just enough emphasis on one or two of the four humors to give each individual a personality. It is unhealthy to upset the balance of the body (for example, by smoking); good health practice should be aimed at restoring and maintaining balance.[81] To the claim that tobacco is an antidote to syphilis, James treats his readers to a racist, nationalist "counter-blaste" of truly Jacobean complexity. The readily intelligible part of it goes like this: Syphilis was brought to Europe by American Indians enslaved by the Spaniards. The Indians used tobacco as a cure for syphilis, which was the reason Europeans started to employ it. But why should we "imitate the barbarous and beastly manners of the wilde, godlesse, and slavish *Indians*, especially in so vile and stinking a custome?" The Indians, "refuse to the world," are slaves of the Spaniards. Since "we," like the French (says the Scottish king to his new English subjects), ought to treat the Spaniards with disdain, should we not disdain even more to follow the customs of their slaves? James does not, however, say definitively that tobacco fails to cure "the Pox."[82]

James's most effective arguments are couched in terms of aesthetics, genteel politeness, and opposition to "luxury." Is it not, he asks, "both great vanitie and uncleanenesse, that at the table, a place of respect, of cleanlinesse, of modestie, men should not be ashamed, to sit tossing of *Tobacco pipes*, and puffing of the smoke of *Tobacco* one to another, making the filthy smoke and stinke thereof, to exhale athwart the dishes, and infect the aire?"[83] It is the "filthinesse" (apparently a moral consideration) of the fact that "an unctuous and oily kind of Soote" is often found in the "inward parts" of "some great *Tobacco* takers, that after their death were opened," rather than its implications for health, which particularly strikes James.[84] Also, the generality of tobacco-taking among the gentry is such that people who "abhorre" tobacco—especially ladies, who James seems to think are particularly sensitive to the filthiness of the custom—are forced by politeness to put up with it. Tobacco smoking is, finally, a form of "luxury," both because it is addictive and weakens the virtuous will (James calls this "lust") and because it leads to ruinous expenditure.[85] All this in 1604, when tobacco cannot have been a significant fashion in England for more than a few years.

Like coffee in later years, tobacco made its initial inroads into Europe without any particular effort by major business interests to create a market. In the late sixteenth century, no existing large business organizations saw market creation as a task they could or should perform. But in England, tobacco soon attracted the reluctant interest of a prominent chartered company, an interest that decisively changed the history of the product. The Virginia Company of London, whose Jamestown colony had clung to the brink of extinction from its establishment in 1607, discovered around 1612 that one of its settlers had managed to transplant broadleaf tobacco success-fully from Spanish America into Virginia.[86] Although pleased that Virginia now produced *something* that might sell in Europe, the company's directors had doubts about tobacco. It had figured in none of the early plans for the colony (such as those were), and it was a private commodity, produced alongside the company's operations and difficult to control. The directors were also afraid of becoming dependent on a fashion that might go up in smoke at any time—a fashion, moreover, that the king was known to loathe. However, as things stood, they had either to accept tobacco or give up the colony altogether. Using an appeal to patriotism linked to a subtle reminder that royal prestige was closely identified with the success of Virginia, they persuaded King James not only to be silent about his version of the evils of tobacco, but also to authorize various advantageous arrangements for Virginia tobacco as against tobacco imports from elsewhere.[87] Serious smokers continued to prefer Spanish-American tobacco, but the tax break gave the Virginia variety substantial access to the English market and allowed it to be sold for a price that attracted customers of middling income. The company, in cooperation with merchants who dealt in exotic goods, even set about attempting to market the product through advertising.

The effort to save Virginia with tobacco contributed to several well-known changes in the nature of the colony: a shakeup of company manage-ment in the late 1610s; a decision to focus on attracting planters through land grants based on the number of people brought over at private expense; and reluctant acceptance of the primacy of privately-produced tobacco (and thus of private production in general) in the economic life of Virginia, because only the lure of profits from the colony's cash crop could attract the amount of settlement that was desired.[88] The decision to establish a system of local self-government in 1618 and the first purchase of African slaves the next year may have been connected to these changes. Officials in England con-tinued to fear that an economy based on a fashion would be insecure and that the colony would expend so much effort on growing tobacco that it would be unable to feed itself. These were reasonable fears, and they would con-tinue to be voiced for some years—especially after Virginia was nearly destroyed by a Native American attack in 1622, which resulted in the replacement of the Virginia Company by direct royal rule.[89] But tobacco turned out to have great staying power. The demand for it continued to grow into the eighteenth century, although not without periods of reversal. Both Virginia and Maryland developed around tobacco, but unlike the monocultures of the West Indian colonies, not to the exclusion of a food-producing sector that met local needs and was able in the eighteenth century to turn toward export as well.

One of the keys to this familiar story was demand for tobacco. Without sustained increases in consumption in Europe, the history of Virginia and Maryland would have been quite different. Why did tobacco enjoy such a satisfactory demand pattern? Apparently for many of the reasons with which we are familiar in contemporary times. There were, of course, the addictive and psychoactive properties of the nicotine in tobacco, noted by James I, which at the very least helped to maintain levels of consumption achieved initially by fashion alone when tobacco penetrated new markets in Europe.[90] But active marketing, much of it taking advantage of the imagery and the cultural meanings of tobacco, played a significant role as well, just as it does today. Throughout the seventeenth and early eighteenth centuries, English merchants, often acting in concert, lobbied for government support in the form of further tax breaks, elimination of domestically grown tobacco, and protection abroad.[91] They established distribution systems in Britain deliberately aimed at "hooking" new users by making large quantities of tobacco available through a wide variety of retail outlets, including taverns, inns, coffeehouses, apothecaries' shops, and eventually general-purpose rural stores. They developed schemes to obtain monopolies on the wholesale supply of tobacco to particular countries (especially Russia) from governments desirous of augmenting revenues through monopolizing or taxing its retail.[92] Often, tobacco interests were driven to these steps not by an overflowing of marketing imagination, but by economic necessity. It turned out that because tobacco growers tended to overproduce over a cycle of years and because existing European markets were relatively easily saturated, without vigorous market expansion the industry would quickly slump—as it did periodically anyway.[93] The kind of control exercised by the VOC over Asian spices was never realized in tobacco (at least not before the twentieth century).

In the first half of the seventeenth century, tobacco marketing heavily featured the two images we discussed previously: tobacco as a cure for disease and a support for health (physical and mental), and tobacco as a symbol of manliness. The first image remained a subject of controversy into the eighteenth century, but a large part of the health-and-diet literature treated tobacco favorably.[94] All through Europe, soldiers continued to adopt the habit, and other young men did so as an expression of their own bellicosity in a bellicose age.[95] In England particularly, tobacco continued to be identified not only with overseas adventure, but also with the entire enterprise of English imperialism. This was appropriate in a way, because the tobacco industry was often artificially maintained by the state as a public token of its dedication to the future of English imperialism as symbolized by Virginia. Walter Raleigh augmented these identifications (one hopes unintentionally) by smoking a pipe to calm his nerves moments before his execution in 1618.[96]

Men were not, however, the only ones who smoked in early Stuart England. Women are sometimes portrayed as smokers in literature on tobacco during the first decades of the seventeenth century—usually in broadsides and pamphlets attacking tobacco. There is no question but that some women smoked tobacco in that period, just as some women did in the late eighteenth and nineteenth centuries when smoking was held to be inappropriate for respectable ladies. In the later periods, if you did not care to be a respectable lady or were not qualified to be one, the main restrictions on smoking (at least in private) did not apply to you. But while some of the representations of female smokers in early-seventeenth-century England are intended to convey their lowly status, not all of them do so. Fashionably dressed ladies also appear.[97] An interesting point about the latter is that they tend to be portrayed in a certain *kind* of fashionable dress style: one that features modified versions of *male* clothing, such as hats, doublets, and visible stockings. In the famous portrait of Pocahontas made during her highly publicized visit to London in 1616–17, she is dressed in this style.[98] Although no tobacco is evident in the picture, Pocahontas was clearly associated in English minds with Virginia's main product, of which her husband, John Rolfe, had been the first English cultivator.

Anthony Fletcher notes this fashion for stylized cross-dressing in his study of early modern English gender history.[99] The fashion was widely adopted by genteel ladies. It was often interpreted by male writers as yet another sign of threatening female aggressiveness. The adoption of tobacco smoking as a complement to the fashion makes sense if we interpret the latter as an attempt by upper-class women to assert autonomy and claim a share of power through appropriating masculine symbols, or alternatively through subverting them. Stylized cross-dressing did not, however, stay in fashion, perhaps because of male opposition or perhaps because it did not become sufficiently well embedded in significant cultural contexts. Fashionable smoking by ladies appears to have declined at the same time and is not much complained about after 1640 or so.[100] One cannot tell for sure, but it is at least possible that, by apparently confirming the masculinity of tobacco through associating it with male dress and yet simultaneously subverting the meaning of the masculinity thus symbolized, the smoking gentlewomen of the early Stuart era helped to provoke a redefinition of tobacco's "masculinity" in the second half of the seventeenth century.

This change can be described in terms of several of the contexts we have discussed. Smoking a pipe of tobacco before or during the exercise of magisterial functions accorded with the increasing emphasis on magistracy as an aspect of (male) gentility. An association between puffing on a pipe and being judicious made its way from this point of origin into many behavior patterns in the eighteenth and nineteenth centuries, including ones incorporated into respectability. For those who believed tobacco to be good for their physical and mental health, smoking was a public way to display their concern for such things within the context of virtue. But it was the context of rational masculinity that provided most of the meaning for smoking and to which male tobacco users most significantly contributed, especially in Britain.

The introduction of the coffeehouse into northwestern Europe in the third quarter of the seventeenth century and its association with images of the Near East brought tobacco into the cultural orbit that revolved around the coffeehouse.[101] Both products were consumed together in Ottoman coffeehouses, so both were consumed together in western European institutions that projected "orientalism" by giving themselves names like The Turk's Head. There was certainly an element of luxurious exoticism to this, but as we saw previously, patrons of coffeehouses quickly came to adopt behavior patterns that centered around political discussion, business, and so forth, from which much of the rest of the context of rational masculinity developed. Tobacco was part of the process. Tobacco had a strong masculine identity, which coffee and tea by themselves did not and which made smoking a particularly appropriate activity in a coffeehouse.[102] Among the many properties of tobacco emphasized in the health literature was its ability to promote evenness of temper, which was an important part of ideal coffeehouse behavior. If smoking did not make you think better, at least it reduced interference from the passions and the worries of daily life and permitted your innate rational capacities to reveal themselves—if you had any. This connection between smoking and emotional stability in support of reason remained strong into (and beyond) the eighteenth century.[103] Thus, in the course of becoming an integral part of rational masculinity, the image of tobacco smoking as a particularly male activity changed, or at least developed a popular alternative form. In its new form, smoking was no longer associated with violent aggression, war and conquest, but rather with male rationality and men's monopoly on the moral strength needed to exercise reason. This type of masculinity was still hegemonial, but it was based not on men's capacity for dominating through physical violence, but on their presumed moral and intellectual capacities.

The earlier associations of tobacco with other images of masculinity (men of action, adventuring, and so forth) did not disappear in the eighteenth century. To the extent that these other images could be integrated into a picture of rational, sober, adult, and yet manifestly virile, heterosexual males (perhaps of the strong, silent type, like the Marlboro Man), they could be made to be consistent with respectability—with just a hint of transgression. The possibility of real transgression was, however, limited in the nineteenth century by the development of a respectable way to smoke that was constructed with primary reference to women, or rather "ladies." Not only was respectable smoking a prerogative of men because the cultural context that gave it meaning applied only to men, but smoking was also assumed, mainly because of its undeniable dirtiness and smell, to be offensive to ladies' sensibilities. This gave birth to a set of smoking rituals that recognized gender differences within the culture of respectability.[104] The withdrawal of ladies after dinner to allow gentlemen to smoke was one of these rituals, as was the requirement that a gentleman request permission to smoke if a lady were present. If a gentleman failed to do the latter, it meant either that he was not respectable or that he did not regard the lady as respectable—or both.

But smoking was not the only mode in which tobacco was consumed. In the seventeenth century, Europeans had begun to adopt the practice of taking snuff. In the eighteenth century, snuffing became extraordinarily fashionable, first in genteel circles, then among people of middling circumstances, and finally, by the nineteenth century in some countries (earlier in Britain), by people of practically all social classes. As Jordan Goodman has shown, contrary to the common view of the history of snuffing, snuff (with its American counterpart, chewing tobacco) became the primary form in which tobacco was used in the Western world in the late eighteenth century. A large part of the rise in tobacco usage in mid-eighteenth-century Europe (reflected in table 7, page 305) was due to the spread of the snuff custom. In some countries (although not in Britain) snuff retained its primary status until the rise of the mass-produced cigarette toward the end of the nineteenth century.[105] Before the nineteenth century, snuff-taking was an activity in which both men and women could legitimately participate, regardless of their social standing.

Snuff probably became popular for a number of reasons: its consumption did not involve many of the health risks that were stressed by the anti-smoking side in the medical debates over tobacco; it had its own medical function, that of clearing the nose and sinuses in cold, damp weather; it did not create lingering smells the way smoking did; and it lent itself to marketing in terms of variety and short-term fashions in aroma, flavor, and accoutrements. What Goodman emphasizes, however, is the consonance of snuff with respectability.[106] Given the fact that snuff achieved popularity before the construction of respectability was completed in the second half of the eighteenth century, it would be better to consider snuff as a product whose use was consistent with several of the contexts of which respectability was eventually composed. It was apparently considered a more refined way of taking tobacco than smoking and thus corresponded to the tendency to redefine luxury in terms of taste. It lent itself to fashion and could represent a claim to genteel status, with the added possibility of claiming virtue as well because of snuff's supposed healthiness. Snuffing avoided the heat and harshness of smoked tobacco, which was supposed to be particularly bad for women, so it was ideal for social rituals involving both men and women. Snuff was also addictive, although snuffers did not use as much tobacco as did smokers.[107]

However, while smoking tended increasingly in the late eighteenth and early nineteenth centuries to be defined by rational masculinity and domestic femininity as elements of respectability, snuffing did not fit into either of those contexts. Their gendering of smoking began to extend to tobacco overall. Precisely because its use did not correspond to a dichotomous gender pattern, snuff may have begun to lose much of its claim to a place in the culture of respectability in the nineteenth century. It is also possible that snuffing was too closely identified with earlier aristocratic fashions to be viable in the bourgeois society of the nineteenth century, but on Goodman's evidence, that is unlikely.[108]

Tobacco's role in rational masculinity remained an important component of its demand basis into the twentieth century—the antecedent of the notion that smoking, under the right circumstances and in the proper dress, shows that you are sophisticated or learned. (Consider the image of the tweed-jacketed college professor with his pipe.) But in the nineteenth century, respectability was also the most important cultural limitation to tobacco use in the West. Ladies (that is to say, respectable women whose behavior patterns were framed by the context of domestic femininity) were not supposed to smoke or, in most countries, to employ tobacco in any form. In part, this prohibition arose from notions about the peculiar physical susceptibility of women to the harshness of tobacco smoke, and partly it derived from tobacco's particular identification with rational masculinity. As the latter context was off-limits to respectable women, so too were some of its central practices. But even more, one of the roles of women that was defined by domestic femininity—to maintain, through a complex set of limitations on male behavior, the foundations of civilized life—required that they abstain from smoking and restrict smoking in their presence. In the next chapter, we will see how this worked.

6

DOMESTIC FEMININITY

TEA AND SYMPATHY

Early in Samuel Richardson's *Clarissa* (published in 1747–48), the heroine
reports the first major instance of the difficulties that her attraction to the
unworthy Lovelace will cause and that will activate the plot of the novel. She
is called to tea with her family in the parlor, where she finds her parents,
aunt, brother, sister, and the footman in their accustomed places but not in
their usual spirits. The brother and sister have informed the parents of
Clarissa's innocent contact with Lovelace. Matters have been arranged so
that Clarissa will eventually be alone with her father, who wishes her to
marry the even more unworthy Solmes and will forbid further visits to the
friend at whose house she met Lovelace. But before Clarissa and her father
can be left alone so he can lay down the law, the ritual of tea must be got
through, with the entire family present. The mother is the center of the action
and the primary person to whom the others defer. She decides that she will
make the tea herself, not Clarissa, who usually performs the task—an obvious, but indirect, sign of her displeasure. The silence of the gathering is
noted, presumably because conversation is the norm. The footman is dis-
missed, but even though the parents are angry and the brother and sister are
gloating at Clarissa's distress, no one brings up the unpleasant point at issue
while the ritual is under way. Only when everyone but Clarissa and her
father have found excuses to leave (after the second dish of tea) does the
practical work of bullying Clarissa begin in earnest.[1]

The situation is a fictional one, but it is consistent with actual practice. It is an instance of formalized, meaningful social intercourse of a kind that fascinated Richardson. Similar scenes are described throughout the novel. Richardson was deeply concerned with the moral meanings implicit in manners, with the symbolic language in which the meanings were expressed, and with the relationships among morality, manners, and the actual behavior of people. So were a great many others in western Europe in the eighteenth century, which perhaps explains why Richardson's novels were so popular—a fact almost incomprehensible to many people today.[2]

The British ritual called "tea" was one of two major meals invented or radically revised in the late seventeenth and early eighteenth centuries that centered around the consumption of overseas imports and that possessed important social and cultural meanings for its participants. The other was breakfast, in the form in which it came down to the twentieth century.[3] The new form of breakfast spread much more widely in Europe than British tea and was probably much more significant in its economic impact. But let us focus on the tea meal for the moment because it leads us directly to the heart of this chapter: the formation of a cultural context built around the home as the core of civilization, around the crucial role of women in the home, and around a definition of femininity derived from that role. (We will follow British practice in the rest of the present chapter and use the word *tea* both for the product and for the meal, except when the ambiguity would be likely to create confusion.)

By the time Richardson wrote *Clarissa* in the 1740s, tea had been established as a custom of families of good standing in Britain for about two generations, although its timing during the day varied throughout the eighteenth and early nineteenth centuries until it came to be fixed in the late afternoon.[4] (The amount of food normally consumed also varied over the same period.) Its origins are obscure, but it seems to have emerged through imitation of the seventeenth-century French aristocratic fashion of salon gatherings.[5] In the course of its subsequent adoption as a general custom of the merely well-off in Britain, its social and cultural significance increased enormously. (In France, tea gatherings remained aristocratic and their fashionability went through cycles, at least until the last decades of the eighteenth century, when the British practice began to be adopted by the less fashionable.)[6]

Some features of tea resembled those surrounding beverage consumption in coffeehouses, but many did not. Tea was a domestic event, not a public one. In the eighteenth century, when tea as a commodity was fairly expensive in Britain, the custom was effectively limited to the middle and upper ranges of society—rather like the clientele of the coffeehouse. But even at midcentury, there were within those limits no obvious class preferences with respect to tea. Tea was taken in the very highest circles (including the British royal family), and it was becoming an emblem of the respectable trades-man's household. When prices came down in Britain in the nineteenth cen-tury, the custom was readily adopted by working-class families in both city and country.[7] From the perspective of social structure, tea was not so much a symbol of the class to which one belonged as it was a means of claiming a standing in society not wholly defined in terms of classes and orders—in a word, respectability.

Tea was not just a meal taken at home, within the household; even more, it was a meal taken with the *family*. Guests could be invited, but they acquired temporary status within the structure of the family while the meal lasted. Certain subordinate household members might take tea with the fam-ily (tutors and governesses in some households, apprentices in others). In general, however, people with the status of servants had their tea separately, with the artificial service "family" downstairs. Tea was not an outwardly directed activity like a banquet, nor was it an occasion to do business or form voluntary associations like a meeting at a coffeehouse. It could be employed to establish or maintain contacts with elements of the outside world, as for example when neighbors and prospective suitors were invited to tea, but the contacts were structured very much in terms of linkage to the family offer-ing the tea. Tea was in a real sense a celebration of the fundamental perma-nent human association: the family.[8]

The fact that tea was a family affair was related to another of its promi-nent features: women not only took part in the meal along with men, but they were also the central, indispensable actors in its ritual. Although in house-holds with servants, the senior woman (usually the wife of the householder) did not prepare the food, at teatime she oversaw the making of the tea and assigned service tasks to various members of the family. Women playing out their roles in the ritual simultaneously ministered to the needs of the family and received the deference that their ministry demanded. It was perfectly acceptable for tea to be taken with full ceremony without men present at all, whereas the reverse was much rarer. Visitors of appropriate status who paid calls on genteel or respectable women in the eighteenth century were given tea in a modified version of the same ritual. Thus the formulation of the tea custom in Britain can be interpreted simultaneously as an aspect of the con-struction of respectability in general and of domesticity, "private life," and a new social and cultural role for respectable women.[9]

The ritual of tea possessed meaning not only as an occasion, but also in terms of the attitudes and demeanor of the participants and the behavior that was expected of them. Although matters pertaining to the family were sup-posed to be discussed, conflict and division were to be avoided—hence the unwillingness of Clarissa's family to speak of the subject foremost in their minds while tea is going on, even though tea is the formal occasion that frames and perhaps sanctions the action her father takes afterward. Tea manifested family solidarity. The presiding woman had a duty to make sure that it did so, and the other participants had a duty to defer to her leadership in this regard. Tea was not just a symbol of the family; it was part of what it meant to *be* a family, a ritual that gave the family as a whole a psychological significance apart from the dual relationships among individuals in it.

Teatime manners were also significant. In addition to the specific ceremonial actions of making, pouring, distributing, and receiving tea (with other comestibles), participants adhered to a well-understood pattern of appropriate behavior. The pattern involved deference between the sexes, general courtesy, and natural (but not rigid) decorum. It was a variety of the pattern of politeness that had emerged in western Europe in the early eighteenth century as an expression of a modified gentility.[10] The meaning of parlor behavior at teatime resembled in some ways that of coffeehouse behavior, but it was not identical. Like its coffeehouse parallel, the teatime pattern manifested an assumption that human sociability was a natural phenomenon, closely allied to reason and moderation. Within the family (the primary institution for fostering sociability), reason and moderation were promoted by activities such as tea. Tea was a training exercise for adolescents and a reminder to adults about how to behave in the world at large. But it was not a replica of the public sphere, as the coffeehouse was. For one thing, although conversation played an important role at tea, it was not supposed to take the form of debate. Although issues discussed in coffeehouses might turn up at tea, they were not discussed in the same way, mainly because they were not intended to result in a decision or consensus. The point of teatime conversation was to promote sympathy and sentimental attachment to other members of the company, not to come to a conclusion. It was bad form to push an opinion too far or to insist that someone else was completely wrong. Moreover, while coffeehouse conversation took place (notionally, and most often in reality) among men, tea was a mixed activity in which the leading roles were taken by women.

The meanings of women's functions in the ritual of tea were quite overt. A woman presided, directing the division of labor; women generally poured, thus symbolically providing sustenance and health. Topics and the manner of conversation were limited by the presumed sensibilities of ladies, and the women—especially the presiding woman—were expected to ensure politely that transgressions of this rule were immediately brought to the attention of the transgressors. The ambience that women maintained was one of support and sympathy, which was symbolized by tea itself. Women thus acted out roles as domestic executives and "civilizers." The symbolic exchange of service by women (pouring and usually distributing the tea) for deference by male participants reflected an ideal vision of the dynamics of gender interaction. This vision was central to the cultural context designated here as domestic femininity.

FEMININITY, DOMESTICITY, AND "SEPARATE SPHERES"

Until very recently, much of the historical research on cultural patterns of femininity in the eighteenth- and nineteenth-century West rested on the assumption that the idea of "separate spheres" provided the main framework around which those patterns were constructed. "Separate spheres" was a formula that held that adult males should dominate a family's relationship to the outside or public world while adult women properly should take direction of the domestic world. Femininity, as a behavioral pattern, was thus defined in two primary ways: in terms of what women were not supposed to do (act like men, in the areas of life that men should dominate), and in terms of what they were supposed to do (act strictly according to a set of norms articulated as a culture of domesticity). The division of spheres was justified on the grounds that it suited the normal genius of each of the sexes while it permitted the characteristics of each sex to restrain the potential for excess present in the other. The differing behavioral characteristics of the sexes derived from inherent, biological features of men and women: tendencies toward either violence or excessive rationality in the case of men, and a superabundance of sentimentality and a relative lack of rational capacity on the part of women.[11]

The existence of the separate spheres doctrine in the late eighteenth and nineteenth centuries is well attested, among other things in an extensive prescriptive literature on gender roles.[12] It clearly bore at least some relation to actual social practice and it certainly affected both public and private life. For one thing, it was a significant means of formally justifying the denial of voting rights to women—that is, of dealing with demands for women's suffrage that arose from the same liberal theories on which most men's claims to political participation were based. It appears to have been the argument most convincing to anti-suffragist women in the nineteenth century.[13] For another, it provided support for laws that gave men hegemony over the instruments of power in society (money, property, access to office) and thereby the means of last resort for subjugating individual women.

Despite the admitted significance of the separate spheres doctrine, recent research has suggested that historians have exaggerated its centrality in defining the cultural context in which Western women lived.[14] A serious blow has been given to the thesis that, before the eighteenth century, women in western Europe enjoyed something like economic equality and parity in esteem with men and that new ideologies of femininity were then constructed by men around the separate spheres doctrine to deprive them of that status.[15] What has emerged is a much more complex, varied, and ambiguous picture. It has been shown that, even on its own terms, "separate spheres" referred much more to differences in emphasis between legitimate male and female activities than to separation of the sexes.[16] Moreover, it appears that much of the work of cultural construction was performed, not by (mostly male) writers of books of advice on conduct for women, but by women themselves, acting out their daily lives.

This expanded view of women's agency in creating and modifying the cultural framework within which they lived can be viewed in different ways.[17] In the terms we are using in the present study, women of elite and middling social standing took a significant role in building a context of domestic femininity around a range of practices and symbolic activities, each heavily laden with meaning: meals such as tea and breakfast, the newly invented enterprise of "shopping," a complex of managerial functions pertaining to household and child-rearing, and so forth. The context was not wholly incompatible with separate spheres thinking, which is probably best considered a product of rational masculinity. "Separate spheres" impinged, perhaps heavily, on domestic femininity, but the latter subverted large parts of it and embedded much of the rest in a set of customs, attitudes, and rituals that afforded women self-respect, a sense of meaning, and a considerable amount of practical autonomy. These desirable features were offset by others, which included the need to submit formally to male supremacy in the public sphere and to accept a regime of emotional and intellectual self-discipline far heavier and far more beset with tension than that assumed by men. Nevertheless, most women who possessed sufficient means adopted the practices associated with domestic femininity, while many other women looked forward to taking the first opportunity that presented itself to do so. It became a central feature of the culture of respectability in the late eighteenth and nineteenth centuries.

Why were European women so attracted to domestic femininity, despite the negative features that were obvious in the eighteenth century to people like Mary Wollstonecraft and that became obvious to more and more others in the course of the nineteenth century?[18] For one thing, many, probably most, of its practical implications for women appeared extremely advantageous when one looked back to the seventeenth century or before (or when some women looked back to their own childhoods in families that had not adopted the new cultural pattern, either out of conservatism or lack of the financial means to do so). The socially sanctioned roles of women, even in well-to-do families, in the seventeenth century were a great deal less attractive and satisfying than were the idealized roles presented by domestic femininity. The latter acknowledged the importance of the wife as executive head of domestic arrangements and a person to whom respect and deference were due (even from the male head of household) because of her assumed virtues and her position of authority, circumscribed as that might be. The women in a family, especially the wife, were the collective axis around which the family's most important functions of nurturing and raising children, promoting morality, and providing psychological support revolved. Women enjoyed, on the whole, considerably less respect in earlier times and therefore had fewer sanctioned grounds on which to respect themselves.[19]

Moreover, the work was easier. In the 1660s, Samuel Pepys's wife, Elizabeth, directed her servants in their housework, but she also performed a great deal of the physical labor herself (including some of the hardest and dirtiest tasks).[20] Pepys, who was quick to react to anything that might lower his standing in the eyes of his fellow state officials, seems to have regarded his wife's role as perfectly normal. Such behavior on the part of the wife of the secretary to the Navy Board would have been unthinkable a century later, when the respectability of a woman's domestic role had come to be connected with her family's status.[21] Moreover, there was no clear symbolic or ritual reinforcement of Elizabeth Pepys's managerial position (except perhaps for signs of deference from the servants). Samuel did go over the household books with Elizabeth each week, but very much in the manner of a merchant auditing the accounts of his clerk.[22]

The ideal of domestic femininity that was celebrated from the eighteenth century onward in the ritual of tea thus provided both psychological and physical advantages to those women who could afford to realize something like the ideal in the arrangements of their families—which goes a long way toward explaining why so many of them wanted to do so. And like many rituals, tea was not just a symbol of an ideal; it was also a tool for achieving it. It was a means through which women, by drawing others (including men) into the ritual and its significations, constructed a more comfortable and rewarding life for themselves than the few alternatives that were practically open to them. The items consumed at the meal—especially tea, the central ritual item—bore distinct meanings in this regard. They represented the things that women were supposed to provide in return for their status: sustenance, health, psychological support, and a model of civilized behavior.

It remains true, however, that the kind of standing and self-respect afforded women in the context of domestic femininity did not entail much practical change in women's traditional exclusion from avenues of power.

Indeed, ideological formulations associated with domestic femininity (such as the separate spheres doctrine) created new ways of explaining why such exclusion was needed.[23] The embedding of domestic femininity in the culture of respectability meant that respectable women were unable for many years to pursue professions except for ones consistent with their domestic or nurturent roles: senior employed housekeeper, governess, teacher, eventually nurse.

But domestic femininity did not wholly exclude women from public life. The prevailing view, shaped within the context of rational masculinity, was that women were not capable of taking a useful part in serious political discussions that took place in the principal public venues: clubs, coffeehouses, or parliaments. According to this view, most of them were not equipped for sustained intellectual debate, and even those who were would only, by the mere fact of their presence, trivialize the proceedings. However, important public issues could be discussed at home, under circumstances in which the male monopoly on connections between the home and public spaces was not challenged. Few commentators saw anything wrong with women influencing men's political views in the privacy of the home or at the points at which the home touched the external world, such as at tea in the parlor. And of course, whether they saw something wrong with it or not, it was bound to happen. Moreover, tea and other, similar occasions involving visits to people in their homes became in the eighteenth century a very important part of the networks of politics, at essentially all social levels and in all western European countries. These occasions both required the presence of women and sanctioned their involvement in what was discussed and decided.[24]

There were also opportunities at least partly outside the home for respectable women to have a public presence. They could become involved in religion (especially of the Evangelical variety), in humanitarian work (such as slave-trade abolition), and, by the nineteenth century, in local party politics. They could write and publish.[25] They could, in these ways, challenge the tendency for the public sphere to be defined solely within the context of rational masculinity. One of the reasons that they could do so was that in the late eighteenth and early nineteenth centuries, ideologists of domestic femininity had extended the idea of women's particular role of upholding morality into a transcendental public task: maintaining civilization itself. This transformation legitimated the active involvement of women in practically any public enterprise that could be framed in terms of protecting or advancing the cause of civilization.

CIVILIZATION

Civilization (like *respectability*) entered the western European languages in its modern form quite suddenly in the latter part of the eighteenth century.

Samuel Johnson's dictionary (1755) carries a technical legal definition of the word (the conversion of a criminal process into a civil one), but that is all.[26] The earliest nonlegal citation in the *Oxford English Dictionary* is dated 1772, and in fact refers to Johnson and his dictionary. The OED quotes Boswell's *Life of Johnson*: "I found him [Johnson] busy, preparing a fourth edition of his folio Dictionary. . . . He would not admit *civilization*, but only *civility*. With great deference to him, I thought *civilization*, from *to civilize*, better in the sense opposed to *barbarity*, than *civility*."[27] Apparently, Johnson regarded *civilization* as an unnecessary neologism. His definitions of *civility* are "Freedom from barbarity; the state of being civilized"; "Politeness, complaisance; elegance of behavior"; and "Rule of decency; practice of politeness."[28] These definitions catch a fair amount of what we understand by *civilization*, but not its expansive (indeed, all-encompassing) historical sense and its connections with the concept of progress. The use of the word overtly raises the discourse of politeness and civility to a higher notional level of significance. This would seem to be the reason that Boswell, like educated Europeans from then on, preferred *civilization* to any of Johnson's equivalents. It also implies a similar raising of other discourses with which the included terms are associated, a tendency that can be seen in politics in the late eighteenth century.[29] The same thing happened with the component contexts of respectability.

Johnson's "civility" encompasses many of the values and behavioral norms that had come to be associated with gentility, virtue, and rational masculinity by the late eighteenth century. "Civilization," however, actively brings these values and norms together and makes them part of a historical process that supposedly leads humankind to general improvement: in other words, "progress." From the late eighteenth century, a "respectable" person was not just a polite, civil, virtuous, and genteel person, but preeminently a "civilized" one. Civilization is something inculcated in people, primarily through the medium of a respectable household. According to notions of domestic femininity, it was the responsibility of women not only to make their households respectable, but to propagate and maintain civilization in its most fundamental senses, as a secular highest good.[30]

This discursive fixing of the basic institution of civilization in the home and the assignment of responsibility for its maintenance to women gave respectable women a significant rhetorical weapon and a means of access to an important (if still subordinate) role in public affairs—as long as that role was consistent with domestic femininity. Mothers working on abolitionist committees were acceptable; mothers voting were not. And as Charles Dickens later insisted through the character of Mrs. Jellyby in *Bleak House*, women who neglected their family responsibilities in order to pursue public interests, however "humane" those interests might be, were to be reprehended.[31]

The connection between civilization and domestic femininity can be seen by looking again at tea. The function of the tea ritual (and of the women who conducted it) in maintaining civilization was implicit in the manners that were supposed to prevail. Civilization was based on a set of attitudes and behavior patterns, including adherence to moral rules, self-restraint, consideration for others, deference to people of real or presumed moral worth, and recognition of one's duty. These could be instilled and reinforced by many means, but the most important was the properly constructed and regulated family. The family molded civilized behavior through socializing and educating children. The lessons of civilized behavior were constantly and symbolically repeated through organized family occasions such as tea, where the central civilizing tasks were performed by women.[32] Sons went off to school or a trade at an early age, thus learning to negotiate the outside world, as was their duty. Daughters remained longer (sometimes permanently) in the home, learning family tasks, perfecting their roles as the guardians of civilization and its rituals—such as tea.

In late-eighteenth-century thought on the subject, progress and civilization were supposed to be afforded by freeing natural human propensities. To greater or lesser degrees, people had a propensity toward rationality. Self-control derived from a propensity toward order and regularity. Both were needed for the achievement of material progress, and both were more notable in men than in women. Sentiment was also natural to humans (especially women) and necessary for their success and happiness. The problem, articulated in various forms and with greater or lesser degrees of optimism about a solution, was that people had other, not so desirable propensities and that even the desirable ones, unless they were in some way balanced or made consistent with one another, put the realization of the advantages of civilization at risk.[33] People liked order, but they (especially men) also had a propensity toward violence. Reason, left to itself and directed toward the achievement of individual desires, could create the ruthless version of civilization that Rousseau attacked. Sentiment, given full sway, could produce incoherence in action and the rule of superstition. The natural human tendencies on which true civilization was built could be overwhelmed by others, or even by excessive development of some "civilized" traits themselves. How was this to be avoided?

One of the means by which the dangers to civilization were to be avoided was, again, the family. Women, with their presumed special access to sentiment, could create in the home and in family life a structure in which rationality and order were "softened," made compatible with a wide range of human needs.[34] The family supplied the basic training and support for civilized behavior, exemplified and taught through rituals such as tea. Gentlemen did not smoke at tea or on other ritual occasions in which ladies were present. Women's presence and their presumed sensibilities required a behavior pattern that reminded men of their own need for self-control in other ways. Neither the elements of civilization based on desirable human propensities nor the harmonious coherence of such propensities could be achieved without extensive inculcation from childhood onward. This became, in theory and, by the nineteenth century, to a considerable extent in practice, one of the most important functions of the nuclear family. Whereas in the seventeenth century it would have been fair to say that nutrition, production, and training for productive skills constituted the main recognized social functions of the family, by the nineteenth century the family's role was much grander: to undergird civilization itself by producing civilized people.[35] Again, this was primarily the duty of women in families, and the most common employment opportunity for a respectable woman unfortunate enough not to have a family of her own was to assist other women who did—for example, as a governess. The tea ritual, therefore, was significant in part because, in celebrating the role of women in the family, it accentuated the importance of both as the foundations of civilized society. Like many other rituals of daily life in respectable families in the eighteenth and nineteenth centuries, tea was practice in civilized behavior—and it was consciously understood as such. It took a lot of tea, sugar, and milk to keep civilization going.

DOMESTICITY AND CONSUMPTION

Studies of English and American households before the eighteenth century have revealed that most families (except for the very richest) possessed relatively little in the way of durable goods.[36] If we contrast households of the late eighteenth and early nineteenth centuries in Britain and America with those of their immediate ancestors at approximately the same social levels, we see that a veritable revolution has occurred. The number, the variety, and the value of household objects have increased severalfold. What has happened?

Economic historians have traditionally emphasized two linked factors: income changes (increases in aggregate amount or in breadth of distribution, or both) and the Industrial Revolution, which is held to have reduced prices for consumer goods and to have supplied some of the increased or redistributed income.[37] As we saw in our earlier discussion of textiles and their relationship to industrialization, these factors are vitally important in explaining the "consumer revolution," especially in the long run, but they are not sufficient by themselves. As Carole Shammus has demonstrated, the significant changes in consumer behavior clearly began well before any conventional dating of the Industrial Revolution, and the key factor directly leading to that behavior was not the amount of family income, but families' decisions to spend their income on certain commodities—and, if necessary, to do the things required to procure more disposable income: to work harder, to situate themselves more fully in the market economy by demanding wages entirely in cash, spending less on drink or charity, accepting the discipline of regular employment, purchasing securities rather than hoarding savings, and so forth.[38]

We could, if we wished, call this interest in objects "materialism," although that term conveys a tinge of moral disapprobation that may obscure our understanding of what was going on. For it was clearly not a question of people wanting to own objects just for the sake of ownership. The commodities that they purchased for their homes had meanings—had, in other words, cultural significance. Obviously, items that could be used or displayed in a house did not possess equal significance, and particular items had meaning only in certain places. In the late eighteenth century, a suit of armor did not belong or have meaning in a parlor; a piano did. Household objects were material enough (and certainly required material processes to produce, distribute, and repair them), but it was not their materiality, their "thingness," that made them desirable, but rather the cultural meanings that they possessed.[39]

As we have seen, changes in the dynamics of European consumption in the eighteenth century were shaped to a considerable extent by the development and interaction of all of the cultural contexts we have discussed—a process that expanded greatly when the contexts were connected together to form the culture of respectability. Both by itself and in connection with respectability, domestic femininity was one of the most influential of all because it informed the setting within which a large part of the consuming was done: the household. It thus gave meaning and motive to much of the increase in demand that accompanied industrialization; it created a substantial part of the motivation for people to adapt their behavior as workers, investors, employers, and managers to the patterns of the advanced capitalist market and industrial production; and it offered a setting within which behaviors essential to an orderly capitalist society could be defined, given meaning, and reproduced over successive generations.

There are a number of ways in which the construction of domestic femininity affected consumption. For example, new forms of childhood were constructed in respectable families, in which children were to be nurtured and civilized as one of the family's main functions. The establishment of separate rooms for children and their activities, the multiplication of items of specialized dress for children at different ages, and above all the emergence of a context of childhood centered around manufactured toys purchased in shops—all these had significant economic as well as social and cultural effects.[40] Another example is the appearance of the structured activity called "shopping" in the last quarter of the eighteenth century in England. This development was much complained about at the time by some men who feared it as an assumption by women of unprecedented economic power, while others encouraged it for a variety of reasons.[41] From the perspective of this study, it can be seen as a direct consequence, not only of the role of women as household managers, but even more of their responsibility for maintaining the domestic ambiance idealized by the new cultural context. This required that informed female shoppers make constant visits to shops.[42] Domestic femininity also had an effect on eating customs and schedules, as we saw in the case of tea at the start of this chapter. As this was a cultural theater in which overseas imports were enormously significant, let us close the chapter by looking at another meal: breakfast.

BREAKFAST

In the sixteenth and seventeenth centuries, most Europeans took their main meal at midday, although where the middle of the day was held to fall varied considerably by region, social level, and occupation, and in any particular country the scheduling changed over time. In some areas and generally among people doing hard physical labor, the midday meal was eaten sometime in the late morning. In other regions and among the higher social orders, the main meal was at noon, in the afternoon, and sometimes in the evening. Almost everywhere, those who could afford it consumed a second, smaller meal, either around the middle of the day if the main meal were late or in the evening if the main meal were early.[43] The main meal typically took considerable time and possessed many ritual characteristics. Before about the mid-seventeenth century, breakfast, although recognized as an activity, did not exist as a meal in the sense that the others did.[44] It was not unusual for people to eat or drink something in the morning between rising and taking the main meal of the day, but it does not appear to have been a daily occurrence. Writing in the late sixteenth century, William Harrison says that Englishmen of all classes eat but two meals per day, in the afternoon and evening—except for children, who do not have the patience to wait so long after waking.[45] We know that Queen Elizabeth I regularly "breakfasted" on bread and beer upon rising in the morning as a health measure, but did not treat it as a meal.[46] In Catholic countries, the question of whether or not a priest who consumed a liquid (such as cocoa) with sugar in it before saying Mass "broke fast" (and thus committed a mortal sin) was seriously debated, which probably means that the custom was fairly widely practiced but also implies that such a breakfast was not regarded as a real meal. If it were, there would have been no question to debate.[47] As late as the 1660s, Pepys (who recorded in his diary on most days where he ate his meals and what he had) refers to his "morning draught" or snack only occasionally. He usually consumed this "breakfast" in a tavern or on the street, not at home, and as often as not without company.[48]

Even in Pepys's day, however, breakfast as a meal in which one consumed particularly "healthy" foods and drinks was putting in an appearance in parts of western Europe. An elite fashion for consuming a morning meal as a support for health was in evidence by the 1650s in the Netherlands. In 1655, the wife of John de Witt, chief executive of Holland, wrote to him reminding him to eat breakfast for his health while he was away from home.[49] We could interpret this new custom as one that developed at the intersection of the contexts of gentility (it was clearly an upper-class practice in its origins) and virtue (it displayed regard for health, and the fact that breakfast was taken early may have suggested that the breakfaster had duties to perform that required him or her to rise long before dinner). It also fit very nicely into the context of luxury, as it permitted the consumption of exotic, good-tasting items (chocolate, tea, and coffee as drinks; sugared and spiced bakery goods as foods) under virtuous circumstances.[50] Breakfast may have been regarded as a healthy meal (we still portray it as such, although what is healthy about it is now explained somewhat differently), but it was not supposed to be a trial to consume. With its heavy emphasis on sugared items and pleasant tastes, it was a morning treat, a comfort to assist in the process of rising from bed.[51]

Although in the 1660s Pepys was still eating or drinking any odd thing in the morning simply because he was hungry, the notion of breakfast as an identifiable daily occasion and as a key to health spread rapidly. By the second quarter of the eighteenth century, Lord Chesterfield was formally (by letter) inviting his young son to breakfast with him, and Samuel Richardson was having Clarissa Harlowe describe breakfast as a ritual meal with as much meaning and importance as tea.[52] Indeed, in *Clarissa* we can see that breakfast was already closely associated with the context of domestic femininity.

Like tea, breakfast was intended to be eaten in the home and, without involving as elaborate a ritual, came to have a similar place in the culture of the family. It incorporated many of the elements of respectability and, symbolically at least, attempted to reconcile some of the contradictions among them within a structure of meaning informed by the domestic and the feminine. For example, the luxurious aspects of breakfast were made compatible with the aspects connected to health and virtue not only by the assumption that the foods and drinks consumed were supposed to be good for you, but also by the fact that comfort and health were provided in the setting of the family and through the agency of the household's women. Unlike tea, from which small children were often excluded and which the husband and father frequently did not attend because of business, the model eighteenth- and nineteenth-century breakfast was something taken together, or in informal sequence depending on time of rising, by everyone in a family. The husband-father "presided" (unlike at tea), but the wife-mother was still a central figure because she either provided the meal herself or took responsibility for its provision by the servants.[53] Conversation among all participants, even the youngest, was acceptable. There were nevertheless tensions present, among other reasons because the implicit code of conduct was not as clear-cut at breakfast as at tea. The senior male had the option, if he wished, of dominating the conversation or enjoining silence, of acting as Oliver Wendell Holmes's "Autocrat of the Breakfast-table." Tea was a ritual celebration of women's role in the family and in the maintenance of civilization; breakfast was a representation of the role of the family itself as a vehicle for physical and spiritual nurture, in which conflicts between members were more likely to emerge than at tea. Conducting a properly run breakfast was essential to the way in which families maintained their respectability—not, as with tea, to the rest of the world, but rather to themselves.

Breakfast was also a major consumption activity. To understand this, we have only to make a quick inventory of the material items present at a family breakfast of the late eighteenth or nineteenth century. We have already mentioned the items that are ingested: chocolate, tea, coffee, breads, rolls, spiced cakes, sugar, butter.[54] Not everything eaten or drunk was of extra-European provenance, but enough of it was that one sometimes suspects the India companies of having invented the modern breakfast in order to sell their products. (They probably did not.)[55] Although it is possible to argue that the same amounts of food and drink would have been taken at other meals if breakfast had not existed, this is far from certain. Three (or four, counting tea) rather than two significant opportunities for food intake in a day may very well lead to more eating overall. In any event, the nature of breakfast, especially its emphasis on featuring whatever passed for healthy eating in a particular era, surely influenced the distribution of demand in favor of those sorts of items. If there were not breakfast today, would there be much of a market for breakfast cereals?

But breakfast (like tea) involves much more consumption than simply eating or drinking. Consider the implements that are used: china plates, porcelain cups, steel or silver-plated utensils, and so forth. These are obviously far more than is necessary to put a little morning sustenance into one's system. They represent a substantial outlay for doing breakfast properly, whether or not one expects company from outside the family. Benjamin Franklin makes an interesting reference to breakfast in his *Autobiography* when he describes his early married life:

> For instance my Breakfast was for a long time Bread and Milk, (no Tea) and I ate it out of a twopenny earthen Porringer with a Pewter Spoon. But mark how Luxury will enter Families, and make a Progress, in Spite of Principle. Being call'd one Morning to Breakfast, I found it in a China bowl with a Spoon of Silver. They had been bought for me without my Knowledge by my Wife, and had cost her the enormous Sum of three and twenty Shillings, for which she had no other Excuse or Apology to make, but that she thought *her* Husband deserv'd a Silver Spoon and China Bowl as well as any of his Neighbours. This was the first Appearance of Plate and China in our House, which afterwards in a Course of Years as our Wealth encreas'd augmented gradually to several Hundred Pounds in Value.[56]

One supposes that the Franklins also moved beyond bread and milk.

One of the great growth industries of eighteenth-century Europe was the production of china—another well-known case of industrialization to manufacture a commodity initially imported entirely from Asia. The manufacture of steel and silver-plated flatware also expanded. Both porcelain and steel utensils were significant products of the early stages of the English Industrial Revolution—especially porcelain.[57] Although these industries responded to a vastly expanding demand that arose from all the meals in a day, not just breakfast, it is also true that the china, flatware, and serviceware for breakfast were specifically designed for that meal. If a respectable family could afford it, they maintained an entire set of items just for breakfast. If they could not afford to do so, the family's respectability would have been—at least in their own minds—questionable, and it would have been incumbent on the adult male(s) in the family to obtain the income necessary to rectify the deficiency. Thus, the fact that breakfast was, through its connection with the context of domestic femininity, an important signifier of respectability probably had a substantial effect on industrialization. Breakfast was one of the many new activities of the eighteenth century that led families to the acquisition of a multitude of new objects.

We should also consider the physical setting of breakfast: usually (when a family could afford it) a room set aside for the purpose or for that and a few other activities. Here again we are dealing with a specific case of a more general tendency: the assignment of functional specializations among the spaces in a house, and their clear demarcation from each other even when the functions performed in two or more separate rooms could actually be combined.[58] Why have separate dining rooms and breakfast rooms, for example, if all that happened in either were simply eating? But of course it was not just eating that occurred. It was the eating and drinking of different things, for different reasons, using different equipment, with different arrays of people present behaving in different ways. If it was possible to afford separate spaces as settings for these different activities, then respectable people would have them or at least aim to have them in the future. And, of course, each separate space required separate, specialized furnishings and decorations.

The context of domestic femininity was central to the construction of respectability in a great many ways. It defined the family as the foundation of morality and civilization, and thus of respectability. It represented the home as a physical and social setting within which other contexts were made conformable to each other: gentility with virtue, virtue with luxury (the "comforts of home"), rational masculinity with all of the others, thereby linking the culture of the home to the very possibility of respectability. It defined a social role for women that was as respectable (if not as powerful or interesting) as that of men. And it established, in the array of goods needed to maintain domestic respectability, an extraordinarily effective engine for demand creation.

7

RESPECTABILITY

The word *respectability* is a late-eighteenth-century coinage; its first citation in the *Oxford English Dictionary* dates from 1785. The primary *OED* definition refers us to the adjectival form: "The state, quality, or condition of being respectable in point of character and social standing."[1] *Respectable* is older. It has had a fairly wide range of meanings since at least the sixteenth century, the earlier ones generally caught by the *OED* entries "worthy of notice, observation or consideration" and "of comparative excellence; tolerable, fair."[2] Before the late eighteenth century, *respectable* did not convey a predominant emphasis on character or morality. It referred to status, and could also be used in the way we would say "respectful." Even *respectable*, however, does not appear to have been a particularly common word. Samuel Johnson's *Dictionary of the English Language*, published in 1755, contains several definitions for the word *respect* but none for *respectable* or *respectability*.[3] It is a fair assumption that if *respectable* had possessed any degree of currency in the mid-eighteenth century or had figured significantly in earlier English literary usage, Johnson would have included it.

By the turn of the century, when Jane Austen wrote *Pride and Prejudice* (eventually published in 1813), she found herself employing "respectable" frequently. Mr. Bingley's sisters "were of a respectable family in the north of England; a circumstance more deeply impressed on their memories than that their brother's fortune and their own had been acquired by trade."[4] Mrs. Bennet "had a sister married to a Mr. Philips, who had been a clerk to their father and succeeded him in the business, and a brother settled in London in a respectable line of trade."[5] A slight but interesting incongruity in usage, a certain degree of tension, shows itself in these passages (which are cited merely because they are the first two times "respectable" appears in the novel). The first could possibly be encompassed under one of the older definitions, but not the second. But neither is inconsistent with later definitions of the word, such as these from the *OED*: "Worthy of respect, deserving to be respected, by reason of moral excellence"; "Of good or fair social standing, and having the moral qualities regarded as naturally appropriate to this. Hence, in later use, honest and decent in character and conduct, without reference to social position, or in spite of being in humble circumstances."

Similar shifts can be seen in other European languages. In French, the equivalent words are practically the same as in English (*respectable* and *respectabilité*), as are their contemporary meanings. They do not appear to have been much used before the nineteenth century and perhaps indicate French recognition of British models for the new culture of respectability.[6] More interesting is the history of the words *honnête* and *honnêteté*.[7] In the sixteenth and seventeenth centuries, they referred to the array of qualities we grouped in chapter 2 under the heading of "magistracy" (probity, moderation, justice, and the like), but these qualities could be connected in the same usages with a variety of others, such as bravery, loyalty, and savoir faire. When Montaigne says that someone is an *honnête homme*, he appears to mean that the person is a man of spirit and that he knows the way of the world. Molière sometimes uses the term in similar fashion, and sometimes to describe a person who is virtuous, sound, and also well mannered or *polis*. Indeed, in the early eighteenth century, *honnête* translated into "polite" in English.[8] Pascal, on the other hand, specifically contrasts the *honnête homme* with the *galant homme*—the upright man with the outwardly polished man. It appears, therefore, that *honnête* and *honnêteté* covered a wide range of meanings within the context of gentility. By the second half of the eighteenth century, *honnête* most commonly referred to the individual qualities associated with the context of virtue. Diderot, for example, played with the word in this sense in *Le Neveu de Rameau*: "I see an infinity of *honnêtes* people who are not happy and an infinity of people who are happy without being *honnêtes*."[9] *Honnête* soon became a standard translation for "respectable."

A similar process can be seen in German. One of the German words that usually translates into the English "respectable" is *anständig*, with its associated noun *Anständigkeit* for "respectability." Until the eighteenth century, *anständig* meant "fitting," in the sense of physically fitting, like clothes, or adhering to a pattern. By the eighteenth century, it had come to refer to "the standard of behaviour expected of a person of breeding"—in other words, genteel or polite behavior.[10] By the second half of the eighteenth century, *anständig* was widely employed to mean "decent." Goethe used *anständig* for "'neat,' 'accomplished,' 'proper,' 'suitable,' 'comfortable,' 'well-mannered,' ... 'worthy,' ... 'honourable.'"[11] In fact, the list of Goethe's uses looks like a catalog of adjectives conventionally associated with respectability.

MODERN TIMES

Naming is not everything, and the histories of words do not always closely track the histories of the things they are supposed to represent. But names generally appear when there is a need for them, and in the late eighteenth century, European languages needed names to denote a cultural phenomenon that was both important and, as something to be referred to in discourse as a single item, new. To investigate what was happening, let us look in some detail at the source of the earliest citation for *respectability* in the *OED*: a novel entitled *Modern Times, or, the Adventures of Gabriel Outcast: Supposed to Be Written by Himself: In Imitation of Gil Blas*.[12] Its author (although he does not name himself on the title page) is John Trusler (1735–1820).

Trusler was a clergyman of the Church of England who made up for the inadequacy of his clerical income by writing and editing books for popular audiences, including an often-reprinted edition of Chesterfield's *Letters*. Judging from *Modern Times*, fiction was not his forte. Although as the title indicates Trusler attempts to reproduce the form of a picaresque novel, the spirit is absent. The hero-narrator is too straitlaced to convey much pleasure in the distresses or the peculiarities of the people he meets and, after the first few pages, too knowing to be naively ironical. Trusler's attempts at satire are labored. The plot serves largely as a way of tying together lengthy speeches of moral criticism on various aspects of contemporary society, some delivered by characters introduced for the purpose, others by the narrator, Gabriel Outcast. The novel is certainly not an unjustly neglected gem of eighteenth-century literature; its author is an archetypal hack, probably trying to imitate Smollett. On the other hand, *Modern Times* is filled with revealing observations about English culture and social attitudes in the 1780s, presented by a writer whose own attitudes tend to be highly conventional.

For one thing, Trusler pays close attention to innovations in language. Not only does he use new words himself (*respectability* for instance), but he takes note of linguistic novelties such as the term *shopping*.[13] In fact, he includes in the novel a clergyman whose real occupation is "neologist"; that is, an expert in the coining and use of fashionable vocabulary. The neologist is supposed to be an object of fun, an instrument for satirizing faddishness and pretension, but his presence (twice) suggests that Trusler considered the conscious production of new words to be a significant characteristic of his times.

As far as I can tell, Trusler uses "respectability" only once in *Modern Times*, in the advertisement to the reader at the very beginning. The author informs us that he "is very sensible that there are in all classes of life, men of honour and respectability."[14] Trusler does not indicate that the word is in any way unusual. We can assume that he took care, in the section that a prospective bookbuyer would probably read first, to avoid words that would not be understood or would be seen as excessively pretentious. Whether or not he actually invented the term *respectability* (which is unlikely but not impossible), Trusler certainly expected that it would be understood from its origin in *respectable*, in much the same way that his contemporaries understood *sensibility* from *sensible*. Of course, as with the sense/sensible/sensibility complex, not every meaning of *respect* or *respectable* is implicitly incorporated into *respectability*.[15] But in reading *Modern Times*, we can get an idea of the range of ways in which Trusler uses "respectable" (which he does frequently), and thus of what he probably expects his readers to understand by "respectability." The range of uses involves ambiguities and inconsistencies, but we can readily detect the links of kinship within a contextual family.

A fuller quotation of the passage in the advertisement that contains "respectability" reveals one part of the range. The author finds it necessary "in this age of slander and detraction" to declare that he is depicting "no particular person, his view being merely to lay before the rising generation the arts and deceptions of the generality of mankind. He is very sensible that there are in all classes of life, men of honour and respectability; but it must be allowed, at the same time, that there are not wanting men of the reverse disposition." Trusler makes similar points several times in the course of the novel. When Gabriel Outcast (fleeing a possible murder charge) is confronted by a band of "marauders," he starts to call them "rascals" but then reflects that there are rascals in every walk of life.[16] In the advertisement, respectability explicitly refers to good character and moral standing regardless of social status, the counterpoint to the rascality that is similarly (although much more generously) distributed among all ranks.

Only two pages into the novel, "respectable" appears in another form. The narrator introduces himself as "the only child of a very respectable, although not very opulent couple."[17] His father belonged to "the younger branch of a good family," with hopes of an inheritance but only a small current income. "Pride of blood" led the father not to put Gabriel out to trade, but rather "made him ambitious of bringing me up, as he called it, a *Gentleman*." Unfortunately for all concerned, Gabriel's parents die from smallpox and he is left without money or any marketable skill apart from his gentility. An uncle to whom he applies for assistance spurns him on the grounds that he (the uncle) had earlier recommended against raising the nephew as a gentleman. Let us see, says the uncle, how far a genteel education will take him without an income to go with it. This leads the narrator, whose real name is Wilbraham, to adopt the pseudonym "Gabriel Outcast." With a little help from the local vicar, he goes to London to seek his fortune.

In this instance, "respectable" refers to gentility based on birth and family, together with an implication that a certain kind of education (a liberal secondary education and training in politeness) goes with that status. But Trusler's use of the term is ambiguous, in a way that may reflect unresolved tensions in his own thinking. Gabriel's father is respectable (genteel) in point of birth, but also genteel in terms of self-image. He clearly has the option of educating his son to trade—which, as it is recommended by a senior member of his own family, is not likely to be seen as a source of dishonor to the family as a whole. The father chooses the genteel option for his own reasons, perhaps to bolster his view of himself as a gentleman, perhaps in anticipation of his inheritance. Trusler does not make it clear whether Gabriel himself would have lost his respectability had he been put out to trade or had he not been taught to be a gentleman. Although this passage, like others, seems to be critical of gentlemanly pretensions and training, at the end of the novel they stand Gabriel in good stead when he receives the inheritance his father had been expecting, enters Parliament, and becomes a government minister. Without the money, he would have no political career, but the money by itself would have been insufficient to procure him one without the education and bearing of a gentleman.

The ambiguity of the respectable/genteel usage appears in other ways. When Gabriel first goes to London, he finds a place as assistant to a Dr. Slashem, the corrupt proprietor of a school where the main lessons to be learned are that money talks and that "to live in the world a man must not be *too* honest."[18] Attempting to escape both the job and the attentions of the schoolmaster's wife and daughter, Gabriel looks through the employment advertisements in the newspapers. He rejects positions that involve labor (apothecary's assistant, for example) or require acting in public in a potentially demeaning manner, but answers an ad worded in this way: "Wanted a person of good address and gentleman-like appearance, to attend a few hours a day in a respectable employ, for which a good salary would be given."[19] He discovers that the position is that of auctioneer's decoy: someone who pretends to be a legitimate buyer and whose role is to bid up prices. Gabriel is offered the job and accepts, on the grounds that it will supply his needs, does not involve physical labor, and allows—indeed requires—him to act outwardly and to dress as a gentleman. As he has previously done in the case of the school, the narrator describes the deceits of his new occupation in considerable detail.

Here Trusler is consciously trying to build humor and moral criticism around the ambiguities of the link between "gentleman" and "respectable." A decoy's gentility is all show: clothes, speech, polite behavior—"gentleman-like," not really genteel. But what is unreal about it? Obviously, no derivation from a good family is required, although one might suppose that a large proportion of the pool of candidates would have such a background. But as to learned genteel behavior, how is that different from the training Gabriel received at his father's orders? Isn't the latter also largely a matter of externals? Perhaps the attribution of respectability constitutes the difference, as something that is internal to an individual as well as external and that has a foundation in good morals. But that possibility is subverted by the juxtaposition of "respectable" and "gentleman-like" in the advertisement, by the actual nature of the job, and by the fact that Gabriel, a gentleman of respectable family, knowingly takes the position.

Gabriel goes through a number of other jobs in the course of the novel's first volume, usually leaving because of some predicament. At one point, he becomes a "collector of news" for a partisan newspaper. The editor explains his task: "'You see, friend,' says he, 'what we want; you may try your hand, and if you can furnish us with the private intrigues of respectable families, you may be constantly employed.'"[20] Gabriel does exactly what is asked, only too well. He charges "a respectable person, of great rank, with high treason."[21] The editor is prosecuted and lays the blame on Gabriel, who has to "secrete" himself. Here, "respectable" appears to refer to well-known people and families enjoying public regard. The newspaper's aim is to show that these people (especially if they support the wrong political party) are unworthy of being respected, either on account of discrepancies between their public characters and their private behavior or because they have betrayed a public trust. In other words, scandal sheet reporting is predicated on popular acceptance of a fundamental component of the context of virtue: that fitness for public responsibility depends on constant demonstration of private morality. Trusler's use of the word *respectable* to denote persons who are supposed to conform to this pattern (and who are therefore vulnerable to the suggestion that they do not) indicates two developments significant for the future: the construction of a discourse of respectability around the context of virtue, and the employment of that discourse to expose hypocrisy, especially through irony.

An example of the latter is seen when Gabriel, having occupied himself with writing sermons for clergymen too lazy or ignorant to prepare their own, decides to pass himself off as a minister.[22] He goes to a "register-office" (brokering agency) to find a situation. He remarks: "As there are register-offices for a variety of *respectable* wants, such as, for houses, servants, whores, etc. so this is a register-office for parsons."[23] Trusler's intention is probably just to extract humor from undercutting the brokerage business (and the ministry), but the fact that he does so by playing on the moral connotations of the word *respectable* shows how peculiarly susceptible respectability is to this kind of treatment.

One other use of "respectable" is worth mentioning. On the occasion noted above when Gabriel flees London and is accosted by marauders, he discovers that they are not fundamentally bad fellows, just a trifle uncivilized—what with threatening to club people on the highway. Most are outcasts, like Gabriel. After hearing a speech by the group's "ruler" in which it is claimed that they have their own forms of honor that are morally superior to those of upper-class English society, Gabriel decides to join them. Only three months later, Gabriel is himself chosen to be their leader, "and I persuade myself from some salutary regulations I proposed and carried, that I placed the company on a more *respectable* footing than it had ever been before."[24]

Homeless, violent clubmen in the woods can be *respectable*? Is this something from W. S. Gilbert? (The previous ruler turns out to be a former high-class shopkeeper's assistant. He delivers the book's main attack on the iniquities of wine merchants, tea dealers, and china retailers. The marauders prefer to assault only bad people, especially smugglers.) Nevertheless, aspects of this joke are no laughing matter. Although the situation is ridiculous, in this case it does not appear that Trusler is using "respectable" ironically. He portrays the marauders as men with a natural sense of right and wrong who are willing to act on it. (There are no women in the gang until near the end of Gabriel's two-year stay; the women inadvertently undermine the moral solidarity of the group and are an important reason that Gabriel decides to leave.) Gabriel describes their society very sympathetically, as a sort of Rousseauian community. Gabriel's "salutary regulations" that make them more respectable have largely to do with the direction of the marauders' attacks. They agree to assault only "suspected" persons and to act "usefully" to the state. Their particular concern is to search out robbers and smugglers, criminals with whom the constituted authorities are too incompetent or too corrupt to deal effectively.

Again there is a public dimension to respectability here, but it is different from the one noted previously. It appears to involve the circumstances under which natural justice and morality, given direction by rational regulation, can break through corrupt institutions of conventional society that condone injustice and immorality. Trusler does not present respectability as a natural state. The marauders are in a natural state before Gabriel's arrival. Rather, respectability is a form of regulation—explicitly described as *self*-regulation—that creates an appropriate connection between what is best in the natural state and what society ought to be. There is ambiguity in this inference due to the silliness of the situation, the many possible readings of "respectable" that have already been suggested, and the fact that when all is said and done, the marauders are still violent men. With regard to violence, however, it is worth remembering that only a dozen years before *Modern Times* was published, a group of (mostly) respectable Bostonians, reacting to what they believed to be an unjust law enacted by a corrupt government, staged an act of ritual violence and dumped shiploads of tea (that great symbol of respectability) into their harbor. Seven years after the book was published, Parisians (by no means of the poorest classes) rioted over the high prices and unavailability of sugar, coffee, and tea—again, symbols of virtue and respectability.[25] Violence is not necessarily incompatible with respectability, if the violence is purposefully directed and reflects consensus about what is naturally right.

Trusler's book thus reveals a spectrum of intersecting meanings that covers much of the range of the nineteenth-century respectable/respectability complex, although ambiguities and inconsistencies among the various meanings are more apparent than they would be in later usage. This suggests a discursive pattern in the process of formation, without all the camouflage possessed by a mature discourse. The notion that respectability can be an attribute of people in all classes coexists uneasily with the idea that respectability is concomitant to gentility—a tension only intermittently relieved by an implicit redefinition of gentility to emphasize acquired manners and moral character. The redefinition is not consistent; sometimes Trusler suggests that the circumstance of being respectable arises mainly from a concern for superficial appearances. There are meanings of "respectable" that relate to public responsibility and behavior, but these, too, are neither wholly coherent nor entirely consistent. There are hints that "respect" requires a positive valuation of oneself by others as well as self-respect. These hints are not, however, pursued. Instances of ironical play with *respectable* anticipate the future, but they also appear to reflect Trusler's perplexity about the present—about the meanings of social distinctions and their relationships to moral standards.

Trusler was by no means the only writer of the 1780s to be confused by these matters, to sense a similar confusion among his audience, and to turn to irony and satire as ways of dealing with it. In the hands of Goldsmith and Sheridan, the result is high literary art, if not satisfactory resolution. In the hands of Trusler, the result is the humor in *Modern Times*, such as it is. Looking back, we can see that one of Trusler's difficulties is that he does not—probably cannot—distinguish between sociocultural analysis based on a descriptive, nonjudgmental approach to what he observes (what we might call "social science") and a moral analysis resting on a comparison between what he observes and a set of explicit or implicit moral criteria. Some of the leading minds of his day (Hume, Adam Smith, Kant) had developed ways of making the distinction and then of reconciling the two frames of analysis with each other, but their work and its implications had not yet been understood by most educated people. It is not surprising that writers like Trusler should often respond with irony or even a "paranoid" approach to inconsistencies among modes of social distinction, individual behavior patterns, and values.[26] What is particularly significant is that Trusler and others of his time sometimes went beyond satirical humor and paranoia to deal with these difficulties—not by means of systematic theory building, as in the social science of Hume and Smith, but by putting together elements of several of the cultural contexts that framed their perceptions of the social world. In so doing, they helped to build the new cultural context of respectability. The breadth of their comprehension of what they were doing varied, but few of them were wholly unconscious of its implications. So let us spend a little longer with Trusler, this time looking for larger patterns within which his usage of the words *respectable* and *respectability* was embedded.

One crucial pattern apparent from what has already been said is Trusler's continual attempt to connect notions of status with those of moral standing. Part of the inconsistency in his use of "respectable" arises from uncertainty about the nature of the connection. Nevertheless, Trusler seems to think that there has been, or perhaps should be, a marriage between gentility and virtue—with the latter bringing a substantial dowry. Sometimes Trusler simply implies that gentlemen should behave virtuously in their dealings with others, especially in public office. This is the note on which *Modern Times* ends, with Gabriel Outcast, now a minister of state, calling on gentlemen in government to behave with integrity.[27] But in other places, the argument is more complicated.

One instance comes in the reminiscences of Gabriel's predecessor as "ruler" of the marauders. At one time in his earlier life, the ruler had been servant to the son of a man with landed income. The son, who had no capabilities besides being a gentleman, was kept on a limited allowance by his father. The father grossly mismanaged the farms that supplied his income, thereby threatening to destroy his fortune and his son's future. The servant, therefore, had no moral qualms about suggesting a plan by which the son defrauded the father, took over the estate, and set up a regime under which careful management produced a modest but secure income sufficient to allow both father and son to meet their obligations and live as gentlemen.[28] Trusler gives no hint in this passage of irony or even mild disapproval of the course of action taken by the son and his servant.

Although it is difficult to reconcile the trick played on the father in this passage with strictly ethical behavior, the result is a situation in which the effects of the father's irresponsibility are neutralized and everyone is better off than before. The important point is that the status of being a gentleman must necessarily be tied to the possession of a moral character that encompasses a great deal more than traditional honor. Honor itself, both for individuals and for their families, is defined broadly to include living within one's means and taking responsible action with respect to the future. In this case, the son was both born and reared as a gentleman, but he must learn to behave as a manager of an estate, not simply its beneficiary. He must display moderation, industry, and the rest of the Franklinian virtues literally in order to remain a gentleman, for if he loses his estate, he will be in Gabriel Outcast's situation. Apart from maintaining fiscal credit, none of this has anything to do with *public* reputation or the exercise of political or hegemonic functions.

Apparently the same virtues can lead one to acquire and maintain status even if one is not born a gentleman. Early in the novel, Gabriel is a temporary inmate of a prison inhabited principally by debtors, whose spiritual needs are met by another prisoner, a "worthy" man. A bill of insolvency releases the debtors but not the worthy prisoner. The latter delivers a valedictory sermon to the debtors just before they are freed.[29] He reminds the debtors that the bill of insolvency does not forgive them or their debts. It is a political act "for the good of society. The more populous a nation is, the richer it becomes, and immuring a number of useful hands, is taking away so many beneficial members of society."[30] They are still morally bound to repay the debts for which they were imprisoned, even though they can no longer be forced to do so and even if their imprisonment was due more to the malice of their creditors than to their own faults. They must restore their credit and attain good standing in the community, which they can do by being honest and working hard. If you follow his advice, the worthy prisoner tells the debtors, "[You] will rise above your enemies, become wealthy and flourishing, be good men, good citizens, and an ornament to your country." He does not say that they will thereby become gentlemen (for all we know, some of the debtors may be gentlemen already in terms of birth and breeding), but clearly the status that counts is that which arises from solvency, wealth, goodness, and citizenship. The education and polish of a gentleman appear to be at best secondary attainments.

Of course, this speech is delivered in jail by a prisoner, in a chapter much of which is devoted to detailing the iniquities of the "trading magistrate" (businessman—justice of the peace) who has illegally incarcerated Gabriel while he decides whether or not to bind the latter over for trial for theft. The magistrate is venal and a moral disgrace to his office, but he is financially very successful and is held in high esteem because he is efficient at prosecuting crimes in cases in which he can obtain a monetary return from doing so.[31] However, neither by his behavior nor by his origins (he was once a "rag-man") can the magistrate be considered a gentleman.

Where this leaves us in terms of delineating Trusler's precise idea of social order is difficult to say; he probably doesn't have a very clear one. Nevertheless, he strongly suggests that, ideally, high status and the possession of a wide range of virtuous character traits should be closely connected. And even if the world cannot conform to the ideal, at least individuals can live virtuously and successfully in it. At the very beginning of *Modern Times*, the narrator says of the adventures he is about to relate, "if they have not a tendency to make men philosophers, they, at least, will teach them worldly knowledge, and shew them, that he is the richest and happiest of mortals, whose resources are within himself, and who depends least upon the assistance of others."[32]

The "worldly knowledge" that the novel is supposed to teach is constructed not just in terms of individual behavior and morality, but also in terms of groups. *Modern Times* is essentially a sequence of judgmental descriptions of aspects of contemporary British life—in particular, urban life in London. Trusler's subjects are sometimes social types such as gentlemen, fashionable women, "foreigners," and so forth, but these are collective representations of individual behavior patterns. Trusler gives us no real social class analysis. What he does focus on is occupations and professions. Through Gabriel's experiences and through speeches given by various characters, Trusler dilates on the deceptions practiced on their clients and customers by teachers, clergymen, physicians, lawyers, government officials, auctioneers, shopkeepers in particular trades, and so forth. His criticisms of the professions follow the conventions of a significant satirical genre of his time: physicians make illnesses worse and are more interested in status than in qualifications; clergymen are lazy and often ignorant; lawyers twist the legal system in order to extract fees.[33] Trusler's criticisms are not original, but they are interesting because of the implicit framework around which they are constructed. Apart from physicians, whom Trusler (the author also of a popular guide to diet and health)[34] treats as completely useless, what is wrong with professions and other occupations is that many of their members behave immorally, which, because of competition, forces the rest to do the same in order to survive. People are as they are: some are good, some are bad, most can go either way. But within a competitive, commercial occupation, those who are good must often limit their goodness to their nonprofessional lives, and those who could be good have no professional encouragement to realize their potential.

Trusler does not give a comprehensive solution to this problem, but the elements of one are implied. Rejecting commerce and competition is not among them. Trusler may complain about the tricks of shopkeepers, but he does so from a perspective that reflects their outlook—as, for example, when he criticizes the new practice of "shopping" in which women of fashion waste the time of retailers by examining shopgoods in detail with no intention of buying, or when he says that the cost of the gentry's governance of local society is borne by the tradesmen who supply them on credit.[35] Rather, the answer appears to lie in two areas: the adoption by *customers* of an appropriate set of virtues, and self-regulation by professions to encourage appropriate behavior among their members and to exclude the unqualified and inherently vicious from their ranks. If customers (especially ladies of the *ton*) were not so given to vanity, if they considered their needs rather than their fantasies when they bought things or contracted services, if they differentiated between luxury and comfort, if they exercised rational judgment and adjusted their purchases to their means—if, in other words, they acted within the scope of the context of virtue—the iniquities of bad professionals, tradesmen, and vendors would be exposed. Competition would force the rest to advertise their high ethical standards and embody them in their commercial practices. (In other words, competition is morally neutral. Whether it results in good or bad depends on the moral context that is consciously constructed around it.) And if occupational groups would organize, not to control production or the market but to promulgate virtuous behavior, that would go a long way toward improving society as a whole. Again, these conclusions are suggested rather than programmatically articulated, but they follow from Trusler's discussions of occupations.[36]

What Trusler gives us, then, is a series of connections between the context of gentility and the context of virtue. The connections mostly take the form of restructuring gentility in terms of virtue and, when aggregated, reflect some of the most essential features of the new culture of respectability. The connections involve not only individuals and certain broad status groups, but also occupations and commercial collectivities. What about other cultural contexts related to respectability? In fact, luxury, rational masculinity, and domestic femininity are all there, connected to each other, to gentility, and especially to the context of virtue.

Trusler reflects the conventional positions in the eighteenth-century debate on luxury—practically all of them. He suggests that many of society's ills can be traced to excess of passionate sensuality, possessiveness, vanity, and fashion.[37] At the same time, Trusler realizes that the purchase of luxury goods—that is, goods desired because they give pleasure in one way or another—is the basis of commercial life, and he clearly has no objection to the power, wealth, and national self-esteem that British commerce has produced.[38] As in other areas, he makes no attempt to reconcile these views formally, but in several places he discusses the factors that were, in his era, already becoming the approach to luxury embodied in respectability: comfort and convenience.

During one of his several flights to avoid arrest, Gabriel is cold and depressed. He exchanges his shoebuckles (he no longer has the shoes that go with them) for a warm coat. "I put it on, and instantly forgot my situation. So much happiness does a little degree of comfort create!"[39] When Gabriel marries his true love, they set up housekeeping in London on a limited income (provided by her father) and manage the conveniences of genteel life without the excesses. They have but one footman and they purchase only the amount of tasteful furniture needed for the modest maintenance of their status and comfort.[40] Moderate, virtuous attention to convenience and comfort are acceptable. "Luxury," in its traditional sense, is excessive and potentially vicious attention to much the same things.

Trusler has a great deal to say on the related issues of femininity and domesticity—none of it particularly original. His representations of women are mostly negative, but so are his representations of men. As we saw in the story of Gabriel's band of marauders, women in general are a threat to the coherence of society because they distract males from men's common purposes, but this unfortunate circumstance is not deliberate and could presumably be controlled by discouraging women from participating in serious social activity. Trusler directs most of his comments toward particular types of women (shoppers, ladies of fashion, prostitutes, actresses), in a way that simultaneously presents his general attitudes and subverts them.

Trusler says that women who "shop" (visit a retail establishment without a fixed intention of buying there) or whose purchases are informed by fashion and novelty are irrational, ignorant of true value, and easily imposed on. Proprietors of china shops, for example, hoodwink their female customers into exchanging their good old china for new stuff by playing to their shallow knowledge and their interest in the latest aesthetic fashions.[41] So much for Trusler's own aesthetic sense and, presumably, that of the china retailers whose triumphs over "stupid" women he relates. He appears to be describing the revolution in midvalue dinnerware accomplished by Josiah

Wedgwood, Wedgwood's competitors, and their many discerning customers.[42] Trusler seems to think that mere age gives value to china, and so he represents a major economic and aesthetic phenomenon of his time (one that we customarily regard in a positive light) as an example of female irrationality and ignorance. Similarly, just after accusing women shoppers of not knowing the value of things, he repeats what is obviously a retailer's complaint about women of quality who deliberately go shopping plainly dressed and not in their carriages so as to avoid being imposed upon by shopkeepers. After expressing the complaint, Trusler seems to have realized that this behavior was not consistent with his portrayal of women shoppers as fools. He tries to deal with the inconsistency by claiming that the behavior is irrational in a broader sense. Shrewd ladies, "instead of going in their own carriage, will pay four shillings for a hackney coach, to save two-pence a yard on a dozen yards of ribband. In a word, they owe this all to their pride, vanity, and parade."[43] Apparently, ladies take pride in a bargain—or perhaps in beating shopkeepers at their own game? One suspects that the ladies in their hired coaches were not, in fact, just undertaking single transactions, but rather using their mobility and anonymity to engage in the subversive activity of comparison shopping.

Trusler clearly does not like the idea of women possessing any degree of independence, although he usually articulates this attitude in terms of sympathy for women forced into a situation of having to look out for themselves. Prostitutes are at the mercy of unscrupulous men (especially magistrates who arrest them in order to be bribed); actresses, though they may enjoy an apparent freedom, are equally vulnerable and can do little about it; women of fashion are the slaves of their own and their husbands' silliness. Modern young women, he says, are forced into immodesty and threatened with the loss of their virtue by current fashions, both in dress ("low stays, narrow tuckers, naked shoulders, and short petticoats") and in the gender of persons providing services to ladies ("men stay-makers, male hair-dressers, menmidwives, and their preparatory visits, all serving to inflame the mind and rouse those unruly passions that would otherwise be asleep").[44] Fashion is not so much a product of feminine weakness as it is a danger against which women need to be protected.

Against these portrayals of female types can be set Miss Wildman, a young lady whom Gabriel eventually marries (and who dies shortly thereafter). Early in the novel, Gabriel saves her from a fate worse than death and is rewarded by her father, who gives him a job as his valet.[45] The Wildman family is wholly respectable in the modern sense; indeed, the father's fondest wish is to see his daughter married "respectably."[46] Both in her father's household and in the one she creates with Gabriel, Miss Wildman is an active member of the family, assisting her husband or father by managing servants and in performing the central tasks of entertaining guests, making social calls, and purchasing. Major buying decisions are shared, with the father or husband having the last word but under a tacit obligation to defer to the woman's judgment (except, presumably, when that judgment is clearly faulty). In many ways, Miss Wildman's domestic role is consistent with those discussed by Amanda Vickery in her study of Lancashire gentlewomen.[47] But Miss Wildman never acts truly on her own. She accepts the guidance of responsible men, in part because she realizes that on her own she would be in danger of making major errors.[48] A properly behaved, self-consciously virtuous woman functions most effectively and is happiest in a well-structured domestic setting in which ultimate responsibility belongs to a man. The ideal domestic setting suggests the sociability of the band of marauders after Gabriel takes over: a mutually agreed framework within which natural sentiments and natural morality are strengthened, protected, and given purpose. In the case of the household, however, this requires direct attention to the inherent weaknesses of women—some of the same weaknesses that destroy the marauders' sodality when women join them. Trusler does not say as much about the reciprocal process whereby women's sensibilities are supposed to moderate the less desirable aspects of male character—an important element of domestic femininity and of respectability. Nevertheless, the idea of the family household as a primary means of socializing everyone in it is certainly present.

One can also detect aspects of rational masculinity in *Modern Times*; for example, in the assumptions about men's roles vis-à-vis women that are embedded in the descriptions of domesticity we have just discussed. There are descriptions also of the structural features of the culture of rational male discourse, such as coffeehouses, clubs, and newspapers.[49] We can derive implications of rational masculinity from many of the things and people Trusler criticizes. But Trusler presents even less of a coherent view of rational masculinity as a whole than he does of the other contexts of respectability. Perhaps Trusler was influenced by sentimental novelists such as Richardson, who tended to downplay the significance of male rationality and emphasize female sensibility.[50] Perhaps he was uncertain, not so much of his own masculinity as of his relationship to the culture of rational male conversation. Or most likely, he simply assumed that his readers comprehended and accepted the context and would apply it to understanding his criticism of modern culture.

Enough of Trusler. We have seen that his novel is interesting not just because it contains an early use of the word *respectability* but also because it gives us a great deal of information about the ways in which respectability as a cultural phenomenon was being put together in Trusler's time—by hundreds, maybe thousands of people in Britain and thousands more in other western European countries and their colonies. Using some of the hints we have derived from Trusler and from earlier chapters, we can now try to describe the new context of respectability as it entered the nineteenth century. We will concentrate primarily, although not exclusively, on Britain because British society appears to have taken the lead, from the mid-eighteenth century onward, in the delineation of respectability.

RESPECTABILITY, SOCIAL STRUCTURE, AND INDIVIDUAL STATUS

In the nineteenth century, the word *respectable* was used most often as an attribute of persons and of families, occupations, and organizations with regard to their social standing. Such usage is suggested by the quotations from *Pride and Prejudice* earlier in this chapter: "respectable family"; "respectable line of trade." One of the most notable features of the culture of respectability was its distinctive presentation of social structure, the one toward which we saw Trusler groping and which we have interpreted as a marriage of the contexts of gentility and virtue (with a bit of luxury thrown in). The marriage involved, among other things, a redefinition of much of the terminology of gentility to correspond to notions of status in the world of respectability. This was confusing, both for nineteenth-century people and for historians since then. Many terms (*gentleman* and *lady*, for instance) also retained their earlier meanings because modified but largely autonomous versions of the context of gentility continued to exist alongside respectability well into the nineteenth century.

Let us look first at some of the implications of respectability for relationships between *individuals* and social structure. We can start by comparing the meanings and connotations of words that derive from *respect* (*respectable, respectability,* and so forth) with those of words developed from *gentle* (*gentleman, gentlewoman, gentry, genteel, gentility,* and so on). Up to the eighteenth century, as we have seen, a "gentleman" was almost always presumed (whether it was true or not) to have been born into a gentry family—a lineage or descent group that passed aristocratic, although not necessarily noble, status from generation to generation.[51] Certain behaviors were expected of a gentleman: protection of his honor, proper attire and manners, some attention to fashion, but technically these were outward signs of something more basic: gentle birth and breeding. The behaviors suggested a person's status as a gentleman, but they did not *constitute* the status.[52] A gentleman who did not behave as a gentleman was still a gentleman, although he could fall into the condition of disgrace through misbehavior. Not all bad behavior led to such a fate. There were even offenses against the criminal law that were not considered disgraceful. One such offense—dueling—was in fact expected of a gentleman when necessary; disgrace arose from failing to do the right thing when presented with a challenge or in the duel itself. Failure to pay gambling debts was disgraceful, but failure to pay a tailor's bill was not.[53] In the former case, a gentleman owed a debt of honor to other gentlemen. In the latter, he owed a commercial obligation to a person who was by definition not a gentleman and therefore had no honor. A disgraced gentleman could be redeemed by doing something extraordinarily gentlemanly, or even just by cleaning up his act. A gentleman who persisted in doing disgraceful things was likely to be suspected quite literally of not really being of gentle parentage at all.

Of course, as we saw in the case of Samuel Pepys, reality was a great deal more complex than theory. Gentility was often contestable ground, which gave considerable scope to those who could employ the weaponry of wit and fashion. Regardless of what the conventions said, some people could, in fact, insinuate themselves into the gentry by behaving appropriately. The "dandies" of eighteenth-century Britain were often examples of this phenomenon. But despite the complications of the real world, the proposition that people were born gentle was still fundamental to the most commonly held ideas of gentility throughout much of the eighteenth century.

As a status designator, "respectability" bore some resemblance to gentility. It could be perceived as inherent in particular individuals and groups, and as such it could have great practical meaning. In her study of law enforcement in mid-nineteenth-century Kent, Carolyn Conley has shown that the primary criterion determining how people were treated by the criminal justice system (for a first offense) was whether or not they or their families were accounted "respectable."[54] Like gentility, respectability could be seen as a concomitant of wealth, or at least of income sufficient to afford the commodities that were the symbols and instruments of the status. At the same time, as with gentility, wealth was seldom viewed as the legitimate essence of respectability. In both cases, the imputation that money constituted the "reality" behind the ascription of status normally implied an accusation of hypocrisy, a suggestion of moral or social criticism.

Nevertheless, respectable status was constructed on a profoundly different basis of assumptions from gentility. A person was respectable if he or she *acted* respectably. Unlike an eighteenth-century gentleman with regard to his gentility, a respectable man (whether a gentleman or not) certainly ceased to be respectable if he were seen to have stopped behaving as a respectable person should.[55] It was perfectly possible for someone to be a gentleman (in the older sense) and not to be respectable. Nineteenth-century novels were full of such persons, who were particularly to be feared as threats to the virtue or the fortunes of ladies.[56] Behavioral criteria were also different. If a gentleman was required to pay his gambling debts but not necessarily his tailor's bill, a respectable man was expected to pay the latter and not to incur the former (or at least not frequently). Like gentility, respectability could be contested discursive ground, but it was a distinctly different ground. The term could be used to indicate someone's high social status, but in principle almost anyone of any class except the lowest could be respectable—and more important, regard himself or herself as respectable. People in the lowest of all classes, the dependent poor and their criminal cousins, could not be respectable. It was presumed that most of them were where they were because they were vicious, and even if they were merely unfortunate, the fact of their relying on charity implied that they had insufficient respect for themselves to be respected by others.[57] But with that exception, respectability provided a distinction to which anyone could legitimately aspire—both in his or her own estimation and in that of other people. Traditional gentility possessed no such capacity. Respectability could be contested with regard to the categories of families who were presumed likely to contain and produce respectable members—for that was the basis on which the notion of a respectable family rested, as opposed to the hereditary designation of gentry families. But regardless of whether or not one believed that some particular family or social group was "respectable," one's belief was a either a response to observed behavior or a reflection of one's estimation of the probability that the family or group would foster appropriate behavior. The contest was *not* over lineage or inherited status.

These very real distinctions between gentility and respectability were sometimes obscured in the nineteenth century by the continued, if attenuated, existence of an autonomous context of gentility and by the fact that the discourse of respectability borrowed part of the terminology of gentility. Members of aristocratic families, especially in countries with titled nobilities, maintained the option of using the term *gentleman* or its equivalents to refer to hereditary gentility and also of adhering to some, at least, of the behavioral patterns of traditional gentility. Adopting these options, however, became increasingly inconsistent with the rest of social reality and exposed those who did so to criticism and ridicule. Even in the highest social circles in Victorian Britain, the terms *gentleman* and *lady* in practice tended to take their meanings from the context of respectability.

These phenomena are reflected in the novels of Anthony Trollope. In the overtly political novels that feature the aristocratic Pallisers, the duke of Omnium—the head of the family—appears as an exemplar of the old gentility in both attitude and behavior, and often as a figure of fun because of that. Significantly, it is his son, Plantagenet Palliser, who possesses (and is possessed by) genuine respectability and who succeeds in politics, becoming chancellor of the Exchequer and then prime minister. A central character in *The Prime Minister* (the book in which Plantagenet achieves that office) is Ferdinand Lopez, a charming but dishonest would-be stock manipulator. Lopez is accepted as the gentleman he presents himself to be because of his manners, appearance, and pretended wealth (although not by the discerning), even though his origins are unknown. When his true character emerges, he is not only disgraced, as a born gentleman would be, but also no longer accepted as a gentleman.[58]

Trollope, of course, was writing about the mid-nineteenth century. But even in the eighteenth, as we saw in the case of Trusler, the relationship between gentility and respectability with regard to individual social status was complex and often confusing. There was more to it than just gentility's tendency to define the elite in terms of birth as against respectability's bias in favor of criteria of moral standing. In essence, respectability prescribed not a particular social hierarchy, but a notion of what the shared characteristics of worthy people in similar places within a social order should be, however the social hierarchy might be constituted. We should probably see the ideal of social organization within the context of respectability (at least in the late eighteenth and early nineteenth centuries) as an overlay that could be placed on existing social structures without necessarily mounting a direct challenge to them. This was true regardless of whether the social structures were construed in terms of orders based on birth and traditional ascribed status or of wealth, or both together. Indeed, part of its appeal may have arisen from the way it allowed people to avoid the age-old issue of whether status should be based on birth or on means.

The ideal could be summarized in this way: Social order is necessary and social differentiation inevitable. Virtue, consisting of an array of characteristics including truthfulness, honesty, moderation, attention to duty, adherence to standard tenets of morality, and so forth, is necessary among some people at all levels and in all segments of society. The practice of virtue should be encouraged, searched for, rewarded, and trusted at all levels. High status, whether seen in terms of belonging to the upper classes or with regard to one's place within any stratum, implies an obligation to act in a particularly virtuous manner. Manifest virtue by itself may or may not be a vehicle for rising from one level of society to another, but it ought to be at least one of the obligatory qualifications for any such movement. In any event, at all levels and in all areas of the social order, manifest virtue, accompanied by evidence of intelligence and knowledge, should be respected—that is, should be grounds for deference from social inferiors and for trust on the parts of peers and superiors. The condition of being respectable implies recognition by others of the virtues a person has displayed and of the worthiness of the person to be entrusted with significant duties that go beyond his or her own interests, or that might (hopefully rarely) require that personal interests be set aside for the general good.

Although this social ideal is most easily presented as a pattern to be applied by people to other people, much of its power arose from the fact that it was very readily internalized. A great many people in the late eighteenth and nineteenth centuries believed themselves to be respectable, acted so as to prove their respectability to themselves as well as to others, and reacted vigorously against suggestions that they were not respectable. One of the best ways to sell something, whether a commodity or a political program, to people who identified themselves as respectable was to create a link between the thing to be sold and such people's respectable self-images. One of the best ways to antagonize such people was to announce that they were not in fact respectable, despite their claims. This was the way revolutions were made.

Apart from its role in allowing people to define themselves and others satisfactorily in relation to a hierarchy, a social perspective framed in terms of respectability could be enormously useful to those actively engaged in the public sphere. It provided a set of criteria for judging some part or all of the prevailing social order—a tool of great value to politicians, social critics, and journalists. It could be used to justify the existing social order, if that order could be described favorably in terms of respectability. (As we have seen, the increasing employment by noblemen of "aristocrat" as a term of self-description in the eighteenth century is an example of this use.) It could also serve as a basis for reform—not so much of structures, institutions, or status groups themselves (although that was possible) as of the behavioral standards, educational norms, and selection criteria applied to the people who belonged to them.

The potential of respectability for supporting reform derived from its uses in judgment and justification. If some significant element of society failed to match the criteria of respectability, then it needed to be reformed until it could be justified according to the same criteria. This kind of reform did not necessarily require social reorganization, rearrangement of classes, "leveling," or other radical responses to perceived inadequacies of social structure. Because the focus of respectability was on actions, reformation of morals and improvement of behavior might suffice, usually together with a revision of the process by which the leading personnel of social groups were trained and promoted. It was possible in the late eighteenth and nineteenth centuries to envision more truly structural reforms within the framework of respectability, but normally it was more useful for reformers, critics, politicians, and social commentators to emphasize a reform of behavior. Thus the Wesleyans, the Evangelicals who spearheaded the British anti-slavery movement, and many other reformist groups that helped to develop the political use of respectability aimed not at reorganizing society, but at improving the ways people acted within it.[59]

One might argue, in conjunction with a tradition going back at least to Halèvy's interpretation of Methodism, that repectability was an inherently conservative historical force in terms of its political implications. It certainly *could* be used in a conservative way (despite the fact that it essentially redefined a large part of the traditional basis of European social hierarchy). But one could also argue on similar grounds that most eighteenth-and early-nineteenth-century cognitive patterns with political implications were conservative—even some of those that came to be part of the "revolutionary" tradition in Europe.[60] People do not normally adopt cultural patterns for informing their daily lives that emphasize violence and danger, or even discontinuity and uncertainty. They do so when they become convinced that it is necessary, and their adherence to such a pattern is notoriously short-lived unless it can be quickly revised to accommodate order and stability.

What is particularly interesting about respectability is that it contained, under the right circumstances, enormous revolutionary potential—as was demonstrated almost as soon as it was put together as a cultural context. This potential made itself apparent when substantial numbers of people who believed themselves to be respectable and thus to be worthy of being respected (by the state, for instance, or by their conventional social superiors) perceived that they were not so regarded. It can be argued that a significant part of the motivation of participants in the American and French revolutions derived from this source. Such motives could not easily have been organized into concerted political action without the existence of a cultural pattern that made sense of them. One might also suggest that, without the existence and concurrent articulation of respectability, it is unlikely that modern Western democratic ideology would have been created in the late eighteenth century because many of its fundamental terms would have been operationally meaningless.[61]

The implications of respectability for social structure also provided a framework around which individuals (almost exclusively men) could construct careers. That respectability played such a role in the nineteenth century is hardly a revelation. Sober, responsible young men who displayed good character by adhering closely to the behavior patterns of respectability were the ideal Victorian employees, the people who would "go far." They wore uniforms—clean, starched collars, suits, hats, and so forth—in earnest of their respectability. In the early eighteenth century, ambitious young employees who dressed in the fashion from which the respectable Victorian work uniform developed (that is, who wore clothing that tried to proclaim the gentility of the wearer) tended to be suspected of lack of seriousness, of wastefulness and social presumption.[62] With the emergence of the culture of respectability, behavior that had previously created tensions between the desire of nonelite men for status and self-esteem and their ability to create a career now could be seen as a key to achieving all aims. In this and other ways, respectability converted what had once been signs of a claim to high birth status (a claim that was easily ridiculed) into signs of moral competence. It validated moral competence as at least the equivalent of birth as a basis for claiming regard and deference from others. Respectability was of course also useful to employers as a means of maintaining desirable standards of behavior among their employees. At the same time, however, it implied at least a theoretical obligation on the part of the employer to show some respect for employees who deserved it.

RESPECTABLE FAMILIES

Family and *home* were central terms in the discourse of respectability in the late eighteenth and nineteenth centuries. Home and family constituted not only the appropriate sphere of women's activity, but the fundamental structure on which much of the respectable world was supposed to rest. Because the culture of respectability absorbed essentially the entire context of domestic femininity that was described in chapter 6, the present discussion can be limited to some of the implications of that context for respectability as a whole.

Respectability heavily emphasized an image of the family as an entity devoted primarily to educating its members in moral behavior and to sustaining their virtue. Respectable people were, in essence, the products of families that performed these functions well. Thus, for real families (except, perhaps, those at the very highest and lowest levels of income and prestige), status depended to a large extent on the ability of the family unit to provide evidence that it lived up to the image. Some of the evidence was derived from actual performance. Badly behaved children, unruly adolescents, and young men or women who went bad all suggested that their families had not done their jobs properly and were perhaps not worthy of much respect. Other evidence was collateral, featuring as criteria a number of common notions about how households were supposed to perform their moral and educational missions. A respectable home and its inhabitants were clean. Respectable people were properly dressed—modestly, as modesty was currently defined, fashionably in the sense of being neither far ahead of current fashion nor far behind, and appropriately for the circumstances—under none of which were they to show disrespect for themselves or for others by not being properly attired. The respectability of a family, and thus an important element of its status, depended on its members being clean and well-dressed in *public*. Equally important, the self-esteem of a family, which derived to a large extent from its members' belief in their own respectability, depended on the same things, whether in public or in private.

In reality, of course, the functions of the family household were vastly more numerous than the ones emphasized in the discourse of respectability. From many standpoints, the role of the family as society's most important unit for commodity consumption is particularly significant. This role was framed by considerations of respectability, including its status implications. As we saw in chapter 6, families manifested their respectability, both to themselves and to the rest of the world, not only in dress but in essentially all the things they bought and used, as well as the ways in which they bought and used them. Simply purchasing a lot of things did not make a family respectable, especially if the things bought were not in common good taste or if they implied adherence to values not consonant with the moral element of respectability. Respectable families in the nineteenth century had to concern themselves with the complicated task of reconciling income to fashionability and taste according to a calculus that was not entirely clear and never static.

Part of the task was to provide a wide range of forms of sensual engagement within a context of luxury that needed to be constantly reconciled to all the other contexts that defined respectability.[63] A respectable family could not purchase paintings, furniture, textiles, or drugs overtly connected to sexuality, but the home was expected to provide a variety of sensual experiences that suggested eroticism or that sublimated sexual meanings—all part of ensuring that the home essentially monopolized sexuality and luxury. As a result, respectable late-eighteenth- and especially nineteenth-century household furnishings were notoriously replete with romanticized sensual associations (oriental objects; overstuffed furniture, especially in public areas where adults of both sexes mixed) or aesthetized references to sexuality (the famous anthropomorphic furniture legs covered by skirts; paintings and statues of nude human forms legitimated by being "art"). Comfort was a primary goal in buying goods for home use—comfort justified by adherence to rules of taste and virtue that precluded sinful luxury and by the role of the home as the proper center of sensuality and emotion.[64] Convenience was also an acceptable reason for buying commodities for home use or for employing servants. Time thus saved could be devoted to the better performance of the family's serious functions. Buying gadgets for their own sake, like hiring servants in order to display wealth, was suspect behavior, but purchasing convenience was appropriate for a respectable family that could afford it.

The respectable home was thus not only an essential structural element of a respectable society; it was also a stimulant for economic demand of unprecedented dimensions. The two roles were closely linked, both in theory and in behavior—a result, in part, of the linking together of the contexts of gentility, luxury, and virtue within the culture of respectability.

RESPECTABILITY, INSTITUTIONS, AND PROFESSIONS

As we saw in Trusler, the term *respectable* also attached itself to associations, organizations, and institutions. The eighteenth century, especially its later years, was an era of accelerating institutionalization in Europe and America. Many informal voluntary associations acquired formal structures, many businesses adopted complex, permanent organizations, and a wide array of new or revised forms of political institution appeared, from the modern political party to the liberal state. Respectability played a discernable, if secondary, role in the shaping of several types of institutions, especially business organizations. It did so mainly by creating the desirable possibility that an association could be considered "respectable" in much the same way a real person could and by laying down a pattern of behavior appropriate to a respectable institution. One of many reasons for restructuring a business partnership or a casual social group into a formal institution was the desire to enforce and present respectability.

For certain types of institutionalization, however, respectability was crucial. One of these was the process of "professionalization"—the movement to institutionalize or reorganize certain occupations in order to improve their standards of performance and to raise their reputations with the public, thereby enhancing the incomes, the status, and the self-regard of their practitioners. Another was the establishment of public associations for the advocacy of particular causes, especially those of a humanitarian nature. The most famous of these associations were modeled on the anti-slavery associations of Britain and the United States, which campaigned for political action to achieve their aims. The role of respectability in humanitarian associations is a very large topic that needs to be covered in a different study. In the present chapter, we will concentrate primarily on professionalization. First, however, we should look at some of the more general relationships between institutionalization and respectability, which we shall do by focusing on business.

Business Institutions

In the seventeenth century, chartered business organizations had made great efforts to proclaim their standing in terms of the existing context of gentility. The English East India Company and the Hudson's Bay Company described themselves as "honorable," not only in their official titles but also in the discourse of their directors and employees.[65] The usage may have implied a great many things (the noble status of some of the stockholders or the companies' exercise of sovereign rights over territory, for instance), but it served mainly to indicate that the companies claimed significant national standing on the grounds of institutional "birth" through royal charter. The Netherlands East India Company was actually a federation of several local "chambers," each a major source of wealth and pride for the city or province in which it was located. Pieter van Dam's *Description* of the company goes into seemingly inordinate detail in discussing the ordering of the representatives of the chambers when they enter, participate in, and leave joint sessions and the many disputes, obviously causing rancor for years, between Amsterdam and Zeeland over these matters.[66] The issues of precedence that exercised the European nobility were replicated in institutional behavior and self-image within the company. The United Netherlands was noted for the importance its citizens gave to collective dignities and provincial rivalries and for the adaptation to organizational use of the language and the cognitive framework of gentility.[67] Van Dam's discussion suggests that these were not trivial matters, but rather a significant part of the way institutions operated within Dutch society.

The chartered companies were a new feature of western European commercial life in the early modern period and a direct result of the widening scope of national government. Under such circumstances, it was natural that the companies would look to the primary context of status signification at the national level—gentility—for cues about presenting themselves. In the eighteenth century, however, most of the proliferation of business enterprises in western Europe took place outside the formal structure of the national state. (This was true in many countries but especially in Britain, where chartered companies fell out of favor during the first quarter of the century.) Among the typical forms of unchartered enterprises were the firm and the membership organization. Lloyd's insurance exchange is an example of the latter.

Although the owners and managers of businesses sometimes attempted to hallow the history of the company,[68] for the most part they were concerned to attach the trappings of gentility individually to themselves. The organization itself was seldom discussed as hereditarily genteel or honorable. Rather, it acquired its status (apart from market status, which resided in profitability and capital) from two sources: the social standing of the people who were identified as its primary customers, and the reputation it had for virtuous dealing by its managers and employees.[69] While in the former sense, a firm was sometimes said to be "genteel," this was a claim merely to being worthy of the patronage of the gentry—and by the nineteenth century, that meant that the patrons dressed, acted, and spent appropriately and that (perhaps) they were therefore allowed more than the ordinary amount of patience in the matter of settling accounts. In both the former and the latter senses, the term that came to be used most frequently to denote positively the status of a business organization was *respectable*, which meant that it had a respectable clientele and that its policies caused its members and employees to act respectably. The moral values and the attendant behavior (actual or reasonably predictable) of directors, employees, and customers thus supposedly underlay the organization's claim to status.[70]

That these values and favored behavior patterns are, for the most part, *useful* for the conduct of business is undeniable. A customer who is treated with respect is more likely to return than one who is not. An employee who believes in his or her own respectability and who shares thereby in the status of the firm is probably less likely to steal and more likely to be loyal. A firm that has a reputation for being respectable may be more likely to pay its debts than one that does not. But it seems unlikely that these patterns were *initially constructed* so as to be useful in this way, that the culture of respectability was formulated by employers mainly to keep their employees honest and to attract customers. Manifest utility was probably only one of several motives leading managers to fit their organizations into a cultural context of respectability. Desire for status and self-esteem was at least equally important. Much of the commercial utility of acting and thinking respectably was embedded in a more general public acceptance of respectability as a pattern for ascribing status, for acting, and for thinking.

Respectable business institutions were not unique to Britain in the late eighteenth and nineteenth centuries. In France, with an aristocratic tradition so strong that it survived revolution and informed the creation under Napoleon of an entirely new, parallel nobility, claims to traditional gentility by the owners of businesses were correspondingly strong, but in general the phenomenon seems to have been much the same as in Britain.[71] The Netherlands was also similar, except that, perhaps because the institutionalization of business started somewhat earlier in the Netherlands than in Britain, many of the characteristics associated in Britain with respectable firms were being attributed to leading Dutch family businesses quite early in the eighteenth century.[72] The only thing missing was a distinctive term. In Germany, the continued viability and aggressiveness of aristocratic culture in the nineteenth century meant that, while firms (like that of the fictional Buddenbrooks family) adopted common European notions of respectability, their owners were strongly tempted to present themselves as gentry in a traditional sense.[73]

Professions

If respectability was a matter of secondary importance to the institutionalization of business, it was central to professionalization. The context of respectability defined much of the moral (as opposed to the technical) aspect of the "higher standards" that the professions adopted in the eighteenth and nineteenth centuries. It served as the framework around which a profession's public reputation was constructed. It provided the criteria according to which professionals, individually and collectively, measured their status and esteem. The were some national differences among Britain, the United States, France, and Germany, but on the whole, professionalization has been relatively uniform in the West since the eighteenth century.[74] This has been due in part to the rapidity with which innovations in professional culture and organization have been taken up in countries other than those of their origins, and partly to the fact that the primary cultural framework of modern professionalism—respectability—was itself very homogeneous. For convenience, we will concentrate on professionalism in Britain in the eighteenth and early nineteenth centuries.

As it happens, this very topic is the subject of an excellent recent study by Penelope Corfield.[75] Corfield concentrates on the three ancient learned professions of law, the clergy, and medicine, with attention also to education and a few others. Her main aim is to test some of the prominent dictums concerning professions, including Foucault's notion that power constitutes knowledge (that is, that the people with power construct "knowledge" as suits them best), Francis Bacon's assertion that knowledge *is* power, and the belief that professionalization is a conspiracy to concentrate in the hands of a small group of experts the power and income that arise from possessing a monopoly.[76] She demonstrates that reality, in the case of Britain between 1700 and 1850, was much more complicated. Although power was an issue, professions that depended on specialized knowledge were not restructured primarily to allow their members to stake out a claim to dominance in society as a whole, nor did their restructuring in fact produce hegemony over the rest of society. Consumers of professional services "had their own agendas" and refused to be putty in specialists' hands.[77] (I think that if Corfield had focused on Germany in the early nineteenth century instead of Britain, she might have found intentions closer to Bacon's formulation, although not to an extent that it would have invalidated her main point.)[78] The enhancement of income is always a consideration with people who sell goods or services in a market, but self-esteem and public regard appear to have been at least equally important objectives, not only as means to power and income, but as goals in themselves. The particular changes that constituted the "professionalization" of the ancient professions—the organization of associations that kept records on members and certified qualifications, conscious improvements in standards of practice and in the education and selection of neophytes, the establishment of codes of professional ethics, and efforts to exclude marginal practitioners from public acceptance as members of the professions—all took place in the full light of publicity, under constant criticism from satirists and the public in general. The formulation of professionalism in the public sphere meant that public expectations about both technical and ethical standards tended to inform the process in practically every instance.

Which raises some questions. What were these public expectations, and why did anyone in the professions care about them? The higher professional ranks (physicians, barristers, and clergymen of the Church of England) had seldom done so before the eighteenth century. These people were at least notionally gentlemen, often by birth and usually by ascription. In each case they had a legal monopoly on access to the most honorific, and usually the most remunerative, posts in their lines of work. Only degree-holding physicians could belong to the Royal College of Physicians in London, with its lock on the carriage trade in health care. Only barristers could become judges. Only ordained, university-educated Anglican clergy could obtain publicly supported livings and promotion to bishoprics. Why should they now care how they were perceived in public or want to change the well-established structures that supported their status and incomes?

One can more easily see why members of the "lesser" branches of the professions—the attorneys, surgeons, apothecaries, and dissenting clergy who had never been considered gentry and were not expected to possess a genteel education—might be concerned about their images. Attorneys (lawyers who handled most of the work of the legal profession but were not permitted to appear before courts or become judges) had especially bad reputations.[79] In England, surgeons were still organized into the same corporation (guild) as barbers until 1745, and apothecaries were not fully recognized as more than a marginal retail occupation, much less a health profession, until later than that, despite the fact that they provided most of the medical care in the country.[80] In a society in which status was distributed on the basis of gentility, to be permanently regarded as (at best) not gentle must have been a daily insult if one thought oneself entitled to better. But why should one think of oneself as so entitled, or hope to get anyone else to agree?

Corfield, like most other historians of the professions, does not directly answer these questions. Her main concern is to respond to the "power" and "conspiracy" interpretations of professionalism—which she does very effectively by demonstrating the significance of self-esteem and desire for social status as motives for professionals to institutionalize their occupations along new lines. She has little to say about why these motives became particularly important in the eighteenth century or why they were framed as they were—apart from general references to tendencies during the period toward a restructuring of the social order along class lines. However, if we look at the points in Corfield's book where she discusses motivation and touches on the cognitive framework of professionalization, we perceive an interesting discursive usage on her part: the words *respectable* and *respectability* appear again and again at the crucial moments—undefined, largely unanalyzed, but assumed to convey significant meaning.

For instance, Corfield remarks that eighteenth-century professionals strove for "self-definition and organization," but that one of their problems was that there were no clear boundaries to their terrain. "Respectable practitioners competed with 'irregular' rivals, who were denounced as 'quacks.'"[81] But surely, that is an important point, not just a difficulty. The principal "boundary" of a profession, as professionalism emerged in the eighteenth century, was the line between the respectable and the not-respectable practitioner, which in the case of medicine was increasingly reinforced by reference to technique and training. "Crucial in the doctors' search for respectability was the need to distance themselves from the untrained 'empirics' and outright quacks."[82] Not until the nineteenth century, however, could they convincingly distinguish their methods as "scientific"—the ultimate technical answer to "quacks." The key to "self-definition" for a professional was to position one's occupation and social description within the boundaries of respectability—"respectability" not as a vague set of attributes, but as a historically specific, meaningful cultural entity. This was true for lawyers as well as doctors. In discussing the decision of a group of attorneys to organize their profession during the first half of the eighteenth century (the first step in the process that eventually produced the Law Society—the solicitors' professional association), Corfield remarks: "Respectability was indeed the desideratum and that could not be achieved without some regulation within the profession."[83] Corfield also emphasizes the relationship between professional registration and respectability. When she interprets the publication of the *Medical Register* in 1783 as an important event in defining the profession of medicine, she describes the 4,592 physicians, surgeons, and apothecaries it listed in England and Wales as "the respectable leaders of the profession."[84]

With regard to the nonconformist clergy and the beginnings of their search for professional acceptance, Corfield says that in the early eighteenth century "the leading churches—Presbyterians, Baptists, Quakers, Congregationalists—grew in respectability rather than in great numbers."[85] It was precisely the ability of the nonconformist denominations to fit themselves into the culture of respectability (of which Wesley was one of the most prominent "makers") that permitted their clergy to present themselves as professionals in the same category as the clergy of the Established Church. It helped other professionals as well: "Regular church-going was one means to prove respectability" for eighteenth-century doctors.[86]

Several other examples could be cited, but the point is clear enough. When Corfield wants to explain the kinds of motivation and behavior that led to the restructuring and institutionalization of the professions in Britain, she tends to employ the words *respectable* and *respectability*. This is not an accident, I think. For one thing, similar terminology is used by some of her sources, and in a highly significant manner. Corfield cites Adam Smith (hard pressed, like most academic economists since his time, to find a way of fitting his own line of work into a production-based analysis) to the effect that professional activity is based on trust, for which not only money but "respect" is returned in payment.[87] One of the prime aims of professionals is to appear to be worthy of the trust of their clients and the public, and thus to be respected. The best way to appear to be worthy is, in fact, to *be* worthy, which requires a fairly exact idea on the professionals' part of what the public respects. But even without cues from the sources, looking at the reasons that Corfield uses the vocabulary of respectability when she does opens up a whole world of historical and cultural meaning—a world that has not been examined very closely in the past.

What has just been said is obviously not so much a criticism of Corfield as of a common tendency among historians to take respectability for granted as a vague, general concept rather than an object of study in itself. In fact, although interrogating Corfield's use of respectability allows us to take her analysis in some cases a little further than she does, it is usually in directions she has already suggested. We can see this if we return to some of the questions that were raised previously about the institutionalization of the professions in Britain.

What were the public expectations to which the professions were responding, and why did the senior ranks of the established professions care about these expectations? Apparently, as Corfield states several times, the public wanted professionals to be *respectable*, and senior professionals found it necessary to respond to this desire—for practical reasons and in order to maintain their self-esteem. Senior professionals perceived a need to be confirmed in their self-ascribed (and, doubtless, sincerely felt) gentility. They found in the eighteenth century, however, that they could not do so by simply asserting their status in manners, dress, and lifestyle (although they were criticized for doing that to excess).[88] They had also to connect their status claims to a set of beliefs, ideas, images, and practices that would make them worthy of trust. The price of not doing so? Expulsion as a group to the margins of *public* regard. As we know from recent histories of the hereditary upper classes of Britain in the eighteenth century, such a fate was a real possibility even for the titled aristocracy in the last quarter of the eighteenth century, despite their possession of vastly more power and wealth than the professionals.[89] For the latter, the danger was even more acute. Were they to be considered publicly irrelevant, it would have meant that they could not have participated effectively in the extended conversations of the public sphere—which was increasingly the criterion of elite status.

In other words, at the core of the processes through which they modernized and institutionalized their professions, English physicians and barristers sought to convert their assumed gentility into a social status (still often referred to as gentility in the eighteenth century) that was defined in fact (and from the late eighteenth century, in name) by *respectability*. They justified their elite status through demonstrating the practical virtues that would lead the public to trust them, both as individual providers of services and as people to whom public responsibility could be safely assigned. In our terminology, they linked gentility to the contexts of virtue and rational masculinity. They established codes of ethics, systems of registration, and courses of study for entry both in order to convince the public of their technical expertise and as a manifestation of their respectability in the senses just described. With regard to the context of luxury, professionals (especially physicians) had to be very careful to appear to keep their standards of consumption within the bounds of acceptable "comfort" and not to indulge aesthetic or sensual tastes beyond what was considered respectable. Physicians, clergy, and various other professionals (but generally not lawyers) found that they could build public esteem by representing themselves as purveyors of "comfort" or "convenience."

So much for the "senior" professionals. Why did the "lower ranks" of the professions—the attorneys, the nonconforming clergy, the surgeons and apothecaries (and eventually the obstetricians and dentists)—believe that they could improve their status and material conditions by imitating (and often preceding) the better-established professionals in making themselves respectable through institutionalization? Again, the answer appears to lie in the existence of a *public* view of the world increasingly structured in terms of respectability. Persons worthy of respect were ones whose status derived from assurance of their virtues (including professional competence), which it was the prime function of professional institutions to certify. Unlike the senior professionals, who found themselves in a defensive position and needing to bolster their gentility, the lesser professionals perceived an opportunity to claim a gentility that they had never previously been very sure about possessing.

In the course of the eighteenth century, as the cognitive elements of respectability were articulated with increasing frequency and connected together in the public sphere, the resulting model of respectable behavior created a framework that people such as attorneys and surgeons and a great many others could acknowledge and imitate. This framework was, as we have seen, an inherent, constitutive part of the "public sphere" itself, and therefore an extremely powerful set of images in a world in which the public sphere was regarded as central to politics, business, and status. Although a significant part of the population was excluded from the pool of people who could conform to the public aspects of respectable behavior (most women, for instance), men who possessed a reasonable amount of income, appropriate manners (which did not have necessarily to be extraordinarily "refined"), and some education, intelligence, and command of the prevailing terms of intellectual discourse could present themselves as candidates for being considered "respectable." They would still, of course, have to demonstrate possession of the moral components of respectability. Assuming that they did, they could—within the framework of respectability—call themselves "gentlemen." That is, they were entitled to esteem themselves as members of a social and moral elite, and they could insist that others regard them in the same way. This was, in essence, what the attorneys, surgeons, and apothecaries were attempting to do by institutionalizing their professions. They were creating a framework for assuring the public and themselves of their genteel status and their right, both as professionals and as individuals, to participate fully in the public sphere.[90]

This interpretation has some significant implications. It helps to explain why the professions were rigorously exclusionary toward women—even more than in the past. As we saw in chapter 6, although women could be respectable in the proper setting and context, they could not be respectable and be direct participants in the public sphere. If the members of a profession wanted their profession (and themselves) to be regarded as respectable, they could not countenance the inclusion of women in their ranks. They had, moreover, vigorously to proscribe groups of allied or parallel practitioners that were typically composed of women.

The efforts of the physicians and surgeons to exclude and undermine midwifery are probably the best-known case of this process. It is traditionally explained in technical terms—as a result of poor health practices on the part of midwives and the appearance of properly trained (and incidentally male) obstetricians in the eighteenth century. There is some debate as to whether or not the "man-midwives" were in fact more successful than their female rivals in conducting safe births. There is, however, no debate about their success—against considerable resistance—in presenting themselves as the appropriate professionals in the field. As they were male and had the other qualifications for respectability, they essentially forced themselves into the ranks of the registered physicians and surgeons, because to have denied them entrance would have cast doubt on the claims of those professions and on their campaign against "unqualified" practitioners such as traditional midwives. By the mid-nineteenth century, most respectable women in western Europe and America preferred to have an obstetrician, or at least some sort of doctor, in attendance at childbirth; employing a midwife called into question the respectability of a woman and her family, for how could respectable people be so careless of their health and that of their offspring?[91]

Another implication of this interpretation of professionalization has to do with the analyses in chapters 4 and 5 of the relationships among respectability, the public sphere, and the formation of the bourgeoisie. The coming together of the elements of respectability created a powerful and attractive model of behavior and social cognition not just for professionals, but for a great many people who acted in public—including, but not limited to, those who operated in commodities markets, in politics, and in literary and artistic production. The specific interests of these people varied, but their common interest in public activity, as well as the opportunity that a display of public worthiness within the framework of respectability afforded for claiming a form of gentility, encouraged them to "buy into" that framework. This suggests, once again, that what defines the "bourgeoisie" or the "middle classes" of the late eighteenth and nineteenth centuries is (at least for men) primarily this common adoption of respectability as a mode of thinking and behaving. Markets and capitalism are important, as are many, many other developments in early modern Europe. But what defines the class that defines modern society, the class with regard to which all the other classes define themselves, is respectability.

8

C O N C L U S I O N

With its description of the new culture of respectability in the late eighteenth century, this book has completed its task. It has given partial answers to the questions with which it began, and partial answers were all that were demanded. One question concerned the nature of the changes in European patterns of consumption that took place in the seventeenth and eighteenth centuries. We have seen that they should be regarded as aspects of several highly dynamic contexts in early modern western European culture. How and why did these changes come about? For a large number of reasons, many of which had to do with the construction or substantial reshaping of the five cultural contexts on which we have focused and the way in which the contexts were linked together to form the culture of respectability. This is not to say that other combinations of events were unimportant. Clearly, without the technological developments that played so large a role in Europe's overseas expansion and industrialization, many, perhaps most, of the new forms of consumption could not have appeared. It is not at all clear that roughly equivalent forms could have taken their places. Had, for example, the technical capacity not existed for transporting large quantities of Asian textiles to Europe or for mass-producing substitutes for them in Europe, the European cultural patterns of which they were a part would have been, at the very least, fundamentally different. Similarly, the complex of developments that produced capitalism affected (and was affected by) changes in European consumption patterns. As we have seen, however, neither changes in consumption nor the cultural patterns in which they were embedded and which gave them meaning can be primarily understood as "products" of these extracultural factors. The cultural patterns that we have analyzed as aspects of contexts possessed as much (and as little) autonomy as capitalism and technology. They, not capitalism or technology, provided the templates for consumer behavior. Moreover, whatever the range of factors that account for the processes of economic and technological modernization in the early modern period, those processes were unquestionably shaped at crucial points by economic demand arising from changes in culturally embedded consumption practices—especially the ones addressed here.

GENTILITY, LUXURY, AND VIRTUE

The most important changes in three of the cultural contexts with which we have been concerned can be summarized briefly, beginning with gentility. Gentility was an array of aristocratic practices, attitudes, social ideas, discourses, and systems of material and behavioral symbols that centered around what it meant to be a gentleman or gentlewomen. Its main features had been established throughout western Europe by the late sixteenth century, when it became the most important means of identifying who belonged to the social elite, the most commonly used map of the battlefields of status, and a significant mode of political behavior. One of its principal features was the assumption that birth and family constituted the foundations of gentility, although in fact the context accommodated a considerable amount of uncertainty and competition over what gentle birth meant. It also incorporated (although not without inconsistency) the notion that the status of gentility was necessarily connected to genteel behavior, a large part of which involved consumption. One of the sources of the many changes that gentility underwent in the seventeenth and eighteenth centuries was an increase in the number, size, and wealth of social groups that claimed elite status. Another derived from the needs of people who, without necessarily claiming such status in traditional terms, wished to assert to themselves and to others their worthiness to be regarded favorably by peers, inferiors, and superiors. Yet another was a set of classic tensions inherent in the context of gentility itself, especially among the genteel behavioral modes built around magistracy, courtesy, and the pursuit of honor. The first third of the eighteenth century saw many conscious attempts to revise gentility from within, by reducing the dissonance among different modes and by advancing "politeness" and notions of duty and moral fitness as more significant markers of aristocracy than birth. These and other alterations had a profound effect. Among other things, they permitted gentility to continue to exist as a more or less autonomous cultural form into the nineteenth century while most of its elements were also incorporated—with somewhat different implications—into the parallel context of respectability. More important, however, were efforts to change gentility by connecting it with elements of other cultural contexts—more important both in their long-term social and cultural effects and in their implications for consumption. Among these developments was the articulation of modern conceptions of "taste" as criteria of gentility, which can be viewed as constructing a bridge between gentility and the rapidly changing context of luxury. They also included the adoption of models from the context of virtue as means of redefining the moral and behavioral aspects of gentility. From these and many other linkages among contexts, the framework of respectability was put together.

The context of luxury was even more dynamic and unstable than that of gentility. It incorporated a wide range of behaviors, discourses, and ideas related to sensual experience—especially, but not only, the sensual experience of commodities. In the seventeenth and eighteenth centuries, tensions that made the context unstable arose from a partial failure of the cultural devices that had in the past, however tenuously, accommodated traditional enjoyment of commodities to traditional views of morality and social order—at least for members of the European elite. Attempts to reconstruct or replace these devices took many forms. Several involved changes in already existing intersections with gentility, while others were intimately connected with the emerging context of virtue. "Taste" is an example of the former, while the emergence of modern notions of comfort and convenience are the most important of the latter. Most were incorporated into respectability by the end of the eighteenth century.

Although the context that has been designated here by the word *virtue* included terms and ideas woven together from many traditions of Western moral discourse, it would be misleading to present it primarily as a repetition or amalgamation of those traditions. The practices that developed within the context were, taken as a whole, quite different from anything that had been seen before, and the arrangement of articulated values that borrowed their forms of expression from moral traditions was novel as well. An unprecedented element of materialism runs through the context of virtue, a materialism formulated in such a way as to appear to be consistent with self-control and (to some extent) even self-denial. Also present is an individualism perceived as fully consistent with the common good. Model behavioral patterns emphasizing personal advancement in wealth, happiness, and sometimes social station are represented as supportive of morality and social order, not their enemies. To try to explain the feat of cultural engineering that produced these results as a recombination of traditions of moral philosophy or religion or as a development in intellectual history (whether or not responding to "deeper" changes in Western society) would be to miss one of its essential features: it was built up from the practices of large numbers of people who created a basic sense of what they were doing by manipulating physical objects and acting toward one another in what they perceived to be meaningful ways. The process by which the context was formed in the seventeenth and eighteenth centuries suggests that the creation of complex symbologies around certain ways of dressing and consuming certain foods preceded (and to a significant extent motivated) the efforts of intellectuals to reevaluate comprehensively the terms of moral discourse. A more or less similar process can be discerned in all the other contexts that have been examined, but it is most apparent in the context of virtue.

The aspects of the context that were used here to illustrate its nature and to explain its relationship to the consumption of overseas products had to do with health and cleanliness. Eating and drinking so as to maintain health, dressing in clean clothing (especially clean underwear), and keeping one's body clean were seen as good things in themselves. Evidence that a person did these things regularly was supposed to be evidence (both to the person himself or herself and to observers) of moral propriety, the basis on which trust should be given and could be claimed. Achieving material success in private life by virtuous means and consuming material goods in a manner that displayed virtue indicated that a (male) person was fit for public responsibilities. This way of understanding was central to the culture of respectability and profoundly important to much of what we understand by "modernity." That it was connected to the major economic changes of the early modern period is undeniable: it appealed to real and would-be members of new economic elites, and it provided strong justification for savings, investment, and consumption practices essential to the world of modern capitalism. But the context of virtue derived from many other needs besides these, and it meant a great deal more to the people who created and adopted it.

MAKERS OF RESPECTABLITY

The preceding chapters gave examples of "people who created and adopted" the contexts of virtue, gentility, and luxury. Before we go on to the other contexts, it might be useful to look briefly at a few examples of eighteenth-century people who contributed to the construction of respectability by creating linkages among these three. The examples that come to mind tend to be prominent individuals acting in the public sphere, but again, one should imagine thousands of other people doing similar things more privately, sometimes under the influence of better-known innovators or fashion leaders and sometimes acting as innovators on their own. For convenience, and in recognition of the leadership of Great Britain in the construction of the primary modes of respectability after about the middle of the eighteenth century, the examples are all Britons.

Lord Chesterfield (Philip Dormer Stanhope, fourth earl of Chesterfield, 1694–1773) was not the only contributor to the development of new modes of politeness in the eighteenth century, nor was he the most important builder of Georgian conceptions of taste. He was, however, unintentionally the author of the most widely read guide to behavior and education for men who wanted to be accounted gentlemen not on the basis of birth, but on the basis of taste and social savoir faire.[1] His letters to his illegitimate son were collected and offered for publication by the son's widow after Chesterfield's death. She and the publishers presumably hoped to make a profit from public interest in a recently deceased statesman and wit, but in fact both the fame of the *Letters* in the late eighteenth century and their popularity in the nineteenth and early twentieth centuries derived more from their advice about manners, conversation, and taste than from concern for their author. The advice was by no means followed exactly. Much of it represented the somewhat idiosyncratic views of an aristocrat on behavioral fashions that soon changed even among the aristocracy, and it incorporated a morality that many readers professed to find unattractive. But the governing assumption behind Chesterfield's advice—that he was writing for a person whose acceptance into genteel society and whose career had (because of illegitimacy) to depend almost entirely on display of gentility and taste—meant that the things Chesterfield said could be appreciated (whether accepted or rejected) by any man believing himself to be in a socially analogous situation (that is, unable to rely on birth as the principal basis of a claim to genteel status). There were a great many people in this situation in the late eighteenth century, and a great many more in the nineteenth century. The clear rationale Chesterfield gave for each of the practices he recommended made them readily understandable to readers and easily adaptable by them to their own circumstances. Thus, Chesterfield's notions of taste and of its role as a necessary emblem of gentility, while neither profound nor wide-ranging in comparison with others of his time, nevertheless had a profound and wide-ranging effect. They supported the idea that gentility was mainly something one acquired through learning, practicing polite behavior, and comprehending current aesthetic consensus. They also helped to create (or at least to articulate clearly) for Chesterfield's many readers one of the vital connections incorporated into the culture of respectability: the link between possessing significant status (still generally indicated by the terms *gentleman* and *lady*) and being able to discourse of sensual experience (verbally and materially) in the vocabulary of "good taste."

Daniel Defoe (1660–1731) supplied so many of the recurring archetypes of modernity (preeminently in the character of Robinson Crusoe) that it would be surprising if he were not also a significant maker of respectability. Defoe contributed to the construction of respectability not so much in his novels as in the highly successful self-improvement books that he wrote in the last years of his life.[2] In such works as *The Complete English Tradesman* (1725, 1727) and *The Compleat English Gentleman* (1729), Defoe developed views of the connection between gentility and the context of virtue that became an essential part of the discourse of respectability. These books were probably read as widely in the eighteenth century as his fiction.[3] They were rhetorically effective because they connected specific topics of personal interest to the reader (how to be a successful business person; how to be a gentleman) with Defoe's views of the proper relationship between social order and individual virtue. *Views* is the correct word, for Defoe's thinking on these matters was not wholly consistent—or at least the ways in which he presented it varied among and within the books. In this, too, Defoe anticipated the future. As we have seen, the relationship between status and virtue was also unclear and often ambiguous in the context of respectability later in the century. As in Defoe's writings, the absence of clarity was hidden behind a presumption of consistency.

One of the key features of Defoe's later writings is an engagement with the relationship between gentlemen and "tradesmen" (businesspeople). Defoe, who claimed to belong to both categories, heavily criticizes the former, largely on the grounds of behavior. While tradesmen are likely to be models of probity, diligence, industry, and care of resources, people who are born gentlemen are generally busy only at succumbing to vice and extravagance and are thus, by implication, no longer fit to rule. Although Defoe can be quite bitter in his criticism of the gentry, he does not advocate an overthrow of the social order by dispossessing them or replacing them with the "middle class." Rather, he emphasizes that the difference between the two groups lies in training and experience. If gentlemen would put their sons into apprenticeship with tradesmen, the sons would learn the practical virtues that commerce requires—virtues, incidentally, that Defoe describes in general categories (moderation, trustworthiness, industry) quite similar to Benjamin Franklin's, not in terms of specifically commercial desiderata. However, because a mercantile education does not provide all the kinds of training that a political elite requires and because there are necessarily certain moral deficiencies in tradesmen's practice (especially a tendency toward economy with the truth in conducting transactions), it is also necessary that a gentleman receive an appropriate gentleman's education. Defoe is not impressed with most of what passes for genteel "classical" education, but training in the more useful abstract subjects such as mathematics and in modern languages, morality, and civility are certainly needed. This is what *The Compleat English Gentleman* is about.[4] From one perspective, and some of the time, Defoe appears to be saying that a hierarchical society ruled by gentlemen is necessary, but that the cultural foundations of such a society need to be maintained by imbuing the gentry with practical virtues that are presently possessed by businesspeople: a marriage of gentility (more or less explicitly defined by Defoe in terms of magistracy and politeness, not traditional honorific behavior) with virtue of a practical kind.

However, Defoe also approaches the subject in other ways. For one thing, he advocates marriage not just of genteel and mercantile cultures, but also of people, which he says already occurs: "The ancient families, who having wasted and exhausted their estates, and being declin'd and decay'd in fortune by luxury and high living, have restor'd and rais'd themselves again by mixing blood with the despis'd tradesmen, marrying the daughters of such tradesmen as, being overgrown in wealth, have been oblig'd for want of sons to leave their estates to their female issue."[5] He pointedly wonders why gentlemen put so much emphasis on descent, when "the highest families begun low, therefore to examine it too nicely, is to overthrow it all."[6] Defoe also suggests nonbiological measures: opening the ranks of the gentry to successful tradesmen, establishing policy advisory boards made up of businessmen, and appointing retired merchants as magistrates—the last two not only on the grounds that such people have important technical knowledge, but even more because they are likelier than others to possess the qualities of magistracy.[7] At times, then, Defoe appears to want to amalgamate classes of actual people, not just their cultures. He claims that such revitalizations of the English aristocracy have occurred before. What he does not advocate is doing without a class of gentlemen altogether.

It is possible to interpret Defoe as claiming political parity with the traditional aristocracy for a distinct "bourgeois" or "middle class" elite. It would be consistent with more of his pronouncements, however, to say that he sees the essence of legitimate elite status as lying in the possession of certain moral and intellectual qualities and in the display of these qualities in public behavior and private practice. Inheritance of status and/or wealth is a natural part of social life, whether for aristocrats or for businesspeople. But the public good requires that those who, as a class, possess high status and therefore exercise public authority also, as a class, possess appropriate qualities that are derived not from birth, but from culturally embedded experience. The public (in the person of Daniel Defoe, the greatest publicist of his day) is therefore entitled to suggest that the contemporary culture most conducive to producing the desired qualities be appropriated for that purpose and harnessed to elements of other cultures as needed. His suggestion could be realized in several ways, but they all involve, as their most central feature, a cultural amalgamation that we have portrayed as an intersection between the contexts of gentility and virtue.

This does not mean that Defoe is insensitive to class antagonisms. His career was punctuated with snubs by his social "betters," and he shows his resentment frequently. The barriers that prevented him from being considered a gentleman by birth were not fictions. But instead of employing a discourse of antagonistic class interests, Defoe argues (in varying, sometimes inconsistent ways) in terms of a public good best realized by an elite defined in part by cultural qualifications—qualifications that he believes that he and others with a commercial background could meet. Social hierarchy is not inherently irrelevant or illegitimate, but it cannot be effective and legitimate unless its mode of operation—including the process of filling its upper ranges—is framed by a set of moral practices that does not derive from the hierarchy itself. Similarly, the fact that the behaviors Defoe identifies as embodying or promoting the right kind of culture are primarily commercial practices is not an accident. He is stating a case for a social and political order that makes adequate space for the market and its leading participants, and he clearly implies that the "failure" of the traditional gentry lies not only in their unwillingness to acquire the virtues the market instills but also in their consequent inability to prosper in the market. But again, the market, the new commercial economy, is not the overt center of Defoe's social view. That center is largely cultural and is defined primarily by a conjuncture of gentility with the peculiar moral framework of the context that is called here "virtue."

Another example of a prominent figure who created linkages among the contexts of gentility, luxury, and virtue is "Beau" Nash (Richard Nash, 1674–1761). Nash was commonly credited in his own time with having turned the city of Bath into the most fashionable health resort in England, a place where the families of aristocrats, professionals, and well-to-do businesspeople jointly participated in rituals of relaxation and enjoyment. Nash, a gambler and the official "master of ceremonies" of Bath, constructed the rituals in order to attract people of all those types (and their money) to the city. The result was not so much an amalgamation of classes through intermarriage or a lowering of the barriers against entry into particular status groups as it was the articulation of a set of practices and discourses that permitted people of different classes to interact comfortably, under circumstances that assured them of the respect they believed to be due them. That various participants in the enjoyments of Bath may have had different views of the nature of the classes to which they belonged was, under such circumstances, a matter of relatively little concern as long as everyone adhered to the same conventions of conversation, dress, and behavior—conventions supposedly established by Nash.[8] Nash contributed to the final elimination of distinctions between aristocratic and non-aristocratic "genteel" dress by prohibiting gentlemen from wearing swords (and boots) in the Assembly Rooms, significantly giving as his reasons the greater comfort of dancing without them and the inconvenience such impediments caused the ladies. He literally codified appropriate behavior for gentlemen and ladies in terms of convenience, comfort, and mutual respect. All paying visitors were supposed to be treated by all others as gentlemen and ladies, which meant essentially that if you were able to afford to visit Bath, dress properly, and follow Nash's rules, you *were* a gentleman or lady, at least while you were at Bath. Moreover, Nash insisted on arranging the entertainments and the physical amenities of the city in accordance with the highest contemporary standards of taste, and to make sure, he enticed to Bath the current arbiters of literary and artistic good taste. Nash (or Bath as a community of local entrepreneurs and transient visitors under the possibly mythical aegis of Nash) thus constructed for the city's "guests" a common gentility defined to a large extent in terms of the new, eighteenth-century standards of the context of luxury: taste, comfort, and convenience.

Of course, Bath also housed baths, which were the ostensible reason for visiting and, in most cases, at least part of the "real" reason. Much of the success of Bath derived from building its reputation around the conscientious pursuit of health. Attendance at the Pump Room was not an onerous duty, but it was expected and it ordered the events of the typical day during the season. Moreover, Nash advertised Bath as a location where *families* could go for health and recreation and where the vices associated with other watering places (gambling, prostitution, and other forms of debauchery) were, if not absent, then at least kept sufficiently hidden or in check that an atmosphere of virtuous innocence prevailed. Gambling took place in decorous circumstances under the scrutiny of Nash himself. Although gentlemen (including Nash) brought their mistresses to Bath, they had to do so discreetly. Freelance prostitution was proscribed. Jane Austen appears to have given an accurate description of the moral as well as the cultural ambience. In our terms, Nash's Bath thus embodied a network of cultural connections among the contexts of virtue (in fact, the particular aspects of that context that were emphasized in chapter 4), gentility, and luxury. It was quite literally a space in which respectability was consciously constructed, and it retained its role as a model for respectability well into the nineteenth century.

Finally, there is John Wesley (1703–1791), the founder of Methodism and a man whose influence on the behavior of people in his century and the following one has long been acknowledged.[9] At first glance, it might seem implausible to cite Wesley and Beau Nash as examples of the same historical phenomenon. Indeed, the two had a famous and highly antagonistic confrontation in 1739, toward the beginning of Wesley's great mission of conversion. (Wesley—according to his own report—came out on top.)[10] Unlike Nash, Wesley had nothing to do with the adaptation of gentility to virtue in the construction of respectability. He did, however, have a great deal to do with generalizing the context of virtue for application to all classes in society. He and other evangelical Christians provided much of the emotional and religious content of respectability, which not only legitimated the new cultural pattern but also imbued it with a force of conviction that leapt over many of its contradictions. In addition, he connected the contexts of virtue and luxury in a way that profoundly influenced consumption practices.

Wesley's contributions in these areas can be understood in part as results of his relationship with the Calvinist traditions of English Puritanism.[11] Wesley was attracted to those traditions and he wanted to rekindle a seriousness and a level of conviction in the Church of England that he thought had been absent since the effective dissolution of Puritanism, but he could not accept a strict interpretation of several central Calvinist doctrines. He agreed that God granted salvation freely to humans, without being influenced to do so by good works or the intercession of the church. He did not, however, believe that salvation was predestined for only a few elect, that there was no guarantee that the souls of the truly faithful were saved, or that most people had to be compelled by the authorities to behave themselves in this life. At the same time, he was repelled by "antinomian" notions that willing acceptance of God's grace, available to everybody, was all that was needed for salvation regardless of one's moral standing. It cannot be said that Wesley worked out his problems with Calvinism satisfactorily in terms of theology, but he did build a highly successful, attractive religious message around applying to them a form of "common sense" that he derived to a large extent from the contemporary contexts of virtue and luxury.

As we saw in chapter 4, the context of virtue as revealed in the writings of Franklin and Blankaart had a decidedly secular, rationalist, materialist cast, despite the influence of Calvinism that can be detected in it. Wesley essentially desecularized the context and brought to it a strong element of emotion and belief, without otherwise seriously disturbing its basic structure. A key feature of the context of virtue (one that became a central element of respectability) was the importance it gave to judgments rendered of a person by his or her peers, based on manifest demonstrations of the person's moral qualities in every visible aspect of life—including the use of commodities. A person's self-esteem and standing in the community were both supposed to depend on such judgments, quite apart from any status that might derive from birth or other forms of ascription. Wesley inserted this feature into the Puritan tradition. In place of the Calvinist process of watching oneself and others closely for signs of God's grace and of election (or the absence thereof), Wesley advanced his model of the Christian Life and his version of justification by faith, both couched to a large extent in terms of virtue, esteem, and respectability. Leading an upright life, under constant examination by oneself and others of one's religious community, was a necessary concomitant to accepting God's grace through faith and thus achieving salvation. Wesley provided guides to the Christian life in his many sermons and tracts, which often dealt with physical appearance, behavior in public, and the use of goods. A good Christian should display neither excessive concern for fashion and expense nor unseemly flaunting of apparent poverty, both of which manifested pride.[12] Clothing should be clean and maintained in such a way that its wearers will be respected by others and by themselves, and so that it will remind them of their duty to God. "Mend your clothes, or I shall never expect you to mend your lives."[13] It was, of course, Wesley who said that "cleanliness is indeed next to godliness."[14] A Christian family did not waste resources on buying fashionable edibles or too much food and drink, but it did not eschew the small comforts that could be afforded and that God provides. Wesley at first disapproved of tea (with sugar), but later changed his mind. In general, luxury (excess) was to be avoided, but moderate pleasure (comfort) was permitted if it took place in the context of a godly family and with the approbation of the community.[15]

Many more examples could be cited, and the ones that have been given could be discussed in much greater depth, but even these bare suggestions provide a perspective on the processes by which respectability was created. Individuals, sometimes as members and leaders of groups, sometimes playing roles in their families, sometimes acting by themselves in private or in public, made respectability. They did so in part by working within and modifying the contexts of culture through which the world made sense to them, and in part by connecting elements of those contexts with each other to create a new context. In none of the above examples can everything the subjects aimed at or accomplished be explained in this way. The cultural contexts we have specified were only a few among the many coherent aspects of the social universe that they actively confronted. Nevertheless, the contexts of virtue, luxury, and gentility played crucial parts in their acts of cultural construction.

RATIONAL MASCULINITY AND DOMESTIC FEMININITY

The two remaining contexts that have been discussed in this study were more complex and connected with a wider range of sociocultural factors even than the first three. Because it is therefore more difficult to describe their formation and their connection to respectability by citing brief examples, summaries will suffice.

Rational masculinity was a loose connection of quite varied cultural items that obtained a large part of its coherence from incorporating within itself certain attributions of ideal characteristics to the male gender. The formation of the context was deeply affected by and, once it occurred, strongly influenced many of the major historical developments of the seventeenth and eighteenth centuries in the West: the construction of liberalism as an ideology, the articulation of modern capitalism, and (most significant) the creation of what Habermas calls the "public sphere." Rational masculinity was neither wholly a part nor wholly a product of any of these phenomena, but it intersected with them in so many ways that it almost certainly would not have taken shape in their absence (again, especially in the absence of the public sphere). By the middle of the eighteenth century, the context incorporated a set of propositions that could be adapted to many uses in public discourse. Its central proposition was that men are, for the most part and with variations, inherently rational and sociable. Their natural capacities in this regard are matched, limited, and sometimes endangered by countervailing factors, including their equally natural tendencies toward violence and selfishness and their desire (at least in "civilized" society) to be accommodating toward women. Women, although capable of reason, are on the whole inherently less so than men, and their judgment is more likely to be swayed by the nonviolent emotions. From these and related notions, a new formulation of gender roles in society was constructed, of which the most famous manifestation was the concept of "separate spheres." "Separate spheres" became a significant part (although in different ways) of both rational masculinity and the context of domestic femininity, and thus of respectability.

Apart from their implications for gender relations, the propositions associated with rational masculinity provided a vital framework, at what we might call a subideological level, for liberal economic and political thinking. If men were basically rational and sociable, then their rationality and sociability fitted them for participation in civil society. (By the same token, the declaration that these were primarily male characteristics explicitly excluded women from such participation.) What was necessary was to define men's sociability in terms of a parallel moral framework that presented individual rationality and rational self-interest as compatible with the good of the community. Part of this definition came from Lockean social theory and its successors, but more of it came from what we have called the context of virtue. The moral qualities emphasized in the context of virtue and the practices in which they were supposed to be manifested, together with general rationality and sociability, became the accepted criteria for direct participation in the public sphere. From about the middle of the eighteenth century in western Europe and the Americas, debates about which segments of the population were qualified to have their interests and opinions directly consulted in the making of state policy (whether by voting or other means) increasingly became debates over which classes possessed and displayed these characteristics and the resources to support them. By the second quarter of the nineteenth century, the issue of franchise extension in western Europe was formulated (by liberals, at any rate, whose ideology was becoming the basis of political consensus) to a considerable extent in terms of which classes were "respectable" enough to be trusted with the vote.[16]

But important as they were, the propositional aspects of rational masculinity were not its essential features, nor were they the first to appear. No one sat down and created the context of rational masculinity by thinking about important social ideas. Rather, it formed from the interactions of people in particular settings in early modern Europe. Among the most important of these settings were the coffeehouses of northwestern Europe in the late seventeenth and eighteenth centuries, with their connections to the global networks of information, commodity, and resource exchange that were described in chapter 5. The close connection of rational masculinity with the public sphere arose largely from the fact that they shared similar origins in location and practice. The propositional aspects of rational masculinity appear to have been derived to some extent by inference and analogy from observing behaviors that had, by the eighteenth century, become customary in male interactions in places such as coffeehouses—places, typically, where overseas commodities were consumed and traded (and worn, in the case of cottons). The values assigned to such commodities in the contexts of gentility, luxury, and virtue made them especially significant as objects around which many of the practices incorporated within rational masculinity developed and from which its propositional elements were derived.

The existence of a culture, or at least an ideology, of domestic femininity is widely recognized by historians, but there has been a tendency to confound it with one of its propositional elements—the "separate spheres" idea—that it shared with (and largely took from) rational masculinity. The context itself was much broader. A large part of it consisted of a set of practices (many of them ritualized, as for example tea-taking) developed by women of means that highlighted the importance of women in social life, particularly in a domestic setting. The purchase and appropriate deployment of commodities were central to these practices: buying and serving luxury comestibles under comfortable circumstances in which luxury was no vice, seeing to the proper attire of family members, conducting the rituals through which families presented themselves to the outside world in the setting of the parlor, and so forth. It is difficult to exaggerate the importance of domestic femininity in shaping consumption of overseas goods and of many classes of European manufactured goods in the eighteenth and nineteenth centuries. Domestic femininity became a vital element of respectability, integrating aspects of all the other constituent contexts and producing, in the modern family, an extremely effective instrument for socializing of individuals, for motivating its members to increase productivity, for generating new economic demands, and for advancing a homogeneity of culture that crossed class lines. Although it might seem that, of all the cultural contexts we have examined, domestic femininity is the one furthest removed from capitalism, it may well have been the most vital to the expansion of the capitalist economy.

Aspects of domestic femininity were formally articulated in eighteenth- and early-nineteenth-century public discourse. The separate spheres doctrine was one of these. It was initially embodied in guides to behavior written by men and reflecting conservative male outlooks on social and cultural change. The doctrine was generally accepted by respectable women as part of the larger context, but primarily as a support for their claims for recognition of their social responsibilities (properly sited in the family), not as the cognitive framework informing the whole. In the nineteenth century, a broader discourse, thoroughly situated in the context of domestic femininity, related women's domestic roles to the definition and maintenance of civilization. It was a discourse through which respectable women could justify participation in public life, as long as that participation was framed in terms of "civilizing" activities rather than political equality with men. It also had profound effects on the ways in which Western political and economic hegemony over the rest of the world was culturally constructed in the nineteenth and twentieth centuries. But the main public formulations of domestic femininity were not formal. They were presented instead in fictional literature by writers such as Frances Burney and Jane Austen and in the pages of the women's magazines that became a major staple of the publishing industry of the nineteenth century.

Respectability, then, was an aggregation of these two overtly gendered cultural contexts, together with the contexts of virtue, luxury, and gentility— an aggregation within which elements intersected with each other in a large number of ways. Respectability was constructed by thousands of individuals and groups seeking hundreds of objectives, but making use of the opportunities for understanding, expression, persuasion, and justification that the contexts provided, and confronting changes in social life that lay outside the limits of the contexts. Commodity consumption was an extremely important aspect of each of the contexts, although in varied ways—so varied as to defy simple explanation. That variety was reduced to some extent by the formation of respectability, but only because it was possible to perceive different kinds of consumption as sharing the characteristic of being respectable.

The complexity of the process that produced respectability and the variety of the practices that came to be connected to it make it difficult to generalize about national differences in its formation before about 1800. One of the reasons that the examples given in this chapter were all British and that much of the discussion in the preceding chapters focused on Britain is that, together with the Netherlands and the former British colonies in the United States, Great Britain was the first country in which what became the classic pattern of respectability was put together. Variations, both in the process of formation and in the array of featured practices, can be noted among countries. In France, for example, with its huge noble class, its government's strong involvement in the formation, extension, and exploitation of aristocratic tastes as an element of national policy developed (before the revolution) a pattern much more heavily weighted toward the contexts of gentility and taste than toward the context of virtue. (The continued centrality of wine, as opposed to tea and coffee, as the preferred liquid ingestible may have been related to this difference.) In Germany, the context of virtue was a very strong element of the emerging culture of respectability, but it tended to be tied much more to the practices of state bureaucracies than was the case in Britain. With regard to the United States, which had relatively little in the way of a hereditary aristocracy, respectability has been seen much more as a social broadening and consequent modification of the culture of gentility developed by eighteenth-century American elites.[17] In the nineteenth century, some of these differences took on more concrete form, but at the same time, the enormous prestige of British political, social, and cultural institutions made the British version of respectability a kind of international model or standard. These are matters that will have to be addressed in a further study. For the purposes of this book, it has been appropriate to acknowledge both the international nature of the cultural changes that have been discussed and the particular importance of Britain in their articulation.

IMPLICATIONS AND FURTHER QUESTIONS

As a way of ending this book, it might be useful to identify some of the implications of what has been said for major historical topics. These will suggest research questions that might be pursued elsewhere.

Industrialization

One of the many heavily debated issues concerning the origins of European industrialization has to do with the role of overseas trade in the

British Industrial Revolution of the eighteenth century. Did Britain's over-seas trade help to cause industrialization by providing profits that were turned into investment capital? Did overseas commerce stimulate industrial development by creating demand, either by tapping new markets abroad or by increasing incomes in Britain and thus expanding domestic consumption? Variations on these positions have been argued in many different ways, with many different kinds of evidence. It has also been claimed, on the basis of estimates that the value of British overseas trade in the eighteenth century was relatively small compared to the total value of domestic production, that extra-European commerce could have had little effect on such a significant economic change as industrialization. [18] The present study suggests that the whole issue may have been misstated. The size of the overseas sector of the British (or any other European) economy relative to other sectors, the mon-etary impact of trade on aggregate industrial demand, on demand for specif-ic products, on general income levels, all these are undoubtedly significant in any overall understanding of economic change. But these factors may be considerably less important in explaining the origins of industrialization than the role played by overseas goods in developing the modes of con-sumption that produced the demand that the leading sectors of the early Industrial Revolution attempted to satisfy. It was not European exports but the products imported into Europe that mattered, and not so much their quantity or value relative to anything else as the kinds of behavior that they stimulated. It was sufficient that imports sold profitably on a large enough scale to encourage European manufacturers to compete for the market through industrial innovation. That the market existed at all was due to the array of meanings that certain imported products had acquired in European culture, to the practices in conjunction with which they were used, and to the motives that led people with discretionary income to adopt (and often to modify) the practices. This was clearly the case with the leading sector of the British Industrial Revolution: cottons. It was also true with the pottery indus-try, where an import from Asia ("china") was first imitated on a restricted scale and then reproduced for much wider sales as a result of industrial inno-vations in the second half of the eighteenth century.

Why should goods produced overseas have performed this crucial func-tion? Several reasons, most of them specific to particular cases, have been presented in earlier chapters. The outlines of a general answer have also appeared. It is not enough to say that these items were rare and exotic and therefore desirable as status symbols. That was certainly part of their initial appeal, but it is not sufficient to explain why demand for them was so dynamic for so long, much less to account for the fact that modernized industrial production in Europe could fill a large part of the same demand.

What was rare or exotic about Manchester cotton (in Europe, at any rate)? They were attractive because adopting the practices in which they were used allowed large numbers of people of varied social standing to manipulate the social and cultural realities with which they were confronted, in many cases to participate in broader, more prestigious patterns of community life than their forebears had been able to do, and, ultimately, to see themselves as respectable persons. It was undoubtedly important that products such as cottons were exotic and fashionable among elites early in their histories as major commodities. What was much more important was that they could readily be produced and distributed in greatly increased amounts when demand presented itself (that is, when they found places in more and expanded European contexts) and that organizations existed that could exploit such demand and make the large-scale adjustments in supply required by rapid changes in consumption practices. In other words, the importance of overseas goods lay not just in the fact that they were from overseas, but also in the fact that supplying overseas goods was a function of entities such as the East Indies companies and the larger networks of which they were a part. Even where large companies did not acquire semimonopoly status (as in the West Indian sugar business), smaller firms participated in the integrated commercial structures discussed in chapter 5. But it was the Indies companies that provided the backbone of the supply mechanism for Asian manufactured goods such as cottons and porcelain. The companies made it possible for new demands and new fashions to be met by changes in the quantities and the specific types of goods supplied—in part because of their efficient organizations, access to large amounts of capital, and global scope, and in part because they alone had access to the manufacturing capacities of India and China under circumstances in which changes could be accommodated, or in some cases foreseen. Profits made by the companies (as well as the profits made by the distributors in Europe who dealt with the companies and by the "interlopers" in the Asian trade whose businesses depended on facilities maintained by the companies) were important mainly because they allowed overseas trading enterprises to flourish, not because they created a vital pool of capital for investment in domestic industries. The nature of late-seventeenth- and early-eighteenth-century Euro-Asian commerce made it possible for the wearing of cottons to acquire the many meanings that it did. If the supply mechanism for cottons had not been as elastic as the network of Indies companies, European interlopers, Indian entrepreneurs, and Indian weavers made it, cottons would not have been available in the quantities and varieties, at the prices, and with the responsiveness to changes in fashion necessary to sustain the practices that developed around their wearing. In order to compete with this network (or, in the case of British cottons, to respond to a demand derived from consumer practices earlier supported by Indian exports that the Indies companies had difficulty filling after 1721), European manufacturers turned to technology and to their own innovations in finance, management, and marketing.

A similar process is illustrated by the much-studied career of Josiah Wedgwood (1730–1795). Wedgwood started as a potter in Staffordshire, a small businessman and master craftsman in an old and stodgy industry that made earthenware products for the everyday use of the nonelite.[19] Although English pottery was not entirely backward, in terms either of technical or stylistic innovation, it was not a very large sector of British manufacturing and not much connected to the cutting edge of the earthenware business: porcelain making.

That enterprise had emerged in Europe entirely as a result of the large-scale importation of Chinese porcelain by the East Indies companies in the seventeenth century.[20] Chinese porcelain rapidly became an elite fashion, partly because of its exotic nature and aesthetic attractiveness, and partly because it fit nicely into genteel dining practices that were already changing to reflect politeness and civility. The widespread adoption of tea drinking enormously increased demand for chinaware, as did many other innovations in daily living affected by, among other things, the changes in the cultural contexts we have examined. The Indies companies noted this, increased their purchases of porcelain, and, by the early eighteenth century, attempted to follow and even anticipate changes in the types of porcelain items demanded. In this, they were fortunate in deriving their supply from a Chinese industry fully capable of responding quickly to the stimuli passed to them by the companies. Even so, because porcelain had become part of so many practices associated with gentility and luxury that its exotic origins were not its only selling points, there was still an opportunity for European manufacturers to move into the market, if only they could figure out how to do it. They never did find ways of exactly reproducing Chinese production techniques (not even Wedgwood managed that), but starting with the Delft chinawares of the late seventeenth century, they came up with various acceptable substitutes. New industries were started under state sponsorship in Saxony and France. Like the Delft potters, they produced items that were ostensibly in the Asian style, but in the course of the eighteenth century they developed their own, often entirely European, shapes, types, and decorative motifs. The Saxon and French industries, however, were highly labor-intensive and focused mainly on expensive items for elite purchase, selling in markets in which their competition came from the highest-quality Chinese porcelain. Other manufacturers sought a wider market for substitute status goods, among people who were not extremely wealthy or traditionally genteel but who wanted to participate in some way in the context of gentility. Even here, a large part of the market throughout the eighteenth century was taken by imported Chinese porcelain, by now often made with European decorative designs.

Most of this passed right by the British earthenware industry.[21] Its sales increased in the first half of the eighteenth century simply because it became standard for most people except the poorest to own at least some earthenware dishes and cups, but its products were in no sense fashionable, nor did they substitute for status-conveying items. Although when Wedgwood entered the business he showed a keen interest in experimentation with materials, methods, and designs, he initially stayed within the confines of the existing Staffordshire markets.

The impetus to change came from Queen Charlotte, wife of George III, who, in an attempt to stimulate the domestic pottery industry, placed an order for a complete porcelain tea service of the highest quality with a Newcastle dealer in 1765, but stipulated that it had to be made in England. The dealer turned to Wedgwood. Wedgwood jumped at the chance, designed a porcelain style to the queen's specifications, applied to it the results of his experiments with material, firing, glazing, printing, and painting, and produced a masterpiece that stimulated orders from aristocrats all over Europe.[22] English pottery had arrived, through porcelain, at the center of a genteel fashion that had commenced with, and continued to be in part sustained by, goods supplied by the Indies trade. But Wedgwood immediately went beyond that. He developed a cheaper, but still high-quality, porcelain patterned on Queen Charlotte's, and he organized a new production process that allowed the pattern to be produced on a relatively large scale for the part of the public that bought china but could not afford to custom-order it. With royal permission, he advertised his product as "Queen's Ware"—the first of the named Wedgwood patterns.

The rest of Wedgwood's story is famous. He entered a partnership with the well-educated and well-connected Liverpool merchant Thomas Bentley, who convinced Wedgwood of the desirability of developing product lines connected with the very latest trends in taste (which ran to the neoclassical). Among the results was Jasper Ware—one of the most prolific (and profitable) media of Enlightenment classicism.[23] Wedgwood was a major pioneer in innovative methods of factory organization, training of skilled workers, research and development, and marketing of manufactured products.[24] In the last capacity, he demonstrated that he understood the nature of the new culture of respectability and he contributed to its articulation. It could be argued that Wedgwood and his china constituted, in themselves, significant connections among the cultural contexts that made up respectability. The practices for which most of his products were intended were central to domestic femininity and to the enjoyment of moderate, comfortable luxury. The products themselves were designed to conform to genteel standards of taste, and consciously sold that way. (Wedgwood usually produced expensive, high-quality versions of his standard lines and built much of his marketing around their use by distinguished aristocrats.)[25] At the same time, the decorative patterns were restrained and chaste, so as to align them also with the maintenance of virtue. (He ordered his designers to hide, if possible, the naughty parts of nude classical figures used as motifs.)[26] Even rational masculinity played a role. To the extent that the eighteenth-century neoclassical aesthetic symbolized or supported the presumption of rationality, Wedgwood's (and Bentley's) stylistic decisions could be connected to that presumption. Perhaps more important, Wedgwood inserted some of his products into contemporary issues in the public sphere. A strong opponent of the slave trade, Wedgwood created the ceramic cameo medallion, sold by the thousands, that became the most famous icon of the abolitionist movement.[27] Although Wedgwood's sales strategies were based in part on the social model of a trendsetting aristocracy and an imitative middle class, the best way of describing his clientele is to say that they were the respectable people of late-eighteenth-century Europe—people who showed their respectability by owning china made by Wedgwood and the competitors who followed his lead.

The story of porcelain and Wedgwood's role in it thus clearly illustrates not only the significance of overseas commodities (especially those imported by the Indies companies) in creating the market that led to many of the innovations of the early Industrial Revolution, but also the way in which the cultural changes that produced respectability were closely intertwined both with overseas trade and with industrialization. Many questions suggest themselves for further consideration, of which one may serve as an example. To what extent did active marketing play a role in all this? Wedgwood's career suggests such a role, but he probably did not invent it. Perhaps the marketing aspect of the expansion of demand for overseas commodities and European industrialization will lead us to an aspect of early modern European cultural change—the development of an "economic culture"—that is not wholly explicable in terms of the standard narratives of the emergence of capitalism.[28]

Consumerism

Several historians of consumption during the past twenty years have portrayed the development of Western modes of consumption in the seventeenth and eighteenth centuries as the birth of "consumerism"—that is, of an identifiable, autonomous sociocultural phenomenon characteristic of the contemporary world—and of a "consumer society" principally characterized by consumerism.[29] The present study suggests that the reality was considerably more complicated and that, at least before the mid-nineteenth century (and possibly later), it is not accurate to treat consumerism as a discrete socio-cultural entity. Rather, the behaviors that we associate with consumerism in our own time were embedded in the cultural contexts we have examined, and when they were brought together into a single pattern, the pattern was not consumerism as that term is usually understood today, but respectability. Most of the meaning that consumption possessed was articulated in terms of respectability—including the moral meaning, the apparent absence of which many critics find distressing in contemporary consumerism. It would an interesting and useful project to trace the process by which a separate culture of consumption detached itself from respectability in the late nineteenth and twentieth centuries—if, indeed, that was what happened. The project might perhaps also consider the possibility that, even today, "consumerism" may not be as distinct and autonomous a phenomenon as we tend to think.

Class

The possible implications of what has been said here about class, and especially about the bourgeoisie or middle class, are too complex to be summarized in a short statement. Historical understanding of class is currently undergoing extensive revision, so that it would take a substantial essay just to situate the implications in contemporary discussions. All that can be done briefly is to suggest a few topics for further development.

All the cultural contexts discussed here were clearly involved in the formation of the Western middle class as a self-conscious social group in the period from 1600 to 1800. In the nineteenth century, respectability was just as clearly a central cultural feature of the "mature" bourgeoisie. But what was the nature of the relationship between this class and the cultural contexts? We have seen that it will not do to postulate the prior emergence of a bourgeoisie defined in any of the standard ways. It is possible to claim that, as separate but intersecting cultural entities, the cultural contexts that constituted respectability developed before the appearance of a self-conscious bourgeoisie and therefore to suggest that the process that produced respectability also helped to produce the bourgeoisie. This claim, however, is complicated by two facts. The first is that, as we have seen repeatedly, the creation, articulation, and alteration of the contexts involved a great many people who could not realistically be considered bourgeois (as well as many people who could). Laying class boundaries does not seem to have been a sustained aim of very many of these people. The same is true of the aggregating process that produced respectability. George III could easily have been discussed as a "maker of respectability" earlier in the present chapter. His deliberately constructed public persona probably did as much as anything else to fix the ensemble of practices, attitudes, and images associated with respectability in Britain, and yet he was in no sense "bourgeois" or "middle class."[30] Second, in the nineteenth century, although respectability was often thought of as being a distinctly middle-class characteristic, many people of other classes were widely regarded as respectable, both by themselves and by others: the "respectable working class," for instance. In some regards, it seems as though the formulation of respectability was connected with the formation of *all* modern classes. This is a puzzle that requires untangling.[31]

One possibility is that classes, as cognitive abstractions with which people identify themselves and which they employ to understand their relationships with others, are formed for essentially political reasons by individuals and groups engaged in public discourse. These individuals and groups may wish, for example, to identify potential supporters and opponents, to mobilize the former and disarm the latter, to connect proposed public actions to conceptions of the common good—even simply to try to make sense of what they themselves are doing. People engaged in this activity must necessarily work with the materials at hand. In the late eighteenth century, respectability and its constituents were not only a prominent part of the cultural equipment of a great many Europeans and European-Americans, but they had also proven their enormous attractiveness. It is not surprising that politicians, journalists, and others concerned with laying out the boundaries of a workable public audience would have used the elements of respectability, as well as occupation and property, for that purpose. It is also not surprising that, because of the attractiveness of respectability, the successful formulations of the class boundaries around the resultant middle class would have been the ones that heavily emphasized it. (The same might also be said for some nonpolitical activities such as identifying the audience for certain types of publications or the market for certain commodities.) Nothing would prevent people excluded from the selected audience from also adhering to the culturel of respectability. Quite the contrary: to the extent that the middle class (denoted as a respectable as well as a propertied sector of society) became the dominant reference group for politics and consumption, its defining cultural practices acquired increased status and attractiveness—especially the ones that were not based on property. It became extremely important for members of classes portrayed as separate from the middle class by the same process that defined the middle class itself (the "working class," for instance, but also the aristocracy) to claim respectability as their own—and to claim that middle-class respectability was, in crucial ways, a sham. Much of the history of the concept of respectability in the late nineteenth and twentieth centuries might be explained in this way.

Gender

This study has shown that highly distinctive gender definitions were inherent in respectability, in large part because of the fact that two of the contexts of which it was composed—rational masculinity and domestic femininity—emphasized gender in terms both of cognition and practice. Respectability continued through the nineteenth century and beyond to shape ideal male and female behavior—including, as we have seen, consumer behavior. One question of interest for further consideration is the nature of the famous Victorian "double standard," the idea that men's deviation from respectable moral standards was, within limits, more acceptable than women's. How much was the double standard part of respectability itself from the beginning, and how much was it an adaptation of respectability to changing circumstances in the nineteenth century? Another question has to do with the influence of respectability on the process by which women eventually gained greater access to public life in the West. It can be argued that one of the results of the triumph of respectability in the early nineteenth century was to limit such access (whether in the form of political participation or in the form of consumption) to channels that reduced its socially subversive potential to levels acceptable to most men. However, because both men and women could be "respectable" in a general sense, and because not all of the indicators of respectability were gender-specific, it became possible for women to see and present themselves as eligible for enhanced public participation on grounds of being respectable in a generic sense, without necessarily attacking the entire edifice of gender differentiation. In the Unites States, at any rate, one of the political strengths of the women's suffrage movement by the early twentieth century was that its leaders and members were eminently respectable. Susan B. Anthony was the successful model of a suffragist, not Victoria Woodhull.

Politics

It has been suggested frequently throughout this study that respectability and its constituent contexts were heavily implicated in political change in the eighteenth century, although generally not as overt components of political issues or programs. The number of nineteenth-century political topics in which an analysis of respectability's role might be important is so large that only a few of them can be listed here. To what extent was respectability an overt, as well as an assumed, aspect of the main European political movements of the nineteenth century? To what extent was the contest over the extension of the franchise seen as a dispute over which sectors of the population were sufficiently respectable to be trusted with the vote? Was the general adoption of respectability a major factor in the creation and success of a politics of humanitarianism—most notably represented by the abolitionist movement? In what ways did respectability inform Western imperialism in the nineteenth century, not only because of the role of humanitarianism in framing the discourse of imperialism, but also because many of the colonial programs of the imperial states came to emphasize the creation of respectable societies abroad, whether white or nonwhite? What effects, consequently, did respectability have on the phenomenon of postcolonialism?

Modernity

Clearly, the formation of respectability was a process closely intertwined with the formation of most of the phenomena that we now call "the modern." A large part of modernity, as we understand it, was given coherence by the culture of respectability. Probably the most important challenge posed by this book is to understand the relationship between respectability and modernity and to show how each has been implicated in the historical career of the other throughout the world since the early nineteenth century.

NOTES

INTRODUCTION

1 Jean-Christophe Agnew, "Coming up for Air: Consumer Culture in Historical Perspective," in *Consumption and the World of Goods*, ed. John Brewer and Roy Porter, (London: Routledge, 1993), 34. Some approaches to the history of consumption, most obviously those employing Marxian models, carry with them networks of implications that meet Agnew's requirements in a formal sense. He was calling for interpretation along a broader range of lines than than those prescribed by established theories.

2 For example, Neil McKendrick, John Brewer, and J. H. Plumb, *The Birth of a Consumer Society: The Commercialization of Eighteenth-Century England* (Bloomington: Indiana University Press, 1982), 9–33.

3 Agnew, "Coming up for Air," 33.

4 Colin Campbell, "Understanding Traditional and Modern Patterns of Consumption in Eighteenth-Century England: A Character-Action Approach," in *Consumption and the World of Goods*, ed. Brewer and Porter, 40–57.

5 T. H. Breen, "The Meanings of Things: Interpreting the Consumer Economy in the Eighteenth Century," in *Consumption and the World of Goods*, ed. Brewer and Porter, 249–60.

6 Lorna Weatherill, "The Meaning of Consumer Behaviour in Late Seventeenth-Century and Early Eighteenth-Century England," in *Consumption and the World of Goods*, ed. Brewer and Porter, 206–27.

7 Maxine Berg and Helen Clifford, eds., *Consumers and Luxury: Consumer Culture in Europe, 1650–1850* (Manchester: Manchester University Press, 1999); John Brewer, *The Pleasures of the Imagination: English Culture in the Eighteenth Century* (New York, Farrar Straus Giroux, 1997); Amanda Vickery, *The Gentleman's Daughter:*

Women's Lives in Georgian England (New Haven and London: Yale University Press, 1998), 164–68.

8   Among the most important of the books that informed the new historiography of consumption were McKendrick, Brewer, and Plumb, *Birth of a Consumer Society*; and Colin Campbell, *The Romantic Ethic and the Spirit of Capitalism* (Oxford: Blackwell, 1987).

9   Important exceptions to this statement are Carolyn Conley, *The Unwritten Law: Criminal Justice in Victorian Kent* (New York: Oxford University Press, 1991); and Richard L. Bushman, *The Refinement of America: Persons, Houses, Cities* (New York: Alfred A. Knopf, 1992). Conley analyzes the meaning and significance of respectability in public perceptions of criminal acts and in the manner in which the law was enforced. More comprehensively, Bushman portrays a movement in taste and manners in eighteenth- and nineteenth-century America from "gentility" to "respectability." As the present book will show, gentility was not the only source of respectability, but it was certainly one of them. It will also attempt to show that Bushman, like most others who have studied social and cultural change at the beginning of the modern era, relies too heavily on determinative models of class relationships and of economic change to explain what happened. Nevertheless, Bushman's perceptions are very acute and his understanding of respectability stands out from almost all other treatments. Compare, for example, F. M. L. Thompson, *The Rise of Respectable Society: A Social History of Victorian Britain, 1830–1900* (Cambridge, MA: Harvard University Press, 1988). Despite the title, the book contains no discussion of the meaning of the term *respectable society* and no reference to "respectability" in the index. It does discuss the "respectable working class" (199, 202–3, 353–54), but with only the barest of hints as to what that term might mean.

Chapter One: Consumption and Culture

1   Neil McKendrick is the main proponent of the eighteenth-century "consumer revolution." See McKendrick, Brewer, and Plumb, *Birth of a Consumer Society*, 9–194. For a discussion and critique of McKendrick's thesis, see Agnew, "Coming up for Air," 23–25.

2   For the classic discussion of the role of demand in the Industrial Revolution and of demand for overseas imports as a precursor to industrial demand, see Elizabeth Gilboy, "Demand as a Factor in the Industrial Revolution," in *Facts and Figures in Economic History: Articles by Former Students of Edwin Francis Day* (New York: Russell and Russell, 1932), 620–39. See also Phyllis Deane, *The First Industrial Revolution* (Cambridge: Cambridge University Press, 1965), 51–68; and Peter Mathias, *The First Industrial Nation: An Economic History of Britain, 1700–1914*, 2nd ed. (London and New York: Methuen, 1983), 191–202. I use the term *Industrial Revolution* in this book in the traditional way, to refer to the large increase in production and in productivity that occurred in certain European manufacturing industries in the late eighteenth and nineteenth centuries, increases notably connected with technological and organizational innovations. In fact, most economic historians now see these changes as threads in a much broader historical fabric, involving considerably more time and more factors than tradition holds. *Industrial Revolution* is used here for convenience. The general thrust of the book, however, not only supports the more current tendencies in the study of industrialization, but suggests that they may not go far enough.

3   Alfred W. Crosby, *The Columbian Exchange: Biological and Cultural Consequences of 1492* (Westport, CT: Greenwood Press, 1972); and Charles Gibson, *Spain in*

America (New York: Harper, 1966), 99–107. One product that would, from the early seventeenth century onward, figure heavily in American exports to Europe was tobacco, which was one of the earliest American commodities to be brought across the ocean (by Columbus, in fact). However, for more than a century after tobacco was introduced to Europe, the Near East, and the rest of the world, little of it was actually grown in America for export. Most was produced locally wherever it was consumed, from plants that had been taken from the Western Hemisphere. The export tobacco industry of the Americas eventually developed not because tobacco could not be grown elsewhere, but because of the commercial and fiscal policies of the major imperial states. See Jordan Goodman, *Tobacco in History: The Cultures of Dependence* (London and New York: Routledge, 1993).

4 K. N. Chaudhuri, *Trade and Civilisation in the Indian Ocean: An Economic History from the Rise of Islam to 1750* (Cambridge: Cambridge University Press, 1985), 67–73.

5 Niels Steensgaard, *The Asian Trade Revolution of the Seventeenth Century* (Chicago: University of Chicago Press, 1974). Several aspects of the creation of the early modern world economy are discussed in the papers collected in James D. Tracy, ed. *The Rise of Merchant Empires: Long Distance Trade in the Early Modern World* (Cambridge: Cambridge University Press, 1990). See also Holden Furber, *Rival Empires of Trade in the Orient, 1660–1800* (Minneapolis: University of Minnesota Press, 1976).

6 See, for example, Ralph Davis, "English Foreign Trade, 1660–1700," *Economic History Review* 7 (1952): 150–66, and "The Industrial Revolution and British Overseas Trade," in Stanley L. Engermann, ed, *Trade and the Industrial Revolution,* vol. 1, ed. Stanley L. Engerman (Cheltenham: Elgar, 1996), 187–201.

7 Gilboy, "Demand as a Factor," 620–39, and Deane, *First Industrial Revolution,* 51–68.

8 Economists tend to pay little attention to the distinction between demand and consumption, assuming that, for their purposes, demand is merely an aggregation of consumption decisions largely made on the basis of price. See, for example, the treatment of the subject in Paul A. Samuelson, *Economics,* 10th ed. (New York: McGraw-Hill, 1976), 58–62. Economists are taken to task for this and other failings in Mary Douglas and Baron Isherwood, *The World of Goods* (New York: Basic Books, 1979), 15–24.

9 This has been true even of some of the very best economic historians. See, for example, Joel Mokyr, "Demand versus Supply in the Industrial Revolution," *Journal of Economic History* 37 (1977): 981–1008.

10 Thorstein Veblen, *The Theory of the Leisure Class: An Economic Study of Institutions* (Fairfield, NJ: Augustus Kelley, 1991); Georg Simmel, "Fashion," *International Quarterly* 10 (1904): 130–55; and Harold Perkin, "The Social Causes of the British Industrial Revolution," Royal Historical Society *Transactions,* 5th series, 18 (1969): 123–43.

11 See William H. Reddy, *Money and Liberty in Modern Europe: A Critique of Historical Understanding* (Cambridge: Cambridge University Press, 1987), esp. 1–33, for a radical version of such a critique.

12 See, for example, Furber, *Rival Empires of Trade.* The chapter entitled "The Craze for Calicoes" (79–124) contains no analysis of the craze for calicoes, and the chapter on tea (125–84) is devoted almost entirely to the ways in which tea was acquired, with the barest mention of consumption—and that only to establish dates.

13 The weaknesses of this argument are demonstrated in Sidney Mintz, *Sweetness and Power: The Place of Sugar in Modern History* (New York: Penguin, 1985). For a recent analysis of the inadequacy of explanations of the consumption of sugar and other comestibles that focus on production and assume a universal taste for such commodities, see Martin Bruegel, "A Bourgeois Good? Sugar, Norms of Consumption,

and the Labouring Classes in Nineteenth-Century France," in *Food, Drink, and Identity: Cooking, Eating, and Drinking in Europe since the Middle Ages*, ed. Peter Scholliers (Oxford and New York: Berg, 2001), 99–118, esp. 99–101.

14 Jordan Goodman, Paul E. Lovejoy, and Andrew Sherratt, eds., *Consuming Habits: Drugs in History and Anthropology* (London: Routledge, 1995).

15 A good summary of the current state of cultural studies from the perspective of historians can be found in the editors' introduction to Victoria E. Bonnell and Lynn Hunt, eds., *Beyond the Cultural Turn: New Directions in the Study of Society and Culture* (Berkeley: University of California Press, 1999), 1–32.

16 Douglas and Isherwood, *World of Goods*; Claude Lévi-Strauss, *The Raw and the Cooked* (New York: Harper and Row, 1969).

17 Marshall Sahlins, *Culture and Practical Reason* (Chicago, University of Chicago Press, 1976). For an excellent example of anthropological analysis of consumption in a historical context, see Grant McCracken, *Culture and Consumption: New Approaches to the Symbolic Character of Consumer Goods and Activities* (Bloomington: Indiana University Press, 1988).

18 See, for example, Jean-Christophe Agnew, *Worlds Apart: The Market and the Theatre in Anglo-American Thought, 1550–1750* (Cambridge: Cambridge University Press, 1986); and Elizabeth Kowaleski-Wallace, *Consuming Subjects: Women, Shopping, and Business in the Eighteenth Century* (New York: Columbia University Press, 1997). See also the imaginative attempt of historical sociologist Colin Campbell to relate consumption in nineteenth-century Europe to the culture of Romanticism: Campbell, *Romantic Ethic*.

19 Probably the most cogent recent analysis of the problem of defining culture for historical purposes is William E. Sewell, Jr., "The Concept(s) of Culture," in *Beyond the Cultural Turn*, ed. Bonnell and Hunt, 35–61. The present book was written before I read Sewell's article, but much of what he suggests about the relationship between culture and the rest of society is echoed in the chapters that follow. Several important general points are made more clearly and economically in that article than in this book. Sewell does not propose the form of analysis in terms of autonomous, interacting cultural contexts that is employed here, but it seems on the whole to be consistent with his suggestions.

20 Michel Foucault comes close to this position. However, in some places (e.g., Michel Foucault, *The Order of Things: An Archaeology of the Human Sciences* [New York: Vintage, 1973], xii–xiii) he suggests that we can discern the causes of change in history once we clearly identify the nature of what it is that changes and adopt a satisfactory notion of "cause."

21 See Marshall Sahlins, "Cosmologies of Capitalism: The Trans-Pacific Sector of the 'World System,'" *Proceedings of the British Academy* 74 (1988): 1–51.

22 See Ralph Linton, *The Tree of Culture* (New York: Alfred A. Knopf, 1955), 33–48.

23 For a brief description of *mentalités*, see Robert Darnton, *The Great Cat Massacre and Other Episodes in French Cultural History* (New York: Vintage, 1985), 3–7. *Épistèmes* are described in Foucault, *Order of Things*, xv–xxiv, 17–30. For paradigms, see Thomas S. Kuhn, *The Structure of Scientific Revolutions*, 2nd ed. (Chicago: University of Chicago Press, 1970), 10–22.

24 Toril Moi, ed. *The Kristeva Reader* (New York: Columbia University Press, 1986), 89–136.

25 Anthony Giddens, *Studies in Social and Political Theory* (New York: Basic Books, 1977), 112–21, presents a theory of "structuration" as the "production and reproduction" of behavior patterns.

26 For examples of this literature, see Douglas and Isherwood, *World of Goods*; and Sahlins, *Culture and Practical Reason*.

27 John Demos, *A Little Commonwealth: Family Life in Plymouth Colony* (London and New York: Oxford University Press, 1971), 21.

28 Mintz, *Sweetness and Power*, 78.

29 This point about commodities is emphasized in Arjun Appadurai, ed., *The Social Life of Things: Commodities in Cultural Perspective* (New York: Cambridge University Press, 1986), 6.

30 See Robert B. Edgerton, *Sick Societies: Challenging the Myth of Primitive Harmony* (New York: Free Press, 1992). For a neurological framework within which notions of conscious meaning are related to individual survivability, see Antonio R. Damasio, *Descartes' Error: Emotion, Reason, and the Human Brain* (New York: Avon, 1994).

CHAPTER TWO: GENTILITY

1 See, for example, McKendrick, Brewer, and Plumb, *Birth of a Consumer Society*; and Perkin, "Social Causes."

2 Pierre Bourdieu, *Distinction: A Social Critique of the Judgement of Taste*, trans. Richard Nice (Cambridge, MA: Harvard University Press, 1984), 466–84.

3 S. A. M. Adshead, *Material Culture in Europe and China, 1400–1800* (New York: St. Martin's Press, 1995), 1, sees the creation of modern status consumption as a subset of a larger "change in material culture . . . called the rise of consumerism," which he describes as a global phenomenon covering the whole period from the fifteenth to the early nineteenth century. Bushman, *Refinement of America*, connects status consumption to the acceptance and transformation of gentility as a cultural form between about 1700 and the early nineteenth century in North America. He dates it a little earlier in England.

4 This is the aspect of status consumption—and of consumption in general—that is most heavily emphasized in studies written in the Marxian tradition. See, for example, Stuart Ewen and Elizabeth Ewen, *Channels of Desire: Mass Image and the Shaping of American Consciousness* (Minneapolis: University of Minnesota Press, 1992); and Stuart Ewen, *All Consuming Images: The Politics of Style in Contemporary Culture* (New York: Basic Books, 1988).

5 Bourdieu, *Distinction*, 318–71.

6 In recent years, it has become customary among historians to use the term *middle class* to refer to the social grouping that they former called the bourgeoisie, mainly, I think, to avoid the suggestion that a Marxian framework of analysis is being employed. Among other things, *middle class* may imply a greater degree of cultural autonomy than *bourgeois*—more of an emphasis on the attitudes of the people so designated as noncontingent factors in their definition. The two terms have never been exactly synonymous: in the Marxian view, the bourgeoisie in a bourgeois society is not in the "middle" of anything. However, a difficulty arises with the *middle* in *middle class*, especially if one tries to define the "middle class" in the context of a vertical hierarchy of classes differentiated primarily in terms of "objective" economic factors such as income, occupation, and control of capital.

This problem is illustrated in the work of American cultural historians. Richard Bushman builds his explanation of the "refinement" of American society around the notion that the "middle class" (defined as "smaller merchants and professionals, ordinary well-off farmers, successful artisans, schoolteachers, minor government officials, clerks, shopkeepers, industrial entrepreneurs and managers") wanted, around the turn of the eighteenth and nineteenth centuries, to "lead a genteel life," which had previously only been available to the upper class (Bushman, *Refinement of America*, xiii). This led them to create a culture of "vernacular gentility" in which the governing virtue was "respectability." But the distinction between upper and middle classes is very difficult to sustain, even on Bushman's own evidence. Most of the upper-class people he cites come from families that correspond to his definition of "middle-class," and the range of "middle-class" occupations includes ones that it would not be incorrect to call "upper-class" (depending on the undefined qualifiers "smaller," "minor," and "ordinary"). Bushman attempts to build an explanation of cultural change around a notion of a "middle class" that is literally in the middle of an economically defined vertical class structure, whereas the class he describes extends from the highest to almost the lowest levels of income and includes practically all occupations except laborers. This is not a "middle" class in socioeconomic terms. It is a class described by *its members' own perception* that they do not belong to an elite—an elite of which the main determinants are cultural in nature. Karen Halttunen, *Confidence Men and Painted Women: A Study of Middle-Class Culture in America, 1830–1870* (New Haven and London: Yale University Press, 1982), 29–30, faced with a similar difficulty, explicitly rejects the idea that the *middle* in *middle class* has any real meaning with respect to income or occupation.

In truth, no consensus has been reached among historians about the meaning of *middle class*, which many continue to use in much the same way as *bourgeoisie*. Here, I will employ both terms interchangeably, using *middle class* when I want to emphasize a perception of "middleness" (generally a self-perception on the part of subjects) and *bourgeoisie* when I address interpretive questions that are usually cast in Marxian terms. The group to which the terms will refer is the same: a self-defined group that formed around (among other things) the culture of respectability in the eighteenth and nineteenth centuries, whose members saw themselves as the primary but not the exclusive possessors of that culture and who constructed images of the classes "above" and "below" them largely in terms of a belief that it was unlikely that more than a minority of people in those classes could be truly respectable. With regard to the traditional model of the bourgeoisie as owners of capital, we will see that this was one factor involved in its members' self-definition, but that consumption in support of respectable status was at least equally important.

7   The distinction between traditional aristocratic gentility and respectability as contexts of status, together with the possibility of using the latter to identify oneself as "bourgeois" even if, by all noncultural criteria, one was no such thing, were exploited fully by Louis-Philippe, the "bourgeois king" of France between 1830 and 1848. See Paul H. Beik, *Louis-Philippe and the July Monarchy* (Princeton: Van Nostrand, 1965).

8   *The Diary of Samuel Pepys*, ed. Samuel Latham and William Mathews, 11 vols. (Berkeley and Los Angeles: University of California Press, 1970–83), 2:226.

9   Ibid., 2:230.

10 For example, ibid., 2:121, 210, 221; 3:55.

11 It is possible that Pepys's specific objection to what Lady Wright says has to do with its political implications. If by "courtiers" she means the people who participate in making policy and the pool from which office-holders are chosen (a reasonable summary of the point of view of the "court" party of the Stuart era), then she is in essence saying that only people who have had the opportunity to become adept at fashions and the practice of courtesy should have access to power. Both on his own behalf and that of the majority of English gentlemen (whether proto-Whig or proto-Tory), Pepys would be bound to disagree.

12 "Montagu, or more properly Mountagu, Edward, first Earl of Sandwich (1625–1672)," *Dictionary of National Biography*, 22 vols. (London: Oxford University Press, 1967–68), 13:679–84.

13 See *Diary of Samuel Pepys*, 1:140. The reference to cognitive dissonance is not entirely generic. The classic theory of cognitive dissonance describes behavior motivated by adherence to two or more inconsistent cognitive frameworks, or by differences between such frameworks and perceived events. Among the predicted responses to cognitive dissonance are ones very similar to those that Pepys appears to demonstrate. See Leon Festinger, *A Theory of Cognitive Dissonance* (Stanford: Stanford University Press, 1957).

14 See, for example, Gregory King's famous late-seventeenth-century table of the elements of England's population in J. D. Chambers, *Population, Economy, and Society in Pre-Industrial England* (London: Oxford University Press, 1972), 38–39. There is a substantial contemporary literature on the status of "gentleman" and the nature of "gentility" in early modern England. Two of the most interesting recent treatments of the subject are in the same book: Keith Wrightson, "Estates, Degrees, and Sorts: Changing Perceptions of Society in Tudor and Stuart Times," in *Language, History, and Class*, ed. Penelope J. Corfield (Oxford: Blackwell, 1991), 30–52; and Penelope J. Corfield, "Class by Name and Number in Eighteenth-Century Britain," in ibid., 101–30. Wrightson shows that "gentleman" meant a number of different things in a social world in which divisions by estates were giving way to divisions by "degrees" and then "sorts." He argues (37–39) that from the sixteenth to the eighteenth century, the term lost the primary reference to birth and military function that had given it meaning in the discourse of estates. Gentility took on new meanings derived from the political functions and the standards of politeness expected of a gentleman, and then became "ultimately a matter of relative wealth and lifestyle" (39). As we shall see, much of Wrightson's approach correlates well with the analysis of gentility presented in this chapter, but his attempt to establish a neat sequence between effective definitions of *gentleman* misses the crucial point that *all* the meanings of the word he gives (and their implications) were current at the same times in the seventeenth and early eighteenth century. This confused situation is, in fact, not unusual, as Corfield points out in her introduction to *Language, History, and Class* and in "Class by Name and Number." It was only partly recognized in Pepys's day, but it was a source of considerable tension and cultural innovation, which we can see in Pepys's behavior. Corfield makes more of the contradictions and tensions inherent in the discourse of gentility, but she still emphasizes a long-term change or sequence in usages without fully explaining how the former were related to the latter. "'Gentleman' had always had a certain ambivalence between a moral and a social definition, and a growing chorus began to stress the older at the expense of the newer" (107, n. 25).

15 In 1587, William Harrison explained it in this way: "We in England divide our people commonly into four sorts, as gentlemen, citizens or burgesses, yeomen, and artificers or laborers. Of gentlemen the first and chief (next the King) be the prince, dukes, marquises, earls, viscounts, and barons, and these are called gentlemen of the greater sort, or (as our common usage of speech is) lords and noblemen; and next unto them be knights, esquires, and, last of all, they that are simply called gentlemen; so that, in effect, our gentlemen are divided into their conditions." William Harrison, *The Description of England: The Classic Contemporary Account of Tudor Social Life*, ed. Georges Edelen (New York: Dover, 1994), 94. (After this relatively clear statement, Harrison in practice muddies the distinctions between gentlemen and citizens and between yeomen and artificers.)

16 On November 8, 1661, Pepys records that the earl of Clarendon, the Lord Chancellor, spoke to him "with great respects" on account of Pepys's great-uncle (not on Pepys's own account)—an event of which Pepys is evidently proud. *Diary of Samuel Pepys*,

2:210. On the other hand, two days previously (2:209), the Lord Privy Seal had complimented Pepys on the quality of his work as a clerk of the privy seal (a fairly subordinate post), and Pepys was proud of that as well.

17 Pepys reveals his predicament poignantly in his entry for July 24, 1661, which records his pleasure at a conversation in his office "with persons of Quality . . . I gave it out among them that the estate left me is 200 l a year in land, besides money [a lie] — because I would put an esteem upon myself." Ibid., 2:140. Technically, Pepys, as secretary, was not a "member" of the Navy Board, but he was entitled to privileges (housing, for example) similar to those enjoyed by the full members. He generally acted as a member, but was always vulnerable to being slighted as a "mere" functionary and thus not quite a gentleman.

18 Ibid., 2:210–11.

19 Ibid., 2:199. "Father Osborne" is a reference to the book that was, in Pepys's time, the most popular of the "advice to sons" genre: Francis Osborne, *Advice to a Son* (1656), which is reprinted in Louis B. Wright, ed., *Advice to a Son: Precepts of Lord Burghley, Sir Walter Raleigh, and Francis Osborne* (Ithaca: Cornell University Press, 1962), 33–114. The specific reference is precept I:29 (50): "Wear your clothes neat, exceeding rather than coming short of others of like fortune, a charge borne out by acceptance wherever you come. Therefore, spare all other ways rather than prove defective in this."

20 Ibid., 2:203.

21 Ibid., 3:77.

22 Veblen, *Theory of the Leisure Class* (Fairfield, NJ: Augustus Kelley, 1991), esp. 22–34, 68–101.

23 For issues concerning the existence or invention of privacy in early modern Europe, see Roger Chartier, ed., *Passions of the Renaissance* (Cambridge, MA: Belknap, 1989), esp. 161–396. (This is volume 3 of Philippe Aries and Georges Duby, eds., *A History of Private Life*, 4 vols. [Cambridge, MA: Belknap, 1987–90]). The notion of "private life" as a construction of the seventeenth and eighteenth centuries presented by Aries and his associates, even if generally correct, probably misses some significant points. Amanda Vickery, for example, has suggested that the important development in genteel households in this period was not a rigid separation between public and private, but rather the development of domestic spaces and rituals (parlors and tea, for example) that created a *connection* between public and private life. See Vickery, *Gentleman's Daughter*, 195–223. Halttunen, *Confidence Men and Painted Women*, 92–123, makes a similar point about nineteenth-century America. These matters will be discussed more fully in chapter 6. Such a regime would have made Pepys's strategy more difficult, but fortunately for him it had not developed in his social milieu in the 1660s. The Pepyses generally socialized away from home.

24 *Diary of Samuel Pepys*, 2:117, 3:228.

25 Note that here, as elsewhere in this book, *gentry* refers to the collectivity of gentlemen (including titled noblemen) in any European society, not (its alternative usage) to a class ranked just below the nobility in English aristocratic society. The word *aristocrat* is (unless otherwise specified) used here to refer to all recognized members of a country's social and political elite, exclusive of urban or commercial elites. It is thus closer in its meaning in this book to *gentleman* and *gentlewoman* than to *nobleman* or *noblewoman*. The latter are aristocrats, but they are not the only ones.

26 Ibid., 1:14, 253; 2:108; 3:79, 240–42.

27 Chartier, *Passions of the Renaissance*, 571–607; Anthony Fletcher, *Gender, Sex, and Subordination in England, 1500–1800* (New Haven: Yale University Press, 1995), 126–53.

28 Montesquieu, *Oeuvres Complètes* (Paris: Editions de Senil, 1964), 538–39.

29 Lawrence Stone, *The Crisis of the Aristocracy, 1558–1641* (Oxford: Clarendon Press, 1965), 184–88.

30 See, for example, *Diary of Samuel Pepys*, 3:7.

31 A point that was often made in the seventeenth and eighteenth centuries. Daniel Defoe, for example, wondered why "our modern pretenders to the title of gentility should lay so much stress upon what they call a long descent of blood" when "the highest families begun low, therefore to examine it too nicely, is to overthrow it all." (Quoted in Michael Shinagel, *Daniel Defoe and Middle-Class Gentility* [Cambridge, MA: Harvard University Press, 1968], 228–29.) For a discussion of the ambiguities of gentility, see Vickery, *Gentleman's Daughter*, 13–37.

32 Stone, *Crisis of the Aristocracy*, 547–86.

33 Andrew Trout, *Jean-Baptiste Colbert* (Boston: Twayne, 1978), 32–47.

34 *Diary of Samuel Pepys*, 3:241.

35 Bushman, *Refinement of America*, 31–38.

36 Corfield, *Language, History, and Class*, especially the introduction (1–29) and the articles by Wrightson (30–52) and Corfield (101–30); Anna Bryson, *From Courtesy to Civility: Changing Codes of Conduct in Early Modern England* (Oxford, Clarendon Press, 1998).

37 Stone, *Crisis of the Aristocracy*, 223–34; Fletcher, *Gender, Sex, and Subordination*, 130–31.

38 Norbert Elias, *The Court Society*, trans. E. Jephcott (New York: Pantheon, 1983), 117–213.

39 *Diary of Samuel Pepys*, 3:81.

40 Two of the standard works in the English literature of magistracy are *Mirror for Magistrates*, ed., L. Campbell (New York: Barnes and Noble, 1960); and Thomas Floyd, *The Picture of a Perfit Common Wealth* (London: S. Stafford, 1600).

41 See J. G. A. Pocock, *The Machiavellian Moment: Florentine Political Thought and the Atlantic Republican Tradition* (Princeton, NJ: Princeton University Press, 1975); and Quentin Skinner, *Liberty before Liberalism* (Cambridge: Cambridge University Press, 1998).

42 Wrightson, "Estates, Degrees, and Sorts," sees this distinction but tends, as elsewhere in the same article, to portray it in terms of a gradual change in elite ideals. "In this new guise, the distinguishing mark of the gentleman became the possession not only of the wealth and leisure but also of the breeding and personal virtues necessary for government, for a more diffuse role of civic usefulness. Gentlemen were defined as governors, and true gentility as the quality and the capacity to govern" (38). This is not incorrect, but the emphasis on sequence obscures the dissonance that arose from the fact that magistracy and other ideals of gentility were *simultaneously* current for much of the early modern period.

43 Stone, *Crisis of the Aristocracy*, 547–86.

44 James Martin Estes, *Christian Magistrate and State Church: The Reforming Career of Johannes Brenz* (Toronto: University of Toronto Press, 1982).

45 Joyce Youings, *Sixteenth-Century England* (Harmondsworth: Penguin, 1984), 320–33, 355–56.

46 Jonathan Dewald, *The Formation of a Provincial Nobility: The Magistrates of the Parlement of Rouen, 1499–1610* (Princeton: Princeton University Press, 1980).

47 Bryson, *From Courtesy to Civility*, 144.

48 Wrightson, "Estates, Degrees, and Sorts," 37–38.

49 This was particularly true in the Netherlands, where cities and their elites predominated, which apparently had a great deal to do with the high level of order and discipline that prevailed. See Jonathan Israel, *The Dutch Republic: Its Rise, Greatness, and Fall, 1477–1806* (Oxford: Clarendon Press, 1995), 677–85. Bryson, *From Courtesy to Civility*, 60–63, argues that in the late medieval and early modern periods, the distinction between urban and landed elites is misleading. Landed elites in many places (Italy, for instance) resided a great deal of the time in cities—a pattern that accompanied the spread of the practices of courtesy and civility in the sixteenth and seventeenth centuries.

50 *Measure for Measure*, act 2, scene 1; act 3, scene 2. *Henry IV* is particularly interesting in its discussion of the context of gentility. In his prankish youth, Prince Henry doubly violates the conventions of gentility: he keeps low company and engages in dishonorable acts (such as highway robbery), and he behaves immoderately, without self-control—an offense against magistracy that he compounds by protecting felons against actual magistrates. Shakespeare, of course, gives him a reason: "Yet herein will I imitate the sun, Who doth permit the base contagious clouds To smother up his beauty from the world, That, when he please again to be himself, Being wanted, he may be more wonder'd at." (*Henry IV, Part I*, act 1, scene 2)—a political strategy of individual self-advertisement. In any event, in *Henry IV, Part I*, Prince Hal is contrasted with Hotspur, who is the perfect exemplar of honorific elite behavior without restraint and who is widely admired for it (by Henry IV, among others). Hal's superiority in Part I emerges as a result not of his adoption of the character of magistracy, but rather of his clearer political insights *and* his willingness to balance the pursuit of honor with the moderation derived from courtesy—something that Hotspur disdains. (See *Part I*, act V, scene 2: Vernon's report to Hotspur of the Prince's challenge to single combat. Of course, Hal's surprising handiness with a sword is also a factor.) It is in *Henry IV, Part II* that Hal finally displays the virtuous deportment of a magistrate and seems to rise not only above Falstaff, but also above the limitations of his own character imposed by his personal political ambitions and by pursuit of honor moderated only by courtesy. (That his success in this regard is not complete is, however, made plain in *Henry V*, where he plunges his country into war out of political ambition and in pursuit of honor. Courtesy is much in evidence in *Henry V*, but it is clearly an ineffective restraint on behavior.)

51 Elias, *Court Society*, esp. 66–116. A succinct summary of historical consensus about the development of courtesy and related phenomena can be found in Bushman, *Refinement of America*, 30–60. Bryson, *From Courtesy to Civility*, 10–12, gives an acute but not wholly unsympathetic critique of Elias and his followers.

52 Chartier, *Passions of the Renaissance*, 167–205, 265–77.

53 Norbert Elias, *The Civilizing Process*, trans. E. Jephcott (New York: Urizen, 1978).

54 For example, in *The Spirit of the Laws*, Montesquieu discusses virtue (which incorporates moderation and self-control) as the informing principle of aristocracy as a form of government, not just as a quality that improves government. Montesquieu, *Oeuvres Complètes*, 537–38.

55 Bryson, *From Courtesy to Civility*, 42–74.

56 Vickery, *Gentleman's Daughter*, 196–202.

57 Lawrence E. Klein, *Shaftesbury and the Culture of Politeness: Moral Discourse and Cultural Politics in Early Eighteenth-Century England* (Cambridge: Cambridge University Press, 1994), 3–14, 123–212.

58 Brewer, *Pleasures of the Imagination*, 3–55.

59 The reality of extreme violence connected with honor and aristocratic dominance in Britain in the late seventeenth and early eighteenth centuries, and the contrast between that reality and the veneer of politeness that supposedly governed manners, is the theme of Victor Slater, *Duke Hamilton Is Dead! A Story of Aristocratic Life and Death in Stuart Britain* (New York: Hill and Wang, 1999).

60 Bryson, *From Courtesy to Civility*, 144–46.

61 Elias, *Court Society*, 244–46, 250–57, discusses the individualism inherent in courtesy. See also Jacob Burckhardt, *The Civilization of the Renaissance in Italy* (New York: Random House, 1954), 272–78, 283–89.

62 Georg Simmel, "Fashion," 130–55. Simmel's theory is discussed in McCracken, *Culture and Consumption*, 93–103.

63 Elias, *Court Society*, 117–213.

64 Quentin Bell, *On Human Finery*, 2nd ed. (New York: Schocken, 1976), 57–89.

65 On the salons, see Carolyn C. Lougee, *Le Paradis des Femmes: Women, Salons, and Social Stratification in Seventeenth-Century France* (Princeton: Princeton University Press, 1976).

66 Colin Campbell's "character-action" model of consumption appears to be consistent with this representation of fashionable behavior. See Campbell, "Understanding Traditional and Modern Patterns of Consumption," 40–57.

67 Michael Grant, *The World of Rome* (New York: Mentor, 1960), 82, 84–85.

68 For a useful summary of the history of the trade in Asian and European silks, see Vilhelm Slomann, *Bizarre Designs in Silk: Trade and Traditions* (Copenhagen: Einar Munksgaard, 1953).

69 An excellent summary of the Asia-Europe cotton trade in the context of the English East India Company's textile business can be found in K. N. Chaudhuri, *The Trading World of India and the English East India Company 1660–1760* (Cambridge: Cambridge University Press, 1978), 277–312.

70 Stuart Robinson, *A History of Printed Textiles* (Cambridge, MA: MIT Press, 1969), 14.

71 Steensgaard, *Asian Trade Revolution*, 22–59.

72 There is a large body of literature on both companies. On the English company, see especially Chaudhuri, *Trading World*. On the VOC, see Kristof Glamann, *Dutch-Asiatic Trade, 1620–1740* (Copenhagen: Danish Science Press, 1958); and Femme S. Gaastra, *De geschiedenis van de VOC* (Leiden: Walburg Pers, 1991).

73 *Thema Thee: De geschiedenis van de thee en het theegebruik in Nederland* (Rotterdam: Museum Boymans-van Beuningen, 1978), 15.

74 Woodruff D. Smith, "The Function of Commercial Centers in the Modernization of European Capitalism: Amsterdam as an Information Exchange in the Seventeenth Century," *Journal of Economic History* 44 (December 1984): 985–1005.

75 Ibid. 994, 996.

76 Glamann, *Dutch-Asiatic Trade*, 91–111.

77 The history of the calico craze is summarized in Beverly Lemire, *Fashion's Favourite: The Cotton Trade and the Consumer in Britain, 1660–1800* (Oxford: Oxford University Press, 1991), 12–21.

78 Robinson, *History of Printed Textiles*, 15.

79 S. William Beck, *The Draper's Dictionary* (London: Warehousemen and Drapers' Journal Office, n.d.), 64, quoting *Weekly Review*, January 31, 1708.

80 Lougee, *Paradis des Femmes*.

81 Ibid.; Marguerite Glotz and Madeleine Maire, *Salons du XVIIIe siècle* (Paris: Nouvelles Editions latines, 1949).

82 Some idea of the extent of the calico craze can be obtained from the business records of Sir William Turner, a merchant draper who was Lord Mayor of London in 1668–69 and in whose retail shop Samuel Pepys was a not-infrequent customer. Turner's papers are held in the Guildhall Library, London, as Mss. 5099–113. In 1664, Turner operated in wholesale trade primarily as the correspondent and partner of a draper in Paris named Pocquelin. Turner exported fine woolens to France through Pocquelin and imported fashionable fabrics made in or imported into France: silks, mixed fabrics, and so forth. The partners moved Holland linens from one country to the other depending on the market. Both dealt with an upscale clientele.

    The fashionable nature of the business is made clear in a letter from Turner to Pocquelin dated August 18/28, 1664: "Pray send mee 6 or 8 pces of the newest rich tabbyes that are to bee had I have here Enclosed sent [*sic*] you a patterne to direct you that those you send should bee as rich and of as new a Fashion as this but if there bee any thing newer so much the better" (Guildhall Library, Turner papers, Ms. 5106/1: Letter Book). Turner did not, at that time, obtain fashionable Asian textiles directly from one of the East India companies, but rather from his correspondent in Paris, who supplied him with goods obtained via Italy as a sideline to his high-fashion business in France.

    However, in the same letter book, in August and September 1664, there are indications of a large demand for printed silks and calicoes that Turner wants to fill but that he cannot because Pocquelin's supplies are too limited. By February of the next year, Pocquelin has sent a large amount of Asian fabric to Turner, which Turner has sold to wholesalers and retailers in London (Ms. 5101/3: Factory Book).

    In later years, Turner's business with Pocquelin appears to have wound down as Turner moved into larger-scale capital investments and as he became an importer, retailer, and wholesaler of fine cloth, a large portion of which was printed calico and silk from India. These he apparently purchased from the East India Company, of which he became a major shareholder. (See Ms. 5105: Booke of Sale.) In 1686, Turner's valuation of his net worth was £47,000, of which about 20 percent was in East India Company stock. (Ibid., fol. 35.) Among other things, Turner's business appears to have been so bound up with calicoes and silks that it was worth his while to keep an extraordinarily large share of his capital in EIC stock, probably so that he could influence the terms on which his supply was afforded.

83 For a summary of the company's strategy, see Chaudhuri, *Trading World*, 277–99; and Sha faant Ahmad Khan, *The East India Trade in the Seventeenth Century in its Political and Economic Aspects* (London: Oxford University Press, 1923), 193–307.

84 CCM, 1677–79, p. 88 (Court of Committees, September 28, 1677). See also the instructions from the East India Company's Court of Committees to its agents in Surat and Bombay, April 3, 1674, and March 5, 1675, IOLR H/34: 13, 23; and in Hugli (Bengal), May 20, 1681, and Fort St. George (near Madras), same date: Letter Book 6 (1678–82), IOLR E/3/89: 349–52.

85 Court of Committees to Hugli, May 20, 1681, Letter Book 6, IOLR E/3/89: 351–52.

86 Court of Committees to Agent and Council in Bengal, August 28, 1682, Letter Book 7, IOLR E/3/90, 21–26. Company relations with Indian wholesalers are discussed in letters to Hugli, December 13, 1672 and December 23, 1674, IOLR H/34: 93, 125.

87 C. W. Cole, *French Mercantilism, 1683–1700* (New York: Columbia University Press, 1943), 36–40, 164–177.

88 The French prohibition against domestic cotton printing was, however, carried out with much greater ferocity than any of the comparable bans later in England. Eli Heckscher, *Mercantilism*, 2nd rev. ed., trans. M. Shapiro, 2 vols. (London: George Allen and Unwin, 1955), 1:173, claims that 16,000 persons lost their lives in France through the enforcement of the calico decrees, primarily through execution and military action. He cites one occasion in Valence on which 77 people were sentenced to hang, 58 to be broken on the wheel, and 631 to be sent to the galleys, while one was freed. No pardons were given. If these figures are correct, mercantilism clearly meant something a good deal more serious in Louis XIV's France than in early Georgian England, where contravention of the Calico Act of 1721 was punishable by a £5 fine on the wearer and a £20 fine on the seller.

89 The politics of the Calico Acts are described in Chaudhuri, *Trading World*, 277–80; and Lemire, *Fashion's Favourite*, 29–42. See also P. J. Thomas, *Mercantilism and the East India Trade* (London: Frank Cass, 1963), esp. 160; William Foster, *The East India House* (London: John Lane, 1924), 68–69.

90 For example, Heckscher, *Mercantilism*, 1:174–75; and Joyce Oldham Appleby, *Liberalism and Republicanism in the Historical Imagination* (Cambridge, MA: Harvard University Press, 1992), 34–57. See also Lemire, *Fashion's Favourite*, 77–114, for the most coherent modern account of the effects of the calico ban on the demand side of the British textile industry.

91 Chaudhuri, *Trading World*, 277–80; Heckscher, *Mercantilism*, 1:174–75.

92 See, for example, the *London Journal* for March 18, 1720 (1721 New Style), in which hysterical denunciation of the South Seas Company and favorable reporting on the Calico Act are closely connected.

93 For a general history of the English cotton industry through the early period of industrialization, see Alfred P. Wadsworth and Julia de Lacy Man, *The Cotton Trade and Industrial Lancashire, 1600–1780* (Manchester: Manchester University Press, 1965). See also Robinson, *History of Printed Textiles*, 15–16.

94 See Chaudhuri, *Trading World*, 177–80, and Thomas, *Mercantilism*. The small size of English silk exports before the second half of the eighteenth century is shown in the tables in Ralph Davis, "English Foreign Trade, 1660–1700"; and "English Foreign Trade, 1700–1774," *Economic History Review* 15, no. 2 (1962): 285–303.

95 Slomann, *Bizarre Designs*; Lemire, *Fashion's Favourites* 12–21, 108–14.

96 Beck, *Draper's Dictionary*, 64. For a classic nationalist and mercantlist approach to textile consumption and the banning of East Indian imports, see John Cary, *An Essay on the State of England in Relation to Its Trade, Its Poor, and Its Taxes, for Carrying on the Present War against France* (Bristol: W. Bonny, for the Author, 1695), 25, 47–55. Not only is it unpatriotic to wear fabrics made abroad, but the very fact that Indian (and French) textiles are fashionable means that they are, by definition, immoral because they are an example of *luxury*. We will discuss luxury in chapter 3.

97 The concept of a substitute commodity has an old pedigree in the economic study of cross elasticities and of the Giffen Effect (the tendency for the prices of some goods to rise in the face of declining income), but the particular formulation employed here, the "substitute status commodity," is my own and is useful mainly for cultural analysis of consumption. It is similar in many ways to the category of "populuxe" or "semiluxury" goods employed by, among others, Maxine Berg to classify many of the products of eighteenth-century European industries. (See Maxine Berg, "New Commodities, Luxuries, and Their Consumers in Eighteenth-Century England," in *Consumers and Luxury*, ed. Berg and Clifford, 63–85.) The latter category, however, is used primarily to explore the ways in which imitation of high-status goods occurs, whereas the notion of the substitute status commodity provides a focus on competition among substitute status goods—that is, commodities belonging to the same category.

98 On the fur business, see Harold A. Innis, *The Fur Trade in Canada: An Introduction to Canadian Economic History*, rev. ed. (New Haven: Yale University Press, 1962).

99 This is one of the points made by John Cary in his classic *Essay on the State of England*. Cary claims (13–14), with great exaggeration, that English light woolens can be made with all sorts of colors and patterns, "some of them so fine and pleasant scarce to be known from Silk." "Our Workmen endeavoring to exceed another they make things to answer all the ends of Silks, Calicoes, and Linnen."

100 See the account book of a Miss Goreing, a rural gentlewoman of limited means but far from impoverished, between 1697 and 1704, preserved in the Chancery Records at the Public Record Office in London: PRO C114/182/32. Miss Georing's annual expenditures ranged between £92 and £138. In 1697, out of total expenses of £93 for a household of herself and two servants, £8/8/16 was spent on silks, just under £1 on calicoes, £1/8/0 on white cottons, £2 on linens, and £15/13/0 on all other fabrics, both wool and mixtures of wool, linen, silk, and cotton. Total expenditures on fabrics and garments amounted to 30 percent of total expenses, as against 55 percent for food. Miss Goreing's distribution of expenditure on textiles can be compared to the bills presented by the tailor William Watts to the dukes of Buckingham and Monmouth in 1667–68, which indicate a much higher proportion of silk to other materials and a heavy use of calicoes in place of European mixed fabrics. The bills (probably unpaid, because they appear to be connected to either a bankruptcy or an inheritance proceeding) can also be found in the Chancery Records: PRO C113/31, parts 1 and 2.

101 For example, Erasmus Jones, *Luxury, Pride, and Vanity, the Bane of the British Nation*, 2nd ed. (London: J. Roberts, 1736), 10. See Lemire, *Fashion's Favourite*, 19, 96–108.

102 Lemire, *Fashion's Favourite*, 35–39, 90–91, 90n.

103 Chaudhuri, *Trading World*, 277–80; Lemire, *Fashion's Favourite*, 83–84. In 1736, the Amsterdam correspondent of the London merchant Thomas Hall wrote: "I will speak to one of our first calico printers about the patterns you desire, but according to my knowledge have your printers in Engeland a better Taste as they have here and you would likewise find them handsomer, but I could forme an instruction very well what sort of patterns to chuse that would make a parcel the most valuable for an Exportation both for Holland and Germanie, where they most are worn." PRO Cl03/132 (letter, Smith to Hall, December 7, 1736).

104 W. W. Rostow, *How It All Began: Origins of the Modern Economy* (New York: McGraw-Hill, 1975), 159, 161–66, makes this argument.

105 The present discussion follows Lemire, *Fashion's Favourite*, 77–96.

106 Robinson, *History of Printed Textiles*, 18–27.

107 Lemire, *Fashion's Favourite*, 77–89.

108 C. Willett Cunnington and Phyllis Cunnington, *The History of Underclothes*, rev. ed. (London: Faber and Faber, 1981), 38–62.

109 Ibid.; Ann Buck, *Dress in Eighteenth-Century England* (London: B. T. Batsford, 1979).

110 Lemire, *Fashion's Favourite*, 15–21, 96–108. In the 1690s, John Cary had claimed that domestically produced English cotton was used mainly for shrouds, "and that chiefly among the Poor, who could not go the Price of finer Linnen" (Cary, *Essay on the State of England*, 54). However, even in the late eighteenth century, it appears that either many of poorer men in England did not possess shirts or that they were at least conventionally regarded as being shirtless. In a novel that we will examine closely in chapter 7, the hero, a man of gentle origins on the run from the law, trades clothing at an inn with a "labouring man," who is sleeping and therefore not consulted on the exchange. The man's outfit consists of leather breeches without strings or buckles, an old scarlet waistcoat, a "thickset" coat, hat, and stockings. No shirt is mentioned. The

hero, however, is careful to state that he himself has retained *his* shirt and pocket hand-kerchief. John Trusler, *Modern Times, or, the Adventures of Gabriel Outcast*, 2nd ed., 3 vols. (London: J. Murray, 1785), 1:209, 211–12.

111 Lemire, *Fashion's Favourite*, 77–114. Some of these changes are reflected in tables 2 and 3. Table 2 shows a growth in English linen imports roughly proportional to population growth in the first three-quarters of the eighteenth century (although the origins of the linen shift decisively from Germany and the Netherlands to Ireland). An increasing British capacity for linen production is shown in the healthy growth of English linen exports (much of which was actually Scottish—a peculiarity of customs reporting conventions). Cotton exports grow from a negligible to a respectable, although not spectacular, amount by the 1770s. At the same time, imports of white calico from Asia (table 3) remain high, although they decline slightly by the mid-eighteenth century. All this seems to show substantial demand for white cottons, linens, and the like. Table 2 shows a decline in imports of silks and mixed fabrics by the middle of the eighteenth century, for which a reasonable explanation would be that English mixed fabrics and cottons are taking their place—an explanation also for the modest decline in white calico imports. Thereafter, the situation changes drastically, as is demonstrated in Mathias, *First Industrial Nation*, 88, 454. Linen imports fall from 10.4 percent to 8.5 percent of total English imports between 1772 and 1790 (which in absolute terms is actually a slight growth), linen exports fall slightly, and imports of raw cotton (the best measure of overall cotton production in England) increase by a factor of five to six times. Cotton exports also increase, but not enough to account for more than a modest proportion of the overall increase in cotton production. By any reasonable inference, both cotton production and cotton consumption in England are skyrocketing, while imports of textiles other than linens decline.

112 Rostow, *How It All Began*, 61–65, 159.

113 See Alistair J. Durie, *The Scottish Linen Industry in the Eighteenth Century* (Edinburgh: Donald, 1979). Eighteenth-century shirting was often of very uneven quality, requiring an improvement in uniformity that was realized in mechanized cotton production but not in linen. A correspondent of the London merchant Thomas Hall wrote to him on February 8, 1736: "The piece of Smith's linen which I bought of you, was a sad bargain. I made it into shirts, which I am sure I have not wore three times each, and I have not one left that I can wear. It was as rotten as Tinder, and after the first washing, you might run your finger's [*sic*] thro' it" (PRO C103/132/31).

114 Lemire, *Fashion's Favourite*, 96–114.

CHAPTER THREE: LUXURY

1 For the history of luxury as an idea and a word, see John Sekora, *Luxury: The Concept in Western Thought, Eden to Smolett* (Baltimore: Johns Hopkins University Press, 1977); and Christopher J. Berry, *The Idea of Luxury: A Conceptual and Historical Investigation* (Cambridge: Cambridge University Press, 1994).

2 Sekora, *Luxury*, 23–31; Berry, *Idea of Luxury*, 126–176. The complexities of the eighteenth-century examination of luxury can be seen in the definitions given in the great dictionaries of the era. The newer approaches are evident in the article by Montesquieu on *luxe* in the *Encyclopédie, ou dictionnaire raisonné des sciences, des arts et des métiers*, 23 vols., facsimile ed. (Stuttgart: Frommann, 1966), 9:763: "Luxury is the use that is made of riches and industry in order to procure an agreeable existence." The older, morally disparaging view is present in Samuel Johnson's *Dictionary*, 2: "Luxury: . . . 1. Voluptuousness; addictedness to pleasure . . . 2. Lust; lewdness . . . 3. Luxurience; exuberance . . . 4. Delicious fare . . . ." "Luxurious: . . . 1. Delighting in

the pleasures of the table . . . 2. Administering to luxury . . . 3. Lustful; libidinous . . . 4. Voluptuous; enslaved to pleasure . . . 5. Softened by pleasure . . . 6. Luxurient; exuberant. . . ." Samuel Johnson, *A Dictionary of the English Language*, 2 vols. (London: W. Strahan, 1755), n.p.

3   Sekora, *Luxury*, 23–62. "It [luxury] could mean many things to many people because its content could be infinitely distended and adjusted. With such dynamic and generative possibilities, it was an idea to be used, not defined"

4   Berry, *Idea of Luxury*, 3–42.

5   See Maxine Berg, "New Commodities, Luxuries, and Their Consumers," 63–85. See also Ann Birmingham and John Brewer, eds., *The Consumption of Culture, 1600–1800* (London: Routledge, 1995); and Brewer, *Pleasures of the Imagination*, 3–122.

6   Campbell, *Romantic Ethic*.

7   John E. Crowley, "The Sensibility of Comfort," *American Historical Review* 104 (June 1999): 749–82.

8   Simon Schama, *The Embarrassment of Riches: An Interpretation of Dutch Culture in the Golden Age* (New York: Alfred A. Knopf, 1987).

9   Werner Sombart, *Luxus und Kapitalismus* (Munich and Leipzig: Duncker und Humblot, 1922).

10   Ibid., 45–69, 111–32.

11   Sekora, *Luxury*, 63–109.

12   For example, Berry, *Idea of Luxury*, 142–73.

13   One of the things that eighteenth-century critics of luxury found most objectionable was the apparent elimination of family distinction as a qualifier for interpreting dress. "People where they are not known," complained Erasmus Jones, "are generally honour'd according to their Clothes." Jones, *Luxury, Pride, and Vanity*, 12.

14   See, for example, Thomas Violet, *A Petition against the Jewes* (London: n.p., 1661), actually a collection of Violet's pamphlets including his anti-Semitic tract. As his petitions are addressed to Charles II, Violet (a member of the Goldsmith's Company of London) does not directly mention royal mistresses. He does, however, lump into one category Jews, East India merchants, and purchasers of "unnecessary trifles" such as Flanders lace and "French baubles" (the last group apparently consisting of loose women of means) as immoral persons who are ruining the country.

15   On sumptuary laws, see Herman Freudenberger, "Fashion, Sumptuary Laws, and Business," *Business History Review* 37, no. 1/2 (1963): 37–48; Youings, *Sixteenth-Century England*, 110–15.

16   See, for example, Thomas Mun, *A Discourse of Trade, from England unto the East-Indies: Answering to Diverse Objections Which Are Usually Made against the Same* (London: Nicholas Oakes for John Pyper, 1621), 5–8 (pro-East India Company); Cary, *Essay on the State of England*, 47–60 (anti-company); Olfert Dapper, *Historische Beschrijving der Stadt Amsterdam* (Meurs: Jacob van Meurs, 1663), 449 (description of wares offered by VOC).

17   Mun, *Discourse of Trade*, 5–6, distinguishes between goods sought for fashion and those employed for other reasons. "Who is so ignorant," he asks, "in any famous commonwealth, which will not consent to the moderate use of wholesome Druggs and comfortable Spices?" At the same time, he tries also to distinguish between "wholesome" uses and those that "please a lickerish taste." The role of the Indies companies in creating an analysis of demand that took the kind of consumption that they satisfied out of the field of moral argumentation is emphasized in much of the literature on the eighteenth-century debate over luxury. See Berry, *Idea of Luxury*, 102–18.

18 On the relationship between taxation of consumption and the social and political structure of eighteenth-century Britain, see John Brewer, *The Sinews of Power: War, Money,
and the English State, 1688–1783* (New York: Alfred A. Knopf, 1989).

19 Ewen and Ewen, *Channels of Desire*, 23–52, 194–202.

20 Robert Louis Stein, *The French Sugar Business in the Eighteenth Century* (Baton
Rouge: Louisiana State University Press, 1988), 100.

21 A Dutch pamphlet of 1680 lists among the virtues of tea that it "stimulates tired
blood," prevents bad dreams, cures headaches, clears the face, improves memory, and
"strengthens the work of Venus serviceably for newlyweds." Reproduced in *Thema
Thee*, 23.

22 Ewen and Ewen, *Channels of Desire*, 53–73; Campbell, *Romantic Ethic*, 58–95; and
especially Rosalind Williams, *Dream Worlds: Mass Consumption in Late Nineteenth-
Century France* (Berkeley: University of California Press, 1982), 1–16, 58–106.

23 Robert Tucker, ed. *The Marx-Engels Reader*, 2nd ed. (New York: W. W. Norton, 1978),
319–29 (an excerpt from Marx's *Capital*, vol. 1, part 1, chap. 1, section 4: "The
Fetishism of Commodities and the Secret Thereof").

24 Cunnington and Cunnington, *History of Underclothes*, 13–14; Iris Brooke, *English
Costume in the Age of Elizabeth*, 2nd ed. (London: A and C Black, 1950), 12.

25 See, for example, Brueghel's *Procession to Calvary* and *The Peasant Wedding* in
Christopher Brown, ed., *Breughel: Paintings, Drawings, and Prints* (Oxford: Phaidon,
1975), 34, 85.

26 The standard works on the Parisian salons are Lougee, *Paradis des Femmes*; and Glotz
and Maire, *Salons du XVIIIe siècle*.

27 See the introduction to Madame de Sèvignè, *Lettres*, 3 vols. (Paris: Gallimard, 1953),
1:7–93.

28 Norman Hartnell, *Royal Courts of Fashion* (London: Cassell, 1971), 43–48.

29 See, for example, the pattern of interaction displayed in the correspondence between
Madame de Sèvignè and the Comte de Bussy Rabutin in Sèvignè, *Lettres*, 1:110–69
passim.

30 See Anne Hollander, *Sex and Suits* (New York: Alfred A. Knopf, 1994), 30–63.

31 Sombart, *Luxus*, 59–70.

32 The central text in this discussion is Edward W. Said, *Orientalism* (New York: Vintage,
1979).

33 These are topics examined by the branch of social psychology called "person perception." See David J. Schneider, Albert H. Hastorf, and Phoebe C. Ellsworth, *Person
Perception*, 2nd ed. (Reading, MA: Addison-Wesley, 1979).

34 Wolfgang Schivelbusch, *Tastes of Paradise: A Social History of Spices, Stimulants,
and Intoxicants*, trans. D. Jacobson (New York: Vintage, 1992), 13–14.

35 *Thema Thee*, 36–38.

36 I am obliged to Brian Cowan for information on virtuoso culture contained in an
unpublished paper.

37 See Said, *Orientalism*, 179–90.

38 See the portrait of Lady Mary Wortley Montague, one of the initiators of the fashion,
in Robert Halsband, ed., *The Complete Letters of Lady Mary Wortley Montague*, 3
vols. (Oxford: Clarendon Press, 1965), facing 1:304.

39 [J. Sowter], *The Way to Be Wise and Wealthy: or, The Excellency of Industry and
Frugality* (London: J. Wilford, 1736), 48; Jones, *Luxury, Pride, and Vanity*, 3–4, 9.

40 Sekora, *Luxury*, 23–62.

41 Ibid., 61–62.

42 Jones, *Luxury, Pride, and Vanity*, 2–16.

43 Ibid., 16.

44 Ibid., 17.

45 Isaac Kramnick, ed., *The Portable Enlightenment Reader* (New York: Penguin, 1995), 247.

46 Sekora, *Luxury*, 23–62; J. T. Cliffe, *The Puritan Gentry: The Great Puritan Families of Early Stuart England* (London: Routledge and Kegan Paul, 1984), 58–62.

47 Cliffe, *Puritan Gentry*, 43–62.

48 Ibid.

49 This attitude is one of those that Max Weber identified as composing the "Protestant Ethic." Max Weber, *The Protestant Ethic and the Spirit of Capitalism*, trans. T. Parsons (New York: Scribner, 1958), 47–78. See also Cliffe, *Puritan Gentry*, 125–45.

50 Victor-L. Tapié, *The Age of Grandeur: Baroque Art and Architecture* (New York: Praeger, 1960), esp. 69–85.

51 See Richard T. Vann, *The Social Development of English Quakerism 1655–1755* (Cambridge, MA: Harvard University Press, 1969), 193–96.

52 Sources on the history of taste are Campbell, *Romantic Ethic*, 138–72; Bernard Denvir, *The Eighteenth Century: Art, Design, and Society, 1689–1789* (London: Longman, 1983), 10–11, 63–116; and Leora Auslander, *Taste and Power: Furnishing Modern France* (Berkeley: University of California Press, 1996), esp. 35–40.

53 See *Lord Chesterfield's Letters to His Son and Others* (London: Dent, 1929), 30–31.

54 Denvir, *Eighteenth Century*, 10–11.

55 On taste and the market for painting in Georgian Britain, see Brewer, *Pleasures of the Imagination*, 201–87.

56 Campbell, *Romantic Ethic*, 161–72.

57 Aileen Ribeiro, *Dress in Eighteenth-Century Europe, 1715–1789* (New York: Holmes and Meier, 1984), 25. Another important example of the adaptation of large-scale manufacturing and consumption to changes in formal taste will appear in chapter 8, where the career of Josiah Wedgwood is discussed.

58 G. J. Barker-Benfield, *The Culture of Sensibility: Sex and Society in Eighteenth-Century Britain* (Chicago: University of Chicago Press, 1992); Brian Cowan, "Reasonable Ecstasies: Shaftesbury and the Languages of Libertinism," *Journal of British Studies* 37, no. 2 (1998): 111–38.

59 *Chesterfield's Letters*, 48–51.

60 See, for example, ibid., 13. Also see Klein, *Shaftesbury and the Culture of Politeness*.

61 *Chesterfield's Letters*, xi.

62 Jean-Jacques Rousseau, "A Discourse on the Arts and Sciences," in *The Social Contract and Discourses*, ed. and trans. G. D. H. Cole (New York: Dutton, 1950), 143–74. See also Henry Mackenzie, *The Man of Feeling*, ed. B. Vickers (London: Oxford University Press, 1967).

63 Crowley, "Sensibility of Comfort," 749–82.

64 The Dutch cultural constructions that Simon Schama describes in his *Embarrassment of Riches* seem similar to many of those Crowley discusses.

65 Crowley, "Sensibility of Comfort," 769–71.

66 John Mullan, *Sentiment and Sociability: The Language of Feeling in the Eighteenth Century* (Oxford: Clarendon Press, 1988).

67 See Crowley, "Sensibility of Comfort," 769–70, which quotes Franklin's analysis of what was wrong with traditional fireplaces as an aggregation of "inconveniencies," the end result of which was discomfort.

68 Steensgaard, *Asian Trade Revolution*, 22–59.

69 The most comprehensive (and breathtakingly brutal) statement of company aims is the 1614 "Discourse" of Jan Pietersz. Coen, later to be the most famous VOC governor-general in the Indies: Jan Pietersz. Coen, *Bescheiden omtrent zijn bedrijf in Indie*, ed. H. T. Colenbrander, 6 vols. (The Hague: Martinus Nijhoff, 1919–1934), 6:451–74. See also K. N. Chaudhuri, *The English East India Company: The Study of an Early Joint-Stock Company, 1600–1640* (New York: A. M. Kelley, 1965), 3–10.

70 Steensgaard, *Asian Trade Revolution*, 209–343.

71 See Chaudhuri, *Trading World of Asia*, 313–28.

72 Violet Barbour, *Capitalism in Amsterdam in the Seventeenth Century* (Ann Arbor: University of Michigan Press, 1963). The classic near contemporary explanation of Amsterdam's replacement of Antwerp is "V. D. H." [Pieter de la Court], *Interest van Holland, ofte Gronden van Hollands-Welvaren* (Amsterdam: Joan. Cyprianus vander Gracht, 1662), 24–35.

73 Glamann, *Dutch-Asiatic Trade*, 2–38.

74 An extremely precise and well-reasoned analysis of the Dutch Baltic grain trade and of the role of the East India trade in it is contained in an anonymous 1631 pamphlet by a Dutch or German merchant resident in Danzig: *Grontlijcke Tegen-bericht Van de waerachtige remedie Der tegenwoordige dierte in de Granen in Nederlandt* (n.p.: Broer Jansz., 1631), esp. 10. A seventeenth-century guide to Amsterdam says of the VOC's headquarters building: "This house is full of everything the Muscovite, the Pole, the High German are looking for." Dapper, *Historische Beschrijving*, 449.

75 Wholesale price fluctuations in pepper and spices are summarized in W. W. Post-humus, *Nederlandsche Prijsgeschiedenis*, 2 vols. (Leiden: Brill, 1943), 1:495–526. See also Glamann, *Dutch-Asiatic Trade*, 73–111. Changes in quantities are less easily summarized. In the late seventeenth century, VOC director Johannes Hudde developed summary tables of quantities sold at the various VOC auctions (with prices), which were sporadically updated thereafter by company officials and which display the tendencies suggested in this chapter. ARA, Hudde Papers, no. 18.

76 C. R. Boxer, *The Dutch Seaborne Empire, 1600–1800* (London: Hutchinson, 1977), 99; Glamann, *Dutch-Asiatic Trade*, 92.

77 This was made clear by one of the main participants in the development of seventeenth-century VOC pricing policy: Pieter van Dam. See van Dam, *Beschrijvinge*, 68:144–299.

78 Glamann, *Dutch-Asiatic Trade*, 111.

79 Posthumus, *Nederlandsche Prijsgeschiedenis*, 1:494–526. The relative stability of demand for pepper can be inferred from table 4, page 302 which shows English East India Company imports of black pepper from 1666 to 1760. Unlike the VOC, the East India Company had no policy of maintaining price stability (and no means of enforcing it even if it had possessed one). The figures in table 4 can be compared to the dynamic increases in importation, and presumably consumption, of sugar (and coffee and tea) shown in table 6, page 304.

80 Glamann, *Dutch-Asiatic Trade*, 141–51.

81 Ibid., 253–54. The argument for raising prices is made in a printed version of an 1692 VOC memorandum, possibly emanating from Hudde: ARA, Vredenburch Papers, no. 11, item 2.

82 Glamann, *Dutch-Asiatic Trade*, 261–65. The extent of VOC domination of the pepper and spice trades is indicated in an internal company report summarizing the amounts of those commodities imported into Europe between 1730 and 1735. Only once (1733) does the total amount of black pepper imported directly from Asia by all the rest of Europe combined exceed 50 percent of Dutch pepper imports. Usually, it is less than 25 percent. Essentially *all* the nutmeg, cloves, cinnamon, mace, and ginger brought to Europe is transported by the VOC. ARA, VOC, no. 7000.

83 The early history of sugar as a commodity is presented by Mintz, *Sweetness and Power*, 19–32.

84 See, for example, P. Nyland, *Den Ervaren Huys-houder* (Amsterdam: Marcus Doornick, 1668), 10, 13–15. The rather broad definitions of *health* and *medicine* when applied to sugar can be seen in *The Treasurie of Hidden Secrets: Commonly Called, The Good-huswives Closet of Provision, for the Health of Her Household* (London: John Wright, 1627), of which chapter 6 (n.p.) consists of recipes that are clearly intended to emphasize the taste and the status implications of sugar, not its supposed healthiness. Richard Ligon, *A True and Exact History of the Island of Barbadoes* (London: Peter Parker, 1673), 96, quotes a saying of a physician named Butler: "If Sugar can preserve both Peares and Plumbs, Why can it not preserve as well our Lungs?" The health-giving qualities of sugar are derived by inference from its other attributes—in this case, its character as preservative.

85 See Richard B. Sheridan, *Sugar and Slavery: An Economic History of the British West Indies, 1623–1775* (Baltimore: Johns Hopkins University Press, 1973).

86 Stein, *French Sugar Business*, 93–105.

87 Sheridan, *Sugar and Slavery*, 22, tabulates the annual averages of colonial sugar imports into England and Wales. He shows that imports more than doubled between the beginning and the middle of the eighteenth century, and because a growing percentage of imported sugar was not reexported, retained imports essentially trebled. The population of England increased only about 20 percent during the same period: B. R. Mitchell, *British Historical Statistics* (Cambridge: Cambridge University Press, 1988), 7.

88 For example, see J. H. Parry, *The Establishment of the European Hegemony, 1415–1715: Trade and Exploration in the Age of the Renaissance*, 3rd rev. ed. (New York: Harper and Row, 1959), at one time the standard short treatment of its subject and an excellent book by most criteria. Parry devotes many pages (100–1, 110–4, 149–61) to the growth of the sugar trade and the West Indian plantation economy, but gives no explanation for the growth of European sugar consumption. Indeed, the question does not even arise.

89 Breughel, "A Bourgeois Good?" 99–118, describes official efforts in the late nineteenth and early twentieth centuries to increase the traditionally very low consumption of sugar by the French working class. He argues that French workers resisted sugar not because of its cost, but because its consumption was identified with their class antagonists.

90 Stein, *French Sugar Business*, 93–105, 120; Mintz, *Sweetness and Power*, 188–90.

91 See, for example, Thomas Short, M.D., *Discourses on Tea, Sugar, Milk, Made-Wines, Spirits, Punch, Tobacco, etc., with Plain and Useful Rules for Gouty People* (London: T. Longman, 1750).

92 Mintz, *Sweetness and Power*, 74–82.

93 Ibid.

94 Mennell, *All Manners of Food*, 40–73; Meister Sebastian, *Koch und Kellermeisterey* (Frankfurt am Main: S. Feyrabend, 1581; repr. 1964), esp. 12–33.

95 A classic example of late medieval exoticism is the (largely fictional) *Travels* of Sir John Mandeville. For instances of exoticism with respect to the pepper and spices of Asia, see [Sir John Mandeville], *Mandeville's Travels*, ed. M. Letts, 2 vols. (London: Hakluyt Society, 1967), 1:119–22, 132–40.

96 See, for example, Parry, *Establishment of the European Hegemony*, 32.

97 Mintz, *Sweetness and Power*, 74–150, supports this view in showing how complex and variable the functional basis of sugar usage was.

98 For an idea of the dimensions of the flood of pepper into Europe in the second quarter of the seventeenth century, see *Lyste Vande Gedenckwaerdige Teyckeninghe op de Peper . . .* (Haarlem: T. Fonteyn, 1639), a list of parcels of pepper signed for by individuals and sitting in the VOC warehouse. The issue of pepper gluts and prices was discussed by the directors of the Amsterdam chapter of the VOC on March 23, 1688: ARA, VOC, no. 243. See also ARA, VOC, no. 7000 (summaries of pepper imports, 1730–35), and Glamann, *Dutch-Asiatic Trade*, 73–90.

99 Glamann, *Dutch-Asiatic Trade*, 91–111. See also Schivelbusch, *Tastes of Paradise*, 3–14.

100 See van Dam, *Beschryvinge*, 68:227–99, for an insider's history of the VOC's attempts to understand its European market for pepper and spices.

101 See W. A. Horst, "De Peperhandel van de Vereenigde Oostindische Compagnie," *Bijdragen voor Vaderlandsche Geschiedenis en Oudheitkunde* 8, no. 3 (1942): 95–103.

102 Mennell, *All Manners of Food*, 62–133.

103 See Meister Sebastian, *Koch und Kellermeisterey*, 12–33.

104 See Nyland, *Ervaren Huys-houder*, 59 (misnumbered 61)–80, for recipes that illustrate this tendency.

105 Mennell, *All Manners of Food*, 20–39, 73.

106 For example, demand for cloves shot up in the 1830s and 1840s and then remained stable, with declining prices due to the extension of production, especially to Zanzibar. See Philip Curtin et al., *African History* (Boston: Little, Brown, 1978), 401–3.

107 The history of sugarbaking is summarized in Mintz, *Sweetness and Power*, 87–96. It is true that sugarbaking employed many of the Asian spices as well, but as the name of the occupation implies, sugar was far and away the most important constituent of confections.

108 J. J. Reese, *De Suikerhandel van Amsterdam van het Begin der 17de Eeuw tot 1813* (Haarlem: I.L.E.I. Kleynenberg, 1908), 28–29.

109 That the practice of sugar courses was not necessarily limited to the extremely wealthy is suggested by *The Treasurie of Hidden Secrets*, a book apparently aimed no higher than the lower gentry. Chapter 6 (n.p.) contains a recipe: "To make Paste of Suger, whereof may bee made all manner of fruits and other fine things with their forme: as Platters, Dishes, Glasses, Cups, and such like things, wherewith you may furnish a Table, and when you have done, you may eat them up."

110 For an excellent summary of these issues and a brilliant contribution to their discussion, see Jan de Vries, "Between Purchasing Power and the World of Goods: Understanding the Household Economy in Early Modern Europe," in *Consumption and the World of Goods*, ed. Brewer and Porter, 85–132.

111 Sekora, *Luxury*, 63–109. See, for example, Jones, *Luxury, Pride, and Vanity*, 4–6. On page 6, Jones asserts that a "man who can afford only to keep the Commandments, must not pretend to stand in competition with him who keeps his Coach and Concubine." Jones obviously misses the distinction between status consumption and what we are calling luxury consumption.

112 Mintz, *Sweetness and Power*, 114–22; Reese, *Suikerhandel*, 30–76. See the rise in sugar imports into England and Wales displayed in table 6, page 304. See also the estimate of British sugar consumption in the eighteenth century in Ralph A. Austen and Woodruff D. Smith, "Private Tooth Decay as Public Economic Virtue: The Slave-Sugar Triangle, Consumerism, and European Industrialization," *Social Science History* 14, no. 1 (1990): 77–97, esp. 99, which shows an increase in per capita consumption from just under five pounds at the beginning of the eighteenth century to over sixteen pounds by the 1760s. Presumably urban averages were higher and rural areas were lower. According to a study undertaken by the scientist Antoine Lavoisier just before the French Revolution, annual per capita consumption of sugar in Paris was 5.3 kilograms, or 11.6 pounds. For France as a whole, however, per capita consumption was only just over 2.0 kilograms as late as the early 1830s—which illustrates both the disparity between urban and rural consumption of sugar and the smaller desire of the French for sugar and sugar products. Breughel, "A Bourgeois Good?" 100, 103.

113 Mintz, *Sweetness and Power*, 3–18.

114 Meister Sebastian, *Koch und Kellermeisterey*, passim.

115 Ibid., 55, 67–74.

116 John Chamberlayne, *A Family-Herbal, or, the Treasure of Health* (London: W. Crooke, 1689), 219.

117 See, for example, William Rabisha, *The Whole Body of Cookery Dissected. . . .* (London: Giles Calvert, 1761); Giles Rose, *A Perfect School of Instruction for Officers of the Mouth* (London: R. Bentley and M. Magnes, 1682); and Patrick Lamb, *Royal Cookery; or, the Complete Court-Cook* (London: A. Roper, 1710).

118 See *The Whole Duty of a Woman* (London: T. Reed, 1737); and the most successful of all English cookbooks before 1800, Hannah Glasse, *The Art of Cookery, Made Plain and Simple* (London: by the author, 1747). There are innumerable later editions of Glasse.

119 Mintz, *Sweetness and Power*, esp. 77–79.

120 Ibid., 93–96.

121 Reese, *Suikerhandel*, 150–57.

122 Mintz, *Sweetness and Power*, 125–26.

123 Chamberlayne, *Family-Herbal*, 120–21, 218–19.

124 Ibid., 105–8.

125 Elizabeth Kowaleski-Wallace, *Consuming Subjects: Women, Shopping, and Business in the Eighteenth Century* (New York: Columbia University Press), 37–51.

CHAPTER FOUR: VIRTUE

1 S[teven] Blankaart, M.D., *De Borgerlyke Tafel: Om lang gesond sonder ziekten te leven* (Amsterdam: Jan ten Hoorn, 1683). Blankaart was also a prominent entomologist and the author of an important book on caterpillars. Natalie Zemon Davis, *Women on the Margins: Three Seventeenth-Century Lives* (Cambridge, MA, and London: Harvard University Press, 1995), 167, 182.

2 Blankaart, *Borgerlyke Tafel.*, 39–43, 84–86.

3 Ibid., preface (n.p.).

4 Ibid., 85; Cornelis Bontekoe, *Tractaat Van het Excellenste Kruyd Thee, Coffi, en Chocolate*, 103, appended to vol. 2 of *Alle de Philosophische, Medicinale, en Chymische Werken van den Heer Corn. Bontekoe*, 2 vols. (Amsterdam: n.p., 1689). Bontekoe states: "If all men had one nature, I should find no difficulty in advising them to drink fifty or a hundred or two hundred cups one after the other; I have myself drunk that much in a morning or afternoon, and not only I, but many people with me have done the same, of whom not one is dead yet." Not surprisingly, Bontekoe was widely reputed to be a quack, but he made a successful career, eventually being named court physician to the Elector of Brandenburg. The author of the introduction to *Alle de . . . Werken* (1:n.p.) reports that Bontekoe met what some regarded as a fitting end: after drinking tea with friends in Berlin, he fell down some stairs while hurrying to make water, and broke his neck. The postmortem, however, revealed that all his internal organs were in perfect condition.

5 Nyland, *Den Ervaren Huys-houder*, 13–14.

6 Reese, *Suikerhandel*, 28–29.

7 Van Dam, *Beschryvinge*, 68:351–52, notes that according to the VOC's 1682 rules for making "presents" of company products to opinion leaders, the packages for ministers of the Reformed Church were not to contain sugar, unlike the packages for everyone else.

8 Blankaart, *Borgerlyke Tafel*, 1–3.

9 Ibid., 84.

10 Robert P. Hudson, *Disease and Its Control: The Shaping of Modern Thought* (Westport: Greenwood, 1983), 176.

11 *The Autobiography of Benjamin Franklin* (New York: Modern Library, 1981), 68–70, 103–16.

12 I remember reading parts of the *Autobiography* dealing with Franklin's scheme of moral perfection in textbooks in at least two different grades at school—with the item about chastity conspicuously made inconspicuous. (In one case, the list proceeded from virtue 11 to virtue 13. In the other, the heading "chastity" was included but Franklin's explication of it was not.)

13 See David Freeman Hawke, *Franklin* (New York: Harper and Row, 1976); and Robert Middlekauff, *Benjamin Franklin and His Enemies* (Berkeley: University of California Press, 1996).

14 *Autobiography of Benjamin Franklin*, 104–5.

15 D. H. Lawrence, "Benjamin Franklin," in *Studies in Classic American Literature* (New York: Viking Press, 1964), 9–21.

16 Fletcher, *Gender, Sex, and Subordination.* 44–59; Patricia Crawford, "Sexual Knowledge in England, 1500–1750," in *Sexual Knowledge, Sexual Science: The History of Attitudes Toward Sexuality*, ed. Roy Porter and Mikulas Teich (Cambridge: Cambridge University Press, 1994), 85.

17 *Autobiography of Benjamin Franklin*, 84–85.

18 Ibid., 84.

19 Ibid., 112, 114–16.

20 Ibid., 104.

21 See Albert O. Hirschman, *The Passions and the Interests: Political Arguments for Capitalism before Its Triumph* (Princeton: Princeton University Press, 1977).

22 See de la Court, *Interest van Holland*, introduction and 15–23.

23 See the articles on *interêt* in the *Encyclopédie*, 8:818–29, especially the article on the moral sense of interest, 818–19.

24 Hudson, *Disease*, 75–88.

25 Sekora, *Luxury*, 23–62.

26 *Autobiography of Benjamin Franklin*, 104.

27 Ibid., 112.

28 Ibid., 15–16, 36–38.

29 Ibid., 112–13, 151.

30 Ibid., 84–85.

31 Ibid., 117–18, 151.

32 See D. S. Hutchinson, *The Virtues of Aristotle* (London: Routledge and Kegan Paul, 1986); and Terence Irwin, *Plato's Ethics* (New York: Oxford University Press, 1995).

33 Jean-Pierre Goubert, *The Conquest of Water: The Advent of Health in the Industrial Age*, trans. A. Wilson (Princeton: Princeton University Press, 1986), 27–29.

34 *Autobiography of Benjamin Franklin*, 102.

35 Weber, *Protestant Ethic*, 64–65, 71–72, 74–75.

36 On the republican or civic humanist tradition, see Pocock, *Machiavellian Moment*. Francesco Guicciardini, a classic "Machiavellian," incorporates a typical republican view of virtue and interest in the speeches that he puts into the mouths of the orators on *both* sides of a 1495 debate on the structure of a new Florentine constitution: Francesco Guicciardini, *The History of Italy*, trans. S. Alexander (New York: Macmillan, 1969), 78–81. One speaker favors election of officials by a "universal council" of all citizens. "Thus," he says, "the distribution of honors and positions not being in the hands of private citizens or of any particular faction or point of view, no one would be excluded by the passion or prejudice of others, but honors would be distributed according to men's virtues and merits" (78). He goes on to say that if most citizens are not brought into the political process on a regular basis, "then, since the citizens are no longer intent upon public welfare but rather on cupidity and on private ends, factions and particular conspiracies will arise . . . the plague and inevitable death of all Republics and governments" (79–80). The opposing speaker, who favors a republic with a much more limited effective franchise, asks whether in a democracy such as the first speaker proposed "an inexpert, inexperienced multitude composed of so great a variety of talents, conditions, and ways of doing things, and each one devoted to his own particular affairs, will be able to distinguish and understand that which men who are wise in public affairs, and devoting all their efforts to no other task, can scarcely discern?" (81). In other words, both speakers set up an opposition between private interest on the one hand and public interest and public virtue on the other. Their argument is essentially about which form of a republic is less prone to being injured by private interests. This is quite different from Franklin, who generally sees the private interests of virtuous persons as being consistent with public interest, or at least not subversive of it.

37 Compare Franklin's view of the basis of benevolence and society with that of David Hume, as explicated in Mullan, *Sentiment and Sociability*, 18–56. Hume, according to Mullan, tried to build a view of society and individuals' relationships to it on the basis of shared sentiment, to which individual rationality and rationally delineated interest are inherently subordinate. The result, while an interesting analysis of society, clearly did not catch on as a standard element of modern culture—unlike Franklin's less sophisticated approach.

38 Fletcher, *Gender, Sex, and Subordination*, 30–43.

39 Blankaart, *Borgerlycke Tafel*, introduction (n.p.).

40 Israel, *Dutch Republic*, 328–98, 610–76.

41 In addition to Weber, *Protestant Ethic*, see A. Whitney Griswold, "Three Puritans on Prosperity," *New England Quarterly* 7 (1934): 475–88.

42 Simon Schama, *Citizens: A Chronicle of the French Revolution* (New York: Knopf, 1989), 602.

43 See Gordon S. Wood, *The Radicalism of the American Revolution*, (New York:Vintage, 1993), 233. In German, *burger* came to mean "citizen" in the modern sense in the late eighteenth century, and it was also the word that carried the class meaning of the French word *bourgeois*—the word, in fact, that Marx used that is translated into English as "bourgeois."

44 *Autobiography of Benjamin Franklin*, 64, 128. This of course does not mean that Franklin may not at one time have *wanted* to be accounted a gentleman, but by the time he wrote his autobiography, he had created his *persona* of being a (highly uncommon) "common" or "natural" man and was not about to call it into question.

45 See, for example, *Autobiography of Benjamin Franklin*, 140–47.

46 As was noted previously, the term *middle class* has come to be used much more frequently by historians in recent years than *bourgeoisie*, partly because of the identification of the latter with Marxist analysis and partly because the foundations of earlier consensus on the meaning of *bourgeois* have eroded. However, *middle class* is not much more satisfactory. Sometimes the term is used to denote a class that is truly in the "middle" and is conscious of its middleness. See, for example, Margaret R. Hunt, *The Middling Sort: Commerce, Gender, and the Family in England, 1680–1780* (Berkeley: University of California Press, 1996)—although Hunt prefers *middling* to *middle class*. Others employ *middle class* as a synonym for *bourgeois* in its broad Marxian or Weberian senses: Shinagel, *Daniel Defoe and Middle Class Gentility*. Still others, not departing very far from Marxist usage, focus on modernizing elites: John Smail, *The Origins of Middle-Class Culture: Halifax, Yorkshire, 1660–1780* (Ithaca: Cornell University Press, 1994).

47 Schama, *Citizens*, 602.

48 An excellent summary of historical research from the 1950s to the 1970s on the eighteenth-century French bourgeoisie is contained in Darnton, *Great Cat Massacre*, 109–13. Reddy, *Money and Liberty*, 1–33, presents a radical critique of "class" (especially the bourgeois class) as a category of historical and social analysis.

49 Mintz, *Sweetness and Power*, 108–19; Sir Percival Griffiths, *The History of the Indian Tea Industry* (London: Weidenfeld and Nicolson, 1967), 14–22; William H. Ukers, *All about Tea*, 2 vols. (New York: Tea and Coffee Trade Journal Company, 1935), 1:35, 49. In France, the sugaring of coffee and tea was a much more limited phenomenon, even at the end of the eighteenth century. See Breughel, "A Bourgeois Good?" 102–4.

50 Mintz, *Sweetness and Power*, 108–19.

51 Griffiths, *Indian Tea Industry*, 3–13; *Thema Thee*, 28. For a more detailed presentation of the subject of this section, see Woodruff D. Smith, "From Coffeehouse to Parlour: The Consumption of Coffee, Tea, and Sugar in North-Western Europe in the Seventeenth and Eighteenth Centuries," in *Consuming Habits: Drugs in History and Anthropology*, ed. Jordan Goodman, Paul E. Lovejoy, and Andrew Sherratt (London: Routledge, 1995), 148–64.

52 Mintz, *Sweetness and Power*, 109.

53 Philippe Sylvestre Dufour, *Traitez Nouveaux et curieux du café, du thée, et du chocolate* (The Hague: Adrian Moetjens, 1685), 15–185 (on coffee), 193–256 (on tea); Ukers, *All about Tea*, 1:23–25; *Thema Thee*, 13–19.

54 Mintz, *Sweetness and Power*, 110.

55 John Chamberlain, *The Manner of Making of Coffee, Tea, and Chocolate* (London: William Crook, 1685), 8.

56 Ibid., 50. Note that the Chinese practice described in Chamberlain of adding some sugar or spices to tea while it is boiling is quite different from the European custom of adding large amounts of sugar *after* the tea is prepared. Tulp's original work on tea was part of a medical treatise: Nicholas Tulp, *Observationes medicae* (Amsterdam: Elsevier, 1652), 4:400–403. Tulp expanded on his observations in a pamphlet that Chamberlain translates and incorporates and that Dufour cites: Nicholas Tulp, *Uitstekkende Eigenschappen, en Heerlyke Werkingen van het kruid Thee . . .* (Amsterdam: n.p., 1675). Tulp was a director of the VOC and is famous as the central (living) figure in the more familiar of Rembrandt's two "Anatomy Lesson" paintings.

57 Jordan Goodman, "Excitantia: Or, How Enlightenment Europe Took to Soft Drugs," in *Consuming Habits*, ed. Goodman, Lovejoy, and Sherratt, 142, n. 61. Samuel Pepys does not mention sugar in his oft-cited entries about tea-taking in the 1660s: *Diary of Samuel Pepys*, 1:253 (September 25, 1660); 6:327–28 (December 13, 1665); 8:302 (June 28, 1667).

58 Bontekoe, *Traactat*, 103–6.

59 Blankaart, *Borgerlyke Tafel*, 84–86.

60 Ukers, *All about Tea*, 1:37–48. Consciousness of the fact that practices had changed with regard to combining tea and sugar can be seen in a pamphlet called *A Treatise on the Inherent Qualities of the Tea-Herb* (London: C. Corbett, 1750). The frontispiece announces that the book was written by a "Gentleman of Cambridge" who has paraphrased and added commentary to a seventeenth-century treatise on tea by Johannes Pechlin, physician to the king of Denmark. The author remarks that Pechlin had written that the "natural Way of drinking Tea" was without sugar, but that "a little Sugar" did not hinder the medicinal workings of tea (10). The mid-eighteenth-century author then goes on in his own voice (possibly with some embarrassment at the inconsistency) to discuss how well-refined sugar adds to tea's color and flavor and which teas are best with large amounts of sugar (not "a little"). In other words, the author, writing at a time when almost everyone in England who takes tea puts a great deal of sugar in it, is attempting to reconcile the practice with a standard treatise from the period before the advent of extensive sugaring.

  In the eighteenth century, the English, among all Europeans, had a reputation for using the largest amount of sugar per cup of tea or coffee, and for sugaring almost without exception. But they were far from alone. James Boswell, studying law at the University of Utrecht in the Netherlands in 1763–64, reports drinking tea with one of the professors: "I was surprised to see that he took sugar like an Englishman, because I had heard so many jokes about the narrowness of the Dutch in that article." *Boswell in Holland, 1763–1764*, ed. F. Pottle (New York: McGraw-Hill, 1952), 43.

61 Various bits of evidence point to this period as the one in which the tea-and-sugar custom came to be widely adopted. For example, the account books of Miss Goreing for 1697–1704 that have been cited previously (PRO C114/182) appear to show an instance of adoption by an English rural gentlewoman. The accounts are very specific with respect even to trivial expenditures. No purchase of tea, sugar, coffee, or chocolate is recorded before 1701. In that year, however, 14s was spent on tea. In 1702, there are entries of £1 for chocolate, 16s for a pound of tea, 15s/6d for a tea table, and 7s for Bohea tea (the first time a type of tea is noted). More tea was purchased in 1703; and finally, in 1704, not only are there specific entries for green and Bohea tea, but there is a single entry for "sagoo" tea and barley sugar together. We may suppose that Miss Goreing observed a new fashion of regular domestic tea-taking (probably on the occa-

sion of social calls) during one of her annual visits to London, bought or ordered some tea upon her return, then acquired the proper equipment for tea rituals, and finally, having become more knowledgeable in matters of tea, began to purchase tea and sugar together. Presumably the fashion had generalized in the capital somewhat earlier than 1700 or 1701.

62 See table 6, page 304. According to Ralph Davis's estimates, England imported on average £630,000 worth of sugar annually in 1699, 1700, and 1701—an increase of more than 50 percent since the 1660s. About 40 percent of that amount was reexported. Davis, "English Foreign Trade, 1660–1700," 164–65. By 1722–24, imports of sugar had increased to £928,000 annually while reexports had fallen substantially, thus indicating a very large increase in domestic sugar consumption in a period in which, as we have seen, the tendency to use sugar in cooking was probably not growing. Annual tea imports in 1699–1701 were valued at £8,000, while in 1722–24 they were £116,000. Because these figures are stated in terms of notional, fixed values of unit quantities of commodities set by the customs, they are probably reliable as to the direction and extent of changes in legal importation, although of course they take no direct account of smuggling. Davis, "English Foreign Trade, 1700–1774," 300–3. According to Chaudhuri, *Trading World of Asia*, 387–89, the English East India Company's tea imports fluctuated greatly in the late seventeenth century. The high point was 13,082 lbs. in 1690. After a period of instability just after 1700 (probably due to the outbreak of the War of the Spanish Succession), company imports of tea rose steadily. Between 1713 and 1720, the company imported an average of about 358,000 lbs. of tea per year. Davis, "English Foreign Trade, 1700–1774," 300–303; and Chaudhuri, *Trading World of Asia*, 359–84, show large increases for coffee at the same time, although with a very strong tendency for tea to overtake and surpass coffee. According to Davis, the value of coffee imported into England around 1700 was about 3.5 times the value of tea. Twenty years later, it was still 2.5 times greater, but by that time, a large proportion of imported tea was smuggled, so the actually amounts of the two products imported were probably much closer. The VOC's imports of tea and coffee into the Netherlands showed a similar pattern, except that coffee maintained a much stronger showing. (Dutch tea imports were buoyed by the fact that the Netherlands was the main source of tea smuggled into Britain.) See Glamann, *Dutch-Asiatic Trade*, 183–243.

63 This was clearly recognized at the time, at least in Britain. For example, a 1731 British broadside entitled *The Dispute between the Northern Colonies and the Sugar Islands, Set in a Clear View* (Goldsmiths' Library Broadside Collection no. 343), referring to developments since the beginning of the century, states: "Whilst the Price of Sugars continued low, the Sugar Islands were very beneficial to us, as they enabled us to undersell the Portuguese, and export great quantities to our Neighbours; but as the general Use of Coffee, Tea, Punch, etc. encreas'd our home Consumption to a very great Degree, the Planters" raised prices. In France, less tea, coffee, and sugar were consumed. Milk seems to have been frequently taken in coffee, without sugar or with very little of it. Breughel, "A Bourgeois Good?" 102–3.

64 Hugh Honour, *Chinoiserie: The Vision of Cathay* (London: John Murray, 1961), 44–86.

65 Chamberlain, *Manner of Making*, 47–48; *Thema Thee*, 26–27; Blankaart, *Borgerlyke Tafel*, 84; Ukers, *All about Tea*, 1:33–35.

66 Ukers, *All about Tea*, 35.

67 Geneviève Bolleme, *La Bibliothèque bleue. La littérature populaire en France du xviie au xixe siècle* (Paris: Julliard, 1971), 27–45; Geneviève Bolleme, *La Bible bleue: Anthologie d'une littérature "populaire"* (Paris: Flammarion, 1975), 332–64. See also the literature cited in Roy Porter, *Disease, Medicine, and Society in England, 1550–1800* (Basingstoke: Macmillan, 1987), 23–31.

68 See, for example, *The Haven of Health* (London: Thomas Orwin, 1589), 112–13. See also Mintz, *Sweetness and Power*, 102–8.

69 Mintz, *Sweetness and Power*, 104–8; Chamberlayne, *Family-Herbal,* 218–19. Compare the recipes for veal and pork dishes in John Murrell, *A New Booke of Cookerie*, 71, 111, 127–28 of *Murrell's Two Books of Cookery and Carving*, 5th ed. (London: John Marriot, 1638), with the equivalent eighteenth-century recipes in Glasse, *Art of Cookery*, 2–3, 35, 142; and Kidder, *Receipts*, 4, 11.

70 *Thema Thee*, 13–19, 23; Chamberlain, *Manner of Making*, 48–52; Short, *Discourses*, 1–76. During the period of the initial fashionability of coffeehouses in the 1660s and 1670s, several attacks on coffee and tea were published in England. These concentrated more on the ambience of consumption than its medical consequences, but some of them suggested that tea especially had an "effeminizing" effect, interfering with male sexual performance. After the controversies of the coffee (and tea) "craze," the attacks died down until tea again came under medical criticism in the eighteenth century. See Griffiths, *Indian Tea Industry*, 23–32.

71 Boxer, *Dutch Seaborne Empire*, 177; *Thema Thee*, 24–25. I have found no evidence in VOC records to support Boxer's suggestion about Bontekoe. No payments to Bontekoe are recorded in chapter 38 of van Dam's *Beschryvinge*, 68:308–58, which is devoted to "gifts" (bribes) and secret payments by the company and which covers the entire seventeenth century. Van Dam's account may, however, be incomplete.

72 Bontekoe, *Alle de . . . Werken*, introduction (n.p.).

73 *Dictionary of National Biography*, 19:1201–2.

74 *Autobiography of Benjamin Franklin*, 17–18.

75 [Thomas Tryon], *A New Art of Brewing* (London: T. Salusbury, 1690), 52–53.

76 See Short, *Discourses*, 32, 43–72.

77 Thomas Tryon, *Tryon's Letters, Domestick and Foreign* (London: G. Conyers, 1700), 183–87. Tryon argues elsewhere that, because the sugar business is so important to England's revenue, consumption of sugar ought to be encouraged. This presumably makes adopting a healthy way of taking sugar all the more important. He also predicts, however, that sugar will be increasingly imported through France and Spain as the soil of Barbados becomes worn out. (He ignores what is happening in Jamaica in his own time.) Tryon sees nothing wrong with this, because importing more sugar from anywhere will lead to an increase in the consumption of items that complement sugar and that the English import "on their own account"—a category that would include coffee and tea, although he does not specify. The decline of sugar production in British colonies would presumably fit well into Tryon's plan for developing manufacturing industries in the West Indies. It is not clear whether Tryon thinks that the fact that the French and Spanish would be abusing slaves to produce sugar rather than the English would be a morally preferable situation. See T. T. Merchant [Thomas Tryon], *Some General Considerations Offered, Relating to Our Present Trade* (London: J. Harris, 1698), 10–14.

78 Tryon, *Letters*, preface and 8–22; Tryon, *New Art of Brewing*, 52–53.

79 Tryon, *New Art of Brewing*, 68–70.

80 Ibid., 79–82, 85–86.

81 See Woodruff D. Smith, "Merchants and Company Directors in Seventeenth-Century European Trading Corporations," *Essays in Economic and Business History* 4 (1986): 1–13.

82 Bontekoe, *Alle de . . . Werken*, introduction, 1:n.p.; Boxer, *Dutch Seaborne Empire*, 177.

83 Dufour, *Traitez Nouveaux*, preface (n.p.).

84 Jürgen Habermas, *The Structural Transformation of the Public Sphere: An Inquiry into a Category of Bourgeois Society* (Cambridge, MA: MIT Press, 1989), 14–140.

85 Even the anonymous "gentleman" who published the *Treatise on the Inherent Qualities of the Tea-Herb* cited above claims to base his statements on the authority of a physician, Pechlin, whom he is translating and paraphrasing.

86 Dufour, *Traitez Nouveaux*, preface (n.p.).

87 Keith Thomas, "Cleanliness and Godliness in Early Modern England," in *Religion, Culture, and Society in Early Modern Britain: Essays in Honour of Patrick Collinson*, ed. Anthony Fletcher and Peter Roberts (Cambridge: Cambridge University Press, 1994), 56–83.

88 Lawrence Wright, *Clean and Decent: The Fascinating History of the Bathroom and the Water Closet* (Toronto: University of Toronto Press, 1967), 23–63.

89 Ibid., 67–78.

90 Thomas, "Cleanliness and Godliness," 57–58. Francis Bacon saw cleanliness as an aspect of decorum: "Cleanness of body was ever deemed to proceed from a due reverence to God." Francis Bacon, *The Advancement of Learning*, in *Selected Writings of Francis Bacon,* ed. H. Dick (New York: Modern Library, 1955), 279.

91 Thomas, "Cleanliness and Godliness," 58, 62.

92 Mark Jenner, "Bathing and Baptism: Sir John Floyer and the Politics of Cold Bathing," in *Refiguring Revolutions: Aesthetics and Politics from the English Revolution to the Romantic Revolution* (Berkeley: University of California Press, 1998), 197.

93 Wright, *Clean and Decent*, 80–88.

94 *Diary of John Evelyn*, 2:430–31. Evelyn visted a "Turkish" bath in Venice in 1645. Charles Webster, *The Great Instauration: Science, Medicine, and Reform, 1626–1660* (London: Duckworth, 1975), 298.

95 Wright, *Clean and Decent*, 76.

96 Webster, *Great Instauration*, 261.

97 For one of the few studies of odor from anthropological and historical perspectives, see Constance Classen, David Howes, and Anthony Synnott, *Aroma: The Cultural History of Smell* (London: Routledge, 1994), esp. 13–92. For changes in attitudes toward odor in connection with cleanliness, see Thomas, "Cleanliness and Godliness."

98 Elias, *Civilizing Process*, 159.

99 Classen et al., *Aroma*, 70–73.

100 Thomas, "Cleanliness and Godliness," 70.

101 Wright, *Clean and Decent*, 139.

102 Ibid., 126–27.

103 Thomas, "Cleanliness and Godliness," 79–83.

104 Albert C. Outler, ed., *The Works of John Wesley III* (Nashville: Abingdon Press, 1986), 249.

105 Classen et al., *Aroma*, 73.

106 Lord Chesterfield recommended cleanliness as a sign of social distinction that conveyed a person's worth. At the end of the eighteenth century, Beau Brummel ruled that men of fashion should control odor by washing thoroughly and using no perfume at all. Thomas, "Cleanliness and Godliness," 70, 76.

107 Ibid., 74–77.

108 Wright, *Clean and Decent*, 173.

109 Carl Van Doren, *Benjamin Franklin* (New York: Viking, 1938), 737.

110 Ralph A. Austen and Woodruff D. Smith, "Images of Africa and British Slave-Trade Abolition: The Transition to an Imperialist Ideology, 1787–1807," *African Historical Studies* (now *International Journal of African Historical Studies*) 2, no. 1 (1969): 69–83.

111 See table 2, page 300, and the discussion of textiles in chapter 2. One interesting point about the role in industrialization played by white cotton for underwear is that it does not wholly conform to either standard type of explanation for the Industrial Revolution: the approach that focuses on supply and technological change, and the one that emphasizes demand. With regard to the first, technological innovation in British cotton production did not create demand for white underwear, any more than it created the demand that it was apparently intended to meet: that for colored calicoes. It did, however, determine that cotton would meet underwear demand, and cotton's availability contributed to the perpetuation of dress styles that demanded much more cotton than was strictly necessary simply for comfort and cleanliness. As to the demand-centered approach, the demand for white cotton for underwear does not seem to have triggered the primary changes in supply (technical innovations), even though purchasers of such items were major beneficiaries of the changes. What this may mean is that explanations of industrialization based on broad, aggregate categories such as "domestic demand for cotton" or "total investment" or "total cotton exports" miss important parts of the dynamics of change that become apparent when one looks at more specific categories and relates them to evidence about the perceptions of producers and consumers. It may also mean that we should not assume that the "causes" of something as complex as industrialization can be meaningfully located only within the category of "supply," or of "demand," or indeed of both together.

112 Thomas, "Cleanliness and Godliness," 70–71, cites Daniel Defoe as stating that, in the 1720s, "nicer gentlemen" changed their shirts twice a day.

113 See Lemire, *Fashion's Favourite*, 10, 199. Crowley, "Sensibility of Comfort," 754n, criticizes Lemire for suggesting that comfort was part of cotton's appeal without giving evidence that comfort was consciously enumerated as a quality of cotton. While this may be a valid objection with regard to the early years of cotton's use in Britain, Lemire does in fact cite evidence for nonelite choice of cotton garments for ease of wear in the latter part of the eighteenth century. Crowley's own portrayal of the construction of comfort as a legitimate category of experience and motivation in that period provides a basis for thinking that the choice was conscious.

114 John Wesley, for example, devoted several sermons and tracts to the moral significance of dress. He railed against luxury and fashionability in dress, demanding that his followers "dress in every point neat and plain" while keeping their clothes and bodies as clean as possible, depending on their professions. *Works of John Wesley III*, 259.

115 As one of the anonymous reviewers of this book cogently pointed out, all this meant considerably more and harder work for women, so that any remarks about "ease" of washing cottons must be taken with that fact in mind. One might also suggest that it helped to make the presence of domestic servants essential in any home whose inhabitants claimed respectability—not just because having servants gave status, but also because of all the work that had to be done.

116 This is true even of the best contemporary treatment of respectability: Bushman, *Refinement of America*, 205–447.

CHAPTER FIVE: RATIONAL MASCULINITY

1   Habermas, *Structural Transformation*, 32–33, 42–43.

2   In the present chapter and the next, frequent reference will be made to some of the leading interpretive themes in the most dynamic new fields in European social and cultural history: family and gender history. For a statement of the general thesis that families changed drastically in structure, function, and affect in early modern Europe (or at least England), see Lawrence Stone, *The Family, Sex, and Marriage in England, 1500–1800*, abridged ed. (New York: Harper, 1979). For the thesis that the roles of women in England altered for the worse in the late eighteenth century because of economic change and the adoption of the "separate spheres" ideology, see Leonore Davidoff and Catherine Hall, *Family Fortunes: Men and Women of the English Middle Class, 1780–1850* (Chicago: University of Chicago Press, 1987). For an attack on this thesis, see Amanda Vickery, "Golden Age to Separate Spheres? A Review of the Categories and Chronology of English Women's History," *Historical Journal* 36 (1993): 383–414; and Vickery, *Gentleman's Daughter*, 1–12. For a treatment of the idea that male gender roles also changed in the seventeenth and eighteenth centuries, in part due to perceptions of a threat from women, see Fletcher, *Gender, Sex, and Subordination*. Fletcher argues (like Davidoff and Hall) that men created and enforced the new doctrine of "separate spheres" in order to maintain their hegemony over women. Vickery, *Gentleman's Daughter*, and Robert B. Shoemaker, *Gender in English Society, 1650–1850: The Emergence of Separate Spheres?* (London: Longman, 1998), 1–14, argue (convincingly, I think) that the "separate spheres" doctrine was at best a statement of some men's perceptions, not a description of reality, and that even the doctrine must be understood as part of a very complex set of cultural and social circumstances in which women's aims were as important as male fears.

3   Coffee is reported to have come into vogue in Constantinople in 1555. Jean Moura and Paul Louvet, *Le Café Procope* (Paris: Perrin, 1929), 13.

4   Steven Pincus, "Coffee Politicians Does Create: Coffee Houses and Restoration Political Culture," *Journal of Modern History* 67 (1995): 807–34; Jean Leclant, "Coffee and Cafes in Paris, 1644–1693," in *Food and Drink in History*, ed. Robert Forster and Orest Ranum (Baltimore: Johns Hopkins University Press, 1979), 86–97—which originally appeared as an article in the *Annales*. It is interesting to note that Leclant makes no mention of the prior English fashion in his explanation of the origins of the enthusiasm for coffee in France, which he dates from the visit of an Ottoman embassy to Paris in 1669.

5   Glamann, *Dutch-Asiatic Trade*, 183; Chaudhuri, *Trading World*, 360–62.

6   Glamann, *Dutch-Asiatic Trade*, 185–87; Dufour, *Traitez nouveau*, 178–85.

7   Glamann, *Dutch-Asiatic Trade*, 207–11.

8   *Old English Coffee Houses* (London: Rodale Press, 1954). What may be the earliest English use of coffee, in the 1630s, also occurred in Oxford and was recorded by John Evelyn: *Diary of John Evelyn*, 1:14–15.

9   Pincus, "Coffee," 807–34.

10   *Diary of Samuel Pepys*, 1:14 (January 10, 1660); 1:20–21 (January 17, 1660); 1:61 (February 20, 1660).

11   *A Proclamation for the Suppression of Coffee-Houses*, December 29, 1675; *An Additional Proclamation concerning Coffee-Houses*, January 8, 1675/76. Goldsmiths' Library Collection of Proclamations, GL 2138, GL 2179.

12   Leclant, "Coffee and Cafes," 91, 93.

13 Moura and Louvet, *Café Procope*, 75–147; *Old English Coffee Houses*, 27–32. Coffeehouses sold many other products, especially tea, and teahouses existed throughout the eighteenth century. However, when people referred generically to shops selling hot stimulants, they called them coffeehouses, cafés, or the equivalent.

14 Although the description that follows is loosely focused on a coffeehouse in Amsterdam at the beginning of the eighteenth century, it is actually a composite based on the secondary sources previously cited and on a variety of primary sources. The latter include James Boswell's journals: *Boswell's London Journal, 1762–1763*, ed. F. Pottle (New York: McGraw-Hill, 1950), esp. 237, 249, 257, 318, 325, 327, 331, 332, 333; *Boswell in Holland*, 43, 101–2; *Boswell in Search of a Wife, 1766–1769*, ed. F. Brady and F. Pottle (New York: McGraw-Hill, 1956), esp. 143–44, 270, 272, 273, 300; *Boswell for the Defence*, ed. W. Wimsatt and F. Pottle (New York: McGraw-Hill, 1959), esp. 65–66, 81, 82, 103, 162, 173, 184. Other sources used are Denis Diderot, *Le Neveu de Rameau* (Geneva: Droz, 1963); Montesquieu, *Lettres Persanes* (Geneva: Droz, 1965), 94–95, 336–38; several London newspapers held by the Goldsmiths' Library, University of London, especially the *Daily Courant* (1720), the *London Journal* (1721–28), and the *Weekly Magazine: or, Universal Intelligencer* (1732–33); and a 1775 inventory of the contents of Joe's Coffee House, at Mitre Court and Ram Alley, London, in PRO, C110/187, part 1 (cause of Williams vs. Yates).

15 Daniel de la Feuille, *Le Guide d'Amsterdam* (Amsterdam: Daniel de la Feuille, 1701), 1.

16 Ibid. 65.

17 Ibid.

18 Ibid. 65–66.

19 *Old English Coffee Houses*, 27–32.

20 Donald J. Matthiesen, "German Parliamentarism in 1848: Roll-Call Voting in the Frankfurt Assembly," *Social Science History* 5, no. 4 (1981): 469–82.

21 Moura and Louvet, *Café Procope*; *Boswell's London Journal*, 318, 325; *Boswell for the Defence*, 184.

22 Pictures of the main rooms of seventeenth- and eighteenth-century English coffeehouses can be found in *Old English Coffee Houses*, 8–9, 21; and a picture of a Paris coffeehouse is the frontispiece to Moura and Louvert, *Café Procope*. Private rooms: *Boswell's London Journal*, 318, 325; and PRO, C110/187, part 1 (inventory of Joe's Coffee House). Size of company: de la Feuille, *Guide*, 65.

23 Pincus, "Coffee," 816, gives evidence that women went to coffeehouses during the coffee craze of the seventeenth century, but he does not make a convincing case for more than casual attendance even then. Most of the evidence we have from the eighteenth century suggests that the coffeehouse was an institution patronized mainly, although not exclusively, by men. Boswell does not mention women as participants in coffeehouse discussions, although because in his time many coffeehouses doubled as restaurants, ladies probably dined in them. Although ladies are known to have visited the Café Procope, a famous picture of its interior (cited in the preceding note) depicting some of the establishment's distinguished clientele shows only one woman: a waitress. In each of the pictures of London coffeehouses also cited in the previous note, the only woman present is the proprietress, who sits in state behind a counter. In terms of customers, at least the public image of the coffeehouse was masculine.

24 Israel, *Dutch Republic*, 337–41.

25 Ibid., 341–48.

26 Pincus, "Coffee," 807–34, emphasizes the presence of men of all classes in London coffeehouses during the period of the "coffee craze" in the seventeenth century. However, "workers," designated as such, do not seem to have frequented coffeehouses in great numbers in the eighteenth century. The pictorial representations cited above in note 23 do not show people who fit that description. But they were not completely absent. Wage-earning persons of appropriate learning and bearing (and presumably dress) certainly did visit coffeehouses. During Benjamin Franklin's first sojourn in England, when he was not yet twenty and was working as a journeyman printer in London, he gained the acquaintance of a surgeon named Lyons. Lyons, he reports, took him to an alehouse in Cheapside "and introduc'd me to Dr. Mandeville, Author of the Fable of the Bees who had a Club there, of which he was the Soul, being a most facetious entertaining Companion. Lyons too introduc'd me, to Dr. Pemberton, at Batson's Coffee House, who promis'd to give me an Opportunity some time or other of seeing Sir Isaac Newton, of which I was extreamly desirous; but this never happened." *Autobiography of Benjamin Franklin*, 52. Franklin does not, however, indicate that any of his friends of similar occupation ever accompanied him to a coffeehouse, nor does he say that he ventured into coffeehouses (or even Mandeville's alehouse) on his own initiative. In each case, Lyons took him. Franklin represents this as a sign of his own manifest excellence at so young an age—as something out of the ordinary. Nevertheless, it is clear that coffeehouses served a fairly wide social clientele, even if they were not all as democratic as Pincus suggests. A surgeon was only a step or two above a skilled artisan in the 1720s, hardly a gentleman in any traditional sense. What we are seeing is a variety of people being drawn to coffeehouses by shared interests, knowledge, and elements of culture, and perhaps beginning to be defined as a class in the process. We should also note that alehouses are not totally outside of the same picture.

27 When Boswell was in the Netherlands in the 1760s, virtually all discussions of serious matters in which he took part were in French. One of his aims in studying in the Netherlands was to improve his conversational French. *Boswell in Holland*, 43, 101–2.

28 This does not mean that behavior could not get out of hand in a coffeehouse, but it was not supposed to and apparently seldom did in the eighteenth century. For an example of coffeehouse discussion, see *Boswell for the Defence*, 65–66.

29 Some examples: a tax bill (c. 1710) addressed to Thomas Bowery, a London merchant, at his house "close by Ratcliffe" or "att the Garter Coffee house in Threadneedle street at 3 or 4 of the Clocke in the afternoone every day," Papers of Thomas Bowery, Guildhall Library Manuscripts Collection, folder 9 (v); letters to Thomas Hall, another London merchant, concerning dealings in the slave trade, some addressed to him at his home in Great Ormond Street and others to him at the "Jerusalem Coffee House, London," PRO, C103/130, bundle 167 (for example, item 29, a letter dated June 2, 1742).

30 Ralph Straus, *Lloyds: The Gentlemen at the Coffee-House* (New York: Carrick and Evans, 1938), 81–95. Specializations were not limited to business matters. Diderot's *Neveu de Rameau* takes place in a coffeehouse that is famous because the best chess masters in Paris congregate to play there.

31 This sort of dealing among brokers and small-scale principals can be followed in detail in the early-eighteenth-century papers of David Leeuw, an Amsterdam businessman. See, for example, his correspondence with the firm of Th. and Hend. Boursse of Middelburg from 1713 to 1725 in GAA, P.A. 88 (Familie Brants), no. 902.

32 Examples of this kind of discussion between merchants, in this case conducted by mail because the discussants lived in different cities, can be found in the correspondence between Jeronimus Velters of Amsterdam and Pierre Macare of Middelburg: GAA,

P.A. 2 (Velters), no. 7. Particularly interesting is a letter of September 25, 1676 (fol. 514–16), which speculates about what would happen if peace broke out between France and the Netherlands.

33 This was the kind of speculative reinsurance practice that Lloyds eventually helped to eliminate. See Straus, *Lloyds*, 87.

34 Montesquieu, *Lettres Persanes*, 94–95 (letter 36).

35 Habermas, *Structural Transformation*, 32–33.

36 David Zaret, "Religion, Science, and Printing in the Public Spheres in Seventeenth-Century England," in *Habermas and the Public Sphere*, ed. Calhoun, 215–16, argues for the primacy of noneconomic factors.

37 See the pioneering study of retailing by Hoh-Cheung Mui and Lorna H. Mui, *Shops and Shopkeeping in Eighteenth-Century England* (Kingston: McGill-Queen's University Press, 1989), esp. 160–200, 249–87 (on tea retailing). The inventory for Joe's Coffee House includes substantial amounts of rum, brandy, wine, cordials, chocolate, and tobacco, as well as equipment for preparing coffee, tea, and cocoa. PRO, C110/187, part I.

38 English tea smugglers are treated as a significant purchasing interest in the Dutch market in the reports sent to the London merchant Thomas Hall by his correspondent in Amsterdam, Diederick Smith, in the 1730s. Whether the smugglers are buying or not has a major effect on prices—and apparently everyone knows who the smugglers are. See, for example, Smith's letters to Hall dated August 14, 1736; October 12, 1736 ("There is no price on Tea now, If the smuggling trade would revive a little it might keep up"); and November 9, 1736: PRO C103/132.

39 *Daily Courant*, February 15, 1720.

40 Examples from one week of one London newspaper: stock and ship sales, *Daily Courant*, February 15, 1720 (New Style); subscriptions, *Daily Courant*, February 16, 1720.

41 Smith, "Function of Commercial Centers," 985–1005.

42 Pincus, "Coffee."

43 *Diary of Samuel Pepys*, 2:124 (June 19, 1661).

44 This theme is developed in more detail (although not with particular emphasis on coffeehouses) in Smith, "Function of Commercial Centers," 985–1005.

45 Straus, *Lloyds*, 47–95.

46 See Pincus, "Coffee."

47 Roy Porter, *English Society in the Eighteenth Century* (Harmondsworth: Penguin, 1982), 245.

48 A classic example of broadside argumentation (one of hundreds that could be chosen) is *The Case of the Merchants Who Export Tobacco* (c. 1713; GLBC 247). This broadside calls for increased tariff protection and lower duties for Maryland tobacco in Britain and for state action to recover markets for English colonial tobacco elsewhere in Europe. The tobacco trade has declined due to competition from other countries, which not only hurts the exporters but also threatens: national defense (less trade means fewer sailors who can be impressed in wartime); the continued functioning of the colonial empire and its markets (Maryland may turn to manufacturing); state revenue (if the trade is destroyed, it will never yield the customs revenues it once did); and national wealth (Britain will have to use money rather than tobacco to buy goods in Holland, Germany, and "Sweedland"). The mode of argumentation is cast in terms of the good of the nation and is apparently rational—even if many of the arguments are quite specious on closer examination.

49 See Darnton, *Great Cat Massacre*, 145–89, esp. 139, and Robert Darnton, *The Literary Underground of the Old Regime* (Cambridge, MA: Harvard University Press, 1982), 1–40.

50 Darnton, *Literary Underground*, 23–24.

51 It is not possible to know what proportion of the tea and coffee imported into western European countries was consumed in coffeehouses in any particular era. For one thing, we don't know the actual amounts imported, because of smuggling. But it is possible to do a sort of mental exercise that shows that the proportion was probably very high, at least with respect to coffee, in the first half of the eighteenth century. A standard rule of thumb is that one pound of ground coffee (which is essentially the same as a pound of coffee beans) is needed to make 10 quarts or 40 cups of coffee (*The Settlement Cookbook* [New York: Simon and Schuster, 1965], 50). Let us assume that the smallest coffeehouses in Paris and London around 1720 would have needed to prepare at least two charges of coffee a day and that each charge must have been at least 40 cups. This is reasonable, given that we know the coffeehouse business to have been highly competitive. Stale coffee or coffee not readily available would have led to disaster for most establishments; they could not have failed to have at least a fair-sized pot of reasonably fresh coffee on hand at all times. If there really were 600 coffeehouses each in London and Paris and each coffeehouse was open, say, 350 days a year, the minimum amount of coffee that would have been purchased by coffeehouses in either of those cities in a year would be (2 lbs. mult. 350 mult. 600 =) 420,000 lbs. Of course, the estimate of 600 coffeehouses may be (probably is) exaggerated, but presumably many of the coffeehouses prepared a great deal more than 20 quarts of coffee each day. At any rate, the amount of coffee imported into Europe annually by the VOC in the years around 1720 was about 1,500,000 lbs. (ARA: VOC 6989). So our estimate of coffee usage in Paris coffeehouses alone would account for about 30 percent of the VOC's coffee imports at a time when the VOC was the main legal source of coffee in France and much of the rest of continental Europe, and the main supplier of coffee smuggled into Great Britain. Whatever the exact figures might have been, coffeehouses must have been responsible for a large part of coffee demand.

52 Short, *Discourses*, 32.

53 Ibid., 43–72.

54 Ibid., 73–76.

55 *London Journal*, February 11, 1720 (1721, New Style), 5.

56 [Sowter], *The Way to Be Wise,* 17. (Although the cited edition of Sowter is dated 1736, the Goldsmiths' Library catalog states that the tract was originally published in 1716; the ascription of authorship comes from the same source.)

57 Consider, for example, the quiet that prevails at the coffeehouse where Diderot situates *Le Neveu de Rameau*. Most of the patrons are either playing chess or silently watching, which makes a striking contrast to the Nephew's subversive conversation. On the other hand, it is somewhat difficult to differentiate completely between gambling and the kind of "insurance" wagering described previously that certainly did take place at coffeehouses. It is also true that White's Club, which became the best-known private gambling establishment in London in the second half of the eighteenth century, originally met at White's Chocolate House. See James Laver, *The Age of Illusion: Manners and Morals, 1750–1848* (London: Weidenfeld and Nicolson, 1972), 43. But establishing a private club with limited membership and its own premises separated gambling from the coffeehouse ambiance, encouraged the adoption of an aristocratic framework of genteel decorum and "honor," and, most important, permitted the management to proscribe "debauchery" and to limit admittance to people who supposedly could afford to lose and knew how to do it gracefully.

58 *Old English Coffee Houses*, 31–32. The inventory of Joe's Coffee House on the occasion of its sale in 1775 shows a moderate amount of alcohol, and also suggests that the coffeehouse doubled as a restaurant. PRO, C110/187, part 1.

59 Certainly not Boswell, who patronized both coffeehouses and alehouses about equally. See *Boswell in Search of a Wife*, 270–73.

60 Although even Wild, when he did advertise his services (finding things that had been "lost"—stolen), gave his address simply as the Old Bailey: *Daily Courant*, August 26, 1720. Consider also a British broadside of 1711 entitled *The Case of Dorothy Petty, in Relation to the Union-Society, at the White Lyon by Temple-Bar, whereof She Is Director* (GLBC 201). Petty claims that she has been running an honest small-claims insurance business. Together with many others, she has been driven out of business by new legislation that gives larger insurers priority in recovery or compensation for losses they have insured. She argues that the act should be modified to allow people like her to stay in business (for the public good, of course; they provide a source of revenue to the treasury). One of the interesting features of this broadside is the evidence it affords of a woman in the insurance business. Apart from that, Petty is clearly very marginal to the financial world: she is a woman; she is located at the edge of the City; the legitimacy of her enterprise is obviously open to question. (She continually emphasizes her honesty and states that she is the daughter of a clergyman. Apparently she fears that the reader will presume that she is running some kind of Wild-type fencing or gambling operation.) All these aspects of marginality are consistent with the fact that she does business in an alehouse. The big insurers are the ones who sit in Lloyds over a cup of coffee. Their legitimacy is supported by the coffee and the coffeehouse. Petty would probably not even be allowed in Lloyds, certainly not to do business, if for no other reason than that she is a woman.

61 Noburu Yoshimura and Philip Anderson, *Inside the Kaisha: Demystifying Japanese Business Behavior* (Boston: Harvard Business School Press, 1997), 68.

62 In general, French society valued wine at a significantly higher level than coffee or tea throughout the eighteenth century (and beyond). Coffee and tea acquired cultural identities in France similar to those they possessed in other countries in northwestern Europe, but not the scope or social breadth. Wine was not connected as closely in French minds with uncontrolled behavior; it was identified more with the notions of taste and aristocracy. See Mennell, *All Manners of Food*, 102–33; and Mintz, *Sweetness and Power*, 188–89.

63 The rules of eighteenth-century coffeehouse conversation can be inferred from sources cited previously. Besides de la Feuille, *Guide*, see *Boswell's London Journal*, 318, 325, 327, 331–33; *Boswell in Search of a Wife*, 300; *Boswell for the Defence*, 65–66, 184.

64 *Lord Chesterfield's Letters*, 7, 9.

65 See, for example, the portrayal of Lord Shaftesbury's social theories in Klein, *Shaftesbury and the Culture of Politeness*.

66 The clientele of Lloyds—who eventually limited their number by subscription—customarily referred to themselves as "the gentlemen of the coffee-house." Straus, *Lloyds*, introduction, 47–80.

67 Emilie du Châtelet (1706–49), perhaps the most prominent woman scientist in France in the eighteenth century, was barred in 1733 from entering the Café Gradot in Paris because of her sex. (The Café Gradot was a favorite meeting place of the leading figures in science and mathematics.) She responded by dressing in a suit of men's clothes to gain admittance—not as a disguise, apparently, but as a protest. Bonnie S. Anderson and Judith P. Zinsser, *A History of Their Own*, 2 vols. (New York: Harper and Row, 1988), 2:88–89.

68 Shoemaker, *Gender in English Society*, 279.

69 Uday S. Mehta, "Liberal Strategies of Exclusion," in *Tensions of Empire: Colonial Cultures in a Bourgeois World*, ed. Frederick Cooper and Ann Laura Stoler, (Berkeley: University of California Press, 1997), 70.

70 Consider in this respect Locke and Montesquieu. In chapter 7 of *The Second Treatise of Government*, Locke discusses two voluntary associations, marriage and civil society—the first in order to undermine the patriarchal theory of the state, and the second in order to establish the basis of the rest of his own political theory. It is clear (although Locke does not say so) that he is using an analogy to the formation of more limited voluntary associations as a way of explaining the nature and construction of society in general, but limited associations appear to play no role in themselves in his political theory. John Locke, *The Second Treatise of Government* (Indianapolis: Liberal Arts Press, 1952), 44–54. In the case of Montesquieu, even when he is dealing with contemporary states and when he is emphasizing the importance of diversity in social organization as a protection for liberty, his units of suborganization are either individuals (the people or the citizens) or hereditary groups (the nobility). "Liberty" is the ability of individuals or hereditary groups, not of people operating in associations, to exercise their wills. See Montesquieu, *Spirit of the Laws*, vol. 11, chap. 2–6.

71 Vickery, *Gentleman's Daughter*; Shoemaker, *Gender in English Society*.

72 Goodman, *Tobacco in History*, 37, 141–43.

73 Jerome E. Brooks, *The Mighty Leaf: Tobacco through the Centuries* (Boston: Little, Brown, 1952), 115–17; Goodman, *Tobacco*, 218.

74 Ralph S. Hattox, *Coffee and Coffeehouses: The Origins of a Social Beverage in the Medieval Near East* (Seattle: University of Washington Press, 1985). Both the Ottoman and the Persian governments attempted to forbid tobacco smoking in the late sixteenth and early seventeenth centuries, but they had no more success than any other government that has attempted the feat. Brooks, *Mighty Leaf*, 77.

75 Brooks, *Mighty Leaf*, 31–35.

76 Ibid., 60–66.

77 Fletcher, *Gender, Sex, and Subordination*, 3–29.

78 Goodman, *Tobacco*, 75–77.

79 Brooks, *Mighty Leaf*, 35–44.

80 James I, *A Counter-Blaste to Tobacco* (Emmaus, PA: Rodale Press, 1954). Although James's authorship of the pamphlet was not officially disclosed for some years, there does not appear to have been any doubt about it from the start. A reading of the pamphlet's foreword (7–9) will suggest why.

81 Ibid., 15–18.

82 Ibid., 11–14.

83 Ibid., 32.

84 Ibid., As James's own habits were reportedly not the cleanest, one is led to imagine that smoking practices in his day were even more obnoxious than those of more modern times.

85 Ibid., 29–36.

86 Alden T. Vaughan, *American Genesis: Captain John Smith and the Founding of Virginia* (Boston: Little, Brown, 1975), 93–112.

87 Goodman, *Tobacco*, 149–50.

88 Ibid., 115–27.

89 Ibid., 129–90.

90 Goodman, *Tobacco*, 37–55.

91 Brooks, *Mighty Leaf*, 81–120, 149–90.

92 Ibid., 151–53; Jacob M. Price, *The Tobacco Adventure to Russia: Enterprise, Politics, and Diplomacy in the Quest for a Northern Market for English Colonial Tobacco, 1676–1722* (Philadelphia: American Philosophical Society, 1961).

93 Allan Kulikoff, *Tobacco and Slaves: The Development of Southern Cultures in the Chesapeake, 1680–1800* (Chapel Hill: University of North Carolina Press, 1986), 78–117.

94 Goodman, *Tobacco*, 77, 78.

95 The relationship between tobacco use and war is worth further research. Larger numbers of men served with organized armies in the Thirty Years' War and the other wars of the seventeenth century than (probably) at any time in Europe's past. It may also be that the great expansions of smoking in the nineteenth and twentieth centuries were connected with periods of war involving national military service: the French revolutionary and Napoleonic wars, the wars of the 1860s and 1870s in Europe and America (which may have been associated with an expansion of the fashion for cigarettes), and the two world wars.

96 Brooks, *Mighty Leaf*, 70.

97 See, for example, the fashionable lady portrayed in one of the plates included in the edition cited here of James I, *Counter Blaste*, 23.

98 Vaughan, *American Genesis*, 74.

99 Fletcher, *Gender, Sex, and Subordination*, 23–24.

100 Although, as Jordan Goodman points out, there is evidence of genteel European women smoking in the late seventeenth and eighteenth centuries, the evidence is fragmentary. In this, smoking differed from snuff-taking, which was clearly practiced by both sexes. Goodman, *Tobacco*, 62–63.

101 Leclant, "Coffee and Cafes," 90–91; *Coffee-Houses Vindicated in Answer to the Late Published Character of a Coffee-House . . .* (London: Lock, 1673). I am obliged to Brian Cowan for this reference and the following one.

102 *The Touchstone or, Trial of Tobacco* (London: n.p., 1673). One of the complaints made in the latter part of the seventeenth century against tea was that it made men effeminate.

103 Josiah Wedgwood begins a letter describing a discussion he had with a business rival about a dispute over a patent in 1771 in this way: "Last night Mr. Palmer & I smoked our pipes together at Newcastle & discuss'd the subject of the Patent." Josiah Wedgwood, *Letters of Josiah Wedgwood*, 3 vols. (1903; Manchester: E. J. Morten, 1973); 2:30 (letter June 13, 1771). In the context of the letter, the smoking of the pipes clearly indicates that the discussion was reasonable and unimpassioned. (It did, in fact, result in a compromise satisfactory to both parties.) Wedgwood and Palmer may or may not have literally smoked pipes together. The detail of smoking, irrelevant to the subject at hand, frames the manner in which the described event was conducted and the process that led to its successful conclusion.

104 Michelle Perrot, "Roles and Characters," in *History of Private Life* 4:173.

105 Goodman, *Tobacco*, 70–85, 90–94.

106 Ibid., 81–83.

107 Goodman ascribes a substantial part of the sluggish demand for tobacco in the eighteenth century to the fact that consumption increases were mainly in the use of snuff. Ibid., 71–73.

108 Ibid., *Tobacco*, 91–93. Goodman suggests that one of the main reasons for the decline of snuff was the rise of the cigarette—a commodity that in the twentieth century crossed gender barriers completely.

CHAPTER SIX: DOMESTIC FEMININITY

1 Samuel Richardson, *Clarissa or the History of a Young Lady*, ed. and abr. George Sherburn (Boston: Houghton Mifflin, 1962), 16–17.

2 Elizabeth Bergen Brophy, *Samuel Richardson* (Boston: Twayne, 1987), 49–81, 110–24; Margaret Anne Doody, *A Natural Passion: A Study in the Novels of Samuel Richardson* (Oxford: Clarendon Press, 1974), 188–215; Mullan, *Sentiment and Sociability*, 57–113.

3 Maggie Lane, *Jane Austen and Food* (London: Hambleton Press, 1995), 28–30.

4 Ibid., 25–54.

5 Ukers, *All about Tea*, 1:33–35.

6 William H. Ukers, *The Romance of Tea* (New York: Alfred A. Knopf, 1936), 200.

7 Mintz, *Sweetness and Power*, 112–50.

8 See *From the Fires of Revolution to the Great War*, ed. Michelle Perrot. Vol. 4 of *A History of Private Life*, ed. Philippe Ariès and George Duby (Cambridge, MA: Belknap, 1987–90), 4:128, 274–77.

9 Ibid., 58–62; Vickery, *Gentleman's Daughter*, 195–97.

10 Vickery, *Gentleman's Daughter*, 196–202.

11 The "separate spheres" thesis is briefly outlined in Shoemaker, *Gender in English Society*, 6.

12 For a sampling of this literature, see ibid., 21–36; and Fletcher, *Gender, Sex, and Subordination*, 376–413.

13 See Brian Howard Harrison, *Separate Spheres: The Opposition to Women's Suffrage in Britain* (New York: Holmes and Meier, 1979).

14 Amanda Vickery has launched the main attack on the preeminence of "separate spheres" in the construction of women's culture in eighteenth- and early-nineteenth-century Britain. See Vickery, *Gentleman's Daughter*, 1–12. See also Shoemaker, *Gender in English Society*.

15 The thesis that Vickery and others attack is summarized in Catherine Hall, "The Sweet Delights of Home," in *From the Fires of Revolution to the Great War*, ed. Perrot, 47–94.

16 Shoemaker, *Gender in English Society*, 305–18.

17 Elizabeth Kowaleski-Wallace, for instance, sees the process generally as women subverting a pattern of behavior imposed, in its overt form, by men, and thus creating a means through which women's conversation evades male domination. She does this brilliantly in analyzing the meaning of tea-taking in eighteenth-century Britain. Kowaleski-Wallace, *Consuming Subjects*, 19–36. Vickery, in *Gentleman's Daughter*, tends on the other hand to emphasize more straightforward forms of female agency, although still clearly within the context of a male-dominated society.

18 Mary Wollstonecraft, *A Vindication of the Rights of Woman* (Mineola, NY: Dover, 1996). Note, however, that Wollstonecraft primarily opposes the personal subjugation of women and the inference from women's inherent nature that they had neither the intellectual nor the moral capacity for autonomous action, public or private. She does

not oppose the presumption that men and women have, in several important respects, different natures, but sees these differences as ones of degree: men, on average, *may* be able to reason more acutely than women because they are less troubled with sentimental considerations, but that very fact means that women have an important social function to perform by supplying the sentimental foundation for such activities as child-rearing. In this, Wollstonecraft did not differ markedly from other women writers such as Frances Burney, Hannah Moore, and Jane Austen, who were among the principal English expositors of domestic femininity of the late eighteenth and early nineteenth centuries (and who hated Wollstonecraft's politics). See Shoemaker, *Gender in English Society*, 40–44, and Hall, "Sweet Delights," 55–57. The crux of Wollstonecraft's argument is the following: "But I insist, that not only the virtue, but the *knowledge* of the two sexes should be the same in nature, if not in degree, and that woman, considered not only as moral, but as rational creatures, ought to endeavour to acquire human virtues (or perfections) by the *same* means as men." Wollstonecraft, *Vindication*, 38.

19 Fletcher, *Gender, Sex, and Subordination*, 59–82, 173–222; Youings, *Sixteenth-Century England*, 370–71. To take one instance in which early modern women before the eighteenth century might seem to have had things better than their female descendents, English widows in the sixteenth century were able to run their own businesses and to choose their next husbands. However, they were under enormous pressure to do the latter as quickly as possible and often paid a considerable price for not succumbing. Even widowed gentlewomen faced a very real threat of forcible abduction and involuntary marriage after rape. Ibid., 124–25.

20 *Diary of Samuel Pepys*, 4:65 (March 2, 1663); 7:14 (January 12, 1666); 7:24 (January 26, 1666); 8:383 (August 12, 1667); 8:384–85 (August 13, 1667); 9:365 (November 17, 1668).

21 Which is not to say that a the role of a respectable married woman in managing her household was mentally or emotionally easy or that it was given the degree of respect it deserved. But it was clearly differentiated, especially in physical terms, from that of servants. Vickery, *Gentleman's Daughter*, 127–60.

22 *Diary of Samuel Pepys*, 3:132 (July 6, 1662).

23 Fletcher, *Gender, Sex, and Subordination*, 376–400.

24 Vickery, *Gentleman's Daughter*, 195–97.

25 Shoemaker, *Gender in English Society*, 209–304.

26 Johnson, *Dictionary*, 1:n.p., s.v. "civilization." The *Encyclopédie* carries the same sense for *civiliser: Encyclopédie*, 3:497.

27 *OED*, 2nd ed., vol. 3.

28 Johnson, *Dictionary*, 1:n.p., s.v. "civility." The *Encyclopédie*, 3:397–98, gives similar entries for the triad *civilité, politesse,* and *affabilité*.

29 The significance of "civilization" and "civility" in late-eighteenth-century republican discourse has been noted by Gordon Wood, *Radicalism of the American Revolution*, 194. Wood does not connect the concept either with respectability or with the roles of women.

30 On the development of the concept of progress, see David Spadafora, *The Idea of Progress in Eighteenth-Century Britain* (New Haven: Yale University Press, 1990), esp. 381–413.

31 Charles Dickens, *Bleak House* (New York: Bantam, 1983), 32–43: chapter 4, "Telescopic Philanthropy."

32 Kowaleski-Wallace, *Consuming Subjects*, 19–36, sees this as a major part of the "text" of the tea ritual, the object of which is actually to control women's conversation. Tea

conversation itself creates a subtext, which appears to subvert not so much the text as its real object.

33 See, for example, the discussion of Scottish Enlightenment thinking on these and related problems in Spadafora, *Idea of Progress*, 253–320. See also Mullan, *Sentiment and Sociability*, 18–56.

34 See the discussion in Mullan, *Sentiment and Sociability*, 57–113, of Samuel Richardson's extraordinarily influential construction of femininity around women's propensity toward sentiment.

35 Fletcher, *Gender, Subordination, and Sex*, 228–32, 396–97.

36 Lorna Weatherill, *Consumer Behavior and Material Culture in Britain, 1660–1760* (London: Routledge, 1988), 25–42; Carole Shammus, *The Pre-industrial Consumer in England and America* (Oxford: Clarendon Press, 1990), 6.

37 See Gilboy, "Demand as a Factor," 620–39.

38 Shammus, *Pre-industrial Consumer*, 3–4, 291–99. See also Weatherill, *Consumer Behavior*, 16–19, 91–111.

39 There have been several significant attempts to account for the changes in economic behavior that occurred at the beginning of the modern era by relating them to alterations in cognitive patterns. Chandra Mukerji, for example, describes the emergence of "materialism" in early modern Europe. Chandra Mukerji, *From Graven Images: Patterns of Modern Materialism* (New York: Columbia University Press, 1983). Colin Campbell argues that nineteenth-century consumption was informed by "hedonism"— a term that, like *materialism*, traditionally conveys moral disapproval. Campbell implies that the modern form of hedonism, which is based on imagination and represents a kind of freedom, should not be so represented. Campbell, *Romantic Ethic*, 58–95. The essays in Berg and Clifford, *Commodities and Luxury*, explore the implications of a number of cognitive patterns. Particularly important is the essay by Berg (63–85). She emphasizes appreciation for novelty and quality of craftsmanship as keys to a context of consumption adopted by "middling" as well as elite people in the eighteenth century. In the present study, most of these cognitive patterns have been linked to broader cultural contexts, especially "luxury." It is quite possible to identify viable alternative contexts that incorporate some of the same patterns but that are not closely connected to the formation of respectability in the late eighteenth century. Brewer, *Pleasures of the Imagination*, could be interpreted as doing this, as could Birmingham and Brewer, *Consumption of Culture*. The key features of this alternative context would appear to be the changing commercial economy, aesthetic tastes, and social structure of eighteenth-century Britain.

40 See J. H. Plumb, "The New World of Children," in *Birth of a Consumer Society*, ed. McKendrick et al., 286–315.

41 The invention of shopping in eighteenth-century Britain has been interpreted recently in widely divergent ways. Vickery, *Gentleman's Daughter*, 161–94, sees it as a relatively straightforward extension of the managerial roles of upper-class women—in other words, an example of conscious female agency. This approach seems compatible with the one taken here. Laura Brown, *Ends of Empire: Women and Ideology in Early Eighteenth-Century English Literature* (Ithaca: Cornell University Press, 1993), places shopping in the context of economic and imperial expansion. In her view, it was men who invented the prevailing images of insatiable woman shoppers as a way of explaining (and displacing any blame for) overseas expansion and capitalism. This seems to me to fail to account satisfactorily for the self-conscious seriousness (obvious to readers of Jane Austen) with which some intelligent women engaged in shopping. Kowaleski-Wallace, *Consuming Subjects*, 73–98, gives a complex interpretation of women's shopping, seeing it in the first instance as a set of practices created as a

means of expanding the commercial economy, but also as a vehicle through which women could consciously develop a subject identity as subverters of commercial rationality. As we shall see in chapter 7, this interpretation provides useful insights into respectable consumption.

42 Vickery, *Gentleman's Daughter*, 161–94.

43 Weatherill, *Consumer Behavior*, 152–56.

44 Weatherill, for example, does not discuss breakfast in ibid., 152–56.

45 Harrison, *Description of England*, 140.

46 Alison Weir, *The Life of Elizabeth I* (New York: Ballantine, 1998), 249.

47 Mintz, *Sweetness and Power*, 99.

48 See, for instance, *Diary of Samuel Pepys*, 2:88 (April 24, 1661).

49 Herbert H. Rowen, *John de Witt, Grand Pensionary of Holland, 1625–1672* (Princeton: Princeton University Press, 1978), 104.

50 Lane, *Jane Austen and Food*, 28.

51 Mintz, *Sweetness and Power*, 106, quotes a 1715 pamphlet by Dr. Frederick Slare extolling the virtues of sugar as part of a healthy breakfast and recommending that it be consumed together with bread, butter, milk, water, coffee, tea, and chocolate.

52 Chesterfield, *Letters*, 12 (1741); Richardson, *Clarissa*, 26–27.

53 See, for example, Richardson, *Clarissa*, 26.

54 Lane, *Jane Austen and Food*, 28.

55 I have looked for evidence that they did in VOC and East India Company records— without success.

56 *Autobiography of Benjamin Franklin*, 100–1.

57 Neil McKendrick, "Josiah Wedgwood and the Commercialization of the Potteries," in *Birth of a Consumer Society*, ed. McKendrick et al., 100–45.

58 Weatherill, *Consumer Behavior*, 6–12.

CHAPTER SEVEN: RESPECTABILITY

1 *Oxford English Dictionary*, 2nd ed., 20 vols. (Oxford: Clarendon Press, 1989), 13:734. The definition continues: "Also with a somewhat derogatory implication of affectation and spuriousness." This refers to a tendency in usage that became increasingly prominent in the late nineteenth century but appears to have been fairly rare earlier.

2 Ibid.

3 Johnson, *Dictionary*, 2:n.p., s.v. "Respect."

4 Jane Austen, *Pride and Prejudice* (New York: Harper and Brothers, 1950), 12–13.

5 Ibid., 25.

6 Paul Robert, *Dictionnaire alphabétique et analogique de la Langue Française*, 6 vols. (Paris: Littre, 1966), 6:851. Most of the following discussion of French equivalents to *respectable* and *respectability* comes from Robert.

7 Ibid., 3:510–11.

8 Vickery, *Gentleman's Daughter*, 197.

9 Robert, *Dictionnaire*, 3:510–11.

10 Keith Spalding, *An Historical Dictionary of German Figurative Usage*, 5 vols. (Oxford: Blackwell, n.d.), 1:61–62.

11 Ibid.

12 Trusler, *Modern Times.*

13 Ibid., 2:38.

14 Ibid., 1:iii. The *OED* citation is 1:vi, which may be from the first edition (also published in 1785). The second edition is followed here.

15 In fact, as Jane Austen's *Sense and Sensibility* demonstrates, by the early nineteenth century some of the meanings of "sense" had come to be seen as dissonant with, if not necessary contradictory to, "sensibility."

16 Ibid., 2:7.

17 Ibid., 1:2.

18 Ibid., 1:26.

19 Ibid., 1:32.

20 Ibid., 1:93–94.

21 Ibid., 1:98.

22 In 1796, Trusler himself published a book of standard sermons for the use of other ministers, engraved in a flowing hand so that they would not even have to be copied by the user. Penelope J. Corfield, *Power and the Professions in Britain, 1700–1850* (London and New York: Routledge, 1995), 104.

23 Trusler, *Modern Times*, 1:107–8. (Emphasis in original text.)

24 Ibid., 2:25. (Emphasis in original text.)

25 See Colin Jones and Rebecca Spang, "Sans-Culottes, *Sans Café, Sans Tabac*: Shifting Realms of Necessity and Luxury in Eighteenth-Century France," in *Consumers and Luxury*, ed. Berg and Clifford, 37–62.

26 A tendency toward "paranoid" approaches to politics, especially under revolutionary circumstances, in late-eighteenth-century Europe and America has been recognized by several scholars. Gordon S. Wood, "Conspiracy and the Paranoid Style: Causality and Deceit in the Eighteenth Century," *William and Mary Quarterly*, 3rd ser., 39 (1982): 401–41, argues that an analytical process that assumes that most undesirable events in society must be due to a deliberate human agency was a natural consequence of accepting Enlightenment ideas of cause and effect. Timothy Tackett, "Conspiracy Obsession in a Time of Revolution: French Elites and the Origins of the Terror, 1789–1792," *American Historical Review* 105 (2000): 691–713, casts doubt on Wood's interpretation in the case of revolutionary France by analyzing the actual incidence of "paranoid"-style arguments in the French national legislatures before the Terror and by pointing out that impersonal forms of explanation for human events (those of Montesquieu and Smith, for instance) were more popular among the revolutionary elites than paranoid ones. Tackett observes that "paranoid" political behavior was generally a response to real threats or ones that could be reasonably suspected on evidential grounds. He also suggests that "paranoid" behavior is likely to be found in societies, as in individuals, in which normal order has broken down. If we take the observation out of a revolutionary context and apply it to the cultural life of the late eighteenth century as a whole, we can see that paranoia—the tendency to blame particular individuals and groups for undesirable sociocultural changes, which we see in Trusler's book—may be one of a number of common attempts to understand and perhaps prescribe actions to deal with change.

27 Trusler, *Modern Times*, 3:190–195.

28 Ibid., 2:55–69. The careful economy practiced by the son is essentially the same as the system presented by Trusler in another book: John Trusler, *The Way to Be Rich and Respectable; Addressed to Men of Small Fortune* (London: for the author, n.d.).

29 Trusler, *Modern Times*, 1:53–58.

30 Ibid., 1:56.

31 Ibid., 1:59–87.

32 Ibid., 1:1.

33 Ibid., 1:75–80, 99–136, 2:89–121, 3:61–79. Corfield, *Power and the Professions*, 42–69.

34 [John Trusler], *An Easy Way to Prolong Life, by a Little Attention to What We Eat and Drink*, 4th ed. (Dover, NH: S. Bragg for W. T. Clap, 1796).

35 Trusler, *Modern Times*, 2:38, 3:40–41.

36 The point about improving consumers' morality and awareness is a reasonable read-ing of Trusler's advertisement to the reader (ibid., 1:iii–iv) and of discussions in 1:25–27, 38, 2:33–38, and especially 3:39–44. Implications for the regulation of pro-fessions can be found in 1:105–6, 2:106–21, and 3:61–79.

37 For example, ibid., 1:63–64, 66–67 (immodest dress and behavior in women encour-aged by modern society); 1:153–70 (fashionable prostitution); 3:106–7 (effects of lux-urious living on health); 3:159–71 ("The Folly of Women of the Ton").

38 Ibid., 1:56, 3:1–18, 190–95.

39 Ibid., 2:2.

40 Ibid., 3:44.

41 Ibid., 2:40–46. Trusler's depiction of women as shoppers corresponds very closely to others analyzed by Elizabeth Kowaleski-Wallace in *Consuming Subjects*, 79–99.

42 See chapter 8.

43 Trusler, *Modern Times*, 2:38.

44 Ibid., 1:63–64.

45 I have no idea what the surname "Wildman" is supposed to signify, for nobody in the family is the least bit wild. If a humorous contrast between the name and the charac-ters is intended, it doesn't seem very funny—but then, neither do many of Trusler's other attempts at wit.

46 Trusler, *Modern Times*, 3:22.

47 Ibid., 1:179–91, 3:19–61; Vickery, *Gentleman's Daughter*, 127–60.

48 See, for example, Trusler, *Modern Times*, 1:153–78.

49 Ibid., 1:94–98.

50 See Mullan, *Sentiment and Sociability*, 57–113.

51 See, however, Wrightson, "Estates, Degrees, and Sorts," in *Language, History, and Class*, ed. Corfield, 39; and Corfield, "Class by Name and Number," in ibid., 107, n. 25. Both suggest in somewhat different ways that assumptions about hereditary gen-tility had worn thin by the eighteenth century.

52 Lawrence Klein's analysis of the third earl of Shaftesbury's view of gentility in rela-tion to politeness suggests that even Shaftesbury, who so strongly emphasized good manners, education, and culture as crucial features of gentility, still assumed that gen-tlemen were born to that status. Klein, *Shaftesbury*, 27–47, 123–53.

53 A clear demonstration of absence of a social obligation on the part of gentlemen to pay tailors' bills can be found in the papers relating to the bankruptcy of William Watt, tai-lor in the 1660s and 1670s to Charles II, the duke of Monmouth, the duke of Buckingham, and a great many other gentlemen who were not notably reliable about clearing their accounts: PRO, C113/31.

54 Conley, *Unwritten Law*, 173–201.

55 Ibid., 174.

56 For example, Rawdon Crawley and Lord Steyn in *Vanity Fair* and Henry Crawford in *Mansfield Park*.

57 Conley, *Unwritten Law*, 146–51.

58 Anthony Trollope, *The Prime Minister* (Oxford: Oxford University Press, 1973), esp. 2–6. Some aspects of nineteenth-century confusion over gentility are discussed, although their problematical character is not resolved, in W. L. Burn, *The Age of Equipoise: A Study of the Mid-Victorian Generation* (New York: W. W. Norton, 1965), 253–67.

59 See the discussion of John Wesley in chapter 8.

60 With regard to this observation, see Gordon Wood's treatment of the American Whigs in Gordon S. Wood, *The Creation of the American Republic, 1776–1787* (Chapel Hill: University of North Carolina Press, 1969), 3–45.

61 This topic will recur in chapter 8. A full discussion will require another book, in which it will be argued that respectability was a significant aspect of revolutionary attempts to change the social order and can be detected in the radical elements in both the American and the French revolutions. This was the case primarily because respectability was *self-descriptive* as well as ascriptive—that is, people felt *themselves* to be respectable, to have self-respect. If the social order, particularly in its political manifestations, blatantly failed to recognize the self-respect with which a large part of the population regarded themselves, and did so on bases such as birth or inherited wealth, that could be a strong motivation for seeking revolution rather than moderate or moral reform. For an excellent analysis of the cognitive framework within which such motives operated, see Wood, *Radicalism of the American Revolution*, 169–89, 229–43.

62 See, for example, Jones, *Luxury, Pride, and Vanity*, 13–16.

63 Campbell, *Romantic Ethic*, 99–137, 173–200.

64 Crowley, "Sensibility of Comfort."

65 As is indicated in the titles of histories of those companies: John Keay, *The Honourable Company: A History of the English East India Company* (London: HarperCollins, 1991); and Douglas MacKay, *The Honourable Company: A History of the Hudson's Bay Company* (Indianapolis: Bobbs-Merrill, 1936).

66 Van Dam, *Beschryvinge*, 63:244–67.

67 The Estates General of the Netherlands (the collective sovereign of the republic) was formally referred to as "Their High Mightinesses." The central committee of VOC directors was called the Heeren 17 (the "Seventeen Gentlemen").

68 As Tony (Frau Permeneder) does in *Buddenbrooks*. Even then, it is as much the Buddenbrooks family as it is the firm that Tony develops as an object of veneration. Thomas Mann, *Buddenbrooks*, trans. H. T. Lowe-Porter (New York: Vintage, 1984), 392–404.

69 The first approach can be seen in the tendency of British firms to seek and advertise appointments as purveyors to royalty. The second can be seen in constant references to "respectable" firms throughout the nineteenth century—including ones in which the usage was satirized, as in act 1 of Gilbert and Sullivan's *The Sorcerer*: "He *could* change you into a guinea-pig, no doubt, but it is unlikely that he would take such a liberty. It's a most respectable firm, and I am sure he would never be guilty of so untradesmanlike an act." W. S. Gilbert, *The Savoy Operas* (London: Macmillan, 1930), 30.

70 The commercial importance of respectability was not a matter just of general ascription. It could also be very specific and practical. In 1808, John Leigh and Company, Liverpool merchants doing business in Ireland and Africa who had just dropped the slave-trading side of their enterprise, were informed by the major Manchester textile firm of Peel, Yates and Halliwell that an order for cotton cloth would not be released until payment in the form of a bill on "some respectable banking House" was received. Apparently neither John Leigh nor his usual commercial correspondents were sufficiently respectable to be trusted by themselves (a judgment that appears to be supported by Leigh's records). PRO, C108/213:76.

71 See Theodore Zeldin, *France, 1848–1945: Ambition and Love* (Oxford: Oxford University Press, 1979), 16–17.

72 See Geoffrey Cottrell, *Amsterdam: The Life of a City* (Boston: Little, Brown, 1972), 213–24.

73 For an example (the banker Gerson Bleichröder, who ended up as Gerson *von* Bleichröder), see Fritz Stern, *Gold and Iron: Bismarck, Bleichröder, and the Building of the German Empire* (New York: Alfred A. Knopf, 1977), 16–19, 59–75. In Germany, respectability was probably more strongly influenced by the traditions and ideals of state bureaucracies than was the case in Britain or the United States. In Germany, the figure of the civil servant was a stock model of respectability long before and to a greater extent than in Britain or the United States.

74 The most comprehensive coverage of professionalization is Werner Conze and Jürgen Kocka, eds., *Bildungsbürgertum im 19. Jahrhundert*, vol. 1, *Bildungssystem und Professionalisierung in internationales Vergleich* (Stuttgart: Klett-Cotta, 1985).

75 Corfield, *Power and the Professions*.

76 Ibid., 1–17, 248–50.

77 Ibid., 246.

78 Some studies of the learned professions in Germany emphasize the widespread belief among their members that their intellectual eminence entitled them to a substantial share of power—which they never actually obtained. See, for example, Fritz Ringer, *The Decline of the German Mandarins: The German Academic Community, 1890–1933* (Cambridge, MA: Harvard University Press, 1969). One could argue, however, that it was not as professionals but as an intelligentsia that the German *Gelehrter* claimed power. Corfield insists that professionals in eighteenth- and nineteenth-century Britain did not constitute an intelligentsia. See Corfield, *Power and the Professions*, 247.

79 C. W. Brooks, *Pettyfoggers and Vipers of the Commonwealth: The "Lower Branch" of the Legal Profession in Early Modern England* (Cambridge: Cambridge University Press, 1986); Robert Robson, *The Attorney in Eighteenth-Century England* (Cambridge: Cambridge University Press, 1959).

80 Jessie Dobson and R. Milnes Wagner, *Barbers and Barber-Surgeons of London: A History of the Barbers' and Barber-Surgeons Companies* (Oxford: Blackwell, 1979); Penelope Hunting, *A History of the Society of Apothecaries* (London: Society of Apothecaries, 1998).

81 Corfield, *Power and the Professions*, 26.

82 Ibid., 143.

83 Ibid., 80.

84 Ibid., 157.

85 Ibid., 122.

86 Ibid., 143.

87 Ibid., 176–77.

88 See, for example, Jones, *Luxury, Pride, and Vanity*, 13–16.

89 Linda Colley, *Britons: Forging the Nation, 1707–1837* (New Haven and London: Yale University Press, 1992), 147–93.

90 A minor character in Jane Austen's *Emma*, Mr. Perry, is an apothecary and the provider of medical care to all the gentry in the neighborhood in which the novel is set. He is described as "an intelligent, gentlemanlike man." Emma does not seem to think that he is actually a gentleman, but Emma is a horrible snob. Jane Austen, *Emma* (New York: New American Library, 1964), esp. 16.

91 On midwives, see Laurel Thatcher Ulrich, *A Midwife's Tale: The Life of Martha Ballard, Based on Her Diary, 1785–1812* (New York: Alfred A. Knopf, 1990). The article under "History of Medicine" in the 1948 printing of the *Encyclopedia Britannica*, 24 vols. (Chicago: Encyclopedia Britannica, 1948), 15:203, states that eighteenth-century midwives were "mostly ignorant, dirty and unskilful, and the resulting loss of life enormous." They are compared with "man-midwives," who supposedly were the opposite and therefore saved lives. It actually is not at all clear that in the eighteenth century male obstetricians had a better success rate in Britain than midwives or that they were notably cleaner or technically more competent. Indeed, it is not unlikely that their unsterilized forceps were transmitters of disease. Porter, *English Society*, 294. The *Britannica* article is evidence of the strength of the cognitive restructuring of medicine in the eighteenth and nineteenth centuries—a restructuring that initially had as much to do with respectability as with science or improved techniques and that continued, down to the twentieth century, to shape attitudes and structure in the medical professions.

     This is not the same as arguing that the substantial replacement of the midwife by the obstetrician in the late eighteenth and early nineteenth centuries was the result of a "male conspiracy." Amanda Vickery, *Gentleman's Daughter*," 94–96, cites her own sources and the work of others including Roy Porter to show that, among the middle and upper classes, women often preferred obstetricians and men tended to resist them. (Trusler, *Modern Times*, 1:64, displays this negative view.) But the reasons Vickery suggests for women's preference for obstetricians have largely to do with not wanting to have one's labor and the events of childbirth spread around by the midwife—in other words, a desire to maintain personal privacy and the privacy of a respectable household.

CHAPTER EIGHT: CONCLUSION

1 See the introduction to Chesterfield, *Letters*, esp. v, xiii.

2 See Shinagel, *Daniel Defoe and Middle-Class Gentility*, 201–45.

3 Pat Rogers, ed., *Defoe: The Critical Heritage* (London: Routledge and Kegan Paul, 1972); John Robert Moore, *Daniel Defoe: Citizen of the Modern World* (Chicago: University of Chicago Press, 1958), 39–44.

4 Daniel Defoe, *The Compleat English Gentleman* (Folcroft, PA: Folcroft Library Editions, 1972).

5 Daniel Defoe, *Plan of the English Commerce* (Oxford: Blackwell, 1928), 61.

6 Quoted in Shinagel, *Daniel Defoe*, 228–29.

7 Ibid., 209–10; Daniel Defoe, *The Complete English Tradesman*, 2 vols. (London: C. Rivington, 1927), 2:237.

8 The standard source on Nash is a hack piece written by Oliver Goldsmith just after Nash's death, which summarizes Nash's mythic history: Oliver Goldsmith, "The Life of Richard Nash," in *Collected Works*, ed. Arthur Friedman, 5 vols. (Oxford: Clarendon Press, 1966), 3:285–398. Goldsmith's account is (slightly) supplemented in Willard Connely, *Beau Nash: Monarch of Bath and Tunbridge Wells* (London: Werner Laurie, 1955). For a comprehensive history of Bath in its heyday that does not emphasize Nash, see R. S. Neale, *Bath, 1680–1850: A Social History* . . . (London: Routledge and Kegan Paul, 1981). See vol. 2 of Jane Austen's *Persuasion* and the first part of *Northanger Abbey* for brilliant fictional representations of Bath as a center of respectable social life at the beginning of the nineteenth century: Jane Austen, *Persuasion* (New York: New American Library, 1964), 113–240, and Jane Austen, *Northanger Abbey* (New York: Lancer, 1968), 16–205.

9 The classic analysis of the social effect of Wesley and his movement is Élie Halèvy, *The Birth of Methodism*, trans. B. Semmel (Chicago: University of Chicago Press, 1971).

10 *The Letters of John Wesley*, ed. B. Telford, 8 vols. (London: Epworth Press, 1931), 1:320.

11 See Bernard Semmel, *The Methodist Revolution* (New York: Basic Books, 1973), 23–109; and Robert C. Monk, *John Wesley: His Puritan Heritage* (Nashville: Abingdon Press, 1966).

12 "Of Dress," in *Works of John Wesley III*, 247–61.

13 Porter, *English Society*, 193.

14 *Works of John Wesley III*, 249.

15 *Works of John Wesley I*, 592–631 (on fasting and greed).

16 See, for example, Thomas Babington Macaulay's famous 1831 speeches in the House of Commons in favor of electoral reform. The thrust of his argument is that the "middle classes" demand a voice in government, and deserve one, because they have become "intelligent" and "respectable." Because of their possession of these characteristics, their interest in state policy is legitimate, and they can be trusted to express it in a responsible way (for example, by electing members of Parliament much like the ones elected at present, rather than radical demagogues). If they are denied the vote and the recognition that it symbolizes, they will, in one way or another, destroy the Constitution. Thomas Babington Macaulay, *The Works of Lord Macaulay*, 12 vols. (London: Longmans, Green and Co., 1898), 11:407–95, esp. 412, 417, 419, 436, 446, 449–52, 458–59.

17 Bushman, *Refinement of America*.

18 See, for example, David Eltis and Stanley L. Engerman, "The Importance of Slavery and the Slave Trade to Industrializing Britain," *Journal of Economic History* 60, no. 1 (2000): 123–44. Much of the discussion of these points focuses on the slave trade and the economic significance of the Atlantic sugar business.

19 For an overview of Wedgwood's life and career, see Anthony Burton, *Josiah Wedgwood: A Biography* (London: Andre Deutsch, 1976).

20 C. J. A. Jörg, *Porselein als Handelswaar: De porseleinhandel als onderdeel van de Chinahandel van de V.O.C., 1729–1794*, Ph.D. diss., University of Leiden, 1978, 1–97.

21 On the state of English pottery in the eighteenth century and the revolutionary changes wrought by Wedgwood, see Robin Hildyard, *European Ceramics* (London: V and A Publications, 1999), 70–91.

22 Burton, *Wedgwood*, 49–51; Wedgwood, *Letters*, 1:38–40 (undated letter, 1765).

23 Hildyard, *European Ceramics*, 81–83; Burton, *Wedgwood*, 35–51.

24 On Wedgwood as marketer, see Neil McKendrick's essay on Wedgwood in McKendrick et al., *Birth of a Consumer Society*, 100–45.

25 See Wedgwood, *Letters*, 1:346 (Wedgwood to Bentley, May 19, 1770) and 1:357 (Wedgwood to Bentley, August 2, 1770).

26 Ibid., 3:109–13 (Wedgwood to his chief designer, J. Flaxman, February 11, 1790). He tells Flaxman (112–13) to avoid nudity in classical figures used for commercial decoration "for none either male or female, of the present generation, will take or apply them as furniture, if the figures are naked."

27 Burton, *Wedgwood*, facing 176.

28 See Woodruff Smith, "The European-Asian Trade of the Seventeenth Century and the Modernization of Commercial Capitalism," *Itinerario* 6, no. 2 (1982): 68–90.

29 See, for instance, McKendrick et al., *Birth of a Consumer Society*.

30 See Christopher Hibbert, *George III: A Personal History* (New York: Basic Books, 1998), 71–87, 96–104, 191–207, 386–95.

31 David Cannadine, *The Rise and Fall of Class in Britain* (New York: Columbia University Press), 1999, 95–96, touches on the subject but almost immediately drops it.

Appendix

Table 1
English East India Company Imports of Asian Textiles, 1666–1760
(all types, in 1,000s of pieces, annual mean for five-year intervals)

1666–1670	165
1671–1675	476
1681–1685	1,046
1686–1690	408
1691–1695	96
1701–1705	302
1706–1710	254
1711–1715	566
1716–1720	542
1721–1725	771
1726–1730	794
1731–1735	805
1736–1740	725
1741–1745	865
1746–1750	678
1751–1755	614
1756–1760	441

Source: Calculated from table C.24 in Chaudhuri, *Trading World of Asia,* 547–48. Data for 1698–1702, when there were two English East India companies, covers only the "old" company.

Table 2
Lawful Imports, Exports, and Reexports of Certain Types
of Textiles: England and Wales, 1699–1701 to 1772–1774
(in 1,000s of £s fixed notional value)

	1699–1701	1722–1724	1752–1754	1772–1774
Calicoes (printed, painted, dyed)				
Total imported (reexport required)	367	437	401	697
Total reexported (mostly to Europe)	340	484	499	701
Cottons (English)				
Exported (mostly to America)	20	48	83	221
Linens				
Total imported	903	1,036	1,185	1,246
NW Europe	798	838	684	415
Ireland	57	114	332	652
Total reexported (mostly to America)	182	232	331	322
English linens exported	—	25	211	740
Silk and mixed fabrics				
Total imported	208	208	112	82
Total reexported (Europe and America)	150	354	281	501
English silks, etc., exported (mostly to America)	80	78	160	189

Source: Tables in Davis, "English Foreign Trade, 1700–1774," 300–3. The notional values assigned by t Customs to units of particular commodities remained unchanged throughout the period and are therefore mea ures of quantity rather than relative or market value. The relationship of reexport figures to imports is ve unclear in the Customs ledgers from which these data arise. Reexport numbers are included as a rough indic tion of the extent of the reexport trade and of demand changes in the areas to which reexports were se Substantial amounts of Asian textiles and other commodities reexported to Europe probably returned as smu gled goods.

Table 3
Imports of White Calicoes into Great Britain, 1718–1770
(in 1,000s of pieces; probably includes checked and striped fabrics;
reexport not required)

1718	1,220
1730	1,126
1740	907
1770	987

Source: Public Record Office CUST 3/20, 3/30, 3/40, 3/70,
Customs Ledgers of Imports and Exports.

Table 4
English East India Company Imports of Black Pepper, 1666–1760
(in 1,000s of lbs., annual mean for five-year intervals)

	EEIC Imports	VOC imports of black pepper for comparable intervals, annual mean, in Dutch pounds:
1666–1670	1,506	
1671–1675	3,418	
1676–1680	4,575	
1681–1685	2,369	
1686–1690	1,524	
1691–1695	514	
1696–1700	1,514	
1701–1705	975	4,635
1706–1710	1,238	4,332
1711–1715	1,195	3,189
1716–1720	2,255	5,160
1721–1725	1,073	
1726–1730	1,179	
1731–1735	2,194	4,158
1736–1740	2,143	
1741–1745	3,601	
1746–1750	2,308	
1751–1755	2,405	
1756–1760	2,219	

Sources: Calculated from table C.14 in Chaudhuri, *Trading World of Asia,*
pp. 529–30; from *Allgemeen Rijksarchief*, Collectie Vredenburch 9, fol. 181–85;
and from *Allgemeen Rijksarchief*, VOC, Kamer Amsterdam, no. 7000.

Table 5
Average Prices of Pepper and Major Spices at
VOC Sales, 1700–1719
(prices per Dutch pound)

	Cloves (in stuivers)	Nutmeg (in stuivers)	Cinnamon (in stuivers)	Pepper (in groats)
1700	75	84	51.3	22.3
1701	75	75	43.9	18.1
1702	75	75	48.4	16.7
1703	75	75	47.9	18.1
1704	75	75	57.1	15.3
1705	75	75	53.8	16.4
1706	75	75	58.0	17.7
1707	75	75	56.4	22.9
1708	75	75	55.1	18.0
1709	75	75	52.5	20.8
1710	75	75	43.6	19.7
1711	75	75	44.0	21.5
1712	75	75	51.0	25.5
1713	75	75	49.5	36.9
1714	75	75	52.5	23.8
1715	75	75	49.9	18.6
1716	75	75	53.6	21.8
1717	75	75	51.9	18.4
1718	75	75	49.8	18.8
1719	75	75	51.8	16.8

Despite fluctuations, the mean sales price of pepper between 1700 and 1719 was 20.4 groats per pound, which is very close to the target price of 20 groats noted in a printed VOC internal document of 1692 as being the company's standard. *Allgemeen Rijksarchief*, Collectie Vredenburch 11, item 2.

Source: Figures from Vredenburch 9, fol. 181–85.

Table 6
Lawful Imports and Reexports of Coffee, Tea, and Sugar:
England and Wales, 1699–1701 to 1772–1774
(in 1,000s of £ fixed notional value; see note, table 2)

	1669–1701	1722–1724	1752–1754	1772–1774
Coffee imports	27 (1.0)	127 (4.7)	53 (2.0)	436 (16.2)
reexports	2	151	84	873
Tea imports	8 (1.0)	116 (14.5)	334 (41.8)	848 (106.0)
reexports	2	267	217	295
Sugar imports	630 (1.0)	928 (1.5)	1,302 (2.1)	2,364 (3.8)
reexports	287	211	110	429
Population, England and Wales (1,000 of persons)	5,058 (1.0)	5,350 (1.1)	5,772 (1.1)	6,448 (1.3)

Index numbers in parentheses ( ) set to base 1.0 = 1699–1701.

Sources: Estimates of population are from E. A. Wrigley and R. S. Schofield, *The Population History of England* (Cambridge, MA: Harvard University Press, 1981), 208–9, and are set at the quinquennial point given by Wrigley and Schofield closest to the first years of the intervals in the table: 1701, 1721, 1751, and 1771. Trade figures are from Davis, "English Foreign Trade, 1700–1774," 300–3.

Table 7
Imports and Reexports of Tobacco: England and Wales,
1699–1701 to 1772–1774
(in 1000s of £ fixed notional value; see note, Table 2)

	1699–1701	1722–1724	1752–1754	1772–1774
Tobacco imports	249	263	560	519
Tobacco reexports	421	387	953	904

Source: Tables in Davis, "English Foreign Trade, 1700–1774," 300–3.

BIBLIOGRAPHY

ARCHIVAL SOURCES AND SPECIAL COLLECTIONS

Amsterdam

Gemeente Archief Amsterdam (GAA)—Amsterdam Municipal Archives

    Collectie Koopmansboeken: 38, 39, 77

    Particulieren Archieven (P.A.):
        1 (Burlamachi): 4, 6, 7, 9, 127, 168–70, 199, 204,
                205, 207, 288, 490, 495
        2 (Velters): 1, 2, 7, 10, 11, 14
        76 (De Graeff): 166, 200
        88 (Brants): 902, 994, 995, 1004, 1036, 1037

The Hague

Algemeen Rijksarchief (ARA)—Netherlands National Archives
    (All Ie Afdeling).

    Levantse Handel: 173(I), 182, 192(I), 192(II)

    Particulieren Collecties
        Hope: 16–18, 82, 83
        Hudde: 18

Radermacher: 82, 115, 116
Vredenburch: 9, 11, 15

Verenigde Oostindische Compagnie (VOC)
    Heeren 17: 101, 106, 114, 108, 221
    Kamer Amsterdam: 230–32, 234, 236–38, 241, 243,
                307, 315, 320–23, 326, 345, 360, 4464, 6963,
                6984, 6985, 6988–91, 6992, 7000, 7012, 7015
    Kamer Zeeland: 7338, 7339, 11087, 13352–54, 13370
    Kamer Hoorn: 14532
    Overgekomene Brieven en Papieren (OB): 1387

West-Indische Compagnie (WIC): 795, 812, 1232

Koninklijke Bibliotheek—Royal Library

Pamphlet Collection (items numbered according to finding
    aid: Knuttel, W.P.C. *Catalogus van de Pamfletten-*
    Verzameling berustende in de Koninklijke Bibliotheek,
    9 vols. [1890–1920; Utrecht: HES Publishers, 1978]):
    Kn. 3233, 3358, 3568, 4154, 4460, 4539, 4636, 5021, 5358, 7454, 7687,
    8183, 8652, 12634, 12635, 13037, 13038, 13951, 14525, 14534

London

Goldsmiths' Library, University of London (GL)

Broadsides Collection (GLBC):
    1: 9, 16, 17, 23, 31, 84, 87, 118, 130 (1–2), 131,
        132 (1), 133 (2–3), 134, 138, 147
    2: 183, 201, 203 (4), 207 (1–3), 210, 217 (1–3, 6),
        220–21, 225 (1–2), 234 (1–3)
    3: 244 (1), 246 (1,3), 247, 278 (1), 281 (1–5),
        282 (1–7), 284, 285, 287, 288 (1–10), 300
    4: 303, 328, 335 (1), 340, 343, 345, 359 (1), 362,
        381, 386 (1–2)

Manuscripts Collection: 56, 408, 448, 741

Newspapers:
    The Daily Courant (1720)
    The London Journal (1720–28)
    The Weekly Magazine: or, Universal Intelligencer
        (1732–33)

Microfilms Collection: MC 35, reels 1 and 2

Proclamations Collection: 1603, 2138, 2179

Guildhall Library

> Sir Charles Banks Papers: Microfilm 217
> Thomas Bowery Papers: Ms. 3041
> Charles Payne Papers: Mss. 5301, 5301A, 5301B
> Sir William Turner Papers: Mss. 5099–113.

India Office Library and Records (IOLR)—now the Oriental and India Office Collections of the British Library

> Series:
> B: 52, 62–66
> E: 3/84, 3/89–90, 3/92–93, 3/97
> H: 7–10, 14, 19, 32, 34–35, 37, 40, 42, 44, 74–75

Public Record Office (PRO)
> Chancery Masters' Exhibits:
> C103/130–33, 192, 204
> C104/126–30, 141
> C106/170–71
> C107/17–20
> C108/43, 132, 213
> C112/60–62
> C113/11–12, 31
> C114/59, 180, 182

> Customs Inspectors' Ledgers:
> CUST 3/20, 30, 40, 70

PRIMARY SOURCES

Austen, Jane. *Emma*. New York: New American Library, 1964.

——. *Northanger Abbey*. New York: Lancer, 1968.

——. *Persuasion*. New York: New American Library, 1964.

——. *Pride and Prejudice*. New York: Harper, 1950.

The Autobiography of Benjamin Franklin. New York: Modern Library, 1981.

Bacon, Francis. *The Advancement of Learning*, in *Selected Selected Writings of Francis Bacon*, Ed. H. Dick, New York: Modern Library, 1955.

Blankaart, S[teven], M.D. *De Borgerlyke Tafel: Om lang gesond sonder ziekten te leven*. Amsterdam: Jan ten Hoorn, 1683.

Bontekoe, Cornelis. *Tractaat Van het Excellenste Kruyd Thee, Coffi, en Chocolate*, appended to vol. 2 of *Alle de Philosophische, Medicinale, en Chymische Werken van den Heer Corn. Bontekoe*. 2 vols. Amsterdam: n.p., 1689.

Boswell for the Defence. Ed. W. Wimsatt and F. Pottle. New York: McGraw-Hill, 1959.

Boswell in Holland, 1763–1764. Ed. F. Pottle. New York: McGraw-Hill, 1952.

Boswell in Search of a Wife, 1766–1769. Ed. F. Brady and F. Pottle. New York: McGraw-Hill, 1956.

Boswell's London Journal, 1762–1763. Ed. F. Pottle. New York: McGraw-Hill, 1950.

A Calendar of the Court Minutes etc. of the East India Company, 1635–1639. Ed. E. B. Sainsbury. Oxford: Clarendon Press, 1907. (CCM) Subsequent volumes:
1640–1643. Oxford: Clarendon Press, 1909.
1644–1649. Oxford: Clarendon Press, 1912.
1650–1654. Oxford: Clarendon Press, 1913.
1655–1659. Oxford: Clarendon Press, 1916.
1660–1663. Oxford: Clarendon Press, 1922.
1664–1667. Oxford: Clarendon Press, 1925.
1668–1670. Oxford: Clarendon Press, 1929.
1671–1673. Oxford: Clarendon Press, 1932.
1674–1676. Oxford: Clarendon Press, 1935.
1677–1679. Oxford: Clarendon Press, 1938.

Cary, John. *An Essay on the State of England in Relation to Its Trade, Its Poor, and Its Taxes, for Carrying on the Present War against France*. Bristol: W. Bonny, for the author, 1695.

The Case of Dorothy Petty, In Relation to the Union-Society, at the White Lyon by Temple-Bar, whereof She Is Director. London: n.p., 1711. (GLBC 201).

The Case of the Merchants Who Export Tobacco. N.p.: c. 1713. (GLBC 247).

Chamberlain, John. *The Manner of Making of Coffee, Tea, and Chocolate*. London: William Crook, 1685.

Chamberlayne, John. *A Family-Herbal, or, the Treasure of Health*. London: William Crook, 1689.

Coen, Jan Pietersz. *Bescheiden omtrent ziyn bedrijf in Indië*, Ed. H. T. Colenbrander. 6 vols. The Hague: Martinus Nijhoff, 1919–34.

Coffee-Houses Vindicated in Answer to the Late Published Character of a Coffee-House . . . London: Lock, 1673.

[Court, Pieter de la]. "V.D.H.," *Interest van Holland, ofte Gronden van Hollands-Welvaren.* Amsterdam: Joan. Cyprianus vander Gracht, 1662. (Kn. 8652).

Dam, Pieter van. *Beschryvinge van de Oostindische Compagnie.* Ed. F. W. Stapel. 7 vols. The Hague: R. G. P. Grote Serie [63, 68, 74, 76, 83, 87, 96], 1927–54.

Dapper, O[lfert]. *Historische Beschrijving der Stadt Amsterdam.* Meurs: Jacob van Meurs, 1663.

Defoe, Daniel. *The Compleat English Gentleman.* Folcroft, PA: Folcroft Library Editions, 1972.

——. *The Complete English Tradesman.* 2 vols. London: C. Rivington, 1927.

——. *Plan of the English Commerce.* Oxford: Blackwell, 1928.

The Diary of John Evelyn. Ed. E. S. de Beer. 6 vols. Oxford: Clarendon Press, 1955.

The Diary of Samuel Pepys. Ed. Samuel Latham and William Mathews, 11 vols. Berkeley and Los Angeles: University of California Press, 1970–83.

Dickens, Charles. *Bleak House.* New York: Bantam, 1983.

Diderot, Denis. *Le Neveu de Rameau.* Geneva: Droz, 1963.

The Dispute between the Northern Colonies and the Sugar Islands, Set in a Clear View. London: n.p., 1731. (GLBC 343).

Dufour, Philippe Sylvestre. *Traitez Nouveaux et curieux du café, du thée, et du chocolate.* The Hague: Adrian Moetjens, 1685.

Eltis, David, and Stanley L. Engerman. "The Importance of Slavery and the Slave Trade to Industrializing Britain," *Journal of Economic History* 60, no. 1 (2000): 23–44.

Encyclopédie, ou dictionnaire raisonné des sciences, des arts, et des métiers. 23 vols., facsimile ed. Stuttgart: Frommann, 1966.

Feuille, Daniel de la. *Le Guide d'Amsterdam.* Amsterdam: Daniel de la Feuille, 1701.

Floyd, Thomas. *The Picture of a Perfit Common Wealth.* London: S. Stafford, 1600.

Gilbert, W. S. *The Savoy Operas.* London: Macmillan, 1930.

Glasse, Hannah. *The Art of Cookery, Made Plain and Simple.* London: by the author, 1747.

Grontlijcke Tegen-bericht Van de waerachtige remedie Der tegenwoordige dierte in de Granen in Nederlandt. N.p.: Broer Jansz., 1631. (Kn. 4154).

Guicciardini, Francesco. *The History of Italy.* Trans. S. Alexander. New York: Macmillan, 1969.

Halsband, Robert, ed. *The Complete Letters of Lady Mary Wortley Montague.* 3 vols. Oxford: Clarendon Press, 1965.

Harrison, William. *The Description of England: The Classic Contemporary Account of Tudor Social Life.* Ed. George Edelen. New York: Dover, 1994.

The Haven of Health. London: Thomas Orwin, 1589.

James I. *A Counter-Blaste to Tobacco.* Emmaus, PA: Rodale Press, 1954.

Johnson, Samuel. *A Dictionary of the English Language.* 2 vols. London: W. Strahan, 1755.

Jones, Erasmus. *Luxury, Pride, and Vanity, the Bane of the British Nation.* 2nd ed. London: J. Roberts, 1736.

Kramnick, Issac, ed. *The Portable Enlightenment Reader.* New York: Penguin, 1995.

Lamb, Patrick. *Royal Cookery; or, the Complete Court-cook.* London: A. Roper, 1710.

The Letters of John Wesley. Ed. B. Telford. 8 vols. London: Epworth Press, 1931.

Ligon, Richard. *A True and Exact History of the Island of Barbadoes.* London: Peter Parker, 1673.

Locke, John. *The Second Treatise of Government.* Indianapolis: Liberal Arts Press, 1952.

Lord Chesterfield's Letters to His Son and Others. London: Dent, 1929.

Lyste Vande Gedenckwaerdige Teyckeninghe op de Peper . . . Haarlem: T. Fonteyn, 1639. (Kn. 4636).

Macaulay, Thomas Babington. *The Works of Lord Macaulay.* 12 vols. London: Longmans Green and Co., 1898.

Mackenzie, Henry. *The Man of Feeling.* Ed. B. Vickers. London: Oxford University Press, 1967.

Mandeville's Travels. Ed. M. Letts. 2 vols. London: Hakluyt Society, 1967.

Mann, Thomas. *Buddebrooks.* Trans. H. T. Lowe-Porter. New York: Vintage, 1984.

Mirror for Magistrates. Ed. L. Campbell. New York: Barnes and Noble, 1960.

Mitchell, B. R. *British Historical Statistics.* Cambridge: Cambridge University Press, 1988.

Montesquieu, Charles le Secondat, Baron de. *Lettres Persanes.* Geneva: Droz, 1965.

——. *Oeuvres Complètes.* Paris: Editions de Seuil, 1964.

Man, Thomas. *A Discourse of Trade, from England unto the East-Indies: Answering to Diverse Objections Which Are Usually Made against the Same.* London: Nicholas Oakes for John Pyper, 1621.

Murrell, John. *A New Booke of Cookerie,* part of *Murrell's Two Books of Cookery and Carving.* 5th ed. London: John Marriot, 1638.

Nyland, P. *Den Ervaren Huys-houder.* Amsterdam: Marcus Doornick, 1668.

Osborne, Francis. *Advice to a Son.* Reprinted in Louis B. Wright, ed., *Advice to a Son: Precepts of Lord Burghley, Sir Walter Raleigh, and Francis Osborne.* Ithaca: Cornell University Press, 1962.

Outler, A. C., ed. *The Works of John Wesley.* 24 vols. Nashville: Abingdon Press, 1984–95.

A Proclamation for the Suppression of Coffee-Houses, December 29, 1675, and *An Additional Proclamation Concerning Coffee-Houses,* January 8, 1675/76. (Goldsmiths' Library Collection of Proclamations: GL 2138 and GL 2179).

Rabisha, William. *The Whole Body of Cookery Dissected . . .* London: Giles Calvert, 1761.

Richardson, Samuel. *Clarissa or the History of a Young Lady.* Ed. and abr. G. Sherburn, Boston: Houghton Mifflin, 1962.

Rose, Giles. *A Perfect School of Instruction for Officers of the Mouth.* London: R. Bentley and M. Magnes, 1682.

Rousseau, Jean-Jacques. *The Social Contract and Discourses.* Ed. and trans. G. D. H. Cole. New York: Dutton, 1950.

Sebastian, Meister. *Koch und Kellermeisterey.* Frankfurt am Main: S. Feyerabend, 1581.

The Settlement Cookbook. New York: Simon and Schuster, 1965.

Sévigné, Marie de Rabutin-Chantal, Mme. *Lettres.* 3 vols. Paris: Gallimard, 1953.

Shakespeare, William. *Henry IV, Part I.*

——. *Measure for Measure.*

Short, Thomas, M.D. *Discourses on Tea, Sugar, Milk, Made-Wines, Spirits, Punch, Tobacco, etc., with Plain and Useful Rules for Goaty People.* London: T. Longman, 1750.

[Sowter, J.] *The Way to Be Wise and Wealthy: or, The Excellency of Industry and Frugality.* London: J. Wilford, 1736.

The Touchstone or, Trial of Tobacco. London: n.p., 1673.

The Treasurie of Hidden Secrets: Commonly Called, The Good- huswives Closet of Provision, for the Health of Her Household. London: John Wright, 1627.

A Treatise on the Inherent Qualities of the Tea-Herb. London: C. Corbett, 1750.

Trollope, Anthony. *The Prime Minister.* Oxford: Oxford University Press, 1973.

Trusler, John. *An Easy Way to Prolong Life, by a Little Attention to What We Eat and Drink.* 4th ed. Dover, NH: S. Bragg for for W. T. Clap, 1796.

——. *Modern Times, or, the Adventures of Gabriel Outcast: Supposed to Be Written by Himself: In Imitation of Gil Blas.* 3 vols. 2nd ed. London: For the author by J. Murray, [1785].

——. *The Way to Be Rich and Respectable; Addressed to Men of Small Fortune.* London: for the author, n.d.

[Tryon, Thomas]. *A New Art of Brewing.* London: T. Salusbury, 1690.

[——]. "T. T. Merchant." *Some General Considerations Offered, Relating to Our Present Trade,* London: J. Harris, 1698.

——. *Tryon's Letters, Domestick and Foreign.* London: G. Conyers, 1700.

Tucker, Robert, ed. *The Marx-Engels Reader,* 2nd ed. New York: W. W. Norton, 1978.

Tulp, Nicholas. *Observationes medicae.* Vol. 4. Amsterdam: Elsevier, 1652.

——. *Uitstekkende Eigenschappen, en Heerlyke Werkingen van het kruid Thee . . .* Amsterdam: n.p., 1675.

Violet, Thomas. *A Petition against the Jewes.* London: n.p., 1661.

Wedgwood, Josiah. *Letters of Josiah Wedgwood.* 3 vols. 1903; Manchester: E. J. Morton, 1973.

The Whole Duty of a Woman. London: T. Reed, 1737.

Wollstonecraft, Mary. *A Vindication of the Rights of Woman.* Mineola, NY: Dover, 1996.

SECONDARY SOURCES

Adshead, S. A. M. *Material Culture in Europe and China, 1400–1800.* New York: St. Martin's Press, 1995.

Agnew, Jean-Christophe. "Coming up for Air: Consumer Culture in Historical Perspective" In *Consumption and the World of Goods.* Ed. John Brewer and Roy Porter. London: Routledge, 1993.

——. *Worlds Apart: The Market and the Theatre in Anglo-American Thought, 1550–1750.* Cambridge: Cambridge University Press, 1986.

Anderson, Bonnie S., and Judith P. Zinsser. *A History of Their Own.* 2 vols. New York: Harper and Row, 1988.

Appadurai, Arjun, ed. *The Social Life of Things: Commodities in Cultural Perspective.* Cambridge: Cambridge University Press, 1986.

——. *Liberalism and Republicanism in the Historical Imagination.* Cambridge, MA: Harvard University Press, 1992.

Auslander, Leora. *Taste and Power: Furnishing Modern France.* Berkeley: University of California Press, 1996.

Austen, Ralph A., and Woodruff D. Smith. "Images of Africa and British Slave-Trade Abolition: The Transition to an Imperialist Ideology, 1787–1807." *African Historical Studies* (now *International Journal of African Historical Studies*) 2, no. 1 (1969): 69–83.

——. "Private Tooth Decay as Public Economic Virtue: The Slave-Sugar Triangle, Consumerism, and European Industrialization." *Social Science History* 14, no. 1 (1990): 77–97.

Barbour, Violet. *Capitalism in Amsterdam in the Seventeenth Century.* Ann Arbor: University of Michigan Press, 1963.

Beck, S. William. *The Draper's Dictionary.* London: Warehousemen and Drapers' Journal Office, n.d.

Barker-Benfield, G. J. *The Culture of Sensibility: Sex and Society in Eighteenth-Century Britain.* Chicago: University of Chicago Press, 1992.

Beik, Paul H. *Louis-Philippe and the July Monarchy*. Princeton: Van Nostrand, 1965.

Bell, Quentin. *On Human Finery*. 2nd ed. New York: Schocken, 1976.

Berg, Maxine. "New Commodities, Luxuries, and Their Consumers in Eighteenth-Century England." In *Consumers and Luxury: Consumer Culture in Europe, 1650–1850*. Ed. Maxine Berg and Helen Clifford. Manchester and New York: Manchester University Press, 1999.

Berg, Maxine and Helen Clifford, eds. *Consumers and Luxury: Consumer Culture in Europe, 1650–1850*. Manchester and New York: Manchester University Press, 1999.

Berry, Christopher,. *The Idea of Luxury: A Conceptual and Historical Investigation*. Cambridge: Cambridge University Press, 1994.

Birmingham, Ann, and John Brewer, eds. *The Consumption of Culture, 1600–1800*. London and New York: Routledge, 1995.

Bolleme, Geneviève. *La Bible bleue: Anthologie d'une littérature "populaire."* Paris: Flammarion, 1975.

——. *La Bibliothèque bleue: La littérature populaire en France du xviie au xixe siècle*. Paris: Julliard, 1971.

Bonnell, Victoria, and Lynn Hunt, eds. *Beyond the Cultural Turn: New Directions in the Study of Society and Culture*. Berkeley: University of California Press, 1999.

Bourdieu, Pierre. *Distinction: A Social Critique of the Judgement of Taste*. Trans. Richard Nice. Cambridge, MA: Harvard University Press, 1984.

Boxer, C. R. *The Dutch Seaborne Empire, 1600–1800*. London: Hutchinson, 1977.

Breen, T. H. "The Meanings of Things: Interpreting the Consumer Economy in the Eighteenth Century." In *Consumption and the World of Goods*. Ed. John Brewer and Roy Porter. London: Routledge, 1993.

Brewer, John. *The Pleasures of the Imagination: English Culture in the Eighteenth Century*. New York: Farrar, Straus, and Giroux, 1997.

——. *The Sinews of Power: War, Money, and the English State, 1688–1783*. New York: Alfred A. Knopf, 1989.

Brewer, John, and Roy Porter, eds. *Consumption and the World of Goods*. London: Routledge, 1993.

Brooke, Iris. *English Costume in the Age of Elizabeth*. 2nd ed. London: A and C Black, 1950.

Brooks, C. W., *Pettyfoggers and Vipers of the Commonwealth: The "Lower Branch" of the Legal Profession in Early Modern England*, Cambridge: Cambridge University Press, 1986.

Brooks, Jerome E. *The Mighty Leaf: Tobacco through the Centuries*. Boston: Little, Brown, 1952.

Brophy, Elizabeth Bergen. *Samuel Richardson*. Boston: Twayne, 1987.

Brown, Christopher, ed. *Breughel: Paintings, Drawing, and Prints*. Oxford: Phaidon, 1975.

Brown, Laura. *Ends of Empire: Women and Ideology in Early Eighteenth-Century English Literature*. Ithaca: Cornell University Press, 1993.

Bruegel, Martin. "A Bourgeois Good? Sugar, Norms of Consumption, and the Labouring Classes in Nineteenth-Century France." In *Food, Drink, and Identity: Cooking, Eating, and Drinking in Europe since the Middle Ages*. Ed. Peter Scholliers. Oxford and New York: Berg, 2001.

Bryson, Anna. *From Courtesy to Civility: Changing Codes of Conduct in Early Modern England*. Oxford: Clarendon Press, 1998.

Buck, Ann. *Dress in Eighteenth-Century England*. London: B. T. Batsford, 1979.

Burckhardt, Jacob. *The Civilization of the Renaissance in Italy*. 1860; New York: Random House, 1964.

Burn, W. L. *The Age of Equipoise: A Study of the Mid-Victorian Generation*. New York: W. W. Norton, 1965.

Burton, Anthony. *Josiah Wedgwood: A Biography*. London: Andre Deutsch, 1976.

Bushman, Richard L. *The Refinement of America: Persons, Houses, Cities*. New York: Alfred A. Knopf, 1992.

Campbell, Colin. *The Romantic Ethic and the Spirit of Capitalism*. Oxford: Blackwell, 1987.

——. "Understanding Traditional and Modern Patterns of Consumption in Eighteenth-Century England: A Character Action Approach." In *Consumption and the World of Goods*. Ed. John Brewer and Roy Porter. London: Routledge, 1993.

Cannadine, David. *The Rise and Fall of Class in Britain*. New York: Columbia University Press, 1999.

Chambers, J. D. *Population, Economy, and Society in Pre-Industrial England*. London: Oxford University Press, 1972.

Chartier, Roger, ed. *Passions of the Renaissance*. Vol. 3 of Philippe Ariès and Georges Duby, eds. *A History of Private Life*. 4 vols. Cambridge, MA: Belknap, 1987–90.

Chaudhuri, K. N. *The English East India Company: The Study of an Early Joint-Stock Company, 1600–1640*. New York: A. M. Kelley, 1965.

——. *Trade and Civilisation in the Indian Ocean: An Economic History from the Rise of Islam to 1750*. Cambridge: Cambridge University Press, 1985.

——. *The Trading World of India and the English East India Company, 1660–1760*. Cambridge: Cambridge University Press, 1978.

Classen, Constance, David Howes, and Anthony Synnott. *Aroma: The Cultural History of Smell*. London: Routledge, 1994.

Cliffe, J. T. *The Puritan Gentry: The Great Puritan Families of Early Stuart England*. London: Routledge and Kegan Paul, 1984.

Cole, C. W. *French Mercantilism, 1683–1700*. New York: Columbia University Press, 1943.

Colley, Linda. *Britons: Forging the Nation, 1707–1837*. New Haven and London: Yale University Press, 1992.

Conley, Carolyn A. *The Unwritten Law: Criminal Justice in Victorian Kent*. New York: Oxford University Press, 1991.

Connely, Willard. *Beau Nash: Monarch of Bath and Tunbridge Wells*. London: Werner Laurie, 1955.

Conze, Werner, and Jürgen Kocka, eds. *Bildungsbürgertum im 19: Jahrhundert*. Vol. 1. *Bildungssystem und Professionalisierung internationales Vergleich*. Stuttgart: Klett-Cotta, 1985.

Corfield, Penelope J. "Class by Name and Number in Eighteenth-Century Britain." In *Language, History, and Class*. Ed. Penelope J. Corfield. Oxford: Basil Blackwell, 1991.

——. *Power and the Professions in Britain, 1700–1850*. London and New York: Routledge, 1995.

——. ed. *Language, History, and Class*. Oxford: Basil Blackwell, 1991.

Cottrell, Geoffrey. *Amsterdam: The Life of a City*. Boston: Little, Brown, 1972.

Cowan, Brian. "Reasonable Ecstasies: Shaftesbury and the Languages of Libertinism." *Journal of British Studies* 37, no 2 (1998): 111–38.

Crawford, Patricia. "Sexual Knowledge in England, 1500–1750." In *Sexual Knowledge, Sexual Science: The History of Attitudes toward Sexuality*. Ed. Roy Porter and Mikulas Teich. Cambridge: Cambridge University Press, 1994: 82–106.

Crosby, Alfred W., *The Columbian Exchange: Biological and Cultural Consequences of 1492*. Westport, CT: Greenwood Press, 1972.

Crowley, John E., "The Sensibility of Comfort." *American Historical Review* 104 (June 1999): 749–82.

Cunnington, C. Willett, and Phyllis Cunnington. *The History of Underclothes*. Rev. ed. London: Faber and Faber, 1981.

Curtin, Philip, et al. *African History*. Boston: Little, Brown, 1978.

Damasio, Antonio R. *Descartes' Error: Emotion, Reason, and the Human Brain*. New York: Avon, 1994.

Darnton, Robert. *The Great Cat Massacre and Other Episodes in French Cultural History*. New York: Vintage, 1985.

——. *The Literary Underground of the Old Regime*. Cambridge, MA: Harvard University Press, 1982.

Davidoff, Leonore, and Catherine Hall. *Family Fortunes: Men and Women of the English Middle Class, 1780–1850*. Chicago: University of Chicago Press, 1987.

Davis, Natalie Zemon. *Women on the Margins: Three Seventeenth-Century Lives*. Cambridge, MA, and London: Harvard University Press, 1995.

Davis, Ralph. "English Foreign Trade, 1660–1700." *Economic History Review* 7 (1952): 150–66.

——. "English Foreign Trade, 1700–1774." *Economic History Review*, 15 (1962): 285–303.

——. "The Industrial Revolution and British Overseas Trade." In *Trade and the Industrial Revolution, Volume I*. Ed. Stanley L. Engermann. Cheltenham: Elgar, 1996.

Deane, Phyllis. *The First Industrial Revolution*. Cambridge: Cambridge University Press, 1965.

Demos, John. *A Little Commonwealth: Family Life in Plymouth Colony*. London and New York: Oxford University Press, 1971.

Denvir, Bernard. *The Eighteenth Century: Art, Design, and Society, 1689–1789.* London: Longman, 1983.

Dewald, Jonathan. *The Formation of a Provincial Nobility: The Magistrates of the Parlement of Rouen, 1499–1610.* Princeton: Princeton University Press, 1980.

Dictionary of National Biography. 22 vols. London: Oxford University Press, 1967–68.

Dobson, Jessie, and R. Milnes Wagner. *Barbers and Barber-Surgeons of London: A History of the Barbers' and Barber-Surgeons' Companies.* Oxford: Blackwell, 1979.

Doody, Margaret Anne. *Frances Burney: The Life in the Works.* Brunswick, NJ: Rutgers University Press, 1988.

——. *A Natural Passion: A Study in the Novels of Samuel Richardson.* Oxford: Clarendon Press, 1974.

Douglas, Mary, and Baron Isherwood. *The World of Goods.* New York: Basic Books, 1979.

Durie, Alistair J. *The Scottish Linen Industry in the Eighteenth Century.* Edinburgh: Donald, 1979.

Edgerton, Robert B. *Sick Societies: Challenging the Myth of Primitive Harmony.* New York: Free Press, 1992.

Elias, Norbert. *The Civilizing Process.* Trans. E. Jephcott. New York: Urizen, 1978.

——. *The Court Society.* Trans. E. Jephcott. New York: Pantheon, 1983.

Encyclopedia Britannica. 24 vols. Chicago: Encyclopedia Britannica, 1948.

Estes, James Martin. *Christian Magistrate and State Church: The Reforming Career of Johannes Brenz.* Toronto: University of Toronto Press, 1982.

Ewen, Stuart. *All Consuming Images: The Politics of Style in Contemporary Culture.* New York: Basic Books, 1988.

Ewen, Stuart, and Elizabeth Ewen. *Channels of Desire: Mass Images and the Shaping of American Consciousness.* Minneapolis: University of Minnesota Press, 1992.

Festinger, Leon. *A Theory of Cognitive Dissonance.* Stanford: Stanford University Press, 1957.

Fletcher, Anthony. *Gender, Sex, and Subordination in England, 1500–1800.* New Haven: Yale University Press, 1995.

Fletcher, Anthony, and Peter Roberts, eds. *Religion, Culture, and Society in Early Modern Britain: Essays in Honour of Patrick Collinson.* Cambridge: Cambridge University Press, 1994.

Foster, William. *The East India House.* London: John Lane, 1924.

Foucault, Michel. *The Order of Things: An Archaeology of the Human Sciences.* New York: Vintage, 1973.

Freundenberger, Herman. "Fashion, Sumptuary Laws, and Business." *Business History Review* 37, 1–2 (1963): 37–48.

Furber, Holden. *Rival Empires of Trade in the Orient, 1660–1800.* Minneapolis: University of Minnesota Press, 1976.

Gaastra, Femma S. *De geschiedenis van de VOC.* Leiden: Walburg Pers, 1991.

Gibson, Charles. *Spain in America.* New York: Harper, 1966.

Giddens, Anthony. *Studies in Social and Political Theory.* New York: Basic Books, 1977.

Gilboy, Elizabeth. "Demand as a Factor in the Industrial Revolution." In *Facts and Figures in Economic History: Articles by Former Students of Edwin Francis Day.* NewYork: Russell and Russell, 1932.

Glamann, Kristof. *Dutch-Asiatic Trade, 1620–1740.* Copenhagen: Danish Science Press, 1958.

Glotz, Marguerite, and Madeleine Maire. *Salons du XVIIIe siècle.* Paris: Nouvelles Editions latines, 1949.

Goldsmith, Oliver. "The Life of Richard Nash." In Oliver Goldsmith. *Collected Works.* Ed. Arthur Friedman. 5 vols. Oxford: Clarendon Press, 1966.

Goodman, Jordan. "Excitantia: Or, How Enlightenment Europe Took to Soft Drugs." In *Consuming Habits: Drugs in Anthropology and History.* Ed. Jordan Goodman, Paul E. Lovejoy, and Andrew Sherratt. London: Routledge, 1995.

———. *Tobacco in History: The Cultures of Dependence.* London: Routledge, 1993.

Goodman, Jordan, Paul E. Lovejoy, and Andrew Sherratt, eds. *Consuming Habits: Drugs in Anthropology and History.* London: Routledge, 1995.

Goubert, Jean-Pierre. *The Conquest of Water: The Advent of Health in the Industrial Age.* Trans. A. Wilson. Princeton: Princeton University Press, 1986.

Grant, Michael. *The World of Rome.* New York: Mentor, 1960.

Griffiths, Sir Percival. *The History of the Indian Tea Industry.* London: Weidenfeld and Nicolson, 1967.

Griswold, A. Whitney. "Three Puritans on Prosperity." *New England Quarterly* 7 (1934): 475–88.

Habermas, Jürgen. *The Structural Transformation of the Public Sphere: An Inquiry into a Category of Bourgeois Society.* Cambridge, MA: MIT Press, 1989.

Halèvy, Elie. *The Birth of Methodism.* Trans. B. Semmel. Chicago: University of Chicago Press, 1971.

Hall, Catherine. "The Sweet Delights of Home." In *From the Fires of Revolution to the Great War.* Ed. Michelle Perrot. Vol. 4 of Philippe Ariès and Georges Duby. *A History of Private Life.* Cambridge, MA: Belknap, 1990.

Halttunen, Karen. *Confidence Men and Painted Women: A Study of Middle-Class Culture in America, 1830–1870.* New Haven and London: Yale University Press, 1982.

Harrison, Brian Howard. *Separate Spheres: The Opposition to Women's Suffrage in Britain.* New York: Holmes and Meier, 1979.

Hartnell, Norman. *Royal Courts of Fashion.* London: Cassell, 1971.

Hattox, Ralph S. *Coffee and Coffeehouses: The Origins of a Social Beverage in the Medieval Near East.* Seattle: University of Washington Press, 1985.

Hawke, David Freeman. *Franklin.* New York: Harper and Row, 1976.

Heckscher, Eli. *Mercantilism.* Trans. M. Shapiro. 2nd rev. ed. 2 vols. London: George Allen and Unwin, 1955.

Hibbert, Christopher. *George III: A Personal History.* New York: Basic Books, 1998.

Hildyard, Robin. *European Ceramics.* London: V and A Publications, 1999.

Hirschman, Albert O. *The Passions and the Interests: Political Arguments for Capitalism before Its Triumph.* Princeton: Princeton University Press, 1977.

Hollander, Anne. *Sex and Suits.* New York: Alfred A. Knopf, 1994.

Honour, Hugh. *Chinoiserie: The Vision of Cathay.* London: John Murray, 1961.

Horst, W. A. "De Peperhandel van de Verenigde Oostindische Compagnie." *Bijdragen voor Vaderlandsche Geschiedenis en Oudheidkunde,* 8: no. 3 (1942): 95–103.

Hudson, Robert P. *Disease and Its Control: The Shaping of Modern Thought*. Westport, CT: Greenwood, 1983.

Hunt, Margaret R. *The Middling Sort: Commerce, Gender, and the Family in England, 1680–1780*. Berkeley: University of California Press, 1996.

Hunting, Penelope. *A History of the Society of Apothecaries*. London: Society of Apothecaries, 1998.

Hutchinson, D. S. *The Virtues of Aristotle*. London: Routledge and Kegan Paul, 1986.

Innis, Harold A. *The Fur Trade in Canada: An Introduction to Canadian Economic History*. Rev. ed. New Haven: Yale University Press, 1962.

Irwin, Terence. *Plato's Ethics*. New York: Oxford University Press, 1995.

Israel, Jonathan. *The Dutch Republic: Its Rise, Greatness, and Fall, 1477–1806*. Oxford: Clarendon Press, 1995.

Jenner, Mark. "Bathing and Baptism: Sir John Floyer and the Politics of Cold Bathing." In *Refiguring Revolutions: Aesthetics and Politics from the English Revolution to the Romantic Revolution*. Berkeley: University of California Press, 1998.

Jörg, C. J. A. *Porselein als Handelswaar: De porseleinhandel als onderdeel van de Chinahandel van de V.O.C., 1729–1794*. Ph.D. diss, University of Leiden, 1978.

Jones, Colin, and Rebecca Spang. "Sans-Culottes, *Sans Café, Sans Tabac*: Shifting Realms of Necessity and Luxury in Eighteenth-Century France." In *Consumers and Luxury: Consumer Culture in Europe, 1650–1850*. Ed. Maxine Berg and Helen Clifford. Manchester and New York: Manchester University Press, 1999.

Keay, John. *The Honourable Company: A History of the English East India Company*. London: HarperCollins, 1991.

Khan, Shafaat Ahmad. *The East India Trade in the Seventeenth Century in Its Political and Economic Aspects*. London: Oxford University Press, 1923.

Klein, Lawrence E. *Shaftesbury and the Culture of Politeness: Moral Discourse and Cultural Politics in Early Eighteenth-Century England*. Cambridge: Cambridge University Press, 1994.

Kowaleski-Wallace, Elizabeth. *Consuming Subjects: Women, Shopping, and Business in the Eighteenth Century*. New York: Columbia University Press, 1997.

Kuhn, Thomas S. *The Structure of Scientific Revolutions*. 2nd ed. Chicago: University of Chicago Press, 1970.

Kulikoff, Allan. *Tobacco and Slaves: The Development of Southern Cultures in the Chesapeake, 1680–1800.* Chapel Hill: University of North Carolina Press, 1986.

Lane, Maggie. *Jane Austen and Food.* London: Hambleton Press, 1995.

Laver, James. *The Age of Illusion: Manners and Morals, 1750–1848.* London: Weidenfeld and Nicolson, 1972.

Lawrence, D. H. "Benjamin Franklin." in D. H. Lawrence. *Studies in Classic American Literature.* New York: Viking Press, 1964.

Leclant, Jean. "Coffee and Cafes in Paris, 1644–1693." In *Food and Drink in History.* Ed. Robert Forster and Orest Ranum. Baltimore: Johns Hopkins University Press, 1979.

Lemire, Beverly. *Fashion's Favourite: The Cotton Trade and the Consumer in Britain, 1660–1800.* Oxford: Oxford University Press, 1991.

Lévi-Strauss, Claude. *The Raw and the Cooked.* New York: Harper and Row, 1969.

Linton, Ralph. *The Tree of Culture.* New York: Alfred A. Knopf, 1995.

Lougee, Carolyn C. *Le Paradis des Femmes: Women, Salons, and Social Stratification in Seventeenth-Century France.* Princeton: Princeton University Press, 1976.

McCracken, Grant. *Culture and Consumption: New Approaches to the Symbolic Character of Consumer Goods and Activities.* Bloomington: Indiana University Press, 1988.

MacKay, Douglas. *The Honourable Company: A History of the Hudson's Bay Company.* Indianapolis: Bobbs-Merrill, 1936.

McKendrick, Neil. "Josiah Wedgwood and the Commercialization of the Potteries." In *The Birth of a Consumer Society: The Commercialization of Eighteenth-Century England.* Ed. Neil McKendrick, John Brewer, and J. H. Plumb. Bloomington: Indiana University Press, 1982.

McKendrick, Neil, John Brewer, and J. H. Plumb. *The Birth of a Consumer Society: The Commercialization of Eighteenth-Century England.* Bloomington: Indiana University Press, 1982.

Matthiesen, Donald J. "German Parliamentarism in 1848: Roll-call Voting in the Frankfurt Assembly." *Social Science History* 5, no. 4 (1981): 469–82.

Mathias, Peter. *The First Industrial Nation: An Economic History of Britain, 1700–1914.* 2nd ed. London and New York: Methuen, 1983.

Mehta, Uday S. "Liberal Strategies of Exclusion." In *Tensions of Empire: Colonial Cultures in a Bourgeois World.* Ed. Frederick Cooper and Ann Laura Stoler. Berkeley: University of California Press, 1997.

Mennell, Stephen. *All Manners of Food: Eating and Taste in England and France from the Middle Ages to the Present.* Oxford: Blackwell, 1985.

Middlekauff, Robert. *Benjamin Franklin and His Enemies.* Berkeley: University of California Press, 1996.

Mintz, Sidney. *Sweetness and Power: The Place of Sugar in Modern History.* New York: Penguin, 1985.

Moi, Toril, ed. *The Kristeva Reader.* New York: Columbia University Press, 1986.

Mokyr, Joel. "Demand versus Supply in the Industrial Revolution." *Journal of Economic History* 37 (1977): 981–1008.

Monk, Robert C. *John Wesley: His Puritan Heritage.* Nashville: Abingdon Press, 1966.

Moore, John Robert. *Daniel Defoe: Citizen of the Modern World.* Chicago: University of Chicago Press, 1958.

Moura, Jean, and Paul Louvet. *Le Café Procope.* Paris: Perrin, 1929.

Mui, Hoh-Cheung, and Lorna H. Mui. *Shops and Shopkeeping in Eighteenth-Century England.* Kingston: McGill-Queen's University Press, 1989.

Mukerji, Chandra. *From Graven Images: Patterns of Modern Materialism.* New York: Columbia University Press, 1983.

Mullan, John. *Sentiment and Sociability: The Language of Feeling in the Eighteenth Century.* Oxford: Clarendon Press, 1988.

Neale, R. S. *Bath, 1680–1850: A Social History* . . . London: Routledge and Kegan Paul, 1981.

Old English Coffee Houses. London: Rodale Press, 1954.

Parry, J. H. *The Establishment of the European Hegemony, 1415–1715: Trade and Exploration in the Age of the Renaissance.* 3rd rev. ed. New York: Harper and Row, 1959.

Perkin, Harold. "The Social Causes of the British Industrial Revolution." Royal Historical Society *Transactions.* 5th series, 18 (1969): 123–43.

Perrot, Michelle, ed. *From the Fires of Revolution to the Great War.* Vol. 4 of Philippe Ariès and Georges Duby, eds. *A History of Private Life.* Cambridge, MA: Belknap, 1987–90.

——. "Roles and Characters." In *Life: From the Fires of Revolution to the Great War.* Vol. 4 of Philippe Ariès and Georges Duby, eds. *A History of Private Life.* Cambridge, MA: Belknap, 1987–90: 167–239.

Pincus, Steven. "Coffee Politicians Does Create: Coffee Houses and Restoration Political Culture." *Journal of Modern History* 67 (1995): 807–34.

Plumb, J. H. "The New World of Children." In *Birth of a Consumer Society: The Commercialization of Eighteenth-Century England.* Ed. Neil McKendrick, John Brewer, and J. H. Plumb. Bloomington: Indiana University Press, 1982.

Pocock, J. G. A. *The Machiavellian Moment: Florentine Political Thought and the Atlantic Republican Tradition.* Princeton: Princeton University Press, 1975.

Porter, Roy. *Disease, Medicine, and Society in England, 1550–1800.* Basingstoke: Macmillan, 1987.

——. *English Society in the Eighteenth Century.* Harmondsworth: Penguin, 1982.

Porter, Roy, and Mikulas Teich, eds. *Sexual Knowledge, Sexual Science: The History of Attitudes toward Sexuality.* Cambridge: Cambridge University Press, 1964.

Posthumus, W. W. *Nederlandsche Prijsgeschiedenis.* 2 vols. Leiden: Brill, 1943.

Price, Jacob M. *The Tobacco Adventure to Russia: Enterprise, Politics, and Diplomacy in the Quest for a Northern Market for English Colonial Tobacco, 1676–1722.* Philadelphia: American Philosophical Society, 1961.

Reddy, William H. *Money and Liberty in Modern Europe: A Critique of Historical Understanding.* Cambridge: Cambridge University Press, 1987.

Reese, J. J. *De Suikerhandel van Amsterdam van het Begin der 17de Eeuw tot 1813.* Haarlem: I.L.E.I. Kleynenberg, 1908.

Ribeiro, Aileen. *Dress in Eighteenth-Century Europe, 1715–1789.* New York: Holmes and Meier, 1984.

Ringer, Fritz. *The Decline of the German Mandarins: The German Academic community, 1890–1933.* Cambridge, MA: Harvard University Press, 1969.

Robert, Paul. *Dictionnaire alphabétique et analogique de la Langue Française.* 6 vols. Paris: Littre, 1966.

Robinson, Stuart. *A History of Printed Textiles.* Cambridge, MA: MIT Press, 1969.

Robson, Robert. *The Attorney in Eighteenth-Century England.* Cambridge: Cambridge University Press, 1959.

Rogers, Pat, ed. *Defoe: The Critical Heritage.* London: Routledge and Kegan Paul, 1972.

Rostow, W. W. *How It All Began: Origins of the Modern Economy.* New York: McGraw-Hill, 1975.

Rowen, Herbert H. *John de Witt, Grand Pensionary of Holland, 1625–1672.* Princeton: Princeton University Press, 1978.

Sahlins, Marshall. "Cosmologies of Culture: The Trans-Pacific Sector of the 'World System.'". *Proceedings of the British Academy* 74 (1988): 1–51.

——. *Culture and Practical Reason.* Chicago: University of Chicago Press, 1976.

Said, Edward W. *Orientalism.* New York: Vintage, 1979.

Samuelson, Paul A. *Economics.* 10th ed. New York: McGraw-Hill, 1976.

Schama, Simon. *Citizens: A Chronicle of the French Revolution.* New York: Alfred A. Knopf, 1989.

——. *The Embarrassment of Riches: An Interpretation of Dutch Culture in the Golden Age.* New York: Alfred A. Knopf, 1987.

Schivelbusch, Wolfgang. *Tastes of Paradise: A Social History of Spices, Stimulants, and Intoxicants.* Trans. D. Jacobson. New York: Vintage, 1992.

Schneider, David J., Albert H. Hastorf, and Phoebe C. Ellsworth. *Person Perception.* 2nd ed. Reading, MA: Addison-Wesley, 1979.

Sekora, John. *Luxury: The Concept in Western Thought, Eden to Smollett.* Baltimore: Johns Hopkins University Press, 1977.

Semmel, Bernard. *The Methodist Revolution.* New York: Basic Books, 1973.

Sewell, William H., Jr. "The Concept(s) of Culture." In *Beyond the Cultural Turn: New Directions in the Study of Society and Culture.* Ed. Victoria Bonnell and Lynn Hunt. Berkeley: University of California Press, 1999.

Shammus, Carole. *The Pre-industrial Consumer in Britain and America.* Oxford: Clarendon Press, 1990.

Sheridan, Richard B. *Sugar and Slavery: An Economic History of the British West Indies, 1623–1775.* Baltimore: Johns Hopkins University Press, 1973.

Shinagel, Michael. *Daniel Defoe and Middle-Class Gentility.* Cambridge, MA: Harvard University Press, 1968.

Shoemaker, Robert B. *Gender in English Society, 1650–1850: The Emergence of Separate Spheres?* London: Longman, 1998.

Simmel, Georg. "Fashion." *International Quarterly* 10 (1904): 130–55.

Skinner, Quentin. *Liberty before Liberalism*. Cambridge: Cambridge University Press, 1998.

Slater, Victor. *Duke Hamilton Is Dead! A Story of Aristocratic Life and Death in Stuart Britain*. New York: Hill and Wang, 1999.

Slomann, Vilhelm. *Bizarre Designs in Silk: Trade and Traditions*. Copenhagen: Einar Munksgaard, 1953.

Smail, John. *The Origins of Middle-Class Culture: Halifax, Yorkshire, 1660–1780*. Ithaca: Cornell University Press, 1994.

Smith, Woodruff D. "The European-Asian Trade of the Seventeenth Century and the Modernization of Commercial Capitalism." *Itinerario* 6, no. 2 (1982): 68–90.

——. "From Coffeehouse to Parlour: The Consumption of Coffee, Tea, and Sugar in North-Western Europe in the Seventeenth and Eighteenth Centuries." In *Consuming Habits: Drugs in Anthropology and History*. Ed. Jordan Goodman, Paul E. Lovejoy, and Andrew Sherratt. London: Routledge, 1995.

——. "The Function of Commercial Centers in the Modernization of European Capitalism: Amsterdam as an Information Exchange in the Seventeenth Century." *Journal of Economic History* 44 (December 1984): 985–1005.

——. "Merchants and Company Directors in Seventeenth-Century European Trading Corporations." *Essays in Economic and Business History* 4 (1986): 1–13.

Sombart, Werner. *Luxus und Kapitalismus*. Munich and Leipzig: Duncker und Humblot, 1922.

Spadafora, David. *The Idea of Progress in Eighteenth-Century Britain*. New Haven: Yale University Press, 1990.

Spalding, Keith. *An Historical Dictionary of German Figurative Usage*. 5 vols. Oxford: Blackwell, n.d.

Steensgaard, Niels. *The Asian Trade Revolution of the Seventeenth Century*. Chicago: University of Chicago Press, 1974.

Stein, Robert Louis. *The French Sugar Business in the Eighteenth Century*. Baton Rouge: Louisiana State University Press, 1988.

Stern, Fritz. *Gold and Iron: Bismark, Bleichröder, and the Building of the German Empire*. New York: Alfred A. Knopf, 1977.

Stone, Lawrence. *The Crisis of the Aristocracy, 1558–1641*. Oxford: Clarendon Press, 1965.

——. *The Family, Sex, and Marriage in England, 1500–1800*. Abridged ed. New York: Harper, 1979.

Straus, Ralph. *Lloyds: The Gentlemen at the Coffee-House*. New York: Carrick and Evans, 1938.

Tackett, Timothy. "Conspiracy Obsession in a Time of Revolution: French Elites and the Origins of the Terror, 1789–1792." *American Historical Review* 105 (2000): 691–713.

Tapié, Victor-L. *The Age of Grandeur: Baroque Art and Architecture*. New York: Praeger, 1960.

Thema Thee: De geschiedenis van de thee en het theegebruik in Nederland. Rotterdam: Museum Boymans-van Beuningen, 1978.

Thomas, Keith. "Cleanliness and Godliness in Early Modern England." In *Religion, Culture, and Society in Early Modern Britain: Essays in Honour of Patrick Collinson*. Ed. Anthony Fletcher and Peter Roberts. Cambridge: Cambridge University Press, 1994.

Thomas, P. J. *Mercantilism and the East India Trade*. London: Frank Cass, 1963.

Thompson, F. M. L. *The Rise of Respectable Society: A Social History of Victorian Britain, 1830–1900*. Cambridge: Cambridge University Press, 1988.

Tracy, James D., ed. *The Rise of Merchant Empires: Long Distance Trade in the Early Modern World*. Cambridge: Cambridge University Press, 1990.

Trout, Andrew. *Jean-Baptiste Colbert*. Boston: Twayne, 1978.

Ukers, William H. *All about Tea*. 2 vols. New York: Tea and Coffee Trade Journal Company, 1935.

———. *The Romance of Tea*. New York: Alfred A. Knopf, 1936.

Ulrich, Laurel Thatcher. *A Midwife's Tale: The Life of Martha Ballard, Based on Her Diary, 1785–1812*. New York: Alfred A. Knopf, 1990.

Van Doren, Carl. *Benjamin Franklin*. New York: Viking, 1938.

Vann, Richard T. *The Social Development of English Quakerism, 1655–1755*. Cambridge, MA: Harvard University Press, 1969.

Vaughan, Alden T. *American Genesis: Captain John Smith and the Founding of Virginia*. Boston: Little, Brown, 1975.

Veblen, Thorstein. *The Theory of the Leisure Class: An Economic Study of Institutions*. Fairfield, NJ: Augustus Kelley, 1991.

Vickery, Amanda. *The Gentleman's Daughter: Women's Lives in Georgian England*. New Haven and London: Yale University Press, 1998.

——. "Golden Age to Separate Spheres? A Review of the Categories and Chronology of British Women's History." *Historical Journal* 36 (1993): 383–414.

Vries, Jan de. "Between Purchasing Power and the World of Goods: Understanding the Household Economy in Early Modern Europe." In *Consumption and the World of Goods*. Ed. John Brewer and Roy Porter. London: Routledge, 1993.

Wadsworth, Alfred P., and Julia de Lacy Man. *The Cotton Trade and Industrial Lancashire, 1600–1780*. Manchester: Manchester University Press, 1965.

Walvin, James. *Fruits of Empire: Exotic Produce and British Taste, 1660–1800*. New York: New York University Press, 1997.

Weatherill, Lorna. *Consumer Behavior and Material Culture in Britain, 1660–1760*. London: Routledge, 1988.

——. "The Meaning of Consumer Behaviour in Late Seventeenth- Century and Early Eighteenth-Century England." In *Consumption and the World of Goods*. Ed. John Brewer and Roy Porter. London: Routledge, 1993.

Weber, Max. *The Protestant Ethic and the Spirit of Capitalism*. Trans. T. Parsons. New York: Scribner, 1958.

Webster, Charles. *The Great Instauration: Science, Medicine, and Reform, 1626–1660*. London: Duckworth, 1975.

Weir, Alison. *The Life of Elizabeth I*. New York: Ballantine, 1998.

Williams, Rosalind. *Dream Worlds: Mass Consumption in Late Nineteenth-Century France*. Berkeley: University of California Press, 1982.

Wood, Gordon S. "Conspiracy and the Paranoid Style: Causality and Deceit in the Eighteenth Century." *William and Mary Quarterly,* 3rd ser., 39 (1982): 401–41.

——. *The Creation of the American Republic, 1776-1787*. Chapel Hill: University of North Carolina Press, 1969.

——. *The Radicalism of the American Revolution*. New York: Vintage, 1993.

Wright, Lawrence. *Clean and Decent: The Fascinating History of the Bathroom and the Water-Closet*. Toronto: University of Toronto Press, 1967.

Wrightson, Keith. "Estates, Degrees, and Sorts: Changing Perceptions of Society in Tudor and Stuart England." In *Language, History, and Class*. Ed. Penelope J. Corfield. Oxford: Basil Blackwell, 1991.

Yoshimura, Noburu, and Philip Anderson. *Inside the Kaisha: Demystifying Japanese Business Behavior*. Boston: Harvard Business School Press, 1997.

Youings, Joyce. *Sixteenth-Century England*. Harmondsworth: Penguin, 1984.

Zaret, David. "Religion, Science, and Printing in the Public Spheres in Seventeenth-Century England." In *Habermas and the Public Sphere*. Ed. Craig Calhoun. Cambridge, MA: MIT Press, 1992.

Zeldin, Theodore. *France, 1848–1945: Ambition and Love*. Oxford: Oxford University Press, 1979.

INDEX

Campbell, Colin, 1, 65, 66
candy, 101–102
capitalism, large-scale commercial, 70–71, 148–149
Castiglione, Baldassare, 40
Chamberlain, John, 122
Charles II, king of England, 28, 36, 43, 45, 141
Charlotte, queen of Great Britain and consort of George III, 241
chastity, 110–111, 114
Chesterfield, Philip Dormer Stanhope, fourth earl of, 82–83, 155, 184, 191, 227
Child, Sir Josiah, 51–52
childhood, 182–183
China, 41, 46, 50, 121, 239, 240
chinoiserie, 123
chocolate, 75, 122, 142, 143, 184, 185
chocolate houses, 139
cinnamon, 86, 92, 95
citizen, 119, 120, 198
civility, 35, 40–43, 155, 179
civilization and civilizing, 40–41, 70, 73, 178–181
    role of women in, 178–81
classicism, 82, 241–242
cleanliness, 108, 115–116, 130–138, 163, 226, 233
    in body, 131–136
    in clothing, 68, 136–138
clergy (as profession), 99, 216, 218, 219
cloves, 86, 88, 92, 93, 95, 96
clubs, 141, 143, 148, 150, 156, 160, 203
coffee, 7, 75, 106, 140–143, 147, 151–154, 159, 161, 162, 163, 184, 185
    consumption with sugar, 102–103, 121–128
coffee craze (seventeenth century), 140–141, 143, 149
coffeehouses, 122, 132, 139, 140–151, 151–157, 159, 160, 161, 167, 172, 174, 203, 235
    women in, 143, 156–157, 278n
Colbert, Jean-Baptiste, 34

comfort, 62, 65, 67, 83–85, 92, 102, 201, 211, 219, 233
commodities
    changes in consumption and demand, 5–8
    imported non-European, 19
    middle-range manufactured, 64–65, 287n
    substitute status, 56–60, 259n
condiments, 92–103
confections, 97–99, 101–102
Conley, Carolyn, 205
consumer demand
    emulation and, 8
    standard explanations of changes in, 7–9
consumerism, 1, 15, 242–243
"consumer revolution," 5–6, 8, 182
consumer society, 1, 6, 25
consumption, 8, 15–16
    changes in early modern Europe, 5–8
    conspicuous, 31–34, 42
    and cultural contexts, 9–12, 223–224, 236–237
    historiography, 1–3
    and families, 211–212
    and status, 25–27, 36, 47, 136–137
convenience, 62, 67, 68, 84–85, 211, 219
cookbooks, 124–125
cookery, 93, 96–97, 100–101
Corday, Charlotte, 135
Corfield, Penelope, 215–218
cotton and cotton textiles, 7, 46–47, 49–60, 60–62, 68, 96, 238, 239
    white cottons, 59–60, 68, 85, 136–138
courtesans, 66, 69, 70, 74
courtesy, 35, 40–43, 224
Cromwell, Oliver, 90
Crowley, John, 65, 83–84
cultural contexts, 12, 160
    change in, 21–23
    components, 15–19, 67
    definition, 13–15
    and meaning, 19–21
culture, study of , 9–23